Ballots, Babies, and Banners of Peace

American Jewish Women's Activism, 1890–1940

Melissa R. Klapper

NEW YORK UNIVERSITY PRESS

New York and London

NEW YORK UNIVERSITY PRESS
New York and London
www.nyupress.org

References to Internet websites (URLs) were accurate at the time of writing. Neither the author nor New York University Press is responsible for URLs that may have expired or changed since the manuscript was prepared.

LIBRARY OF CONGRESS CATALOGING-IN-PUBLICATION DATA
Klapper, Melissa R, author.
Ballots, babies, and banners of peace : American Jewish women's activism, 1890–1940 / Melissa R. Klapper.
pages ; cm
Includes bibliographical references and index.
ISBN 978–1–4798–5059–4 (pb : alk. paper)
ISBN 978–0–8147–4894–7 (cl : alk. paper)
ISBN 978–0–8147–4895–4 (e)
ISBN 978–0–8147–4946–3 (e)
1. Jewish women—United States—Political activity—History—20th century. 2. Jewish women—United States—Social conditions—20th century. 3. Women—United States—Political activity—History—20th century. 4. Women—United States—Social conditions—20th century. 5. Women—Suffrage—United States—History—20th century. 6. Women and peace—United States—History—20th century. I. Title.
HQ1426.K57   2012
305.48'89240730904—dc23   2012035354

New York University Press books are printed on acid-free paper, and their binding materials are chosen for strength and durability. We strive to use environmentally responsible suppliers and materials to the greatest extent possible in publishing our books.

Manufactured in the United States of America

10 9 8 7 6 5 4 3 2 1

Lovingly dedicated to my niece, Sophie Fine,
latest in a long line of strong Jewish women.

CONTENTS

ACKNOWLEDGMENTS

I take great pleasure thanking the many people who helped me with this book. Writing a book may be a solitary undertaking, but the process is no such thing. Without the encouragement, support, and faith of family, friends, colleagues, and a variety of institutions, taking on a project this size would indeed have been a thankless task.

First, let me express my gratitude to the unsung heroes of history, the archivists and librarians whose work preserves the past. Although too many in number to mention individually, the devoted professionals at the American Jewish Archives Center, the American Jewish Historical Society, the Harvard Medical Library, the Historical Society of Pennsylvania, the Jewish Museum of Maryland, the Minnesota Historical Society, the Philadelphia Jewish Archives Center, the New York Public Library, the North Carolina Office of Archives and History, the Rowan University Campbell Library, the Swarthmore College Peace Collection, the Schlesinger Library on the History of American Women, the Social Welfare History Archives, the Sophia Smith Collection, the Upper Midwest Jewish Archives, and the YIVO Institute for Jewish Research made my research possible. As this list indicates, I traveled far and wide while working on this book, and I would also like to thank all those who offered me home hospitality and made my research trips even more enjoyable: Arlene Bernstein, Beattie Broide, Phil and Sylvia Barack Fishman, Ruth Langer and Jonathan Sarna, Ferne and Mitchell Klapper, Sue and David Klapper, Elky and Reuven Pelberg, and Riv-Ellen Prell and Steven Foldes.

An array of institutions provided fellowships and grants. Many thanks to the American Jewish Archives Center, the Association for Jewish Studies Women's Caucus, the Frankel Institute for Advanced Judaic Studies at the University of Michigan, the National Endowment for the Humanities, the Peace History Society, Rowan University, the Schlesinger Library, the Sophia Smith Collection, and the YIVO Institute for Jewish Research. I am especially grateful for the continuous support of the Hadassah-Brandeis Institute, an unparalleled home for Jewish women's studies.

The list of colleagues who have contributed in some way to this book is a long one. I am fortunate to be part of a genuinely encouraging and just plain nice group of people in the Department of History at Rowan University. Special thanks to my Rowan colleagues Dianne Ashton, Emily Blanck, and Janet Lindman for thoughtful comments on early versions of several chapters. It has been a pleasure to work with Jennifer Hammer at NYU Press again. Thanks to Naomi S. Cohen, Asya Vaisman, and Sebastian Schulman for rendering into such beautiful English some of the Yiddish sources I identified. Participants in the Philadelphia-area American Jewish studies reading group and the Frankel Institute for Advanced Judaic Studies Fall 2011 seminar on Jews and politics offered useful feedback at critical junctures. Joyce Antler, Sylvia Barack Fishman, Anna Igra, Leslie Ginsparg Klein, Deborah Dash Moore, Riv-Ellen Prell, Shula Reinharz, and Jonathan Sarna all helpfully commented on various parts of the book along the way. I owe special gratitude to Pam Nadell, for generously reading multiple drafts of the entire manuscript and for many years of encouragement, and to Alice Kessler-Harris, for consistently and enthusiastically challenging me to think bigger and for continuing to uphold the gold standard of mentorship.

My family and friends have been living with this book nearly as long as I have. I am so appreciative to Devorah Taitelbaum, Rivkah Fischman Weiss and family, Sara Esther and Yaakov Kader, Malka Miriam Mandel, Ashley Klapper Pressman, Yael and Michael Buckstein, Sarah Gersten, Janet and Danny Eisenberg and family, and Yoni and Zevi Jacobson and family for their friendship and encouragement, without which I might have drowned in a sea of footnotes. Most of all, I am grateful for the love and support of Ferne and Mitch Klapper, my parents, and Jennie, Josh, Dovie, and Sophie Fine, my sister, brother-in-law, nephew, and niece.

ABBREVIATIONS OF ORGANIZATION NAMES

ABCL	American Birth Control League
AWSA	American Woman Suffrage Association
BCCRB	Birth Control Clinical Research Bureau
CCAR	Central Conference of American Rabbis
CL	Consumers' League
ICW	International Council of Women
IWSA	International Woman Suffrage Alliance
LWV	League of Women Voters
NAWSA	National American Woman Suffrage Association
NCCCW	National Committee on the Cause and Cure of War
NCFLBC	National Committee on Federal Legislation for Birth Control
NCJW	National Council of Jewish Women
NCPW	National Council for Prevention of War
NFTS	National Federation of Temple Sisterhoods
NWP	National Woman's Party
NWSA	National Woman Suffrage Association
PMC	People's Mandate Committee
VPL	Voluntary Parenthood League
WCTU	Women's Christian Temperance Union
WILPF	Women's International League for Peace and Freedom
WPoU	Women's Political Union
WPU	Women's Peace Union
WRL	War Resisters League
WTUL	Women's Trade Union League

Israel's women, like women of other faiths, are interested in all causes that tend to bring people closer together in every movement affecting the welfare of mankind.
—Hannah Greenebaum Solomon, 1894[1]

Sinai Temple, E. G. Hirsch Scholarship, Hadassah Home Club for Working Women, Ruth Home for Working Girls, Scholarship Association, Council of Jewish Women, United Jewish Drive, Lincoln Center Camp, Chicago Heart Association, Service Council, Women's International League for Peace and Freedom, Blind Service Committee, Civic Music Association, Jewish Consumptive Relief Society, League of Religious Fellowship, Chicago Woman's Aid, Woman's City Club, Red Cross, Mothers' Aid to the Lying In Hospital, Lincoln Center, Chicago Woman's Club, Art Institute.
—List of Jennie Franklin Purvin's charitable contributions, 1926[2]

The summer of her seventeenth birthday found Jennie Franklin enjoying a merry whirlwind of social activities with her circle of friends in Chicago. But on August 23, 1890, Jennie marked the day itself by solemnly writing in her diary, "It is high time for me to definitely shape my career and awaken to the duties of a woman." Some of the "duties of a woman" seemed obvious to a middle-class adolescent Jewish girl at the turn of the twentieth century, and Jennie dutifully fulfilled them. She graduated from high school, helped out in the faltering family business, frequented public lectures, read a great deal to keep up her education, and in 1899 married the businessman Moses L. Purvin and subsequently had two daughters. Even as an adolescent Jennie had been both a model young American woman and a model young Jewish woman, attending synagogue services, being confirmed, participating in Chicago's Hebrew Literary Society, socializing with other young Jews like her future husband, and consulting with her congregational rabbi for advice on starting out on "the road I wish to travel." Neither Jennie nor anyone else in her milieu saw any contradiction between Jewish and female identity. Of all the Hebrew Literary Society events she wrote about in her diary, she relished most the debates on such subjects as racism and woman suffrage, secular topics given serious attention in an explicitly Jewish setting. Once married, she not only focused on her private life at home with her husband and children but over the decades also expanded her civic activities. Within the Jewish community, Jennie took on leadership roles in her synagogue sisterhood, the Chicago section of the National Council of Jewish Women (NCJW), and the Chicago Woman's Aid, a middle-class Jewish women's benevolent group.[3]

Participation in Jewish women's organizations neither confined Jennie to a strictly Jewish public life nor precluded her steadily expanding commitment to the large American women's social movements of the day. Interested in suffrage from her adolescence, as an adult she immersed herself in the cause still further as she, like other American women during the Progressive Era, realized that disenfranchisement limited their power to achieve meaningful social reform. Members of a Jewish women's organization that she served as president wrote a poem in her honor that reflected her commitment to suffrage:

> Jennie has the habit of being President,
> On the next election her thoughts are now intent;
> Looking to the future, to Nineteen Sixteen
> What "Votes for Women" count for plainly can be seen.[4]

The following decade, Jennie encouraged the Chicago Woman's Aid to become involved with the burgeoning birth control movement by sponsoring the clinics that the Illinois Birth Control League set up during the 1920s. The league recognized the importance of local women's organizations in its work. Its 1926 annual report approvingly singled out the Jewish women's group for regularly sending a delegate to its meetings and providing volunteer personnel to the clinics.[5] Additionally, from the earliest years of the 1900s, Jennie devoted herself to a variety of women's peace organizations, especially the Chicago branches of NCJW and the Women's International League for Peace and Freedom (WILPF). She attended the 1923 National Council of Women biennial meeting as an NCJW delegate with a special interest in the parts of the program devoted to peace activism.[6] To each of these secular movements she brought a Jewish sensibility, often carrying out her activism through Jewish women's organizations. The contemplative, aspiring Jewish girl she had been had now become a thoughtful, active Jewish woman who believed in her responsibility and power to make a difference not only to her own Jewish family and community but also to the wider world.

Jennie Franklin Purvin symbolizes Jewish women throughout the United States during the late nineteenth and early twentieth centuries who developed a distinctive activist identity that drew on both their gender and their religious or ethnic identities. At various moments they foregrounded each of these.[7] American Jewish women who wanted to be both good Jews and good women found themselves negotiating sometimes competing, sometimes complementary demands, and they daily made complex choices as their understandings of their American, Jewish, and female identities fluctuated. Participating in major American women's social movements gave them the opportunity to make those choices. Significantly, Jewish women, who could, at least theoretically, hide their ethnic, religious, and cultural differences rarely chose to do so. They generally opted to sustain an open Jewish identity of some kind while participating in American women's movements, discovering convergences in values shaped by gender, class, national, and religious or ethnic identity. They drew on these common values when becoming involved with social movements, whether their paths to engagement led them to activism as individuals, as members of Jewish organizations, or as members of women's groups.

Judaism and Jewishness signified different things to different people. Jews could be Jewish without attending synagogues or speaking a particular language or subscribing to ideals of either particularism or universalism. The problem of what being Jewish meant—and the nature of the religious, cultural, and social responsibilities that Jewish identity entailed—figured prominently in the ways that American Jewish women saw their own activism. The complexity of Jewishness in the United States intersected with women's movements at the point of American Jewish women's early feminist activism.

The confluence of identity and activism was never static for these women. Changes in gender roles during the first half of the twentieth century affected religious and ethnic women and women's organizations, including Jewish women's groups. Class and religious differences shaped American Jewish women's social and political activism as well. So, too, did the exponential growth of American Jewry that resulted from mass migration at the turn of the century and the concomitant struggle to find a stance that balanced traditional culture with a rapidly modernizing American society. Various permutations of anti-Semitism played a role in both limiting and directing Jewish women's social and political activism and sometimes shaped their relationships with their non-Jewish activist counterparts. Jewishness mattered to them, especially a communal tradition of caring and support and a sense of social justice. All these factors promoted Jewish women's important involvement in early twentieth-century feminist movements.[8]

The turn of the twentieth century ushered in a prolonged moment of great reform energy in the United States. Women used the language of municipal housekeeping to justify an expansion of their roles outward from their private homes into the public sphere. They also summoned the rhetoric of maternalism, a term that signifies a collective belief in gender differences based on motherhood as the foundation for reform. Municipal housekeeping and maternalism opened many doors for women's activism and to a limited extent enabled cross-class alliances founded on essential ideas about womanhood and motherhood.[9]

For Jewish women, the ferment of reform offered possibilities for acculturating into American society as well. As Jews and as women, they grappled with becoming modern American citizens. However, not all women's movements invited their participation. The Women's Christian Temperance Union, for instance, organized on the basis of religious identity, welcomed few Jewish women.[10] Some Jewish women preferred to direct their public activities toward explicitly Jewish causes like Zionism or to work in the heavily Jewish milieu of the labor movement, both forms of activism that have received considerable scholarly attention.[11] But a significant number of Jewish women, who have been virtually ignored by historians, chose instead or in addition to focus their energies on the great women's social movements of the first part of the twentieth century: suffrage, birth control, and peace.

Not as radical as socialism or communism, not as Jewish as Zionism, the suffrage, birth control, and peace movements nonetheless offered Jewish women exciting opportunities to be swept up in gendered activism without abandoning Jewish meaning. All three causes emerged from the larger nineteenth century woman's movement, always about more than voting rights, and from working-class women's traditions of labor activism. Women's claims to equality, justice, and authority extended beyond suffrage, yielding equally feminist movements such as birth control and peace, both fundamentally concerned with structural social and political change, and both insisting on the collapse of the gendered divide between public and private.[12] For Jewish women, radicalism in these social causes also emerged from Jewish traditions of taking care of the community that found expression in the labor movement and in American feminism.

These movements overlapped with one another chronologically and together formed a cluster of feminist activity. The suffrage movement, revitalized in 1890 by the merger of two competing groups into the National American Woman Suffrage Association (NAWSA), attracted growing numbers of supporters and finally began to achieve notable successes in state campaigns during the 1910s that culminated in the passage of the Nineteenth

Amendment in 1920.[13] Meanwhile, though contraception was hardly a new phenomenon, the birth control movement as such began during the mid-1910s. By the 1920s and 1930s, the establishment of birth control clinics and repeated attempts to change legal restrictions on contraception transformed it into an increasingly popular cause.[14] The peace movement similarly boasted a long history, stretching back at least to the early nineteenth century in the United States, but the proliferation of women's peace groups during and after World War I closely linked peace activism to feminism for the first time.[15]

For all three social movements, World War I proved a turning point. Women's ability during the war to fill roles and jobs traditionally held by men impressed many Americans favorably. Mainstream suffrage leaders struck something of a bargain with President Woodrow Wilson, offering women's cooperation in war work in exchange for his support for a constitutional amendment enfranchising women. The devastations of World War I energized the peace movement, which worldwide attracted millions of people determined never again to allow such a catastrophe. Because many social critics pointed to a link between overpopulation and war, World War I also provided the impetus for some activists to adopt birth control as another method of ensuring world peace, the wealth of nations, and the health and happiness of citizens everywhere. Following the success of the suffrage movement after the war, both the birth control and peace movements grew in strength, number, and activity during the 1920s and 1930s as some former suffragists, along with many new activists, turned their attention to them.[16]

From this perspective, the "doldrums" decades between suffrage victory and the so-called second wave feminism of the 1960s and 1970s did not exist in the United States.[17] These decades of meaningful women's activism reshaped many gendered relations of power, albeit not conclusively enough to satisfy later generations of women. The birth control and peace movements exemplify this obscured feminist history. They were not alone; working-class industrial feminism and middle-class Equal Rights Amendment activism also flourished during this period.[18] That not all the women involved in social movements during the 1910s, 1920s, and 1930s would have claimed the term "feminist" changed neither the significance of their activism nor their achievements. No understanding of twentieth-century U.S. history, let alone American women's history, is possible without full consideration of these social movements.

Furthermore, no understanding of these movements is possible without Jewish women. Exploring American Jewish women's activism inspires rethinking of ethnicity and gender roles during the first decades of the twentieth century, especially in reference to the meaning of community membership, citizenship, and women in public life. This is not just a question of "contribution history." Middle-class Jewish women may not typically have been leaders of the suffrage movement, but they were heavily involved in ways that other suffrage scholars have overlooked, and working-class Jewish women who were labor leaders played key roles in suffrage campaigns. Jewish women's leadership and grassroots activism, from within and outside Jewish communal organizations, actively shaped birth control and peace by encouraging these movements to encompass a greater diversity of interests while still underscoring gender as the most powerful identity factor underlying feminist activism.[19] No history of either birth control or peace in the United States, which is to say, virtually no previous history of those movements, is complete without analyzing the impact of Jewish women's presence.[20] Similarly, the history of American Jews is incomplete without considering the importance of women's activism in shaping the American Jewish community during the period of its greatest consolidation.[21] American Jewish women brought awareness of feminist issues to the American Jewish community, particularly through the extensive American Jewish press coverage of suffrage, birth control, and peace. They challenged the social, political, and cultural constraints on women at every turn. In so doing, they established organizations among the most active women's groups in the United States, expanded their causes internationally to include Jews and women in other places, and experimented with reconciling their multiple identities as women, Jews, and Americans.

American Jewish women were a diverse lot, and even a study of just a brief period, let alone one that spans several generations, needs to reflect that diversity.[22] Complicated divides in religious observance and affiliation, class status, national origin and citizenship, cultural and ethnic heritage, political persuasion, geographic location, and attitudes toward Americanization provided any number of axes along which Jewish women in America expressed their diversity. Neither was the American Jewish population writ large the same in 1940 as it had been in 1880. Yet none of these undeniable differences mean that the very term "American Jewish women" is only a historical convention. Historical actors wrote, spoke, and thought of themselves as American Jewish women, an identity category they both chose and were sometimes relegated to by others for whom none of the internal fissures within American Jewry mattered as much as the Jewishness, however defined, of that community. During the early twentieth century, when anti-Semitism appeared all too frequently even within apparently progressive political movements, American Jewish women managed to reconcile their many differences to fight against prejudice and discrimination.

Many of the most salient changes experienced by Jews in America during this period stemmed from the mass migration that brought their numbers from approximately 250,000 in 1880 to nearly 5 million in 1940, with the children and grandchildren of immigrants contributing to this number despite the immigration restrictions of the mid-1920s.[23] A revival of Jewish tradition and practice preceded mass migration among an influential cadre of urban, well-educated, American-born Jewish sons and daughters during the 1870s and 1880s, yielding a host of new institutions whose very names proclaimed the promise of a synthesized identity, such as the *American Hebrew* newspaper (1879) and the American Jewish Historical Society (1893).[24] But the arrival of nearly 2 million mostly eastern European immigrants between 1880 and 1925 transformed virtually every facet of American Jewry.

Orthodox and Conservative Judaism joined Reform Judaism as formal religious denominations, with groups like Young Israel advocating an Americanized form of Orthodoxy and a newly reorganized Jewish Theological Seminary combining in the Conservative movement traditional Jewish law with modernization. Each denomination was thus by definition progressive in its own way, though many of the most prominent social reformers affiliated with Reform Judaism. Motivated by a potent combination of genuine concern for the new immigrants and a not unrealistic fear of increased anti-Semitism, the established American Jewish community engaged in philanthropic endeavors across the United States that offered tremendous resources to newcomers but generally insisted on rapid acculturation as the price of entry. Many immigrant Jews responded with a mixture of alacrity, gratitude, and suspicion; few wished to reject Americanization altogether, yet most wanted to make choices on their own terms about what and how fast to change. By the 1920s, immigrants and children of immigrants had often moved into positions of leadership in Jewish social service agencies, which became models in their fields.[25]

In the cities where most new immigrants clustered, an ethnic economy not just of commerce but also of culture and politics flourished, with Yiddish, at least for first-generation immigrants, as a critical identity marker. Like their western European predecessors, some of whom came to the United States as political refugees following the European upheavals of 1848, some eastern European Jewish immigrants arrived with radical convictions that many native-born Americans viewed with dread. Already attracted in large number to the "isms" that had penetrated every corner of European Jewry—socialism, Bundism, Zionism—the new arrivals and their children after them utterly transformed the political character of American Jewry.[26]

And where were Jewish women in this welter of religious affiliations, class identities, geographic locations, political movements, degrees of Americanization? Everywhere. The same municipal housekeeping rhetoric and gendered notions of the moral high ground that paved the way toward an expansion of American women's public role enabled women to occupy prominent positions in Jewish communal life. The same feminization of religion that transformed women into central religious figures in Protestant churches occurred in the liberal denominations of American Judaism, especially within Reform Jewish congregations. Changes in traditional Jewish ideas about and limitations on women became central to the modernization of Judaism within both synagogues and the larger community. As mothers, immigrant Jewish women were seen as key to the success of future generations of American Jews, and there was widespread consensus within the community that middle-class Jewish women were best equipped to help them. Working-class and immigrant Jewish women often resented middle-class Jews' attitude that they must change in order to succeed, but that did not stop them from taking advantage of resources offered by the wider Jewish community or even from hoping that their children would have very different lives than their own.

A brief introduction to the National Council of Jewish Women (NCJW), featured prominently throughout this book, provides a case study of changes within the American Jewish community and both differences and similarities among American Jewish women, on the one hand, and between Jewish and non-Jewish women in the United States on the other. Founded in 1893 as a result of the World's Parliament of Religions at the Chicago World's Fair, NCJW was the first independent national Jewish women's group. Led by Hannah Greenebaum Solomon, who had been the first Jewish woman invited to join the Chicago Woman's Club, it quickly became the major Jewish women's organization in an era of American women's large-scale organizing. The NCJW originated with an explicitly religious and philanthropic mission but soon, like other turn-of-the-century American women's groups, turned toward a program of progressive reform. Deeply concerned about Jewish immigration to the United States, the mostly American-born, middle-class NCJW members wanted to ease immigrants' transition to life in America. Although their activities were at times tinged with an element of social control, NCJW became a major innovator in all kinds of social reform. Its commitment to ensuring the safety and well-being of young Jewish women traveling alone set a new standard in the deployment of a national philanthropic network as well as the cooperation of voluntary and government agencies.[27]

The NCJW's Americanization, citizenship, and religious education efforts during the first decades of the twentieth century are relatively well known. Much less well known is the kind of political activism that played an increasingly central role in NCJW programs during the interwar years. During those decades, NCJW supported birth control and peace. These commitments located NCJW, still mostly middle class in composition although now with a significant membership of second- and third-generation American Jewish women, far to the left on the political spectrum of American women's organizations. Though it was certainly the case that secular activism facilitated their insistence on greater equity in Jewish communal affairs, Jewish women harbored feminist goals outside their own religious communities as well.

NCJW members found a consonance of values in mainstream and Jewish thinking about women and saw no contradiction in expanding their activism as Jewish women to encompass an array of causes. As its former national president Marion Misch explained, NCJW was primarily a Jewish organization for a number of reasons. It honored famous and inspiring Jewish women in history and held them up as role models; followed Jewish injunctions to be charitable and serve the needy in the community; offered religious as well as social or service programming; and maintained constant awareness of the important lessons of Judaism. However, none of these commitments precluded taking those role models or injunctions or programming or lessons into other fields of endeavor. When NCJW became involved in causes outside the Jewish community, the organization did not leave Jewishness behind but took its religious and cultural identity along to enhance and facilitate its work. Misch herself exemplified this pattern, as she had served on the executive board of the International Council of Women while occupying leadership positions in NCJW. External observers also noticed the ability of NCJW to expand its activities while retaining Jewish identity. In her 1934 history of American women, Inez Haynes Irwin wrote of NCJW, "No other of the sectarian organizations has done so much work apart from sanctuary or temple."[28]

During the interwar years, NCJW, along with other Jewish women's organizations, carved out a new role in the public sphere for women eager to see Judaism and Jewishness as sources of activism. Middle-class Jewish women in particular used American women's associational life to demonstrate their acculturation. Working-class Jewish women, especially political radicals, were more likely to cast a jaundiced eye on the promise of universal sisterhood, but they nonetheless joined national and transnational organizations both inside and outside the Jewish community. All these women worked with men, often closely, to support their causes, particularly when trying to help persecuted Jews worldwide. But they also flocked to women's organizations and feminist movements in ways that illustrated the primary importance of their gender identities.[29]

Interactions of gender, religion, politics, and class lay behind every manifestation of American Jewish women's activism before World War II. Jewish women of all class backgrounds and political stripes, middle-class matrons as well as working-class leftists, committed themselves to suffrage, birth control, and peace. On the surface they seemed to be focusing their energies on secular movements, but they often saw their activism as an extension of their religious or culturally traditional roles rather than as a rejection of Judaism or Jewishness. During the early twentieth century, American Judaism experienced profound transformations, including serious reconsideration of women's roles. At the same time, much of American society committed to progressive reform and reevaluated women's status more generally. At the nexus of all these changes, American Jewish women found in women's social movements causes that bridged the sacred and the secular.

American Jewish women believed that their activism could alter relations of power. Activists influenced definitions of citizenship through the suffrage movement, reproductive rights through the birth control movement, and international relations through the peace movement. Gendered activism brought Jewish women into political spaces where their perspectives as women and Jews generated a unique sensibility. Because Jewish women were so prominent in these causes, especially birth control and peace, where they held positions of leadership and provided significant numbers at the grassroots level, their activism illustrates the intensely personal nature of women's politics during the first decades of the twentieth century. "The personal is political" is a mantra most often associated with feminists of the 1960s and 1970s. Yet the insight that public and private structures of power are inextricably linked and constitutive of each other applies to earlier periods as well. Feminist activists of the first half of the twentieth century were not likely to chant about "personal politics," but their activism nonetheless expressed the deep connections between the personal and the political, between private and public.

Of the three movements, suffrage was the most traditionally political because women pressed for their right to vote as an expression of power in the public sphere. Activists argued that modernity required an expansion of private responsibility outward from the family to the neighborhood to the community to the municipality to the state to the national government. Suffrage campaigns brought Jewish women into previously male-dominated spaces of political life. Jewish women also gradually began to claim an expanded public role in their synagogues and religious communities, imbuing their gendered, supposedly private religious spheres with political significance.

Like suffrage, birth control also embodied personal politics. Women contended that they should exert private control over their own fertility rather than delegating public power over their bodies to the state. As part of their process of acculturation, Jewish women wanted the freedom to choose upward mobility over large families and to take both health and economic reasons into account when deciding how many children to have. Jewish women also mounted religious and ethical arguments, made possible by the space Jewish law provided for family planning. Based on their own experiences, an important cadre of activist Jewish women doctors believed that women could make more valuable contributions to public life, as professionals and political beings, if they could shape their personal lives themselves.

Peace activism encompassed personal politics as well. A women's peace movement based on ideas about universal motherhood appealed to Jewish women, who often appreciated the traditional Jewish valorization of mothers and thus found in maternalism a bridge between American women's political and social interests and their own. The collective action and politicized motherhood involved in peace work transformed Jewish women's groups, already linked by family, community, and history to Jews overseas. Jewish women in the peace movement eventually faced special challenges when the specific, existential threat that Hitler and Nazism posed to Jews and Judaism threatened their universalist commitment to ideals of peace.

All these connections provided the basis for a group defined by the supposedly private matter of religion to bring multiple Jewish sensibilities to public issues and political concerns. Jewish identity also brought a distinctive sense of internationalism to activists seeking change in relations of power across borders as well as within nations. New forms of mobilization and assertiveness emerged at the same time for women and Jews in open Western societies, a phenomenon of timing that encouraged Jewish women to develop a politics of activism. Like Jews in most countries at the turn of the century, women developed alternative political strategies to compensate for their absence from the arena of electoral politics. Their activism used the mechanics and tools of informal politics to encompass meaningful social reform.

A consistent feature of many Jewish women's lives across borders of class and national origins, activism contributed to shared experiences that belie a historiographic tradition pitting established American Jews against newcomers. If anything, immigrant Jewish women, often with greater previous exposure to radicalism, found expansion of their public activity to be a natural extension of their legacy of public roles and may have set the standard of activism.[30] By the 1920s and 1930s, with American Jewish women now encompassing new immigrants, daughters and granddaughters of immigrants, and women whose families had been in the United States for generations, activism in women's movements simultaneously offered Jewish women a chance to acculturate based on shared gender norms and an opportunity to claim Jewish identity as something of value for American society overall.

Due in part to women's activism, American Jewry became heavily associated with liberalism and progressivism, which both encompassed and, to some degree, moderated the radicalism that some eastern European Jewish immigrants had brought with them to the United States. Organizations such as NCJW, the National Federation of Temple Sisterhoods (NFTS), or the Workmen's Circle Ladies Auxiliary, which many women used as vehicles for their activism, simultaneously established Jewish communal autonomy and forged connections to other American political constituencies that viewed activism as a critical instrument of expression and dissent within sovereign states. The American Jewish community debated suffrage, birth control, and peace from religious, political, social, and cultural perspectives and generally provided a supportive environment to women and their causes. Exploring American Jewish women's activism as individuals and as members of both Jewish and nonsectarian organizations helps reconstruct, understand, and analyze modern Jewish political identity.

Jewish women in the United States and Europe achieved recognition during their own time as major players in the suffrage and especially the birth control and peace movements, yet standard accounts of women's activism barely mention them. The historiography on American Jewish women refers only minimally to any pre–World War II political activism outside of socialism, the labor movement, or Zionism, yet many Jewish women found their activist homes in gendered social movements less obviously connected to Jewishness. The lacuna results in part from a more general absence of Jewish women from narratives of American women's history. The neglect may be due in part to a historiographic perception of Jews as "just" white that does not reflect a more complicated historical reality; during the period covered in this book, Jewish women were not always perceived or accepted as white, though their participation in women's movements contributed to their acculturation. The connections among Jewish women's religious and cultural convictions, their ethnic and class backgrounds, and their political activism has been lost by scholars of both American Judaism and historians of American women. The former, even now, tend to discount both Jewish women's spiritual lives and the power of politics in American Jewish history. The latter rarely acknowledge the presence of Jewish women in social movements they assume to have been either Christian or secular in nature. This omission is particularly surprising given the widespread acknowledgment that religion motivated much of American women's collective action. In part, then, this entire book is a project of documentation and restoration.[31]

Beyond that project, American Jewish women embodied the tensions that virtually all immigrant ethnic groups confronted in balancing the obvious benefits of Americanization and acculturation with the preservation of their heritage. Contested meanings of "Jewishness," which could signify religion, ethnicity, culture, or even race, further complicated the issues. Some American Jewish women approached social movements from Jewish and female perspectives, while others initially paid little attention to their Jewish identity. During the 1930s, however, they were all forced to deal with the implications of growing anti-Semitism in domestic life and foreign affairs. Their struggles to define American Jewry at home and then—in some cases for the first time—to consider the ramifications of Jewishness as a force operating across national borders illustrates the complex issue of multiple and transnational identities in the modern world.

Jewish women's experiences also illuminate the conditional alliances within the early twentieth-century women's movement, exemplified in the Women's Trade Union League (WTUL), which brought together working-class women and their middle-class allies to support women's organizing and improve their work conditions. As many Jewish women workers and allies in the WTUL discovered, gender identification could unite women across barriers of class, culture, ethnicity, religion, and nationality (and, to a lesser extent, race), but only when those involved could successfully prioritize gender over all other identity claims.[32] Both gender solidarity and feminism were larger than maternalism; not all feminists or Jewish women were maternalists. Still, it is unsurprising that so many Jewish women spoke of suffrage, birth control, and peace in maternalist terms because motherhood served as an important link between American and Jewish gender identities, especially for middle-class women. Motherhood also bridged religious, class, and national differences among Jewish women both in the United States and internationally. As a result, the language of maternalist politics, while never encompassing all of feminist activism, served ideological and instrumental purposes for most Jewish women in the suffrage, birth control, and peace movements. Like other universalist ideals of the period, however, maternalism ultimately proved to be contingent, if not entirely illusory.[33]

The history of American Jewish women's early feminist activism also complicates recent efforts to conceive of American Jewish history as stretched between two opposing poles of communalism and dispersionism. Broadly defined, communalist history emphasizes self-proclaimed and self-identified Jewish individuals, organizations, and institutions, while dispersionist history encompasses anyone of Jewish descent, regardless of his or her engagement with communal Jewry and identification as Jewish. Proponents do not argue that the binary approaches are irredeemably divided.[34] Still, the complicated lives of the women in this book disrupt any borders between communalism and dispersionism. Because notions of identity are fluid rather than fixed, it is impossible to differentiate between some kind of public Jewry and private individuals who happen to be Jewish. American Jewish actors of the past, blessed with free will, a shifting social, economic, and cultural landscape, and the possibility of a sort of voluntary Judaism not available elsewhere, very often found their Jewish identities changing over time and in response to circumstances. There were women in the peace movement, for example, who never gave much thought to being Jewish until the crisis of the 1930s cast a whole new light on what that meant, and their personal identities changed accordingly. They, and countless others like them, cannot be so neatly dismissed as dispersionists or even converted communalists.

The heavy involvement of Jewish women's organizations in secular causes like birth control and peace upends any firm distinction between inward-looking communal organizations and outward-looking dispersionist activities. Both NCJW and NFTS, for instance, were founded with explicitly religious missions but, caught up in the era of progressive reform and a general expansion of women's public activities, came to see secular activism as part of their Jewishness and religious mandate. The Jewish identity of these organizations provided the basis for their significant nonsectarian activities, which were then widely recognized by the larger social movements in which they participated. The same was true for countless individual women who found that Jewish identity, with or without religion per se, provided the major source of motivation for their commitment to effect change in the wider world. For them there was no conflict between communalist and dispersionist activism. Innumerable Jewish women joined Jewish groups and secular movements at the same time. Changes in Jewish communal organizations both shaped and were shaped by relationships with disparate political and social movements as brokered by Jewish women and men who moved easily from one to another.

Anti-Semitism further disrupts the communalist/dispersionist model.[35] Jewish women activists, and by extension all Jews in America, may have had control over their own identities, but not over their identification. In the most benign sense, even those American Jews who felt no connection to the

Jewish community writ large were often identified as Jews by others. Some resisted this identification mightily, while others resigned themselves to it. In a less benign sense, Jewish women in secular social movements, especially those who took on leadership roles, were always aware that their colleagues saw them as Jewish. Sometimes that did not matter much; sometimes it did. The blatant anti-Semitism of parts of Elizabeth Cady Stanton's *Woman's Bible* frightened some Jewish women away from the suffrage movement; some birth control spokespeople adopted eugenicist rhetoric that many Jews found alarming; peace organizations for a long time refused to acknowledge the unique nature of the threat to Jews under Nazism. Whether they liked it or not, even the most dispersionist Jews then found themselves encountering communalist issues. By setting boundaries that were not always immediately apparent, anti-Semitism affected American Jewish women's activism. Given the appeal of feminist activism to Jewish women from a variety of backgrounds and the heretofore unexamined role Jewish women played in the suffrage, birth control, and peace movements, consideration of anti-Semitism must recast our understanding of both American Jewish history and the history of American feminism.[36]

* * * *

This book proceeds both thematically and chronologically, drawing on a tremendous range of long-neglected archival materials as well as published primary sources and periodical literature in English and Yiddish. The first chapter traces Jewish women's suffrage activism from the creation of NAWSA in 1890 through the ratification of the Nineteenth Amendment in 1920 and its aftermath. Jewish women primarily worked for suffrage as individuals, though intense debate flourished among Jewish women's groups. There were some Jewish anti-suffragists as well. The American Jewish press devoted considerable time and space to suffrage, and rabbis aired the issue within the community. The cross-class and international dimensions of Jewish women's activism were apparent in their involvement in suffrage, as was the anti-Semitism that set some limits on their activism. By the end of the suffrage campaign, some Jewish women had begun to draw parallels between expanding their civic roles as American citizens and their religious roles in synagogue and communal life.

Chapter 2 establishes the continuities and new directions in Jewish women's activism during the 1920s, when Jewish women in growing numbers worked for a broader feminist agenda, like their non-Jewish counterparts. Even before the suffrage victory this agenda had included women winning greater control over their bodies. During the 1920s, an explosion of birth control activism veered away from its radical roots and engaged ever more "ordinary" women and men. Jewish women became a significant consumer constituency for the birth control movement, challenging the restrictive legal environment. American Jewish culture generally supported contraception, although pockets of resistance persisted.

The third chapter analyzes the expansion of American Jewish women's peace activism, which also predated suffrage victory but achieved new power and recognition during and after the First World War. Throughout the 1920s, Jewish women's organizations devoted considerable resources to the cause, regardless of the suspect radicalism of peace work. Significant numbers of American Jewish women joined nonsectarian women's peace groups as well and won the respect of peace leaders at home and abroad, although Jewish women were disappointed to encounter anti-Semitism within these groups. The American Jewish community conducted a lively debate about the relationship between peace and Jewishness. Multiple motivations fueled Jewish women's peace activism, including religious imperatives, class identity, maternalism, and notions of international sisterhood.

Chapter 4 explores the challenges and successes that Jewish women in the birth control movement encountered during the 1930s. Most Jewish women supported the strategy of increasing the number of birth control clinics, and Jewish women's organizations took up the cause in large numbers. Growing professionalization provided Jewish women with expanding opportunities as birth control doctors, activists, and consumers. The economic depredations of the Depression made contraception increasingly acceptable to both a general and a Jewish public, and a series of court decisions in which Jewish women figured prominently as attorneys and defendants moved birth control squarely into the mainstream. This chapter also examines the relationship between birth control and eugenics. Although the very word has a sinister overtone today, during the 1930s eugenics was a respectable, quasi-scientific approach to population and birth control that many Jewish leaders and laymen supported—even as a form of similar scientific racism undergirded Nazi policies in Germany that were about to throw Jews everywhere into crisis.

The fifth chapter probes a new set of challenges confronting Jewish women in the peace movement during the 1930s. As the international scene deteriorated, the Depression spread worldwide, and Hitler rose to power, the female and Jewish identities that underlay American Jewish women's peace activism steadily came into conflict with each other. Eventually most Jewish women in the peace movement faced an agonizing choice between their political beliefs and their religious, ethnic, and cultural identities. In the face of perceived indifference on the part of peace organizations to the plight of Jews under Nazism, Jewish identity ultimately prevailed. Decades of committed peace work at home and abroad, meaningful friendships, and synthesis of gender and religious identity could not withstand what most American Jewish women considered an existential threat to the survival of Jews and Judaism.

The conclusion of *Ballots, Babies, and Banners of Peace* reflects on the motivations of Jewish women engaged in early feminist activism. It considers the importance of fluid, but ever-present, Jewish identity to every kind of social movement in which Jewish women became involved. Women's social activism during the early twentieth century illuminates the gendered paths toward acculturation taken by various elements of the American Jewish community. The conclusion pays special attention to the impact of Jewish women on American women's feminist activism and the importance of recovering their voices in order to understand the foundational, critical involvement of Jewish women in postwar feminism.

1

"We Jewish Women Should Be Especially Interested in Our New Citizenship"

American Jewish Women and the Suffrage Movement

> Womanhood has occupied an unique place in Jewish life and we should be among the first to welcome the assumption of those responsibilities of citizenship by womankind which are an inevitable part of the new order of democratic life that lies before us. No one ought to be more sympathetic to the ideal of enfranchisement than Jews, who as a people have long known the hardship and the bitterness of unjust and proscriptive political discrimination.
> —Maud Nathan, 1917[1]

On a spring day in 1911, suffragists in New York enjoyed an entertaining break from their serious but often frustrating activism. Prominent women dressed in the fashions of decades past presented earlier arguments for and against women's enfranchisement. One notable speaker, wearing a hoop skirt in style fifty years ago, took an anti-suffrage position as befit her old-fashioned lack of enlightenment. This tall, elegant woman was Maud Nathan, whom the audience recognized as one of the most renowned activists in the United States and abroad. The satire was strengthened by the fact that everyone in the audience surely knew that one of the most outspoken real-life anti-suffragists was none other than Nathan's own sister, Annie Nathan Meyer.[2]

Of all the American Jewish women who participated in the suffrage movement, Maud Nathan was probably the best known at the turn of the century. The daughter of an elite Sephardic Jewish family, Nathan was born in 1862 and grew up in both New York and Green Bay, Wisconsin. At age seventeen, she married her cousin Frederick Nathan and settled in New York. Their only daughter died in childhood in 1895, and, with the encouragement of her husband and the cushion of considerable financial resources, Nathan turned her attention to affairs outside the home. She belonged to her synagogue sisterhood and the National Council of Jewish Women (NCJW) and

Maud Nathan. Courtesy of the Jacob Rader Marcus Center of the American Jewish Archives

was otherwise involved in Jewish communal affairs but also felt strongly that she did not want her life to be "bounded by the walls of the synagogue." Still, Nathan was proud to be Jewish and trumpeted her religious identity as loudly as her membership in the Daughters of the American Revolution. When she felt it necessary, she staunchly defended Jewish tradition and Jewish women. She believed that Jewish women had a special civic responsibility that could best be demonstrated through social reform and political participation.[3]

Suffrage activism was not the only focal point for the expansion of women's public roles at the opening of the twentieth century, but it was an obvious choice for women who, like Nathan, refused to accept lives "bounded" by political barriers, cultural norms, or social conventions. Jewish women in America encountered all of these limitations through the further complication of religious and/or ethnic traditions that imposed structurally similar, though not identical, boundaries on gender roles in both public and private expressions of Judaism and Jewishness. Class identity also played a role, as working-class Jewish women sometimes saw suffrage as a tool for achieving economic equality rather than an end in itself. Still, suffrage promised greater integration into the civic body, a major concern for Jewish women at a time when "genteel" prejudice was pervasive and less genteel forms of anti-Semitism were on the rise. Though not all Jewish women drew direct links between political rights for women and an expanded role in the synagogue or Jewish community, many did. A minority opposed the changes that suffrage might bring to traditional Jewish family life or to what they saw as the valuable role differentiation of women and men. The American Jewish community confronted these concerns throughout the early twentieth century, conducting a sustained discussion of the issues. American Jewish women's notable participation in the suffrage movement opened up possibilities for what full citizenship might mean for them as women and as Jews.

Nathan's activist career illustrates the interweaving of these themes and strands of identity. Her political activity began with the Woman's Municipal League of New York, founded at the turn of the century by elite women interested in rooting out municipal corruption. As the best public speaker in the group, Nathan addressed audiences large and small all over the city. Her Lower East Side speeches were translated into Yiddish by Minnie Rosen, whom she knew from the New York Consumers' League (CL). She had become involved in the CL at the behest of the prominent philanthropist Josephine Shaw Lowell, who encouraged Nathan to assuage her grief after her daughter's death by helping to improve the lives of working women in New York. As president of the CL from 1897 through 1927, decades that both preceded and postdated her suffrage activism, Nathan campaigned for consumers to buy only goods produced by "white label" factories and stores that agreed to specific sets of regulations designed to improve women's working conditions.[4]

Nathan's CL experience with legislators who would pay no attention to the views of disenfranchised women galvanized her. As she explained, "My experience in investigating the conditions of women wage earners warrants me in making the unqualified statement that some of the evils which these women suffer would not exist if women had the right to place their ballots in the ballot box." She encouraged working-class women to support suffrage in order to protect their own interests. Her 1908 pamphlet *The Wage Earner and The Ballot* argued that in suffrage states the age of consent was higher, illiteracy rates were lower, women were paid more for civil service jobs, there was better enforcement of protective labor legislation, and there were stronger child labor laws. Nathan never thought that the vote would be "a panacea for all evils in this world and the next." However, she genuinely believed that women were essentially different from men and had unique contributions to make to public life that required direct political expression through the vote. She thus brought both a gender and a class analysis to suffrage activism.[5]

First in New York and then on the national scene, Nathan's oratorical prowess helped her ascend to the top of the suffrage ranks. She also deliberately courted publicity, hoping to disrupt the stereotypes of disheveled, mannish suffragists. A 1908 profile of Nathan in *The Woman's Journal* described her as "tall, stately, beautiful, and always beautifully dressed." The article recounted an incident at a suffrage hearing when a heckler who assumed that all suffragists were unattractive hollered at her, "That one's an Anti—I know by the look of her!" Nathan felt it was important to emphasize that women voters would be more, not less, womanly once enfranchised. She thought that while militancy might be necessary in England, in the United States what she called "stunts" did a more effective job preserving activists' femininity. She claimed to have innovated a variety of stunts, including writing suffrage skits and plays, addressing audiences during theater intermissions, giving "silent speeches" on placards in store windows, and speaking from automobiles stationed in crowded areas.[6]

Nathan put forward both practical and ideological arguments for suffrage. In a prize-winning essay written in 1917, she explicitly addressed both the justice and the expediency of enfranchisement for women. Justice, she explained, decried the anti-democratic status quo of disenfranchisement, which left women paying taxes and otherwise affected by legislation they had no role in instituting. Expediency required that now that modern life had removed some domestic duties from the home to the government, making the home a more public place and the public arena more homelike, women were the most practical choices for many government positions and elected offices. Full citizenship for women would make them better wives, mothers, teachers, citizens, and patriots. Nathan believed that the expansion of women's education and the growth of women's clubs had combined to create a population of American women who were not only ready for but also deserving of enfranchisement.[7]

As the most famous American Jewish suffragist, Nathan was regularly called upon to contribute to the American Jewish press. In a 1912 *American Hebrew* article titled "Jewesses in the Suffrage Movement," Nathan expressed her lack of surprise that "the Jewish women . . . are taking their place in ever increasing numbers among those who are struggling for full emancipation." To her, the considerable political experience and interest of many working-class Jewish women, in addition to the reform agenda and social consciousness of middle-class Jewish women, explained Jewish women's excitement over the prospect of suffrage. As she consistently did in explaining her own motivations, Nathan linked women's Jewish heritage to their activism. "Political equality appeals to the imaginations of the descendants of Miriam, Deborah, and Esther," she wrote.[8] Not only was there no contradiction between Jewishness and American citizenship, there was congruity, making activist American Jewish women's identities particularly rich and meaningful.

Jewish women's involvement in the suffrage movement embodied a fundamental consonance between Jewish identity and American progressive politics but also demonstrated the continuing inhospitality of some elements of American society. Gender solidarity in the form of ideas about universal womanhood was not enough to overcome class differences, racial prejudices, and religious discrimination within any women's reform cause at the turn of the century. Jewish support for suffrage despite these barriers reflected the growing importance and public role of women within the American Jewish community. Suffrage activism gave middle-class Jewish women a way to acculturate through women's associational life and working-class Jewish women a way to combine economic and political claims to social justice. Regardless of their background, all American Jewish women grappled with becoming modern American citizens through their participation in political movements and social reform, relying on gender as a bridge between national and religious or ethnic identity. Jewish suffrage activism thus provided critical connections among social integration, American Jewish citizenship, and modern womanhood.

A Brief History of the Suffrage Movement in the United States

The beginning of the woman suffrage movement in the United States is usually dated to the Seneca Falls, New York, convention called in 1848 by Elizabeth Cady Stanton and Lucretia Mott. This convention produced the "Declaration of Sentiment" that modeled itself on the Declaration of Independence and called for a host of women's rights. Although Stanton insisted on the inclusion of women's enfranchisement, the controversial proposal did not immediately receive widespread support. One who did latch onto the idea was Ernestine Rose, whom later Jewish suffragists held up as a model even though Rose herself rarely acknowledged her Jewish background. Since many of the more radical women's rights advocates of the antebellum years were also committed abolitionists, it was not until after the Civil War that what scholar Ellen Carol DuBois calls an "independent women's movement" dedicated primarily to suffrage gained real power.[9]

In 1869 Wyoming became the first territory to grant women full enfranchisement, and the first suffrage amendment was introduced into Congress.

That year also marked a major split in the movement that slowed it down for several decades. The American Woman Suffrage Association (AWSA) and National Woman Suffrage Association (NWSA) differed sharply in their reaction to the Fifteenth Amendment, which enfranchised African Americans but, for the first time, included the word "male." Lucy Stone, Frederick Douglass, and other AWSA leaders believed that this was "the Negro's hour" and supported the Fifteenth Amendment, while Elizabeth Cady Stanton, Susan B. Anthony, and other NWSA members strongly opposed any measure that would, as they saw it, enfranchise former slaves at the expense of women. Another fundamental disagreement about whether to work for a federal amendment or individual state amendments weakened the execution of both strategies.[10]

The post–Civil War era was ripe with possibilities for women's progress on many fronts, but political gains were limited at best. During Reconstruction, the Supreme Court rejected the idea that the Fourteenth Amendment established the supremacy of national rather than state citizenship and, in the 1875 case *Minor v. Happersett*, ruled that the Constitution did not consider suffrage an automatic right of citizenship. Despite this denial of women's right to the franchise, suffrage never disappeared from the national scene and was brought before Congress nearly every term during the 1870s and 1880s, though progress was minimal.[11]

During this period it became increasingly evident that far from being the only useful instrument, the vote was but one of many implements stored in the political toolbox. Women, African Americans, Native Americans, not-yet-naturalized immigrants, and countless other groups recognized the power of enfranchisement, rarely discounting the vote as merely symbolic, yet they developed numerous strategies to function as political actors even without it. White women in particular, unfettered by additional burdens of racism, deployed a range of approaches to exert political power despite their formal voicelessness. They formed women's lobbies, gathered millions of signatures on petitions, organized around both special causes and broader women's interests, pulled strings and persuaded individual men of the righteousness of their causes, forced male legislators and politicians to recognize women's influence, cooperated with men on legislative efforts, and expanded women's domestic responsibilities in ways that increasingly legitimized their presence in the public arena.[12]

The reunification of AWSA and NWSA in 1890 brought new life to the suffrage movement. Although the merger was in many ways an admission of weakness, the new National American Woman Suffrage Association (NAWSA) revitalized older women's rights activists, who had already seen progress toward many of their earlier goals, such as married women's property rights and higher education for women, and also attracted significant numbers of new members into the fold by promising to keep the focus on suffrage. The younger generation of activists, many of them already experienced clubwomen, were accustomed to the idea of joining mass women's movements organized around specific issues and responded to new tactics that brought higher visibility to suffrage than it had enjoyed for several decades. Many of the younger suffragists had been radicalized by their frustration with the limitations that disenfranchisement put on their reform activities. Women entering the professions encountered intense discrimination that they hoped suffrage would help to diminish. The time also seemed ripe for changing public ideas about what the vote meant. As the United States gained power over new peoples and territories during the late nineteenth century, the question of voting as a mark of civilization came to the forefront. This made it easier for women to begin pushing in earnest for a federal amendment at a time when voting was widely seen as a state right. Individual state campaigns continued—the 1893 victory in Colorado buoyed the spirits of all American suffragists—but the movement's focus turned to the federal level.[13]

Suffrage rhetoric continued to rely on tropes of both justice—as citizens women should justly have the right to vote—and expediency—giving (white) women the vote would ensure the right kinds of decisions would be made by the right kind of people. However, there was also a pragmatic shift in suffrage logic from the natural rights of individuals to their national rights as citizens. This approach appealed especially to the thousands of immigrant women arriving in the United States daily at the turn of the century, most of whom were concerned with political and economic citizenship in their new home.[14]

A new generation of leaders contributed to the suffrage movement at the turn of the twentieth century and the decades that followed. NAWSA at first trod familiar paths, holding annual conventions, circulating petitions, and fending off the increasingly sophisticated National Association Opposed to Woman Suffrage. NAWSA grew ever larger and attracted new groups of women, particularly in the South. The development of new tactics in state referendum campaigns after 1910 gradually pushed NAWSA toward a more aggressive stance that included public demonstrations such as parades and even civil disobedience. Carrie Chapman Catt, who had spent a decade at the head of the International Woman Suffrage Alliance (IWSA), became president of NAWSA in 1915 and immediately put her tremendous administrative talent to work organizing the most effective campaigns yet.[15]

One of the challenges facing NAWSA was the divide between those who advocated for greater militancy and those who preferred more accommodating tactics. The British movement, which received a great deal of American press coverage, provided constant examples of both the promise and the peril inherent in such activities as pickets, work stoppages, attacks on property, arrests, and hunger strikes. The two women leading the faction that advocated more direct action were Alice Paul and Lucy Burns, both of whom had been radicalized while studying in England. When they returned to the United States, they joined NAWSA in the hopes of giving what they saw as a staid organization a jolt. In 1912 Paul became the chairman of NAWSA's Congressional Committee. She and Burns began to cultivate awareness, fundraise, and lobby, which did increase NAWSA membership. Frustrated by the lack of success in lobbying for the federal amendment, in 1913 they created the Congressional Union for Woman Suffrage, drawing in some of NAWSA's younger, better educated, more professional women. Catt, however, feared that the direct action tactics proposed by the Congressional Union would do the suffrage movement as a whole no favors. In 1916 Paul and Burns left NAWSA altogether, forming the National Woman's Party (NWP). This organization was only a fraction of NAWSA's size, but the militancy with which it conducted its campaign garnered a great deal of attention and also presented American suffragists with a legitimate choice of organizations.[16]

During World War I, NAWSA supported the war effort in the hopes of winning over President Woodrow Wilson and public opinion, which turned out to be a successful strategy. Regardless of the war, NWP sustained its opposition to any politician who did not support suffrage, picketing the White House and continuing its use of militant tactics. NWP members were arrested and went to prison, where their hunger strikes and work stoppages may have won some sympathy for the cause and certainly attracted constant publicity. After the war ended, and in the wake of numerous state suffrage victories during the preceding few years, the Nineteenth Amendment was finally passed in 1919 and ratified on August 18, 1920.[17]

The Variety of Jewish Women's Suffrage Activism

American Jewish women had many motivations for joining the suffrage movement and then had a variety of experiences once they became involved. Relatively few reached the level of prominence or influence of Maud Nathan, but the eventual suffrage victory would not have been possible without the grassroots support of women and men from diverse social, economic, cultural, ideological, and geographic locations. Jewish women's motivations, activism, leadership, and sometimes willingness to embed their suffragism in a particularly Jewish context made them a force to be reckoned with in the women's movement. They attracted more attention at the time than they have from subsequent historians; reconstructing their participation complicates the image of a primarily white, Christian, middle-class movement, although there is no doubt that the suffrage movement was often inhospitable to those perceived as "other" in terms of ethnic, religious, class, or racial background.[18]

American Jewish women took a number of paths toward the suffrage movement. Some first became involved while attending college. Irma Cain, a 1907 Vassar graduate, attended secret midnight meetings at a nearby cemetery, as Vassar outlawed suffrage groups on campus. During Belle Fligelman's senior year at the University of Wisconsin in 1913, she was invited to speak at a public suffrage hearing at the state house because she was president of the women students. This opportunity made her think hard about all the reasons to support suffrage. After she graduated, she returned to her hometown of Helena, Montana, just in time to throw herself into the state campaign there, which succeeded in enfranchising women in 1914. She joined cars full of women who drove around the city honking horns, waving banners, and tossing suffrage literature into the streets.[19]

Other Jewish women underwent a kind of conversion experience. Elizabeth Hirshfield, a teacher who was also president of the Buffalo NCJW section, became a suffragist during the late 1890s when she discovered how much less she was paid than male colleagues. She joined the Buffalo Political Equality Club and published a pamphlet titled *Concerning Woman Suffrage*. Augusta Lord-Heinstein, a Boston physiotherapist, turned into an activist after attending an anti-suffrage meeting and becoming so disgusted by the speakers' attitudes toward women that she was at local suffrage headquarters by nine o'clock the next morning. Suffrage became a family project; Lord-Heinstein marched in parades with her husband and her children. Her daughter Lucile displayed a "Votes for Women" banner in the office of her medical practice for decades.[20]

A few Jewish women found that their commitment to suffrage was bound up with their religious identity. As an adolescent during the 1870s, Rebekah Bettelheim Kohut struggled with Judaism, even though her father was a rabbi. Several of her non-Jewish teachers encouraged her to view Judaism more favorably, pointing to notable Jewish women like the biblical judge Deborah, the Italian Renaissance poet Sara Copia Sullam, and the renowned American reformer and educator Rebecca Gratz. Kohut began to wonder what these women would be like in her own day and decided that "comparison suggested itself with the women of the day who were fighting the battle for the emancipation of their sex." Kohut's suffragism was also due to the less noble belief, shared by many suffrage leaders, that American women should receive the vote before immigrant men. She grew up in California, where such prejudice was rampant even among otherwise socially conscious people. Her father pointed out that their Chinese servant might become a full citizen before she, Rebekah, finished college, but she never would unless she and other women fought for their rights.[21]

For Kohut, as for other American Jewish suffragists, geography mattered. Because some states enfranchised women before others and some never did give women the vote until forced to by the Nineteenth Amendment, suffrage supporters' experiences were shaped by location. Activists who moved around found that they were needed in different ways in different places. Miriam Allen De Ford's career provides one example of these shifting needs. When Miriam was fourteen years old, her mother, the scion of an old Philadelphia Jewish family, sent her to local suffrage headquarters to stuff envelopes and hand out literature. Both mother and daughter marched in the occasional suffrage parade. In 1907 De Ford was part of the Philadelphia contingent at a national parade in New York, an experience she enjoyed so much that she repeated it several times. She never encountered real violence at these parades, though the crowds of onlookers sometimes jeered and mocked the marching suffragists. From 1912 through 1915 De Ford lived in Boston, where she began to carve out a career for herself as a journalist. She joined the Massachusetts Woman Suffrage Society, which published pamphlets and every evening sent out speakers. De Ford volunteered as one of the soapbox speakers and addressed crowds of people once or twice a week. She had been a committed suffragist for more than a decade by the time she moved to California, where women were already enfranchised. De Ford cast her first ballot there in 1916. Her new location meant that there was not much for her to do for suffrage on the local scene, though she did continue to write pro-suffrage articles in the run-up to the campaign to ratify the Nineteenth Amendment.[22]

Social as well as physical geography also played a role in activism. Born in Louisville, Kentucky, in 1878, Amy Schwartz Oppenheim had no interest at all in politics until she married and moved to New York City in 1900. Surrounded for the first time by politically active women and encouraged by her husband, Oppenheim became a founding member of both the Women's National Republican Club and the Women's City Club. She discovered, like many of her clubwomen counterparts, that disenfranchisement severely constrained women's power to affect policy or effect social change. She moved in the same social circles as Nathan, who served as her political mentor and inspired her to join the suffrage movement. In 1915 Oppenheim was one of several wealthy women asked to join the finance committee of the Equal Franchise Society of New York. Oppenheim and Nathan frequently corresponded about suffrage and society events, including some that took place within the elite Jewish community of New York City. As her involvement deepened, Oppenheim became interested in developing her own oratorical skills in order to do more than just offer her administrative and financial support to the movement.[23]

Oppenheim's interest in becoming a better speaker demonstrated the extent to which suffrage drew women into public activity in new ways during the first decades of the twentieth century. By taking their cause to the streets, suffragists garnered more publicity than they ever had before. However, disapproval of public suffrage activities did not swiftly disappear.[24] As a freshman at Boston University in 1906, Jennie Loitman Barron founded a suffrage association that held rallies and staged plays, but not on school property, since the college refused to grant permission. Before one of the plays could be performed, a group of anti-suffrage students kidnapped the leading man, but he managed to escape and arrive in time for the show to go on. Barron endured taunting, including a college editorial that described her as "mannish," but she persisted and became a well-known street speaker throughout New England.[25] At one 1915 rally in Framingham, she said:

> If you men should ask us for the vote, should we say, Mr. Carpenter, your sphere is at the bench; Mr. Blacksmith, your place is at the forge; Mr. Chauffeur, your place is in the garage; Mr. Clerk, your place is in the shop and therefore you should not have the ballot for that would take you out of man's chosen sphere of being the bread winner of the world and of fathering the race. No, that would be as absurd an objection as to argue that "woman's place is in the home" should disqualify her to vote. The ballot today may protect the home just as it is the effective means of protecting everything else.[26]

Barron kept up her suffrage stumping even after becoming a lawyer, despite the damage her public appearances might have done to her career.

American society, only gradually accepting the presence of women in the public arena, still demonstrated some ambivalence toward the spectacle of open air rallies and parades. Although these activities drew far more people to the cause than lobbying the corridors of power ever could, the brazenness took some time to gain acceptance. When Fligelman began to give speeches on street corners in her hometown, her disapproving stepmother, who did not even oppose suffrage, at first would not let her sleep in the house. Every time Kohut spoke publicly about suffrage, she faced opponents who demanded to know who was taking care of her children, along with hostile listeners who jeered that she should be wearing trousers. Like other suffragists working in public venues, she tried to defuse these situations with humor, often asking her female hecklers who was home taking care of their children while they stood there objecting to her.[27]

Jewish Ambivalence toward the Suffrage Movement

Rebekah Kohut's hecklers undoubtedly included Jewish women, since she was one of the most visible American Jewish women of her day and spoke often to Jewish audiences. Though there were fewer prominent Jewish women in the anti-suffrage movement than in the suffrage movement, there was no consensus on the issue within the American Jewish community. During the period just following the reunification of NAWSA, the leading example of a Jewish anti-suffragist was Rachel (Ray) Frank. A teacher and journalist from San Francisco, Frank had caused a stir in 1890 when she presided over Yom Kippur services in Spokane Falls, Washington. She helped create Jewish congregations there and in other Western towns and cities, effectively functioning as the first Jewish woman religious leader in America. She never accepted a formal pulpit position or the title of rabbi, but she earned a national reputation and delivered an address on "Woman in the Synagogue" at the Jewish Women's Congress held at the Chicago World's Fair in 1893. NAWSA leaders naturally assumed that Frank would support their cause but were dismayed to find that she often spoke out against it instead. In a speech on "The Jewish Woman and Suffrage," Frank argued that the ballot was unnecessary for reform. She suggested that Jewish women put their own houses in order before turning their attention outside the home. An 1895 interview in the *San Francisco Bulletin* revealed that Frank did not believe in universal suffrage at all. She thought the vote "should be granted strictly according to the intelligence and capacity of the individual for government" and criticized suffragists as too "silly and volatile" to deserve enfranchisement. In the same interview, Frank stated that "I am not a suffragist because I do not believe that a woman can properly fulfill her home duties and be out in the world, too." No one could accuse Frank of hypocrisy; when she married the physician Simon Litman in 1901, she promptly retired from public life.[28]

Just as Maud Nathan was perhaps the most visible Jewish suffragist, her younger sister Annie Nathan Meyer was probably the most conspicuous

Jewish anti-suffragist. Meyer received even less formal education than her sister and spent much of her time remedying the deficit by organizing study circles and enrolling in university extension courses for women. She married Alfred Meyer in 1887 and joined him in affiliating with the Ethical Culture Society in Manhattan rather than her family's historic synagogue, Congregation Shearith Israel. She had one daughter, who died in a mysterious accident shortly after marrying. Though she did not renounce Judaism or a Jewish social life and sometimes served as a representative of Jewish women, she was less embedded in the Jewish communal world than her sister. Meyer first achieved public prominence in her role as a founder of Barnard College, which opened in 1889 as a self-sustaining liberal arts college affiliated with Columbia. She was active in Barnard's fund-raising and administration for decades and tirelessly advocated the expansion of women's educational and employment opportunities. Meyer was also a prolific author of plays, novels, and sociological surveys.[29]

Despite a resume that seemed tailor-made for suffragism, Meyer became one of the most visible "antis." She claimed that higher education for women and women's enfranchisement were completely separate issues. Like Frank, Meyer believed that suffrage would diminish the importance of women's

Annie Nathan Meyer.
Courtesy of the Jacob
Rader Marcus Center of the
American Jewish Archives

duties in the home, arguing that no one should have to leave her home to improve it. She also strongly rejected what she called "spreadhenism," the idea that women were inherently superior moral beings who would therefore transform the world if they could vote. Meyer's concern that such attitudes would inevitably devolve into hatred of men found expression in such literary works as *The Dominant Sex*, which was published (but not produced) in 1911. In this play, a heated polemic against suffrage and clubwomen, the main character neglects her home and child and shows nothing but icy contempt for her husband.[30]

Suffragists and anti-suffragists stayed abreast of what the other camp was doing, and the spectacle of two sisters opposing each other drew attention. The press reported it when Meyer was invited to a 1907 luncheon in honor of Susan B. Anthony at which Nathan was the main speaker. The sisters engaged in spirited battles via dueling letters to the editor. When Meyer wrote to the *New Republic* in 1916 to reiterate her case against suffrage and to claim that "men. . . [are] always ready to consider special legislation whenever women's peculiar needs require it," Nathan fired back in the same magazine. She pointed out that male politicians barely considered the non-voting women in their districts as constituents and thus did little to protect them in non-suffrage states. Nathan also derided Meyer's avowal of support for the presidential candidate and non-suffragist Woodrow Wilson, noting that his rival, the pro-suffragist Charles Edward Hughes, "naturally cares not at all how many voteless women turn from him to Mr. Wilson."[31] As was the case with the Nathan sisters, both suffragists and anti-suffragists fed off each other's activism and rhetoric. In terms of organizational strategy and structure, NAWSA and the National Association Opposed to Woman Suffrage actually resembled each other. For example, in December 1916, Josephine Dodge, president of the latter organization, wrote to Meyer to update her on the great success of the recent national convention, to thank her for producing anti-suffrage pamphlets, to outline a congressional campaign, and to denounce the "extreme actions of the opposition." Such a letter, from tone to word choice to content, could just as easily have been written by NAWSA's president Carrie Chapman Catt to Nathan.[32]

Though only a few Jewish women avowed anti-suffragism as loudly as Meyer, many more viewed the suffrage movement with suspicion. They considered many suffrage leaders xenophobic at best and anti-Semitic at worst. They were excluded from major women's organizations that either professed Christianity explicitly, such as the Women's Christian Temperance Union, or assumed the Christianity of its members, such as the National Council of Women. Working-class Jewish women, especially in urban areas, feared the outright missionizing of many of the women's social reform organizations with which they had contact. They had no desire to work with evangelizing Christian women, even on an issue about which they might have agreed. On a practical level, traditionally observant Jewish women found it difficult to participate in the suffrage movement when parades, rallies, and conventions were routinely held while they were observing the Sabbath on Friday nights and Saturdays. On a theoretical level, the shift from suffrage arguments based on justice to expediency further distanced Jewish women. Expediency arguments—that suffrage would ensure social improvement by empowering the best people—tended to strengthen racial ideologies and hierarchies by focusing on educated, white, native-born, middle-class women as deserving the vote. At a time when Jewish racial identity was not fixed and increasing numbers of foreign-born Jews were neither educated nor middle class, expediency arguments seemed exclusionary to immigrants of many different backgrounds.[33]

Mainstream suffrage leaders had never done much to encourage Jewish women's participation in the woman's movement. They did not turn Jewish women away, but many of their pronouncements and actions seemed positively hostile to Jewish observers. Susan B. Anthony and Elizabeth Cady Stanton's newspaper *The Revolution* had published an 1869 article that referred to Jews as "a useless portion of society." When the *Jewish Messenger* complained, the editors halfheartedly apologized but also took the opportunity to criticize the American Jewish press for its supposedly retrograde attitude toward women. In 1878, the prominent suffragist Matilda Joslyn Gage denounced the New York Iroquois tribes' rejection of citizenship, which would include voting rights for men, because such citizenship would eliminate their tribal sovereignty. Bitterly she wrote of the average suffrage supporters, "She, educated, enlightened, Christian, in vain begs for the crumbs contemptuously cast aside by savages." Like Gage, many suffragists saw themselves as Christian as much as white or female.[34]

Always the radical thinker, Stanton fought to remove Christianity as an integral part of suffrage identity, but her efforts only made things more difficult for Jewish suffragists. Stanton arrived at the 1885 NWSA convention in Washington, D.C., with a list of resolutions indicting Christianity and other religions for teaching and reinforcing female inferiority, a theme she had been sounding for decades. A committee watered down Stanton's resolutions but came up with a version that blamed religion's attitude toward women on "dogmas incorporated in religious creeds derived from Judaism."[35] Jewish women in attendance protested to no avail. When the convention voted down the resolution, it was because NWSA did not want to alienate Christian women, not because NWSA was concerned about anti-Semitism. A few years later, the famed suffrage orator Anna Howard Shaw delivered a talk at the 1888 International Congress of Women that expressed hostility to Judaism in relation to its purported attitude toward women. Shaw also blamed the failure of repeated South Dakota suffrage campaigns during the 1890s on the voting records of counties with heavy immigrant Jewish populations.[36]

At the end of the nineteenth century, Stanton remained the primary face of what some American Jews saw as the outright anti-Semitism of the suffrage movement. In 1895 she presided over the publication of the radical Woman's Bible, which critiqued the Bible from a feminist perspective and reinterpreted biblical events from the standpoint of women's experiences. The historian Kathi Kern has argued that Stanton, a religious liberal and freethinker, believed that ethical relationships among people comprised the highest religious ideal. To both Jewish and non-Jewish observers, however, Stanton's Woman's Bible cared not at all about ethical relationships with Jews. Her contributions denounced the "God of the Hebrews" for the low status of women and characterized the history of the Jews as notable for "corruption, violence, lust, and petty falsehood." Though not all the contributors to the hugely controversial Woman's Bible took this tone, and a few even drew on elements of Jewish mysticism as providing a basis for more female liturgical images, many of the authors Stanton gathered wrote equally explicit anti-Semitic statements. Ellen Battelle Dietrich, commenting on the two creation narratives in Genesis, attributed the second narrative, in which Eve is created out of Adam's side, to "some Jew, in an endeavor to give 'heavenly authority' for requiring a woman to obey the man she married."[37]

Jewish women did speak out against the Woman's Bible. According to Stanton, a group of Jewish women came to see her to protest her attack on their religion. They claimed that women were held in the highest regard in Judaism, but Stanton turned them away by pointing out that traditionally observant Jewish men each day thanked God for not making them women. NAWSA tried hard to dissociate itself from Stanton's text, realizing that any connection to such a radical take on religious tradition and authority would doom the cause among Christian women, let alone Jews. Suffrage groups all over the United States issued statements like that of the Equal Suffrage Association of North Carolina, which repudiated the "so-called Woman's Bible" and stated very clearly that the suffrage movement was about the political status of women, not religion.[38] The damage was done as far as many Jewish women were concerned, however, and it is likely that one of the reasons some Jewish women's organizations never endorsed suffrage was residual anger and fear related to Stanton's *Woman's Bible*.

Subsequent developments reinforced Jewish fears about suffrage anti-Semitism. Harriot Stanton Blatch shared some of her mother's prejudices. During her European travels as a young woman she wrote disparagingly of Jews, and upon returning to New York to work for suffrage, she complained about the challenge of convincing "the biggest Jewish city to convert from its Germanic and Hebraic attitudes toward women." Catt, who would later champion Jewish causes during the 1930s, during her suffrage career blamed the foreign-born element in New York for the 1915 referendum defeat. She referred to "the foreign vote" and "men of other races and nationalities," but everyone assumed she meant Jews, and the defenses published in response to her statements were largely written by Jews, about Jews. NWP leaders took Alice Paul's anti-Semitism for granted. As the NWP organizer Mabel Vernon said to an interviewer about her friend and colleague Rebecca Hourwich Reyher, "She's Jewish, and have you detected Alice's antagonism for Jews?" Reyher, along with Anita Pollitzer, Caroline Katzenstein, and other Jewish NWP activists managed to work with Paul, quite closely in some cases, but they were aware of the tensions. The NWP supporter Alva Belmont, even while ostensibly praising cultured and educated Jewish women in public life, still wrote about Jews as a race apart and criticized "the average Jew" for being overly "sensitive and jealous of his prerogatives."[39]

Unease with their place in the American suffrage movement extended to Jewish women's involvement in the international women's movement, where they also occupied an ambiguous position.[40] On the one hand, a disproportionate number of leading women activists in Europe were Jewish, and Jewish women from all over the world supported the international women's movement in significant and noticeable numbers. On the other hand, through the 1920s, most Jewish women in the international movement, with the exception of those belonging to the Palestine branch of the IWSA, presented themselves by nationality rather than religion. Aletta Jacobs, the first woman doctor in the Netherlands, exemplified this pattern. She neither denied nor emphasized her Jewishness as she worked within the International Council of Women (ICW), helped spearhead the suffrage group that met separately at the 1899 ICW meeting in London, and then attended the founding meeting of the IWSA in Berlin in 1904. Jacobs became the correspondent who sent quarterly reports on the Dutch Association for Woman Suffrage to IWSA's president Catt.[41]

For all her lack of interest in emphasizing her own Jewish identity, Jacobs did not overlook Jewish women as important and disproportionate supporters of the women's movement internationally. In 1900 she asked Hannah Greenebaum Solomon to send her NCJW materials to include at an exhibition on women at the upcoming World's Fair in Paris. While on a suffrage trip with Catt in 1906, she wrote to Rosika Schwimmer, a radical activist usually even less interested in her Jewish origins than Jacobs, "It is remarkable that they are always Jewish girls. With us and everywhere else. Courage and spirit are found most in these girls." Catt also acknowledged this phenomenon and was pleased to recruit Rosa Manus at a 1908 meeting in Amsterdam. Manus, considerably more Jewishly identified than either Jacobs or Schwimmer, became an IWSA stalwart and remained especially close to Catt.[42]

Of all their generation of activists, Nathan and, to a lesser extent, Solomon, were the only American Jewish women to become seriously involved with the international women's suffrage movement before World War I. Both participated in the founding IWSA meeting in Berlin in 1904, where Solomon reported learning a great deal but also encountering some blatant anti-Semitism. Nathan attended a number of IWSA meetings in Europe during the next decade. Writing in 1913 about five different international congresses she had attended over the summer, she remarked with satisfaction that men the world over were "imploring women to come to their aid" in solving the "evils that have grown up in a man-made civilization."[43] Nathan played important roles as a translator and parliamentarian at international meetings and, along with other Jewish women in leadership roles, may have helped Catt and other IWSA leaders recognize the importance of religious diversity to a truly international women's movement. Before the 1913 IWSA meeting in Budapest, Catt announced:

> For the first time in the woman movement, it is expected that Hindu, Buddhist, Confucian, Mohammedan, Jewish and Christian women will sit together in a Congress uniting their voices in a common plea for the liberation of their sex from those artificial discriminations which every political and religious system has directed against them.[44]

Still, Nathan experienced some discrimination at the international congresses she attended and was disappointed but not surprised that anti-Semitism made occasional appearances in the international women's movement as it did in the suffrage movement at home. Her involvement with the CL also alerted her to the issue of class identity, which, like religious prejudice, disrupted the ideal of universal sisterhood theoretically underlying much of the organized suffrage movement.

Class and Ideological Distinctions in the Suffrage Movement

Though in the largest sense the suffrage movement prioritized gender identity, in practice, class and gender were deeply imbricated. A cross-class alliance existed in the suffrage movement, but the relationships were often tense.
Because inflections of American Jewish identity were also tied to class for Jewish women, different aspects of suffrage activism served the different needs of
American Jewish women. Many middle-class Jewish women saw working for
suffrage as a way to promote their acceptance into American women's organizational life, while many working-class Jewish women saw enfranchisement
as a means of achieving both political and economic citizenship. In all cases,
Jewish women fought for suffrage not only to win the vote but also to locate
themselves in polities they could help shape as citizens, workers, and mothers.
The importance of suffrage thus crossed class boundaries but looked different
when women of varying perspectives shifted the angle of their analysis.

As one example, suffragists became accustomed to linking economic disabilities to disenfranchisement. Not all of the suffrage leaders of the 1890s
and early 1900s saw the need to reach out to working women, but most of
them acknowledged that only by wooing wage-earning women to the cause
could they create a truly mass movement. Women who were already engaged
in public workplace activity and understood the link between political rights
and economic independence were natural candidates for suffrage activism.
The experiences of the Votes for Women Club in San Francisco and the Equal
Suffrage League of New York proved emblematic. The Votes for Women Club,
founded in part by the Jewish activist Selina Solomons, attracted immigrant
women by offering cheap meals, suffrage literature, and a commitment to
linking political and economic demands. The San Francisco organization
consciously set out to create a cross-class suffrage movement by emphasizing all women's shared interests and desires. The "Human Flower Show"
showcased the members' babies to demonstrate "that the offspring of suffrage
women were the finest in the country." The Women's Committee of Protection
fought vice. Child welfare and protest against vice were causes all women,
regardless of background, could come together to support while also agitating
for voting rights.[45] Organizations such as the Equal Suffrage League of New
York City, founded by a group of women including Maud Nathan, were often
open to wider constituencies than NAWSA, as it was easier for local groups
to understand that working women's economic interests made them obvious candidates for conversion to the suffrage cause.[46] In a city like New York,
with a large and rapidly growing Jewish population, visibly Jewish leaders like
Nathan helped provide links between communal life and political activism.

Several additional organizations brought New York Jewish working women into the suffrage movement in unprecedented numbers during the early twentieth century. In 1907 Harriot Stanton Blatch, probably the most class-sensitive suffrage leader, formed the Equality League of Self-Supporting Women, which included both industrial laborers and professional women. The organization, which changed its name to the Women's Political Union (WPoU) in 1910, targeted single working women. The Jewish labor leader Rose Schneiderman helped Blatch appeal to issues of women's work that cut across class, and she addressed the group's first mass meeting in April 1907. A large percentage of the working-class membership was Jewish. That same year, the National Progressive Women's Suffrage Union was founded to encourage garment workers, a heavily Jewish group, to take direct action. The organization sponsored open-air meetings, parades, solicitations at beaches and amusement parks, street meetings, and demonstrations. The Lower East Side branch of the Political Equality League boasted an entirely Jewish board and provided social services as well as suffrage activism to a Jewish constituency. The Wage Earners' League, founded in 1911 by Women's Trade Union League (WTUL) leaders Schneiderman and Leonora O'Reilly, held meetings and created a Yiddish press committee to attract Jewish women interested in combining union membership and suffrage activism. Only workers could be full members. Clara Lemlich, the firebrand who had achieved notoriety as a labor leader during the 1909 garment workers' strike, became the chief organizer for the Wage Earners' League.[47]

Even though of all these organizations only the WPoU achieved longevity, the growing militancy of Jewish female garment workers like Lemlich helped create and then sustain mass support for suffrage among working women. Olga Gross, a young Jewish worker in Philadelphia, wanted so badly to contribute to the cause that she bought a hundred-pound sack of peanuts, made peanut brittle, sold it during her lunch hour and donated the proceeds to the local suffrage headquarters. A group of labor organizers already accustomed to cross-class alliances with feminist reformers, often through WTUL work, also played a vital role in recruiting working women during the 1910s. Schneiderman spoke for many when she said, "I think that I was born a suffragist, but if I hadn't been I am sure that the conditions of the working girls in New York . . . would have made me one." Working-class women across the country shared Schneiderman's conviction that the vote was necessary to improve their lives.[48]

For all the success in organizing women workers in New York and elsewhere, the suffrage movement continued to be plagued with cross-class tensions. For example, Blatch at first supported the 1910 shirtwaist-maker strike in New York, but when conflicts arose between the WTUL and other groups representing the broader women's movement, Blatch sided with the wealthier women, angering Schneiderman. Blatch also received criticism for not using union labor in her own suffrage organization, an ongoing issue that ultimately led the WTUL to dissociate itself from WPoU and even, for a few years, to drop suffrage as a priority. A clash of cultures remained a barrier for working-class suffragists. When one well-known Jewish organizer attended a suffrage meeting at a Gramercy Park mansion, she asked for a coat check number when the butler took her coat, unused to such grand service.[49]

Probably the biggest problem confronting the delicate cross-class suffrage alliance was the relationship between suffrage and socialism. Many middle-class suffragists could not countenance the idea of doing anything to support socialism, but since socialists were likely to support suffrage, conflict was inevitable. As author Charlotte Perkins Gilman's satiric verse "The Socialist and the Suffragist" explained:

> Said the Socialist to the Suffragist:
> My cause is greater than yours!
> You only work for a special class,
> We for the gain of the General Mass
> Which every good ensures!
> Said the Suffragist to the Socialist:
> You underrate my Cause!
> While women remain a subject Class
> You never can move the General Mass
> With your Economic Laws.[50]

When the International Socialist Women's Secretariat formed in 1907, it was pro-suffrage as a matter of course, but the Second International, the coalition of labor and socialist parties that directed international socialism from 1899 through 1916, decreed that women's suffrage should come through the party organization rather than the women's movement. This decision posed a challenge to women activists who did not want to give up their association with suffrage groups, which were finally expanding to include working women. In the United States, the cross-class alliances that had gradually become features of the suffrage movement heightened the problem. Jewish immigrant women who prioritized class over gender consciousness did not want to derail socialism's larger goals but still believed that suffrage was key to women's emancipation.[51]

Socialist suffrage was somewhat ideologically distinct. The historian Mari Jo Buhle has explained that the socialist perspective considered suffrage related to class struggle, with women's fate aligned with the "political reconstruction" of the working class. A 1908 article in *The Socialist Woman* contended that the mainstream suffrage movement was far too genteel to be effective and that working women were the true heirs to the radical pronouncements made at the Seneca Falls convention sixty years earlier. Working women understood that they needed both an economic and a political agenda, since they competed with men in the labor market as well as the political arena.[52]

Politically radical Jewish women never assumed that enfranchisement would solve all of women's problems. At the turn of the century, the most eloquent articulator of this position was the anarchist Emma Goldman. In essays titled "Woman Suffrage" and "The Tragedy of Emancipation," Goldman challenged what she saw as conservative suffragists' claims that enfranchisement would not remove women from the home. For Goldman, the home was a prison for women who needed to break their chains through a process of internal development rather than the granting of external citizenship. "The right to vote, or equal civil rights, may be good demands, but true emancipation begins neither at the polls nor in court. It begins in woman's soul," she wrote. Although Goldman hoped that emancipation would allow women to embrace their full humanity, she was not optimistic that suffrage would purify politics; she remained convinced that social revolution was first necessary to reconstruct class, rather than gender, relations. She referred to suffrage as a "modern fetich" [*sic*] and worried that a focus on suffrage would blind women to the true sources of their oppression.[53]

Later socialist critics of the suffrage movement disagreed with Goldman about the necessity of the vote but denounced too narrow a focus on enfranchisement, which they considered only one piece of a much larger puzzle. Lemlich argued that suffrage was important primarily as a means of allowing women to help themselves rather than relying on consistently unreliable men. In the pamphlet *Relieving Working Women of the Burdens and Responsibility of Life*, Lemlich stated baldly that men had never relieved women of their responsibilities before, so it was fatuous to pretend that this was their motivation for opposing suffrage. Writing with undisguised anger that "every man is responsible for the ruin of every woman," she reminded her readers that no one protected working girls and that plenty of married women shared economic responsibility for the home. Lemlich believed, or at least hoped, that enfranchised women would create a world with fewer burdens for all. Her colleague Jennie Matyas, a socialist labor organizer, viewed women's enfranchisement primarily as a practical parallel to their economic participation. She nonetheless took every opportunity to promote suffrage activism among women workers. Every time she was arrested for disorderly conduct while stumping for the union, she spent her time in the holding block or prison cell talking to other women and encouraging them both to join a union and to work for suffrage. She later said, "I felt that as a working woman I should have the same right to exert my influence and to assume my responsibility of citizenship in the community as I had in my union."[54]

Pauline Newman became one of the most visible socialist women who worked for suffrage. Already an experienced garment worker and labor organizer, in 1908 the seventeen-year-old Newman ran as the Socialist Party candidate for secretary of state of New York. The largely symbolic campaign included a suffrage plank. Newman traveled the state to speak about socialism, often in the company of the renowned Eugene V. Debs. While in Philadelphia organizing for the International Ladies Garment Workers Union and WTUL in 1911, Newman was recruited by Alice Paul to address working-class audiences. The WTUL suggested to Carrie Chapman Catt that the New York State campaign should develop an industrial section led by a union woman. Catt agreed that it was a good idea to have a wage-earning woman target other workers and accepted Schneiderman's suggestion of Newman as the best candidate for the job. At first, Newman was concerned that her radical politics would present a problem, but Catt did not view Newman's socialism as a stumbling block and sent her on a tour throughout upstate New York with the special task of convincing organized labor to support suffrage. Newman spoke at countless union meetings and on innumerable street corners.[55]

Ideological niceties thus did not automatically limit the activities of socialist Jewish women engaged in suffrage work. The Wage Earners' League for Woman Suffrage, for example, affiliated with NAWSA rather than the Socialist Party Women's Committee in order to secure financial support. Still, unhappy with the idea of subordinating economics to politics, the Socialist Party established its own suffrage clubs under the Jewish socialist Theresa Malkiel's leadership.[56] The socialist suffrage clubs published material in Yiddish and fed articles to the Jewish press. They sent women door-to-door on the Lower East Side and staged demonstrations and torchlight parades. However, the fault lines between suffrage and socialism grew wider with time. A prominent socialist with no sympathy for independent women's organizations warned Schneiderman that working for suffrage rather than socialism was acting "like a bad doctor who pretends to cure his patient by removing the symptoms instead of removing the disease itself."[57] Malkiel, who wrote a pro-suffrage column for the popular Yiddish newspaper *Forverts* (*The Forward*) and founded socialist suffrage clubs that combined political activism with social programs, was constantly frustrated both by the Socialist Party's lukewarm backing and by Jewish women's apparent tendency to prioritize either suffrage or socialism. After the 1915 New York referendum defeat, the Socialist Party withdrew its support for the suffrage clubs altogether. Malkiel protested and tried to sustain a network of socialist suffragists but did not succeed. She eventually bowed to party discipline, though she continued to work for suffrage on her own.[58]

Jewish Women and Suffrage Campaigns

The experiences of socialist suffragists like Newman and Malkiel with organizing the working class illustrate Jewish women's gradual move into positions of suffrage leadership, particularly in statewide campaigns. By 1910, the failure of most state referenda and the apparent lack of interest of both major political parties in women's enfranchisement led many suffragists to worry that they would never win the vote. Just as the reuniting of NWSA and AWSA in 1890 had marked the beginning of a new stage in the suffrage campaign, so did a few key victories just before World War I contribute to the movement finally gaining some momentum, in part by further emphasizing cross-class alliances.

Jewish women played notable roles in these finally successful campaigns. One of the most important occurred in California, which enfranchised women in 1911 after a hard-fought struggle. The first major campaign in California had been in 1896, when Susan B. Anthony and Anna Howard Shaw canvassed the state and recruited such Jewish women as Hannah Marks Solomons and her daughter Selina, both active in Jewish communal life and reform activities in San Francisco. Selina Solomons tried organizing in her own wealthy neighborhood and also in a working-class immigrant area, which was home to a large German and Irish population, but to little avail. Both immigrants and native-born Californians voted against suffrage. After Washington State adopted suffrage in 1910, Solomons joined a group of activists determined to win suffrage for California. She even wrote a suffrage play, *The Girl From Colorado*, which dramatized the impact an enfranchised visitor from Colorado had on a group of California women, including one character named "Aunty Suffridge" who was converted to the cause by the time the curtains rang down. Keeping in close contact with national leaders throughout the state campaign, California suffragists finally prevailed. Solomons gleefully went to her polling place the morning of her first election and announced, "Good-day, fellow citizens. I've come to vote."[59]

Nevada saw renewed activism at the same time as did California. In 1911 the new Nevada Equal Suffrage Association supported a suffrage bill in the state legislature. Felice Cohn, a Jewish lawyer who was Nevada's first female assistant U.S. attorney, wrote the bill. The measure passed but had to be reconfirmed during the next legislative session before any public referendum was possible. Cohn led a successful lobbying campaign, and the suffrage bill was reconfirmed by the Nevada legislature in 1913. In Nevada, as in California, fault lines appeared in the suffrage movement. Cohn clashed with Anne Martin, president of the Nevada Equal Suffrage Association, fearing that Martin's affiliation with the militant Congressional Union/ NWP would threaten the suffrage bill as it came up for public referendum. The conflict subsided, and the Nevada suffrage bill became part of the state constitution in 1914.[60]

State by state suffrage victories led to growing impatience in other parts of the country and in NAWSA's central headquarters. "Women to Men," a poem published in *The Woman Voter* in 1912, expressed this restlessness and even anger at men:

> We are they that wept at Babylon,
> And still are they that weep;
> We have watched the cradles of the world,
> And hushed its sick to sleep;
> We have served your folly and desire,
> And drunk your cruel will:
> You have smiled on us with far contempt—
> Are you smiling still?[61]

Carrie Chapman Catt, who had been putting her tactical skills to good use as president of the IWSA, was emphatically tired of both waiting and smiling. Forced by the outbreak of World War I to shift her focus back home, she felt the time was ripe to move the entire American suffrage movement toward what she called the "winning plan." As of 1915, NAWSA assigned suffrage associations varying tasks depending on the status of suffrage in their states. This multilayered strategy engaged more women than ever before at every level of suffrage campaigning.[62]

Catt's experience running the 1915 New York referendum campaign just before she assumed NAWSA's presidency helped her come up with the winning plan. That campaign was the most organized ever conducted, even though it ultimately failed. The 1915 fight brought all kinds of Jewish women new opportunities for suffrage work. Jewish women helped fill Carnegie Hall at the November 6, 1914, meeting to kick off the referendum, with several wealthy Jewish women and men making substantial donations to the campaign. Activists in New York's Woman Suffrage Party reached out to working-class Jewish union members who hoped the vote would improve their economic power and to middle-class Jewish social workers who hoped the vote would lead to social reform legislation. The 1915 campaign included a variety of innovative tactics, many dreamed up by Nathan along with Catt and Harriot Stanton Blatch. In July 1915 Blatch paraded a "Liberty Torch" throughout upstate New York, relying on local activists to drum up large crowds wherever the procession appeared. A few weeks before the referendum, suffragists including Lillian Wald, the beloved founder of the Henry Street Settlement, took over boxes in all the major theaters in New York City. They draped the boxes with bunting and flags and displayed signs reading "Vote Yes on Woman Suffrage Nov 2."[63]

Excitement built as the referendum date neared. Even Jewish high school students like Berta Ratner joined the campaign. Berta and her sister Eva spent their evenings canvassing for the Woman Suffrage Party and distributing literature at street meetings. They also monitored the polls on election day. As Berta wrote in her diary, "Reported at poll at 22-Tompkins Ave. . . . Had a wonderful time there until 7 in evening as watcher and picket. My district won . . . Eva's district also won." When the dust settled after the polls closed, however, the suffragists had been defeated. Other states that handed the movement defeats in 1915 included Massachusetts, New Jersey, and Pennsylvania. Suffrage leaders gritted their teeth and grimly vowed to schedule a new referendum as swiftly as possible. Embodying this spirit, Berta wrote to a friend, "We rather pride ourselves on the good showing that we made, altho, a good many people consider a defeat—a defeat, pure and simple. But to us, it was a glorious victory in that we learned so much of existing conditions that were outside our interests before that time." She continued to campaign for suffrage after the 1915 defeat, was certified as a "Women's Watcher" for the 1917 state referendum, and jubilantly attended a district celebration after the suffrage triumph that year.[64]

In the aftermath of the 1915 defeat, suffrage leaders cast about for an explanation. Blatch, openly angry, blamed immigrants for the loss in a statement to local newspapers. Attempting damage control on behalf of the people she lived and worked among, Wald pointed out that the suffrage cause did better in immigrant areas of New York City than in almost any other part of the city or state. Statistical evidence indicated that the strongest support for suffrage came from middle-class Jews living in Harlem and working-class Jews living on the Lower East Side. Blatch would hear none of it, and although she typically used the terms "foreign born" or "immigrants," it became clear that she usually meant to single out Jews as scapegoats.[65]

Wald worried that such prejudices might compromise Jewish support for the suffrage movement, but that did not prove to be the case. In the successful 1917 referendum, 78 out of 100 pro-suffrage districts in New York City were heavily Jewish, and within the Jewish districts, 76 to 93 percent of the total vote was pro-suffrage.[66] New York became the first eastern state to give women the vote prior to ratification of the Nineteenth Amendment in 1920. All these numbers reflect the number of Jewish men who supported suffrage, as they were the only ones able to cast votes. Jewish women in these districts likely supported suffrage at even higher rates.

In 1917 suffrage leaders showed more appreciation for Jewish and other immigrant women.[67] A short story about the 1917 campaign, published in a popular suffrage collection, made a Jewish woman the protagonist. In "The Nail," Mirra Volshen, a working girl from the Lower East Side, supports suffrage and finds sympathizers among Jewish union members and socialists. While canvassing, Mirra meets Mendel, who opposes suffrage because he does not think women need it. Mirra tells Mendel that working women are not protected by men and therefore require the vote. She also explains the economic value of domestic labor and points out how frequently women support households on their own, especially in immigrant communities. Out on the street campaigning, Mirra gets hurt. Mendel brings his sister Martha to visit the convalescent, and Martha tells Mirra that Mendel has been learning about suffrage by reading and attending meetings. When a factory fire kills many women workers, Mendel is completely converted to the cause. He begins to speak in public about women's exploitation and economic needs, explaining that the vote will give women the tools they need to improve their lives. The story ends, naturally, with Mirra and Mendel's marriage. The fact that a story with Jewish protagonists was published in a suffrage collection intended for general readers is significant. "The Nail" not only appealed to Jewish readers but also made the point that Jewish women's support was crucial for suffrage victory in New York and elsewhere.[68]

Meanwhile, Jewish activists like Rebecca Hourwich Reyher in Massachusetts and Gertrude Weil in North Carolina worked to garner support for the federal amendment presented to Congress. Local conditions shaped their strategies. Reyher, working in a state with a significant immigrant population, pointed to other bills in Congress that would grant citizenship to foreigners in the army and enfranchise soldiers under the age of twenty-one. Should not women receive the same privileges for their own contributions to the war effort, she asked?[69] Weil's particular challenges stemmed from the influential liquor lobby in North Carolina and, even more significantly, racial tensions. In a 1919 letter to Congressman Sam Brinson, Weil tried to convince him that opposition to suffrage from liquor and vice interests should make it clear that supporting suffrage was the right thing to do. She argued that even if Brinson did not approve of the types of politically active women he saw in the West, genteel southern ladies from North Carolina would be different if enfranchised. Weil was less forthcoming about racial issues. She admitted that the problem of enfranchising African American women was real and serious and would have to be solved locally by the states, but she asked Brinson not to hold back white women because of the "Negro problem."[70]

Most of the American Jewish women in the suffrage movement, like most women of all backgrounds, supported suffrage without taking on leadership roles. But more than a few became, like Weil, prominent on the local and state levels. As a student at Smith College in 1900, one of the first Jewish students there, Weil had not evinced much of an interest in suffrage. She wrote, "I'm so everlastingly tired of hearing girls talk politics and the method of electing president." However, after graduating, returning home to Goldsboro, North Carolina, taking up various social reform causes, and becoming increasingly frustrated by what she saw as the limitations on women's influence, she changed her mind. Weil helped found the Goldsboro Equal

Gertrude Weil at a suffrage demonstration. Weil is standing at the far left. Courtesy of the North Carolina Office of Archives and History

Suffrage League in 1914 and ultimately became president of the North Carolina Equal Suffrage League. Deploying all her reform connections to publicize the cause, she also tried to draw in the members of the North Carolina
Association of Jewish Women, which she and her mother had helped establish. She attended numerous NAWSA conventions and treasured her copies
of the programs, pins, and ribbons she received there.[71]

By 1918 Catt acknowledged Weil as the leading suffragist in North Carolina. Catt wrote to Weil in April 1918 that while it would be helpful if the
Republican Party in North Carolina adopted a suffrage plank, no resolution should be introduced unless it would definitely pass. Not all suffragists
in North Carolina agreed with this decision, but Weil, with Catt's backing,
had the final say. When the federal suffrage amendment was finally about to
come up in Congress, Catt urged Weil to produce as many letters and tele-
grams of support as possible to be sent to the North Carolina congressional
delegation. Weil called on everyone she knew in the state to back the federal amendment. One of her Jewish clubwomen acquaintances wrote, "I am
undecided in my views, but if you really believe it will do any good to have
women nosing around the polls then you can have my sanction." This letter demonstrates the extent to which personal connections mattered in the
suffrage movement, which relied on not only committed activists but also
women and men who held much less definite opinions on the matter. During the final ratification campaign in 1920, Weil wrote to all of the members
of the Equal Suffrage League of North Carolina, encouraging them to obtain
as many signatures as possible on pro-ratification petitions. Although North
Carolina did not, in the end, ratify the Nineteenth Amendment, Catt spoke
glowingly of Weil's efforts.[72]

Another Jewish woman who achieved prominence on the state level was
Caroline Katzenstein, a successful agent at the Philadelphia Life Insurance
Company. She began her suffrage work in 1910, explaining later that "I found
that democracy was to many persons, then as now, only a name." Katzenstein
and a friend went to the Philadelphia shopping districts before dawn to write
"Votes for Women" in colored chalk all over the sidewalks. She took Alice
Paul, just returned from England, to her first street meeting in Philadelphia.
Katzenstein and Paul worked together the whole summer and into the next
year, taking over street corners to give speeches and distribute pamphlets.
They alerted the media to ensure newspaper coverage of their activities.[73]

In 1911 Katzenstein served as the Pennsylvania delegate to the NAWSA
convention in Louisville. She joined the Membership Committee, which that
year made the important decision not to admit groups that advocated limited suffrage, such as enfranchisement that required literacy tests. NAWSA

decided that the franchise should not be limited for either women or men, a determination that was not popular with southern suffragists who were less interested in doing away with Jim Crow laws than securing voting rights for white women.[74] Back home, Katzenstein ran suffrage headquarters as executive secretary of the Equal Franchise Society of Pennsylvania. She sold suffrage candy, postcards, buttons, pins, and notepaper to help keep the office open. The most popular items were washcloths emblazoned with "taxation without representation is tyranny." In 1912 she helped bring the NAWSA convention to Philadelphia. Despite Katzenstein's best efforts, the 1915 suffrage referendum in Pennsylvania, as in New York and elsewhere, failed.[75]

After the referendum disappointment, Katzenstein became convinced that a federal amendment was necessary and switched her loyalty from NAWSA to NWP. She felt that political work in Washington, D.C., would be the most effective. Katzenstein did not move to D.C. full time, since she needed to keep her insurance job, but she became both the publicity chairman and the executive secretary of the Pennsylvania branch of NWP. Her old friend Alice Paul sent her on a national suffrage tour in 1916, for which she took a leave of absence from work. Katzenstein became increasingly radical and was involved with NWP's Watchfire Demonstrations in 1919, which burned President Wilson in effigy. Unlike other participants, Katzenstein was not sentenced to jail, and she remained unrepentant, believing that Wilson's intransigence had called such symbolic violence on his own head. Once ratification finally appeared in sight, Katzenstein, who was also interested in settlement houses and the international peace movement, asked to be released from NWP to do other work. Paul agreed to her request and wrote back, "I am sure you know perfectly well that I have always felt you were one of the corner-stones upon which the work has been built."[76]

Although Katzenstein ended up becoming a NWP stalwart, like most other NWP members, she had started her suffrage career by getting involved with NAWSA. By 1916 the contrast between the organizations was posing a problem for many activists. For some longtime Jewish suffragists, though, there was no dilemma. Under NWP auspices, Mrs. Harry Lowenburg of Philadelphia showed no compunction about sneaking into a December 1916 joint session of Congress and disrupting President Wilson's speech by unfurling a banner that read, "Mr. President, What Will You Do for Woman Suffrage?"[77] In contrast, Sadie Jacobs Crockin never considered leaving NAWSA for NWP and expressed grave doubt about the efficacy of militancy. Although Crockin had herself been involved in parades and lobbying in Baltimore, activities deemed unladylike and strident only a few years earlier, she could not countenance the idea of picketing the White House or, even more inconceivably, being arrested for doing so and actually going to prison. Crockin thoroughly approved of the way that the Equal Suffrage League of Baltimore kept the most "modern" women—those with bobbed hair who rode bicycles—in desk jobs and dispatched the more traditionally ladylike activists to carry out suffrage work.[78] Many older Jewish suffragists, leaders like Hannah Greenebaum Solomon and Rebekah Kohut, also expressed reservations about NWP activities.[79] It is possible, though, that at least some of the suffragists who publicly abjured NWP may have secretly welcomed the chance to appear less radical in the public eye. The movement may actually have benefited from the split.

NAWSA and NWP were quite different in tone and temperament and attracted different kinds of people, including different groups of Jewish suffragists. Despite their generally more radical outlook, most working-class women preferred the more conservative NAWSA because its leaders often had ties with the social reform community that had successfully worked on protective labor legislation for women. Many working-class women also disagreed with NWP's single-minded focus on the vote. NAWSA, too, was focused heavily on enfranchisement, but at least in theory NAWSA was also concerned with a somewhat broader array of women's issues.[80] Not all working-class Jewish women preferred NAWSA, however. Ernestine Hara, for example, supported NWP tactics wholeheartedly. Born into an anarchist family, Hara was a self-described "general radical" who even as a young woman already had strong ideas "about the repression of women in many fields of political and public life." She marched in suffrage parades and, at a socialist convention in New York in 1917, was recruited by a NWP member to join the team currently picketing the White House. Hara knew she might be arrested and even go to jail, but she found that "kind of romantic" and went to Washington anyway. NWP paid her fare, room, and board. She immediately joined the picketers, who worked in groups of four for several days and were then usually arrested and replaced by other teams. They walked back and forth in front of the White House gates, displaying banners in the suffrage colors of purple, gold, and white. They were harassed by onlookers who made obscene comments. During Hara's time in D.C., someone even fired a gun through NWP headquarters windows. Hara was arrested in due course. NWP bailed her out of the city jail, but she was sentenced to the infamous Occoquan workhouse in nearby Lorton, Virginia, after she made a pro-suffrage statement at the trial. While in jail, Hara joined other suffrage prisoners in refusing to work. Hara's group did not go on a hunger strike, but she found the food so inedible that she became quite sick. Although after her release she was tempted to picket again, she decided she could not bear the idea of going back to prison. Instead, she returned to New York and continued to participate in major suffrage parades and other NWP activities.[81]

The more typical NWP activist was a single, professional, middle-class woman like Anita Pollitzer. Eventually becoming Paul's right-hand woman, Pollitzer initially became involved with the Congressional Union. While teaching at the University of Virginia, she visited Washington every weekend to lobby for a federal amendment. Pollitzer was very popular in NWP as someone who was both more likeable and more approachable than Paul. A NWP insider described her as a "messenger on roller skates," willing to do anything that needed to be done and intensely loyal to Paul.[82]

Rebecca Hourwich Reyher was another Jewish woman more ideologically inclined toward NWP than NAWSA. Returning home to Washington, D.C., for the summer of 1917 after a year at the University of Chicago, she picketed with NWP, finding that the most difficult part was standing so still that all attention would be focused on the banners rather than the women holding them. Reyher was amused and sometimes dismayed by Paul's need for tight personal control, but she agreed with both her tactics and her reasoning. Paul recognized Reyher's gifts as an organizer and sent her on a suffrage tour through the South, mostly to provide publicity and make arrangements for NWP lobbyist Maud Younger, though Reyher gave speeches as well. The suffrage tour proceeded smoothly, with Younger's automobile creating a sensation wherever the group went, and Reyher found the press coverage fair and favorable even though another of the main speakers, Jeanette Rankin, attracted some ire for her pacifist stance after the United States had entered World War I. Paul was particularly pleased by the ability of the team to recruit prominent professional women like the lawyer Sue Shelton White of Tennessee, who became an NWP mainstay and one of Reyher's closest friends. While in the South, Reyher frequently confronted racial tensions. As a progressive, she was more outraged than Weil by the way racism framed the southern suffrage movement, but she acceded to Paul's directive not to address the subject on the campaign trail.[83]

Following the southern campaign, Reyher got married, afterward refusing Paul's request that she be arrested and write about her prison experiences. For a while, Reyher ran the New York NWP office. She learned to draw people in by arranging attractive window displays and making cheap suffrage literature readily available. As a fund-raiser, she also came to realize how many wealthy women were totally dependent on their husbands, with no access to cash of their own. With this lesson about the importance of economic independence continually before her, she accepted a job organizing the Massachusetts NWP operation and saw her husband only on the weekends. The

Massachusetts campaign kept Reyher very busy; when asked about her hob-
bies, she retorted "Such indulgences are not for suffragists—not until the federal amendment is ratified."[84]

Paul appreciated Reyher's success and recalled her to national headquarters, but by then Reyher was pregnant and again annoyed Paul by refusing
to participate in a demonstration that both women knew might turn violent. Reyher gave birth to a daughter in May 1919 and took a year off. After
the Nineteenth Amendment was finally ratified, she reactivated NWP's New
York headquarters in preparation for the Equal Rights Amendment (ERA)
campaign. She also helped set up the Chicago NWP headquarters, but with
a child and an unsuccessful writer husband to support, Reyher found that
continuing NWP work was not lucrative enough. She helped Paul organize
the 1923 convention in Seneca Falls and remained both a NWP member and
an ERA supporter for the rest of her life, but she never worked full time for
NWP again.[85] Unlike some other suffragists, she could not indulge in the luxury of voluntary activism.

When the United States entered World War I, the split between NAWSA
and NWP deepened, leading many suffragists to make a final choice. Catt,
though personally pacifist, offered President Wilson NAWSA's support for
the war effort with the tacit understanding that he would then back enfranchisement, which he eventually did. The NWP, however, continued to oppose
any government that did not support women's suffrage, including President
Wilson's wartime government.[86]

Like many activists, Amy Schwartz Oppenheim had worked for suffrage
through both NAWSA and NWP. After one NWP outburst against the government in June 1917, she reluctantly resigned. As she wrote, "I have always
enjoyed working with you . . . and it is not easy for me to take this step. I do
not approve of the action taken yesterday in Washington. . . . The noble and
heroic women of Europe and America are doing more to keep the cause of
Woman Suffrage going everywhere than any attack or threat could possibly
accomplish." Oppenheim continued to work for suffrage, but she, like others,
found it difficult to sustain loyalties to both NAWSA and NWP.[87] For her,
suffrage work must not only enhance but also embrace her patriotism, something that she felt continuing to work with NWP would preclude.

Oppenheim's dilemma highlighted the problems Jewish women faced
when their activism seemed to conflict with either their American or their
Jewish identities. Oppenheim experienced a particular kind of discomfort
during a moment of world crisis, and she never questioned her support for
suffrage. But there were also Jewish women who continued to feel ambivalent or even opposed enfranchisement because a large swath of American

society as a whole still saw political activism as unwomanly, and middle-class American Jewish women tried mightily to live up the ideal of American womanhood. The prejudice against them encountered by some Jewish activists further complicated commitment to suffrage as an assertion of American Jewish identity. Although ultimately the American Jewish community on the whole supported suffrage, an internal debate persisted.

Jewishness, Judaism, and Suffrage

The role of Jewishness in Jewish suffragists' activism varied, but from the turn of the century on, Jewish women became noticeably more willing to bring their Jewish identities with them into their activism. Unlike Ernestine Rose, the antebellum women's rights advocate, Hannah Greenebaum Solomon, Nina Morais Cohen, and Sadie American, among others, remained highly visible as Jewish women as they became involved in the national suffrage movement during the 1890s. Cohen, for example, like Solomon and American a founder of NCJW, wrote suffrage articles for *North American Review* and offered home hospitality to Susan B. Anthony and Anna Howard Shaw when they attended a national suffrage conference in Minneapolis in 1901.[88] Throughout the country, women who played prominent roles in Jewish organizations supported suffrage. Frances Wisebart Jacobs, a major figure in Denver's Jewish community who earned a national reputation as Denver's "Mother of Charities" during the 1880s, believed women should vote to make the world a better place, saying in 1888 that "if we had votes in the coming election we would secure what we want" in the way of a reform agenda.[89] Furthermore, most of the innumerable Jewish women who supported suffrage affirmed their Jewish identity in some way. Working-class Jewish suffragists like Rose Schneiderman and Pauline Newman lived in heavily Jewish neighborhoods and belonged to Jewish labor, socialist, or Zionist organizations. Middle-class Jewish suffragists like Solomon, Cohen, and Jacobs also tended to live in Jewish enclaves and belonged to an array of socially conscious groups.

Although many prominent Jewish women leaders supported suffrage, they did not necessarily express their convictions through their Jewish organizations. The *Atlanta Constitution* called Sophie Weil Brown "one of the most interested workers in the Suffrage League" in 1917, yet the Century Club, the Jewish women's organization of Columbia, Georgia, in which Brown held office, did not work for enfranchisement. Despite the great interest and significant support of individual Jewish women from all walks of life, no major American Jewish women's organization endorsed suffrage until 1917. When in 1915 NAWSA sent questionnaires to the presidents of each state suffrage association, asking for list of other pro-suffrage groups, only Arkansas listed a Jewish women's group. The only Jewish suffrage organization in the world was the Jewish League for Women Suffrage in England, a fairly militant group that pushed for immediate enfranchisement for all women and also considered the relationship between Jewish women's political roles and religious lives.[90]

Mainstream suffrage groups found it puzzling that Jewish women's organizations were reluctant to endorse suffrage when they were otherwise known for being socially progressive. While visiting Washington, D.C., to speak at the Mother's Congress in 1896, the NCJW leader Rebekah Kohut was embarrassed when the NAWSA leaders Anthony and Shaw cornered her and demanded to know why Jewish organizations did not take their place among American women's groups fighting for their rights.[91] As Kohut explained repeatedly over the next twenty-five years, it was not the case that Jewish women's groups never discussed suffrage. Many of them did, increasingly often as the twentieth century unfolded. The Atlanta NCJW section, for instance, regularly addressed the issue, devoting a full program to suffrage in March 1914 and urging members to follow the debate closely. But in Atlanta, no major women's organization—Jewish or not—formally endorsed suffrage. The sisterhood of the Hebrew Benevolent Congregation of Atlanta affirmed that Jewish women exerted power in society with or without suffrage.[92]

Of all the Jewish women's organizations in the United States, the NCJW would have been the obvious group to join the suffrage movement, but it never officially did. It routinely worked with other women's organizations that either originated as pro-suffrage groups or adopted that position later. Pauline Steinem of the Toledo section of NCJW believed that "the perfect equality of man and woman is founded on divine wisdom" and argued that women's wider experiences would enhance their abilities as mothers and homemakers.[93] Suffrage became a common topic for NCJW sections across the country. In Charleston, a 1908 program considered "Various Methods of Voting." In Minneapolis, the $100 that a January 1914 special event brought in was split between the NCJW's section treasury and the local Equal Suffrage League. At the national level, prominent suffrage speakers like Carrie Chapman Catt regularly addressed NCJW Triennial conventions. But still NCJW did not officially endorse suffrage.[94]

At least one Jewish suffragist condemned NCJW and other Jewish women's organizations in harsh terms for their lack of support. In a 1915 feature in *American Hebrew*, a New York–based publication with a national audience aimed primarily at American-born Jews oriented toward religious reform, the anonymous critic blamed Jewish women for remaining forty to fifty years behind the times. The critic sardonically suggested that perhaps "the Jewish woman so naturally finds herself the equal of the man . . . that it is unnecessary for her to seek political equality, since she can affect her pressure for social good without going to the ballot." The author immediately dismissed her own rhetorical feint, however, declaring that it was impossible for Jewish women so engaged in communal organizations and efforts not to realize that the "pleasant man who was so chivalrous as long as she limited her activities would become a violent opponent if she touched the sacred political and social usages for which he was responsible." The article concluded by warning Jewish women that they were doing themselves no favor by staying out of the great movement of their time.[95] Given the heavy involvement of so many Jewish women in suffrage work, it seems likely that the author was directing her opprobrium toward Jewish women's organizations rather than toward individual Jewish women.

For NCJW, the situation came to a head in 1917. By this time individual sections, such as that of Jamaica, New York, were sending Catt and NAWSA their own letters of support for suffrage.[96] Kohut promised her suffrage colleagues that a resolution would pass at the 1917 Triennial. The resolution read:

> Whereas, The question of Equal Suffrage is now one of great moment; and Whereas, Every body of women organized for progressive work along lines of special and civic betterment is forced to recognize the imperative need for woman's enfranchisement; and Whereas, This organization is co-operating with all groups organized for bettering conditions for women and children; be it Resolved, That the National Council of Jewish Women, in Convention assembled endorse the bill now pending in Congress providing an Amendment to our Federal Constitution granting to all the women of the United States the same political rights now enjoyed by the men.[97]

The resolution emphasized social welfare and alliances with other women's organizations, both features of NCJW widely supported by the larger membership. Kohut and many others were utterly shocked when the resolution failed to pass.

It is still not entirely clear why NCJW never endorsed suffrage despite the marked support for enfranchisement shown by many members and sections. The NCJW chronicler Faith Rogow has suggested that influential anti-suffragists may have swayed the group, or at least have condemned the resolution so loudly that the convention might have tried to avoid further controversy by rejecting it. It may also have been the case that NCJW members simply did not see suffrage as a particularly Jewish issue, or even part of their mission at all, and therefore preferred to take their positions on it outside NCJW. The roots of this stance were evident in an 1893 speech given by NCJW founder Carrie Shevelson Benjamin. Benjamin urged "that woman's sphere may comprise, among other things, suffrage, dress reform and charity, but that the greatest of her duties is charity." If politics would interfere with philanthropy, than perhaps NCJW should steer clear.[98]

By 1917, though, NCJW had long moved away from its roots as a group devoted to religiously inspired charitable works and had made itself into a large, dynamic, progressive women's organization routinely involved in political matters. In addition, as soon as women got the vote in states like New York, NCJW members eagerly embraced their new political roles. At an anniversary meeting of the New York NCJW section in May 1918, one speaker said, "One year ago, a woman's organization was a group of women that had combined . . . merely for the purpose of conducting a discussion of what they think should be done. To-day a women's organization is a group of those who politically are the equals of man."[99] These were hardly the words of anti-suffragists or those who believed women had no political role to play.

NCJW's recalcitrance remained all the more difficult to understand as other major Jewish women's groups did finally begin to endorse suffrage. The historian Mary McCune has argued that Jewish women in NCJW, the socialist Workmen's Circle, and Hadassah, the American women's Zionist organization, experienced heightened gender consciousness during World War I, leading to greater support for suffrage. The working-class, socialist members of the Workmen's Circle endorsed suffrage in 1917 despite earlier conformity to the Second International's disdain for the bourgeois suffrage movement. In 1918 Hadassah, which more typically focused on events and conditions in Palestine, sent a telegram to President Wilson instructing him to support suffrage and pointing out that women in Palestinian Jewish villages already had the right to vote.[100] It may be that the middle-class, largely American-born membership of NCJW simply could not bring itself to issue a formal endorsement of suffrage when a proportion of its membership either did not care about suffrage or actually opposed it.

For all of NAWSA leaders' disappointment in the reluctance of Jewish women's organizations like NCJW to take a stand, Jewish communal support for suffrage grew steadily. Anyone who paid attention to the large number of American Jews who discussed and endorsed enfranchisement, advanced particularly Jewish reasons to support women's voting rights, and conducted lively suffrage discussions in the Jewish press could not help but agree with *The Woman Voter* that "it is a well known fact that the Jewish people are in favor of the movement."[101] Though there was no Jewish suffrage organization per se, there was also no anti-suffrage Jewish group, and even Jewish anti-suffragists rarely made explicitly Jewish arguments to support their position, as their pro-suffrage counterparts often did.

A variety of reasons explains widespread Jewish communal support for the cause. The historian Elinor Lerner has argued that middle-class, American-born Jewish women were often better educated and more socially conscious than their non-Jewish counterparts, characteristics that tended toward greater progressivism in general. Working-class Jewish women, whether immigrants themselves or the daughters and granddaughters of immigrants, were steeped in a culture that valued Jewish women's economic contributions and fostered political awareness, which frequently led to other forms of public activism, such as membership in unions or participation in charitable and communal organizations. Jewish immigrants who arrived in the United States with previously developed radical ideas and organizational experience often believed that American democracy was fatally compromised by its exclusion of women from the direct political process. Particularly in large urban areas, the Socialist Party was heavily Jewish and hoped that suffrage would lead to greater electoral success by adding women to the number of socialist voters.[102]

Jewish communal support for suffrage steadily expanded. Men as well as women explored the issue. The Men's League for Woman Suffrage in New York, for example, listed a number of prominent Jewish men as office holders and advisory committee members. One of them, Maud Nathan's husband Frederick, supported her enthusiastically, accompanying her to suffrage parades and a number of international conferences. Though ill, he went in a wheelchair to vote for enfranchisement in the New York referenda of 1915 and 1917. In 1915, just before the renowned attorney Louis Brandeis's historic appointment to the Supreme Court, *The Woman's Journal and Suffrage News* was delighted to report that at a recent Zionist convention in Boston Brandeis had stated, "In the great Jewish commonwealth the equality of rights and women stand uppermost," an opinion he held for women in the United States as well. Meyer London, a Jewish socialist who represented the Lower East Side in Congress, proclaimed emphatically in a September 1917 address to the House of Representatives that his constituents were rabidly pro-suffrage and demanded a federal amendment immediately to rectify the great wrong of women's disenfranchisement. London helped secure the 1917 referendum in New York as well.[103]

Rabbis played a significant role in the Jewish suffrage movement. Though it was hardly the case that all American Jews cared deeply about rabbinical opinion, which was not unanimous in any event, rabbinical endorsement was important to a movement that had long sought clerical approval. Numerous rabbis' statements appeared in suffrage pamphlets containing clergy endorsements. In one such pamphlet, Samuel S. Cohen, rabbi of Chicago's Zion Temple, neatly combined both traditional and progressive ideas about women in his statement: "Good mothers and faithful wives use the ballot for the purpose of protecting their homes and children and in some instances even their husbands against the spread of the contagion of immorality."[104] Rabbis Aaron G. Robison, Joseph Krauskopf, and W. H. Fineshriber invited suffrage leaders like Nathan to speak at their synagogues at a time when it still came as something of a shock to see a woman addressing a congregation from the pulpit. In some cases, rabbis supported suffrage even when their congregants remained ambivalent. In San Francisco, rabbi Martin H. Meyer aroused some ire when he not only delivered several pro-suffrage sermons but also taught the girls in his confirmation class about the importance of having the vote.[105]

Due to the presence of denominations within American Judaism, no official, unitary Jewish institutional endorsement was possible, but suffrage did gain support from across the religious spectrum. Rabbis contributed to the debate by bringing explicitly Jewish arguments to bear. In 1917, the Reform movement's Central Conference of American Rabbis issued a pro-suffrage statement after previously defeating similar resolutions. Two years later, the Orthodox rabbi Jacob Levinson published *The Equality of Women from the Viewpoint of Halakhah*, which evaluated evidence both for and against suffrage from the perspective of traditional Jewish law and concluded that enfranchisement was permissible and even desirable, given the important actions taken in the public interest in the past by Jewish women role models such as Deborah and Esther.[106]

Of all the rabbis who lent their names and support to the suffrage movement, the most prominent was Stephen S. Wise, a leading figure of American Jewry throughout the first half of the twentieth century. His opinions and activities carried tremendous weight within the Reform Judaism with which he was primarily identified and in the immigrant community to which he ministered at the progressive Free Synagogue he founded in New York. Wise had first become interested in suffrage during his tenure at Temple Beth Israel in Portland, Oregon. After moving to New York in 1907, he kept in touch with suffrage friends in the West like Abigail Scott Duniway, and he continued to speak for enfranchisement during his frequent travels across the country.[107]

In his essay "Woman and Democracy," published in 1915, Wise delved into the many positive justifications for supporting suffrage. He began by expressing his conviction that the "sound and wise" leadership of women in the movement itself demonstrated the fitness of all women for full citizenship and equal political rights. He pointed out that even the most impassioned believers in women's domesticity must, in these modern times, accept the fact that millions of women in the United States and elsewhere were no longer primarily occupied in the home due to their participation in the industrial workplace. Moreover, he added, "wifehood and motherhood are not completely adequate as a life-calling for women in the home." If social reform and political interests did not fill the void in their lives, the consequences would be to the great detriment of all of society. Some of Wise's pronouncements were controversial, as when he said that "woman's life must cease to be relative to man. Woman must make and shape her own life, and she must no longer be expected to live in terms of relativity, in terms of dependence, in terms of complement." Perhaps aware that not all his congregants would be comfortable with such an outright feminist statement, he moved swiftly to further arguments about the inclusive meaning of modern democracy, the need for wage-earning women to have a say in policy that affected their lives and working conditions, and the danger of the current state of women exerting political influence without the accountability that enfranchisement would bring. Wise concluded, "the vote of women will not be better than the vote of men, but better than the vote of men will be the vote of men and women together."[108]

Noticeably absent from Wise's essay, though it appeared in a synagogue publication, was an explicitly Jewish approach to suffrage. Other Jewish activists more frequently drew on Jewish traditions and culture. Nathan nearly always presented justifications for suffrage in religious terms when speaking to Jewish groups. During a speech at Temple Mishkan Israel in New Haven in 1912, Nathan took for her text a passage from the biblical prophet Isaiah and emphasized the opportunities suffrage would bring Jewish women to "safeguard and protect the home," the traditional source of their strength and power. At a rally in Philadelphia attended by thousands just before the 1915 Pennsylvania referendum, Nathan used Jewish identity in a different way to promote suffrage. She proclaimed, "The Jewish people, more than any other, ought to realize the benefits of freedom. . . . Let the Jewish men of Pennsylvania be true to their traditions and vote for a square deal on election day."[109]

Nathan had good company in making explicit Jewish suffrage appeals. Several of the participants in a major symposium published in *American Hebrew* in 1915 did so as well. Lillian Wald, not in the least observant herself but nonetheless a frequent spokesperson for Jewish interests, noted that there had been a natural progression from the Old World Jewish woman who wielded a great deal of power in the home to the New World Jewish woman who demanded equal influence outside it. Rebekah Kohut pointed out that the biblical commandment to "Honor thy father and thy mother" equated the respect children should have for both parents and reflected the fact that "the position of the Jewish woman has always been as high, if no higher, than that of the female among contemporary nations." Kohut, who enjoyed an unusually good religious education, no doubt knew of some of women's legal disabilities in traditional Jewish law and culture, but she also knew of the high status of Jewish women in other arenas and focused on suffrage as a natural extension.[110]

By the time of the symposium's publication in September 1915, suffrage was a frequent topic of discussion in virtually all American Jewish periodicals in both English and Yiddish. The steady press coverage testified to the great interest of American Jews from all walks of life in what was rapidly becoming one of the most momentous political issues of the day. As one *American Hebrew* article put it in 1914, "Whether we are suffragists or antis, or are occupying that most uncomfortable place, a seat on the fence, we find ourselves sooner or later discussing suffrage. It has crept into our favorite magazines, our heart-to-heart talks, and the family table conversation. Suffrage is in the air."[111]

The 1915 symposium was contrived by presumably sympathetic editors, and they asked the well-known suffragist journalist and welfare worker Sophie Irene Loeb to organize the forum. The editors were also aware that some American Jews opposed enfranchisement and made sure that they were also represented. Annie Nathan Meyer received ample space to air her views, as did anti-suffragists Mrs. Henry Seligman and Helen Lauterbach. Seligman and Lauterbach advanced fairly simplistic arguments, with Seligman insisting that women "as a whole would make inferior voters" and should focus on influencing their husbands and sons at home, and Lauterbach contending that "in neither Philosophy, Art, Science has woman ever shone" and that her preference was to be "governed by men—the more virile the better." By 1915 these attitudes rang hollow even for the mostly middle-class readership of *American Hebrew*.[112]

Meyer's opposition to suffrage took a more sophisticated form. She began by expressing her conviction that American democracy was so successful a political system that it neither needed nor demanded further enfranchisement of more voters. She reserved the main thrust of her argument for a full-bore attack on feminism. "The two issues, suffrage and feminism," Meyer wrote, "cannot be kept separate and they are both inspired by a spirit of unrest and discontent." She accused feminists of condemning the domestic woman for passive inferiority, for eschewing the pleasure and responsibilities of hours devoted to culture and a wise use of leisure, for propagating the view "that nothing in life counts save an activity that may be measured and paid for," and for promoting independence as the highest virtue when the conditions of the modern world cried out for increasing interdependence instead. Meyer had no personal objection "to the economically independent woman, either as an exception or a misfortune, but with every scrap of force within me I decry her as an ideal." Many agreed with most of Meyer's points, and indeed the conflation of suffrage and feminism, which seemed natural to some suffragists, had presented a real obstacle to gaining the mass support of American women ever since the Seneca Falls convention.[113]

The pro-suffrage contributors to the *American Hebrew* symposium all countered Meyer's arguments. Wald pointed to the increasing overlap between government and home responsibilities in an age of social reform and municipal housekeeping, and she believed women's enfranchisement was therefore vital to the development of a modern democracy. A major figure in recently successful campaigns for mothers' and widows' pensions, Hannah Einstein commented on the improvement of conditions for mothers and children that would follow enfranchisement of women. Finally, Nathan unleashed an avalanche of statistics to attack her sister's arguments, demonstrating both the undeniable and growing presence of women in the workplace and the positive results of women's political power wherever they had it.[114]

Regardless of *American Hebrew*'s due diligence in presenting both sides of the question, overall the influential periodical consistently supported suffrage. A May 1912 article commented with approval that Jewish women who had marched in a recent suffrage parade included working women, school girls, and socialites. A few months later, the columnist Adele Rabinovitz cited the biblical judge Deborah as a Jewish model of a woman advising men. This piece praised the conditions of a modern world in which Jews could be recognized as human beings and still retain their full Jewish identity and made the same argument for women receiving full recognition as human beings while still retaining their essential womanliness. A 1914 article dismissed as ridiculous the notion that if husbands were to be found for all the suffragists, they would drop their claims, pointing out that plenty of wives and mothers also insisted on the vote. When the Jewish agricultural colony of Woodbine, New Jersey, conducted its own vote on enfranchisement, *American Hebrew* noted the overwhelming victory of the suffragists and editorialized, "This is what was to have been expected when one bears in mind the fierce longing for democracy which dwells in the heart of Jews of Russia." *American Hebrew* supported suffrage in both the 1915 and 1917 New York referendum campaigns and continuously published profiles of leading Jewish women to show how deserving all Jewish women were of the vote.[115]

Coverage of suffrage was just as widespread in the Yiddish press. The interest of the Yiddish press and its readers in suffrage provides another example of the Jewish communal culture and context within which suffragists operated. Though *American Hebrew* boasted the widest circulation of the English-language American Jewish periodicals, the Jewish newspaper with the widest reach of all was the Yiddish *Forverts*. A socialist, politically progressive daily, *Forverts* was read by tens of thousands and exerted considerable influence over working-class and immigrant Jews. It was one of several Yiddish periodicals that commented often on suffrage and kept their readers abreast of developments not just in the United States but also abroad.[116]

Discussions of suffrage appeared throughout *Forverts*. In 1909 a Jewish man wrote to the popular "Bintel Brief" advice column about a regular discussion group he attended. When the group began to debate suffrage, the correspondent was startled to discover that many in the group feared that suffrage would destroy family life. He strongly disagreed, writing that women were not slaves to men and should not be dependent upon them. He pointed out to the other members of his discussion group that they had recently commemorated Abraham Lincoln's one hundredth birthday in honor of the emancipation of the slaves—should they not, as good socialists and Jews, work for the emancipation of women?[117] This letter was significant for the writer's assumption that the advice columnist and, presumably, readership of *Forverts* would agree with him and also for the evidence it provides that not all politically progressive Jews automatically supported suffrage.

Unlike some of the *American Hebrew* writers, *Forverts* writers rarely justified suffrage on the grounds that women were morally superior or needed to protect the home. Instead, they considered suffrage merely a question of social justice, taking women's political participation for granted. During the ten years following the publication of the "Bintel Brief" letter, *Forverts's* coverage of suffrage increasingly assumed overwhelming support from the working-class American Jewish community. The "Notes From the Women's World" column analyzed progress made toward passing a federal suffrage amendment but also went beyond suffrage to criticize women's legal disabilities in New York and elsewhere. By 1918 the main topic of the women's page of *Forverts* was the suffrage movement, though historians disagree over the role women's issues played in the periodical overall.[118]

Meanwhile, other important Yiddish periodicals also debated the issue. *Der Fraynd* (*The Friend*), the socialist Workmen's Circle monthly publication, ran a regular feature about women, including material on such topics as suffrage workplace parity. Forced by Second International policy to regard the women's movement per se as hopelessly bourgeois, *Der Fraynd* nonetheless supported women's right to vote along with their right to work and unionize. The periodical also kept readers informed about women's rights in other countries. In December 1914, *Der Fraynd* published a lengthy article titled "The Struggle for Women's Rights in the World." This piece traced the origins of the women's rights movement to prehistoric matriarchies and emphasized the modern push toward equal rights for all, rather than the dominance of any one group over another. Listing suffrage victories at home and around the world, *Der Fraynd* saw the American movement as only one expression of epochal change that would affect men and women everywhere. When writing about the final push to secure a federal suffrage amendment in 1919, Dr. Esther Luria, a regular *Der Fraynd* contributor, took a similar approach. She reviewed the history and current statistics of the American suffrage movement and reproduced the seven planks of the new League of Women Voter's platform for the post-suffrage era. Interestingly, Luria also took the opportunity to bash the South, full of "accursed states" that continued to deny rights to blacks as well as women. This approach likely appealed to her already politicized readers, who were accustomed to analyzing issues in terms of oppression and mastery.[119]

Some of the Jewish periodicals that took a stand on suffrage were less radical than *Der Fraynd* or *Forverts*. *Di Froyen Velt*, which loosely translated its own title as the *Jewish Ladies Home Journal*, targeted a more religiously and politically conservative population of Yiddish speakers. *Di Froyen Velt* included a column called "From the Women's World" in each of its issues during its brief run in 1913. An analysis of the 1913 issues reveals that while the monthly magazine supported suffrage, it roundly condemned any hint of militancy. The April 1913 column reported the havoc wrought by suffragettes in England who had recently broken numerous windows and even set some houses on fire. By contrast, in the United States, *Di Froyen Velt* commented approvingly, "everything is carried out in a respectable manner, without wars and acts of violence, only with consideration, propaganda, and peaceful demonstrations." A few months later, the "From the Women's World" column described militant British suffragette Emmeline Pankhurst's controversial bid to go on a lecture tour in the United States with a combination of disdain for Pankhurst and admiration for a country that prized free speech so highly.[120]

During the summer of 1913, the magazine reported on the IWSA meeting in Budapest, men's participation in the New Jersey campaign, the suffrage victory in Illinois, and, once again, the difference between American and British tactics.[121] *Di Froyen Velt* quoted New York's mayor, William Jay

Gaynor, as suggesting that England's problem with militant suffragettes could be solved if the government found husbands for them. He had no objection to suffrage but felt that in the United States agitation was milder because there were fewer unmarried women. *Di Froyen Velt* sarcastically wondered if the mayor knew what kind of reaction these ill-advised, ignorant comments would provoke. The July issue also contained a brief item on women serving on juries that displayed *Di Froyen Velt*'s leftover ambivalence toward some of the implications of equality for women. An all-women jury in San Francisco had been empaneled in a case with a female defendant, but it proved difficult to find female jurors because

> each woman tried to wriggle out of it with excuses: this one has a baby in her arms, this one a sick child, this one a sick father, this one can't leave the house, and so on. It seems that voting rights are not such a piece of cake there when the responsibilities that these rights carry with them are also required.[122]

Though generally supportive of suffrage, *Di Froyen Velt* and its more traditional audience was less convinced about other aspects of feminism.

Since the final years of the campaign increasingly narrowed in on the vote as a single issue, supporting the movement became easier for somewhat more conservative American women like the *Di Froyen Velt* readers. The intense focus on women's enfranchisement rather than an entire feminist program emboldened Jewish women who had previously been unsure how to react to women's political activism to join the final push. The more acceptable suffragism became for American women in general, the more acceptable it was for American Jewish women who did not wish to compromise any aspect of their identities or community affiliations. When suffrage finally became a reality, it served as a springboard for some women to become involved with other feminist activism. It also allowed others to savor being part of a victory that they approvingly felt was meaningful but would not challenge social structures in any significant way. Like all the other fault lines within the suffrage movement, this one, too, became immediately apparent in the wake of the final victory.

The Aftermath of the Nineteenth Amendment

Ratification of the Nineteenth Amendment had immediate effects on huge numbers of jubilant American women. Longtime suffrage activists like Gertrude Weil rejoiced in the hard-fought victory. Weil's relatives congratulated her as soon as they heard about ratification, writing "Hurrah for suffrage and Tennessee! You surely have worked strenuously and faithfully and we are proud of you." She received another letter as well, from a man who grumpily congratulated her for winning the vote but complained that Jewish women like her should know better than to rejoice over the elevation of black people who, according to the Bible, he claimed, were meant to be forever cursed. Weil apparently did not respond to this letter, though she did keep it and she must have known that many southerners would have agreed with its sentiments. Instead, she focused her attention on working with Carrie Chapman Catt and others on a new campaign to support federal legislation for maternal and child welfare.[123]

In states that enfranchised women prior to 1920, women had already begun to vote with enthusiasm. After the successful 1917 suffrage referendum in New York, nearly 50 percent of the Socialist Party registrations in New York were women, illustrating the fact that new women voters embraced suffrage within the context of previously existing political loyalties and interests. Now women across the United States prepared to join them, with many acting on preexisting partisan loyalties.[124]

Suffragists had to make major readjustments after finally winning the right to vote. Women who had pursued enfranchisement with a kind of tunnel vision found themselves at something of a loss. Fortunately for the women's movement in general, however, many activists and probably the majority of suffrage leaders had always taken a broader view of women's political potential. As the historian Nancy Cott has argued, there was a striking similarity between women's political participation before and after 1920. Women continued to use voluntary organizations as a base of political influence. The vote was critical but not necessarily transformative of women's political behavior. Some of the major women's organizations, including NCJW, joined forces in the Women's Joint Congressional Committee to try to parlay suffrage success into social welfare legislation. As voters, the women members of the organizations represented by the Women's Joint Congressional Committee expected that they would have more power to effect legislative changes, but their maternalist goals remained much the same after suffrage as they had been before. Even the National Association Opposed to Woman Suffrage continued down the path it was already on, morphing into the Woman Patriots and opposing many Women's Joint Congressional Committee reforms as inviting too much government interference into the home.[125]

One of the organizations with which many Jewish women became involved in order to make their mark as voters on "the affairs of the time" was the League of Women Voters (LWV).[126] The league was NAWSA's successor organization and earned broad support from Jewish women. As Jennie Franklin Purvin explained to Chicago NCJW members, "We Jewish women should be especially interested in our new citizenship, since we are ambitious to see our own homes and our city, the big home of us all, taken care of." A few years later, Purvin also invited LWV to a meeting of the Chicago Conference of Jewish Women's Organizations to present the "Every Woman to the Polls" campaign. Other Jewish suffragists also continued their political activity under the aegis of LWV. The Boston suffragist Jennie Loitman Barron attended the second national LWV convention in Cleveland in 1921 and worked with a national committee of attorneys to standardize U.S. laws affecting women. In Montana, the former suffrage street speaker Belle Fligelman Winestine became active in her local LWV chapter and eventually ran for state senate with LWV support. Even Jewish women who had opposed suffrage became involved with LWV. Ray Frank Litman helped organize a LWV chapter in Urbana-Champaign, Illinois, and Annie Nathan Meyer was one of many anti-suffragists who joined LWV to ensure that newly enfranchised women, even those whom they felt did not really deserve the ballot, would have access to political education.[127]

Just as NWP had presented an alternative to NAWSA, it also presented an alternative to LWV in the post-suffrage era.[128] The LWV developed a broad platform of maternalist reform goals, such as voter education, child welfare and peace, but NWP focused narrowly on an Equal Rights Amendment (ERA), which it first proposed in 1923. Not all NWP suffragists agreed with this strategy or with Alice Paul's fierce determination to retain control of NWP, but Paul prevailed on all counts. During the spring of 1922, Rebecca Hourwich Reyher opened an ERA headquarters in New York, which rapidly became the central arena for the clash between opposing forces.[129] On one side were NWP forces, which insisted that true equality could be achieved only through legislating absolute legal parity between men and women. On the other side were arrayed the WTUL, CL, and a host of social reform groups that favored protective legislation for working women and feared the consequences of gender-blind legal status. The NCJW strongly opposed the ERA, which it felt would undercut its commitment to motherhood, hurt working women, and ignore the patent differences between men and women.[130] Jewish women took up visible positions on both sides of the debate. During the 1920s and 1930s, the labor leader Pauline Newman and NWP officer Anita Pollitzer frequently met in public debate over the ERA, as did the WTUL president Rose Schneiderman and NWP representative Reyher.[131] These women respected each others' abilities but were firmly convinced that their opponents were hurting women's cause by believing as they did.

Both LWV and NWP achieved some success during the 1920s, though neither ever had anything like the mass membership NAWSA could boast during the last years of the suffrage campaign. Members of the two groups held starkly different positions on the ERA, but they also shared interests, such as the state of other countries' struggles for suffrage and women's status.[132] The LWV member Setty Swartz Kuhn, a clubwoman from Cincinnati, and pro-ERA Reyher traveled together to Russia, parts of Europe, and Palestine in 1928–29, and both of them made an effort to learn about the condition of women in every country they visited. Reyher attended a presentation of the League of Greek Women for Women's Rights in Athens. In Palestine, Reyher and Kuhn had tea with Dr. Rosa Welt Strauss, secretary of the Jewish women's suffrage group, who blamed British officials' anti-Semitism for the slow movement toward political equality there. Reyher felt that Zionist leaders were also to blame: when she asked them about it, they laughed her off. Although Reyher was dubious at best about Zionism, she did appreciate the Jewish women she met who were insisting that any Zionist constitution include equal suffrage as a fundamental right.[133]

While former suffragists continued to do battle over such issues as the ERA, they also spent a great deal of time assessing the results of suffrage in the United States. None of them would have rolled back enfranchisement, but many were forced to admit that the radical changes they had been expecting failed to appear. Within just a few years of enfranchisement, women were already considering its ramifications. Some former suffragists marveled at the modest effects voting rights seemed to have had on other areas of women's lives. Iphigene Bettman, an LWV member, found it surprising that younger women, like her, who had marched in suffrage parades and rejoiced over the Nineteenth Amendment, still felt guilty when they went to bars and "tittered" when they discussed sex.[134] Rokhl Herman, a socialist journalist, was less surprised that suffrage had not changed the world. She believed it had always been foolish to expect that votes would alter women's lives without concomitant changes in working conditions. She wrote in *Der Fraynd* in August 1923 that "The fate of the working women is closely tied to the fate of the whole working class. She should fight its battle and its victory will bring her worthy liberation."[135] Economic, not political emancipation, was key.

In 1924, the LWV publication *The Woman Citizen* sponsored a symposium asking "Is Woman Suffrage Failing?" That such a symposium appeared less than five years after enfranchisement indicates the anxiety many former suffragists felt. Several Jewish women participated. Molly Lifshitz, secretary of the White Goods Workers Union, found the title question of the symposium insulting. No one ever asked men if their suffrage was a failure, she pointed out, even though they had been voting for far longer and there were many problems in the world. She thought women's groups could be more effective now that they had more respect from men in business and politics, but she also considered it a mistake to expect any more from women voters than from men. The socialist Rose Pastor Stokes was less convinced by the utility of suffrage when political parties only served to express class interests anyway. Like Emma Goldman before her, she agreed that enfranchisement had raised women's political awareness but dismissed as insignificant any political development that did not lead to fundamental change in class relations and structures of governance. Finally, WTUL leader Schneiderman stated, "I am just as disappointed in women's suffrage as I am in men's suffrage." She admitted that it was proving difficult to convince women to accept the political responsibilities from which they had once been barred, but she also firmly believed that a process of political education could and would encourage working women to make the best use of their votes by representing their own interests.[136]

Conclusion

Once the Nineteenth Amendment was ratified in August 1920, Jewish women moved to apply their new rights to their sense of Jewish communal status as well as American citizenship. Immediately after winning the vote, the members of the sisterhood of The Temple in Atlanta successfully demanded representation on the synagogue board. As they explained, "in this age of woman's suffrage, the Sisterhood should demand the right to have a real working voice."[137] Synagogues across the country took similar steps. Temple Beth-El of Providence, Rhode Island, enlarged its board in 1921 to allow women to vote and hold office, and local Jewish communal leader Marion Misch won election as a trustee shortly thereafter. Misch firmly believed that "Jewish women are . . . esteemed not only supreme in their households, but as direct agencies for influence upon the affairs of the time."[138] Even Jewish women's organizations that had not formally supported suffrage, such as NCJW, reacted excitedly to enfranchisement. The Cincinnati NCJW section immediately organized a citizenship class so that Jewish women could become "intelligent voters." Constance Sporborg, president of the New York NCJW section stated, "Now that our organization has 3,000 voters as well as 3,000 members, its influence can be more direct.[139] For Jewish women like these NCJW members, suffrage had implications in both their political and their religious lives.

Suffrage activism offered Jewish women opportunities common to all American women but also particular to them. Suffragists gained valuable organizational and administrative skills, developed their writing and public speaking abilities, learned to lobby and petition, became familiar with the inner workings of political systems, insisted on their own humanity and civic equality, grew accustomed to thinking of women as a political force to be reckoned with, and dared to make demands on local, state, and national power structures. Jewish women shared in this acquisition of skill and power but made additional gains as well. The focus on women qua women ironed out some—though not all and certainly not racial—ethnic, religious, cultural, and even class distinctions and allowed Jewish women of many backgrounds an important entree into American women's associational life. Jewish women's organizations achieved major recognition as both targets of and propagators of suffrage organizing. Individual Jewish women's leadership eased the acceptance of Jewish women into other areas of American life, though never entirely erasing the anti-Semitism that left some Jewish women persistently uneasy. Finally, Jewish women began to see direct connections between civic and religious enfranchisement, drawing on all elements of the suffrage movement to reinforce their claims to wider, more meaningful participation in Jewish communal and religious life. This connection between the heretofore private realm of Jewish women's religious activity and their now solemnized public roles as voting citizens transformed American Jewish women's notions of modern citizenship. Their new status launched them into further realms of social and political activism inflected by both their gender and their Jewish identities.

2

"I Started to Get Smart, Not to Have So Many Children"

The American Jewish Community and the Early
Years of the Birth Control Movement

I would not live in constant fear of bringing another child into the
world, which meant death for me.
—Rose Heiman Halpern, 1934[1]

In January 1917, a woman described by a *New York Times* reporter as "poorly
clad" joined nearly a hundred others in applauding the lawyer Jonah Goldstein during his defense of Ethel Byrne, on trial for her role in the pathbreak-
ing birth control clinic her sister Margaret Sanger had opened in Brownsville,
Brooklyn, the past October. Goldstein argued that women did not seek to
eliminate childbearing but to make motherhood voluntary and within wom-
en's control. Thirty-five-year-old Rose Heiman Halpern, with six children
from ages sixteen months to ten years and a husband who earned seventeen
dollars a week, did not have the wherewithal to dress up for court, but she
did have the means to become involved with a cause that she immediately
saw would be of great benefit to her and other women like her. As soon as
she heard about the Brownsville clinic, Halpern volunteered to distribute the
Yiddish, Italian, and English handbills that Sanger had prepared, and she was
one of the first to receive contraceptive services before the clinic was shut
down. She attended all the trials related to the case, often with her children
in tow, and presented a bouquet of flowers from the mothers of Brownsville
to Sanger upon her release from jail.[2]

Immigrant women like Rose Halpern desperately sought out birth control as a means of preventing, or at least ameliorating, poverty, high infant
and maternal mortality rates, illness, and barriers to social mobility. In so
doing they followed in the footsteps of middle-class women who had for
more than a century used a variety of techniques and tactics to reduce their
family size.[3] A mercilessly logical approach to childbearing saw contraceptive
efforts as a necessary accommodation in an industrializing economy that
rendered children drains on, rather than assets to, the family economy.[4] Yet

Rose Heiman Halpern and her six children greet Margaret Sanger on the courthouse steps, 1917. Corbin/Bettman Archive

few women or men viewed the creation and sustenance of families primarily from this coolly rational perspective. Although women's roles were changing at the turn of the century, only the most radical argued against the notion that women's primary destiny was motherhood. This role identification was especially strong in Jewish culture and tradition, which for centuries had reified motherhood as the divinely mandated purpose of women. The gradual transformation of Jewish womanhood in the new world continued to elevate motherhood even as some other elements of Jewish gender roles modernized, in part because the value of women as mothers was shared by the middle-class American conventions so many immigrants longed to adopt and adapt for themselves.[5]

The birth control movement thus could have presented a real dilemma for Jewish women, as it offered on the one hand a path toward the "modern" American family and on the other a seeming rejection of women's traditional place within Judaism. But because most saw birth control not as a rejection of motherhood but rather as an improvement upon it, the movement instead endowed childbearing with a voluntary, positive spirit with obvious ancillary benefits in terms of health, marital relations, and social mobility. Due to the premium that Jewish law puts on the lives and well-being of mothers, as evidenced by considerable rabbinic discussion and sanction of some contraceptive practices, few tradition-minded American Jewish women worried overmuch about the religious implications of birth control, and secular Jewish women cared not at all.[6] Instead, American Jewish women became avid consumers as contraception increased in effectiveness and availability. Though not all elements of the community embraced birth control, American Jewish women generally continued the patterns of falling fertility rates that had already begun in eastern European Jewish communities.[7] And for some women like Rose Halpern, birth control became not just a personal or family choice but also a critical social cause worth supporting with enthusiasm.

Halpern, who immigrated to the United States in 1902, was no stranger to political causes. In Vilna she had belonged to the same radical reading group as her brother, who was arrested and sent to Siberia. After arriving in New York, she joined the Socialist Party along with her new husband William, a garment worker and trade unionist who would eventually run unsuccessfully for the New York State Assembly on the Socialist Party ticket. By 1916 the family lived in a small, crowded Brownsville apartment with diapers boiling on the stove next to the soup pot. After having six children in rapid succession, Halpern had not had an uninterrupted night of sleep in more than a decade. Her interest in the nascent birth control movement came first and foremost from her own personal experience, though her political background probably predisposed her to become interested in the movement as a whole rather than seeing contraception as an individual affair.[8]

Remaining involved with the movement long after the original Brownsville clinic closed in 1916 and the related trials concluded in 1917, Halpern became one of Sanger's acolytes. She accompanied Sanger to give testimony at a state assembly hearing in Albany in 1925. Every time the birth control movement achieved some kind of victory, such as the Federal Council of Churches' decision to condone contraception in 1931, Halpern wrote Sanger a congratulatory note. She attended a testimonial dinner to Sanger in 1932 and made an impromptu speech, to which Sanger responded with a heartfelt letter of appreciation. In 1934 Sanger invited Halpern to testify about birth control before Congress. Halpern immediately accepted, writing "I am only too happy to do my bit for you and the cause of all womanhood," although she was embarrassed to have to accept the offer of paid expenses. A savvy organizer, Sanger no doubt valued Halpern as an individual but also wanted a clearly working-class woman to appear before Congress. She asked Halpern not to let her "ambitious daughters" dress her up too much, warning "We do not want you to look too fashionable or the point of your appearance will be lost." At the hearing, Halpern testified that " I could safely say that

Mrs. Sanger had saved my life, as I could not stand any more births" after seven pregnancies in eleven years. She played her role well, as evidenced by a *Chicago Daily Tribune* report that found the personal accounts of the "plain people" even more impressive than the testimony of doctors, lawyers, and clergy members. Halpern and Sanger kept up a correspondence over a period of decades, and Halpern made small donations to the cause whenever she could. As an eighty-year-old woman, she attended a memorial service for Sanger in 1966, honoring the important role the birth control movement had played in her life.[9]

Rose Halpern was only one of countless American Jewish women who became deeply invested in the birth control movement as consumers, activists, and professionals. The fact that a significant number of Jewish women were involved in radical politics meant that they were exposed to constant discussion of issues like contraception, voluntary motherhood, free love, autonomy, and women's control of their own bodies. Even if they were not so obviously politicized, both working-class and middle-class Jewish women could easily identify their own interests and the benefits that limiting their childbearing would bring to their families. Given the marked drop in the Jewish birthrate in America, it is probably no exaggeration to say that more Jewish women than not had some experience with birth control.[10] Their mass participation helped shape the movement in significant ways and sparked intense discussion of birth control within the American Jewish community during the first decades of the twentieth century.

Continuities and New Directions in Jewish Women's Activism during the 1920s

Even before the suffrage movement reached its final victory with the ratification of the Nineteenth Amendment, there were strong links between suffragism and participation in other political movements of the day. During the 1917 cost-of-living boycotts in New York, fueled by working-class, mostly Jewish women with some help from middle-class allies in the Women's Trade Union League (WTUL) and other reform organizations, a cadre of socialist women attempted to direct attention to suffrage, arguing that votes were necessary for all women's causes. At the height of the boycott in February 1917, a Mother's Anti-High Price League Committee combined 158 organizations that represented the wide range of women's activism, including the birth control movement. Critics of women's activism tended to lump together its various iterations. When the federal government banned a socialist monthly, *The Masses,* in 1917 for expressing pacifist views and opposing conscription, it also, as a matter of course, condemned the periodical for supporting birth control and feminism.[11] The tendency of both insiders and outsiders to emphasize these links made it difficult for women who tried to defend their causes by dissociating themselves from radicalism. The pervasive image of Jews as radicals further complicated Jewish women's activism in movements that sometimes eyed them with suspicion.

The pattern of connecting and even conflating activist causes predated the end of the suffrage movement and provided opponents of the birth control movement, in particular, with ammunition. They linked birth control to suffrage as a violation of the natural role of women as mothers. In 1915 the judge presiding over William Sanger's trial for disseminating Margaret Sanger's *Family Limitation* pamphlet made his distaste quite clear, stating, "If some persons would go around and urge Christian women to bear children, instead of wasting their time on woman suffrage, this city and society would be better off."[12] References to Christian women notwithstanding, a sizable contingent of Jewish women suffragists supported the birth control movement, which was actually more radical during the years when it overlapped with the end stage of the suffrage movement than it would be later. A February 1917 article in the first issue of *Birth Control Review*, then under Margaret Sanger's direct editorship, inquired "Shall We Break the Law?" and responded with an emphatic yes. Both suffragists, especially the more militant National Woman's Party (NWP) members, and early birth control activists used direct action, violation of existing laws, and arrest as tactics to draw attention to their causes.[13] As a result, suffragists were denounced as free love radicals, and birth control activists were condemned as strident feminists. Feminism, a word claimed and used by growing numbers of women during the first decades of the twentieth century, did in fact provide a link among all causes that activists believed would improve the status of women and helps explain the significant overlap of strategies, networks, personnel, donors, and visions for the future among women devoted to a variety of causes.[14]

By 1920 the birth control movement had, to some extent, turned away from its radical roots in an effort to attract the support of more wealthy women, professional women, middle-class women's organizations, and the medical establishment. Still, activists flush with the victory of the suffrage campaign who hoped to remain in the political arena found birth control an attractive possibility for the new focus of their attention not only because they believed in it, though many surely did, but also because they understood that feminism did not begin and end with suffrage. As one example, Viola Kaufman, a suffragist and teacher, went to work for Sanger's American Birth Control League (ABCL) as an organizer and lobbyist shortly after the passage of the Nineteenth Amendment and bequeathed the birth control movement $12,000 when she died during the mid-1930s.[15] Many others like Kaufman recognized that women still faced major obstacles in their fight for rights and segued easily from suffrage to birth control as a logical continuation of feminist activism.

A Brief History of Birth Control in America

There was birth control long before there was a birth control movement in America. For centuries, a market thrived in everything from herbal concoctions and "French letters" to douching solutions and womb supports, unperturbed by failure rates and undisturbed by regulation. By the mid-nineteenth century, purveyors of all manner of contraceptives advertised in the mainstream press, and the typical American woman could resort to a wide variety of aids in her quest to have fewer children. The popularity of that quest was evident in the national birthrate, which for white women dropped from 6.14 in 1840 to 4.55 in 1870 to 3.56 in 1900 to 2.51 in 1930.[16] Even abortionists, though portrayed in medical and moral literature as nefarious creatures, could practice their trade quite profitably. Married middle-class couples as well as desperate working girls employed their services; in fact, married middle-class couples were more likely to be able to afford their fees.[17] Technology sided with couples wishing to procure some form of contraception, as vulcanized rubber improved the efficacy and convenience of both condoms and cervical caps. Other medical breakthroughs facilitated the development of spermicidal gels.[18] Even though a cloud of secrecy purportedly hung over the contraceptive market, family limitation via means other than abstinence was entirely possible, if never foolproof, even in a world that condemned explicit discussion of such matters as distasteful.

Not until the so-called Comstock Law of 1873—technically the Act for the Suppression of Trade in and Circulation of Obscene Literature and Articles of Immoral Use—was the distribution of information about contraception declared obscene and therefore illegal. As a result of a potent combination of factors, including technological innovation and mass production of contraceptive devices, concerns about the falling birthrate of native-born white Americans during a period of mass migration, fears about public morality tied to rapid urbanization, and the personal efforts of the anti-vice crusader Anthony Comstock, contraception became significantly less available and even less effective during the late 1800s than it had been during the mid-1800s, when a relatively free market had enhanced quality and accessibility to some degree. By the mid-1880s, a number of states had passed legislation even more restrictive than the federal laws, criminalizing not only distribution but also use of contraception and, in some cases, forbidding doctors to give their patients medical advice related to contraception. Through coded advertisements, surreptitious exchanges between doctors and patients, and euphemistically labeled merchandise, contraception was still available to some American women, but mostly those who could afford to pay for medical care and merchandise. Poor women had few options by the beginning of the twentieth century.[19]

The birth control movement, in the United States and in other countries like England, where a similar environment of legal repression had taken hold, developed in this context. Though historians have periodized the birth control movement in several different ways, nearly all agree that the early twentieth century was significant as the first stage. The earliest years of the birth control movement in the United States, prior to World War I, saw a grassroots effort to publicize the problem and then the first failed attempts to open birth control clinics. During the 1920s, the birth control movement as led by Margaret Sanger and Mary Ware Dennett, among others, took up increasingly professional lobbying through such organizations as the ABCL and the Voluntary Parenthood League (VPL). A new set of clinics, carefully calibrated to local circumstances, opened in a number of states. Throughout the 1920s and early 1930s, activists pushed for legislative change, though they did not always agree on what those changes should be, while the number and size of clinics grew steadily. By the mid- to late 1930s, a series of court decisions had eased legal restrictions on contraception, leaving the movement to change its focus to the professionalization of birth control services and the expansion of access. Along with the shift to medicalization and professionalization came the greater involvement of men as leaders, with Dr. Robert Latou Dickinson's Committee on Maternal Health gaining influence in the national movement. Women often retained considerable power at the local clinic level.[20]

The historian Gene Burns has argued that public attention to birth control was episodic rather than continuous and that legal changes often occurred during periods of dormant interest. A 1933 study of changing American social attitudes noted that following extensive magazine coverage of birth control from 1915 to 1918, a general lull in public discussion lasted until 1930–31, when the volume of media coverage peaked again.[21] However, the ebb and flow of the movement does not mean there was not steady activism—and steady use of contraceptives—throughout the first few decades of the twentieth century.

The birth control movement in America had at least two incubators. One was the leftist political milieu of those who believed in a link between revolutionary class struggle and women's reproductive control. The other was early twentieth-century feminism, which at first probably preferred temperance or abstinence to contraception but still made a strong claim for women's personal choice and thereby opened the door to birth control. As a result of these dual incubators, birth control came to be associated with a cultural complex of more or less radical social reforms.[22] Even middle-class professionals in the birth control movement who pursued socially acceptable lives and careers typically maintained some kind of connection to radical politics. During the early 1920s, for example, the Jewish doctors Ben Zion Liber, Abraham Stone, and Hannah Mayer Stone, highly visible birth control advocates all, taught at the Labor Temple in New York and introduced sex hygiene and contraception to worker education.[23] Given the conservative, even repressive, political climate of the late 1910s and 1920s, however, women and men whose primary commitment was to birth control often found it politic to hide the radical roots that might have brought them into the movement in the first place. It also became necessary to reposition birth control as both morally and medically desirable in order to win mainstream acceptance. In addition to the strategies of activists, the behavior of consumers also helped shape the movement, especially as working-class women's perspective that birth control was a fundamental economic need rather than a convenient luxury grew more prevalent across class boundaries.[24]

Radical Roots

The vibrant world of radical politics in the United States, particularly in urban areas, formed an important context for the birth control movement in its early years. The heady brew of socialism, anarchism, unionism, communism, feminism, and other movements contributed both leaders and grassroots activism to the birth control cause and drew in Jewish women from a variety of backgrounds. Margaret Sanger, associated with socialism and the feminists of Greenwich Village, launched an opening salvo when she not only published *The Woman Rebel*, a magazine insisting on the right of free access to contraceptive information and devices, but also mailed it, thereby violating the Comstock laws. She was arrested in August 1914 and refused a trial postponement in October, whereupon she fled to Europe. While in Europe, Sanger educated herself about birth control techniques and medical advances.[25]

Meanwhile, the larger American birth control movement slowly began to develop. At an Academy of Medicine meeting in New York in May 1915, thousands of people gathered to protest the New York state law that made it a crime for a doctor or any other person to give out information about contraception. Dr. Abraham Jacobi argued that it was in the best interests of the state to ensure that all children be healthy and fit, a standard that birth control could help promote. Other speakers pointed out that since doctors were entrusted with life and death decisions, they should certainly be entrusted with the power to teach sexual hygiene and contraception. They claimed that women should have the right to decide how many children to have, echoing one of the main points in *The Woman Rebel,* and also compared the United States unfavorably to the many countries in Europe where both science and law supported birth control. Most of the people in attendance at the meeting signed cards endorsing the work of the newly formed Committee on Birth Control.[26]

The fact that one of the earliest mass birth control meetings was held under the auspices of the Academy of Medicine reflected the important role that doctors played in the early movement, although the largely male medical establishment was soon to decry many elements of birth control activism, particularly that of women's leadership.[27] Activists within the profession found it necessary to mount a series of arguments on behalf of the birth control movement. Children's health provided one consistent argument. In 1909 Dr Alice Hamilton, a pioneer in industrial medicine and public health, studied the birth and death rates of 1,600 poor families in Chicago. She found that child mortality rates were much higher in large families, so she argued that birth control would help poor people improve the health of smaller families. Dr. Rachelle Yarros, a Jewish veteran of the social hygiene movement who lived and practiced medicine at Chicago's famed Hull House, refuted the most common misconceptions about birth control in a 1916 issue of the journal *Surgery, Gynecology and Obstetrics.* Yarros wrote that the mere removal of legal obstacles to the free dissemination of contraceptive information was not enough. She called for a public education campaign that would promote "the new ideal of sex, which embraces a single standard of morals for both men and women as well as rational scientific ideals of the need of greater self-control."[28]

Yarros expected criticism for introducing this controversial perspective on the relations of the sexes into what was supposed to be an article on the practical aspects of birth control, but she insisted that the modern woman possessed such a fundamentally different attitude toward her social role that it was necessary for doctors to consider at least some feminist arguments, whatever they wished to call them, in order to care for their patients in this new century. Without participating in the birth control movement, she warned, doctors would be abandoning their responsibilities. "It is the physician," Yarros stated, "who should lead in this enlightenment and he should not leave it to the quacks." Such articles failed to convince the profession as a whole. As late as 1927, the editors of the *Journal of American Medical Association* refused to publish a paper on birth control, noting that the material should not be disseminated to the entire medical profession and encouraging publication in a more specialized journal instead.[29] Birth control remained a radical movement for the time being.

The two radical Jewish women most prominently associated with birth control were Emma Goldman and Rose Pastor Stokes. Neither felt a particular attachment to Judaism per se, but both spoke frequently at explicitly Jewish venues and were often identified as Jewish by the press.[30] Goldman, born in Lithuania in 1869, immigrated to the United States as a sixteen-year-old, already inspired by ideas about political and personal freedom. At a young age she became a popular and impassioned public speaker. She initially lectured in German and Yiddish, but her growing command of English made her a visible figure among large American-born audiences as well. Strict government controls on free speech meant that Goldman was often arrested for preaching anarchism, and she was in and out of jail over a period of several decades. She helped establish the Free Speech League in 1903 and gained near celebrity status as either the most courageous or most dangerous woman in America.[31]

During the late 1890s, Goldman studied midwifery in Vienna, giving her a medical basis for her interest in birth control. She attended a neo-Malthusian conference in Paris in 1900 and added birth control to her lecture repertoire, viewing contraception as a tool of revolution.[32] Goldman also used her publication *Mother Earth* as a venue for birth control advocacy. She regularly ran notices for the *American Journal of Eugenics* that urged "the importance of quality rather than greater number of children" and demanded "the right of woman to control her own person." In her essay "The Hypocrisy of Puritanism," Goldman argued that misplaced Puritanism affected women the most by forcing chastity on unmarried women and uncontrolled childbearing on married women. Comparing Anthony Comstock and his ilk to the Russian secret police in their enthusiasm for interfering in the private lives of citizens, she pointed out that puritanical attitudes toward birth control only resulted in a higher rate of abortion among American women.[33]

Not, at first, wishing to go to jail, Goldman did not initially discuss specific methods of contraception in her lectures. She felt that birth control was part of a wider struggle and only gave out specific information privately. However, once Sanger got into trouble after the publication of *The Woman Rebel* in 1914, Goldman felt that she either had to avoid the subject altogether or become more explicit. In her Yiddish lectures to Jewish audiences, she gradually began to speak in greater detail about contraceptives. Goldman made the transition to actively distributing information in Jewish venues because she expected to find sympathetic audiences there. She assumed she would be arrested for these activities and took to bringing a book with her so that she would have something to read in jail. In August 1915 she and her partner Ben Reitman were arrested and fined $100 after a lecture in Portland, Oregon, but they won on appeal.[34] When Sanger returned from Europe in 1915 to stand trial for her own obscenity case, Goldman raised money for Sanger's defense. After Sanger's young daughter died, Goldman wrote to express her sincere condolences but also to urge her not to give up her important work. She sent Sanger the forty dollars she had collected on her behalf at a recent lecture. "The Birth Control question has now taken hold of the public as never before," Goldman reminded Sanger, suggesting that a lecture tour across the country would "pull you out of yourself and at the same time give the movement an impetus of great force."[35] Sanger took Goldman's advice and came to appreciate the relative openness of Jewish audiences to radical ideas, writing of her 1916 lecture tour that "Average well-to-do persons hesitated except for the Jewish leaders in civic affairs who, as soon as they were personally convinced, showed no reluctance in aligning themselves publicly."[36]

Despite the obvious personal relationship between the two women—Goldman repeatedly referred to Sanger as "dear" in her letter—Goldman resented the fact that Sanger had so quickly become the face of the movement in America. Her grudge against Sanger took on a life of its own and lasted a long time. Two decades later Goldman's former lover and partner in birth control activism wrote a prose poem to the author of a history of contraception protesting

> I mean your prejudice against the RADICALS
> Is so great that you COULD not give them credit
> Emma Goldman
> More than any one person in America
> Popularized B.C.
> She was Margaret Sanger's INSPIRATION
> No that ain't the word.
> Margaret imitated her and denied her.[37]

Goldman continued to work for birth control, but when she wrote in *Mother Earth* of her February 1916 arrest and subsequent jail time, she did not even mention Sanger's name. A Jewish social worker in New York who attended Goldman's trial described her as a "short, rather dumpy looking woman." Her appearance may have been unprepossessing, but she emerged from her prison term unbowed, still determined to continue speaking about birth control in public, which she frequently did until her main interests turned elsewhere once the United States entered World War I.[38]

When Goldman completed her two-week prison term, she was met with a celebratory birth control meeting at Carnegie Hall. One of the organizers proclaimed that "We will achieve victory which will be equal to the right of labor to organize and the abolition of negro slavery."[39] Another of the featured speakers, Rose Pastor Stokes, was determined to use Goldman's release from prison as a means of publicizing birth control to as wide a public as possible. Stokes was, by 1916, as well known a radical figure as Goldman. She and her family had come to the United States from Russia during her childhood, and by the age of twelve, she was working at a cigar factory in Cleveland. Stokes had a natural literary gift and became a columnist for the religious daily *Yidishes Tageblat* (*Jewish Daily News*), writing in English about a variety of Jewish topics and labor politics. After moving to New York, she met and married James Graham Phelps Stokes, a non-Jewish millionaire reformer. Their marriage across class, social, and religious boundaries made headlines everywhere and even inspired a novel, Anzia Yezierska's *Salome of the Tenements*. They both joined the Socialist Party in 1906, and Stokes became a prominent spokesperson for a variety of radical groups and causes, including birth control. Stokes and Goldman corresponded and agreed that if large numbers of women publicly distributed contraceptive information, the arrests would have to stop.[40]

Stokes delivered a major speech at the May 5, 1916, Carnegie Hall meeting that welcomed Goldman home after her prison term. One of her most important points was the condemnation of a system "that operates to keep the knowledge of contraception from the mothers of the poor and blinks the fact that the comfortable classes obtain that knowledge from their highly paid physicians." The class inequities that left most vulnerable the working women who needed the most help enraged Stokes. She denounced the hypocrisy of the enforcers of Comstock laws who, based on the size of their own families, apparently themselves ignored those laws as they pertained to contraception. She spoke about both the human and material costs of uncontrolled reproduction and dismissed religious arguments against birth control as mere superstition, doomed to make way for the progress of science. Unusually for the time, Stokes deployed the rhetoric of rights in her discussion of birth control, declaring that "since science has shown the way, the mothers of the world should have the power and the right to control birth." She addressed the last

Rose Pastor Stokes. Courtesy of the Library of Congress

part of her speech to the hostile journalists and policemen she assumed were in the audience, stating that she had no wish to go to jail but could not pass up the opportunity, even in their presence, to pass out contraceptive information to any who wished to have it. Stokes knew that her social connections made her arrest much less likely than Goldman's had been.[41]

As a result of this speech, along with countless editorials and letters to the editor, Stokes became deeply identified with the cause. In 1916 she wrote *The Woman Who Wouldn't*, a play that delivered a subtle but definite birth control message. In the play, set in an impoverished mill town, the main character, Mary, is pregnant but refuses to marry the father because he loves someone else. Mary leaves home and raises her daughter herself, eventually becoming a famous labor organizer. The birth control element of the plot comes from Mary's older sister Jennie, who, dismayed to learn that she is to have yet another child, says, "Poor folks like me an' Henry ain't got no right t'bring children into the'world. If it's a sin, I say it's less a sin preventin' 'em than bringin' 'em into a life of bitter poverty."[42] Many working-class women agreed with this moral sentiment, regardless of the legal status or the practical means necessary to live by it. Sanger corresponded with Stokes about the numerous women who contacted them for instruction in contraceptive techniques and requested that Stokes contribute to *Birth Control Review*.[43]

Like Goldman, however, Stokes saw birth control as a part of a revolutionary struggle for personal and political freedom, and contraception gradually
slipped down her list of priorities. Sanger's initial interest in birth control
had also sprung from larger commitment to leftist politics, but she found
frustrating the Socialist Party's attitude that birth control, like feminism in
general, was a distraction. After her first clinic was closed down, she purposefully began to distance herself from radicalism and framed birth control as a separate issue in a successful bid to increase its respectability and
thus acceptability. Sanger and Stokes remained correspondents, but Stokes's
earlier prominence as a birth control advocate had faded by 1920, at least
in part because Sanger was reluctant to shine a spotlight on someone like
Stokes, who had loudly denounced the United States' entry into World War
I. By 1925, when Sanger asked Stokes for a message to be read at the upcoming international birth control conference in New York, Stokes refused and
wrote back that the only way to achieve their once-shared goals was through
communism.[44] While still supporting birth control in theory, Stokes's agenda
had shifted. However, the priorities of hundreds of thousands of other American Jewish women interested in birth control had not.

Jewish Women as Birth Control Consumers

The Jewish women who became a significant constituency for the birth
control movement rarely chose childlessness. Jewish women in the United
States shaped their birth control practices in response to the Jewish values
of having children and raising families. As early as 1890, a Jewish immigrant
woman writing to her mother in Poland explained that in her new San Francisco home, "it is the custom that if a woman wants to, then she has a baby,
and if she does not, she does not have any. . . . It is terrible that at home
women suffer only hardships and childbearing. And the children do not have
it so good either because the parents are not able to take care of them when
they have so many."[45] A study of the 1910 census concluded that second-generation Jewish women's fertility dropped by nearly half to match the fertility
rates of the native-born white population. They were less likely than either
native-born white women or other ethnic women to remain childless or
delay childbearing after marriage, but significantly more likely to space children and to cease childbearing after reaching what they considered optimal
family size.[46] In 1910, even before the birth control movement began in earnest, Jewish women averaged 4.1 children compared to Italian women's 6.5

children. Native-born white women averaged only 2.6 children, illustrating both the greater access of the middle class to contraceptive information and the widespread interest in family planning as an economic strategy.[47]

Before birth control clinics became common, contraception was certainly possible for Jewish women, but it was less effective and generally men's prerogative. Fannie Shapiro married an Americanized cigar maker, and they agreed to delay having children so they could save some money first. However, she relied on him to take care of her, describing herself as "naive to life," and before she knew it, she was pregnant with their first child. After Louise C. had two sons within a year and a half, her husband's friend told him to "use the fire escape," but withdrawal was hardly foolproof. Neither was the suppository solution that Florence W. and many of her women friends bought at the local drug store. Contraception was most effective when couples worked together, as was the case with Helen C. and her husband, who learned from friends that they could use condoms to prevent unwanted pregnancies.[48]

When contraception did not work, abortions were an alternative to going through with unwanted, physically and economically dangerous pregnancies.[49] Sarah Rothman had an abortion when she found herself pregnant soon after giving birth to her daughter. Tanya N 's mother, unable to counter her husband's refusal to use condoms, ended up limiting her family by having twelve abortions. They knew the risks of illegal abortions, but these women were often desperate. As Dora G. reflected sadly later in life, "Why do you think I had so many miscarriages? The miscarriages I didn't have to feed, I only had to feed the living children." Edna B. had just begun a teaching job when she discovered she was pregnant. Her husband agreed with her that the timing was wrong to start a family and, after consulting with his friends, made all the arrangements for an abortion.[50]

A network of friends and family helped Jewish women circulate birth control information. Emma L. remembered that "About one month before my marriage, my mother said, 'You have to take care of yourself.' I said , 'I know,' and that was the end of the conversation. I knew she meant contraception." Whether discussed openly or not, contraceptive information spread rapidly in Jewish communities. Ida Richter wanted children but conferred with friends because she was determined not to repeat her mother's mistakes, a sentiment her mother heartily approved. Ida recalled, "I had two children. . . . I started to get smart, not to have so many children. My mother, after I was married six years and I only had two children, says 'Oh if I only knew what to do, I wouldn't have [had] twelve children.'" When Henrietta Moscowitz Voorsanger's first child was born prematurely less than nine months after her wedding, Sanger, a friend from New York feminist circles, wrote to scold her "in a spirit of fun" and illegally mailed her a box full of diaphragms, contraceptive jellies, and pamphlets. Voorsanger's doctor delightedly confiscated most of the materials Sanger sent so that he could help patients who, unlike Voorsanger, did not yet understand the possibilities of birth control.[51]

Jewish Women and the Legal Environment

Voorsanger's doctor was pleased to get his hands on the contraceptives not only so he could educate his patients but also because the illegal materials were difficult to obtain, even for physicians. One of the constant problems facing birth control consumers and activists was the repressive legal environment. Prior to 1900, nearly a third of the people arrested for violating the Comstock laws were not convicted, and those who were tended to receive very light sentences unless they were repeat offenders. However, Margaret Sanger's arrest after the publication of *The Woman Rebel* in 1914 led to more stringent enforcement, which ironically ended up doing a great deal to publicize the cause. A number of activists in the United States believed that the best way to avoid leaving birth control in the hands of quacks was to fight for the repeal of federal and state laws that relegated contraception to the category of obscenity. Under Mary Ware Dennett's leadership, the National Birth Control League formed to fight the New York state penal codes that included contraceptives in a list of illegal drugs. However, the National Birth Control League refused to help Sanger with the revolutionary, albeit short-lived, clinic in Brownsville, setting off a long-lived rivalry between Sanger and Dennett and their supporters.[52]

Jewish women were intimately involved with the protracted legislative and judiciary proceedings that accompanied the birth control movement. Along with Sanger and her sister Ethel Byrne, the Jewish social worker Fannia Mindell was also arrested at the Brownsville clinic in 1916, which had seen nearly five hundred patients in ten days. Mindell came to trial in early 1917 for distributing prohibited literature, specifically Sanger's *What Every Girl Should Know*. She received a fifty-dollar fine for the charge but later won on appeal. Numerous Jewish women who lived in Brownsville and had visited the short-lived clinic were subpoenaed in Byrne's trial and waited all day at the courthouse in Brooklyn, equipped with nursing babies, pacifiers, and kosher food. They sat next to wealthy representatives of the National Birth Control Committee, creating at least the appearance of a cross-class birth control alliance. Rose Pastor Stokes commented to the press that these women who had gone to the clinic for information could not afford to have any more children. Despite accusations of anti-Semitism levied against

Flyer advertising the Brownsville birth control clinic in English, Yiddish, and Italian. Courtesy of Sophia Smith Collection, Smith College

Byrne by the prosecution, which accused her of trying to prevent the birth of Jewish babies, Jewish mothers from Brownsville also participated in a Carnegie Hall protest rally on her behalf.[53]

Sanger's trial began on January 29, 1917, and was attended by a number of Jewish women, both clinic patients like Rose Halpern and members of the Woman's Committee of One Hundred that had formed to support Sanger. This group of New York City women included many of the people who would become prominent birth control advocates over the next decades, such as Sanger's rival Dennett, future ABCL supporter Juliet Rublee, and Katharine Dexter McCormick, who decades later funded research on oral contraception. Sanger was convicted and served thirty days in prison. After an initial appeal was rejected, Judge Frederick Crane of the New York Court of Appeals ruled in 1918 that doctor-prescribed birth control acquired for the purpose of curing or preventing disease—but not directly for contraception—was legal as a matter of public health. This decision did not legitimize birth control per se, but it did remove the stigma of immorality and encourage doctors to become the initiators of birth control prescription. The ruling enabled Sanger to open the Birth Control Clinical

Research Bureau (BCCRB) in 1923 and also allowed manufacturers to sell condoms for disease prevention.[54]

Even after Sanger began to work primarily through legal channels, much as Dennett did, the two women's differing approaches shaped the entire movement. First through the National Birth Control League, which dissolved in 1919, and then through the VPL, which Dennett founded immediately thereafter, she preferred legislative action rather than more radical activism. The VPL lobbied to remove contraception from the aegis of federal and state obscenity laws and favored the widest possible access so that all women could get birth control on demand in multiple venues, with the free market acting to ensure quality.[55] Sanger gradually abandoned the most radical forms of direct action and instead came to believe the birth control movement could succeed only with the support of the medical profession. She and the ABCL she founded in 1921 pushed for "doctors-only bills" that would exempt doctors from legal restriction on birth control. Dennett feared that such a bill would benefit only economically secure women who already had access to medical care, while Sanger insisted on the importance of women receiving safe and effective instruction from doctors on an individual basis. Though the ideological differences between the two were real, personality clashes widened the rift. Sanger badly wanted to be the most visible birth control activist and saw no benefit in ever cooperating with Dennett. She practically shut the VPL out of the first American birth control conference, and the two women lost little opportunity to snipe at each other.[56]

Both VPL and ABCL met tremendous resistance to their legislative programs. The situation was exacerbated by the welter of state laws with which they had to contend. At the time of the ABCL's founding, for example, there were at least four categories of states in terms of restrictions on birth control. Some states restricted the dissemination of both oral and written birth control information, with no exception for doctors; some states forbade the circulation of written birth control information; some states allowed doctors to distribute birth control information to cure or prevent diseases; and some states permitted doctors to give out contraceptive information. Much as the suffrage movement had done, the birth control movement found it necessary to work for changes to both state and federal law. As usual, VPL and ABCL disagreed over how best to do that. However, both groups did come to support the clinic as the most important birth control delivery mechanism. Even Sanger, busily declaiming the importance of doctors-only bills, insisted that doctors and nurses should distribute birth control through independent, not-for-profit medical facilities free of the organizational control of American medicine. On this, if on few other issues, Dennett concurred, and both ABCL and VPL supported the creation of birth control clinics. These clinics primarily served poor women who had no other access to private medical care.[57]

From the inception of the birth control clinics, Jewish women made use of them with alacrity. One Jewish immigrant woman wrote in her Yiddish autobiography that she knew if she did not want to have too many children, she needed to get "fixed" by Sanger. Helen Isaacson stumbled across the BCCRB in New York by accident just four days after her marriage. She was so impressed that she sent all of her friends there for contraceptive advice as they got married.[58] The New York Academy of Medicine criticized independent birth control clinics for hiring women doctors, some of them immigrants with accents, and placing clinics in settlement houses and tenement areas, but these were the very features that made birth control so appealing to working-class Jewish women, who could get what they needed close to home.[59] Once ABCL and VPL launched a succession of popular clinics, women's control of contraception, and particularly the most up-to-date contraception in the form of diaphragms, became more feasible and significantly more effective. Few Jewish women who came to the clinics paused to consider the legality of their actions. Their presence was noted in the detailed information compiled by birth control doctors and often published in annual reports and journal articles. In 1925 Dr. Hannah Stone reported that the proportion of Protestant (38.8%), Jewish (32.6%) and Catholic (26.2%) clients at the BCCRB in New York more or less paralleled the city's population statistics. In other cities the proportion of Jewish clients was considerably higher, demonstrating the extent to which Jewish women became birth control consumers. During the early years, opponents of the movement tried to convince Jews that birth control leaders wanted specifically to reduce the number of Jews being born, but the numbers of Jewish women taking advantage of available contraception suggests that they generally dismissed this ploy out of hand.[60]

Birth Control and American Jewish Culture

While there is no doubt that Jewish women became avid consumers of birth control, their choices did not preclude considerable debate on the topic within the American Jewish community. No denomination of Judaism ordained women as rabbis at the time, and women rarely played prominent roles as explicators of Judaism. It is thus unsurprising that men conducted much of the early public Jewish discussion, though the observably declining birthrate among American Jewish families calls into question the relationship between public rhetoric and private behavior. Both Margaret Sanger and Mary Ware Dennett reached out to rabbis to provide a Jewish seal of approval for birth control. They recognized that even though not all American Jews were particularly concerned with religious approval of their private practices, rabbinic endorsement was nonetheless an effective way to proclaim Jewish support. Some liberal rabbis became early enthusiasts. One of Sanger's rabbinical conquests, Edward Israel of Baltimore's Har Sinai congregation, emerged as a mainstay of the birth control movement. He pushed the Central Conference of American Rabbis (CCAR), the Reform movement's rabbinical association, to endorse birth control, and Israel himself offered frequent testimony at legislative hearings. Stephen Wise, the progressive rabbi of New York's Free Synagogue, was also an admirer and correspondent of Sanger. He wrote regularly to his state and federal representatives urging them to support birth control bills, which would ease access to contraceptive information. Wise's associate rabbi, Sidney Goldstein, became one of the most prominent rabbinic voices endorsing birth control.[61]

In the wake of William Sanger's recent arrest for distributing birth control information, Goldstein addressed the Free Synagogue in December 1915 on the topic of "Birth Control as a Moral Issue." He first insisted that it was entirely appropriate for religious leaders such as himself to discuss the issue of birth control, pointing to the late-eighteenth-century Anglican minister Thomas Malthus, whose theories of population control constituted one of the major intellectual strands of the modern birth control movement, often known as neo-Malthusianism. He then contended that the final stage of contemporary social progress was to improve the quality of children being born. Goldstein admitted that "it is perhaps impossible to completely eliminate defectiveness from human society" but entertained several strategies for attempting to do so, including certification of both physical and mental health before marriage, remanding of the "socially incompetent" to custodial care, and sterilization of those deemed defective by the state and medical community. To Goldstein, as to many supporters of eugenics theory during the early twentieth century, if the state had a legally acceptable interest in the "health, morals and general welfare of the public," as recent court decisions on such issues as protective labor legislation for women seemed to indicate, then it was only natural for the state to exercise its legitimate interests in controlling the population.[62]

The second half of Goldstein's lecture addressed the issue of voluntary motherhood and the need to make contraception available without legal restrictions. He dismissed the idea that birth control would have a negative impact on the health of the community, adducing studies of the Netherlands, where birth control was widely available to the entire populace. The death rate there had fallen even faster than the birthrate as the health and well-being of the Dutch people improved. Professing outrage over the accusation that birth control would lead to immorality, Goldstein asked whether opponents of birth control thought so little of women that they assumed that the availability of birth control would lead all women "to a saturnalia of unchastity." Finally, he conjoined spirituality, science, and morality in his defense of birth control, arguing passionately

> The God who speaks through the long ages of evolution, whose mighty message science is slowly translating into the accents of the human tongue, teaches a doctrine that is not contrary to our own. He reveals to us the fact that the lower down we go in the scale of life, the less limitation we find placed upon the spawning process; the higher we rise the more controlled and restricted becomes the power of reproduction.

This peroration reflected the telling title of Goldstein's talk; he approached birth control as a *moral* issue rather than a *religious* one. As such, very few of his arguments were rooted in a particularly Jewish theology or philosophy, even though they were addressed to a Jewish audience.[63]

Beyond the level of rabbinic pronouncements on the subject, the American Jewish community also dealt with a whole complex of issues surrounding the early birth control movement. Since Yiddish was the primary language of many immigrant and working-class Jews in America, the availability of Yiddish materials on birth control was important. The Grand Street Press of Literature and Knowledge published several Yiddish editions of Sanger's *What Every Girl Should Know* and *What Every Mother Should Know.*[64] Early birth control clinics produced very detailed, widely disseminated Yiddish instructions for the use and care of diaphragms that concluded by advising Jewish women to "remember the thousands of women who use this method and have been helped."[65] The Yiddish press also carried a constant stream of articles on the topic of birth control. The newspaper *Forverts* could not give specific contraceptive advice for legal reasons, but the paper generally supported family limitation to improve the lives of mothers and facilitate social mobility.[66] The 1918 edition of Ben Zion Liber's Yiddish tome *Dos Geshlekhts Lebn (Sexual Life)*, which he dedicated as "a gift to the Jewish people" included some cautiously worded contraceptive advice and a photograph of Sanger. Liber's monthly Yiddish magazine *Unzer Gezund (Our Health)* also disseminated some contraceptive information. Adele Zametkin's 1930 *Der Froys Handbuch (The Woman's Handbook)*, very popular in Yiddish-speaking households, included an entire section on sex hygiene.[67]

Leonard Landes's Yiddish booklet *Geburts-kontrol* (*Birth Control*), written during the mid-1920s for a working-class audience, approached the topic from a number of angles. Landes, a doctor working in New York's immigrant Jewish community, wanted his readers to understand that they could master nature rather than be enslaved by it and that contraception was neither a sin nor anything new under the sun. For him, economic and health imperatives were paramount rather than religious injunctions, though he cited biblical stories to bolster his points. Landes explained that in modern society, the relationship between husband and wife centered on more than just the goal of bringing children into the world. Although he admitted that there could be national reasons to encourage the birth of many children or to reduce the number of children born in poor countries without resources, he believed that birth control was primarily an individual question and that couples need not make decisions based on such concerns as "race suicide," resource scarcity, or even rabbinic authority. Relating multiple anecdotes of helpless husbands, hopeless wives, and endangered children, he grimly pounded home his thesis that no one should be forced to have unwanted children who could not be properly cared for.[68]

Landes condemned a system that left wealthy people with "the best medical means to protect themselves from having children when they do not want them. . . . They do not ever take any risks. They do not endanger their health or their ability to mother children later. Those who want to have children can have them at the time they want to." He reserved his harshest words for the laws that forbade even doctors like him from giving advice about birth control. It is likely that his Yiddish-speaking readers would have recognized their very real problems in the stories he told. Certainly, Landes was hoping they would adopt the birth control solutions he recommended but could not discuss in detail.[69]

Both the flowering of interest in and the varied responses to birth control were also evident in the Yiddish theater, a central American Jewish cultural institution. The production of at least two Yiddish plays on the subject, Harry Kalmanowitz's *Geburth Kontrol, oder, Rassen Zelbstmord* (*Birth Control or Race Suicide*) and Samuel B. Grossman's *Di Flikhten fun a froy in Geburt Kontrol* (*A Woman's Duty in Birth Control*) literally dramatized the importance of the issue within the American Jewish community.[70] Many Americans, Jewish or not, clung to the idea that women's whole purpose in life revolved around bearing children and that any interference with this function represented a crime against nature, from the secular perspective, and a sin against God, from the religious one. Though other scholars have adduced these two plays as evidence for widespread American Jewish support for birth control, a close reading clearly demonstrates that in at least some quarters there remained deep ambivalence toward birth control, gender relations, and the American Jewish condition of the early twentieth century.[71]

When *Birth Control or Race Suicide* premiered at New York's National Roof Garden Theater in July 1916, Yiddish theater was at high tide in America.[72] There were twenty Yiddish theaters in New York alone, with theaters in Baltimore, Boston, Chicago, Detroit, Los Angeles, Newark, Philadelphia, and St. Louis as well. The four main theaters in New York presented 1,100 performances a year to two million patrons for ticket prices ranging from twenty-five cents to a dollar, a significant amount in an era when the average male worker earned ten dollars a week and the average woman even less. The authors of Yiddish plays were swift to gauge the interests of the theatergoers, and around World War I the number of plays set in America increased noticeably.[73] The Yiddish theaters sought to draw in as many audience members as possible, but there was recognition that some topical plays would be controversial. Children under sixteen were not allowed to see *Birth Control or Race Suicide*.[74]

The four acts of *Birth Control or Race Suicide* follow the central characters of Rosa and Benjamin Gutman over a period of approximately ten years, starting from shortly after their wedding. Other characters include Jakey and Alice, their children; Harris and Hinda Simon, the slightly older couple with whom Rosa boarded when she was a working girl; Nakhmen, Benjamin's friend from the old country, and his wife, Etty; and Jacob Rosenberg, a life insurance agent. Some of the characters represent the stock figures of the Yiddish stage, especially the always-joking Harris and the sharp businessman Jacob.

The issue of birth control makes scant appearance in the first act of the play, despite its title. Benjamin and Rosa live in a nice apartment with good furniture, which Hinda good-naturedly compares to her own poor possessions. Harris advises Benjamin that he must swiftly train Rosa to be a good wife, saying, "You have to know how to handle them, brother. Take, for example a young colt. If you spoil him, he'll jump around; and then when you want to harness him, he won't allow it. . . . It's the same with a young wife." Benjamin insists that Rosa is already a good and loyal wife, and later in the scene she thanks him for freeing her from the shop and becoming her beloved husband and building such a nice home. Together they decide to buy a life insurance policy from Jacob. Later, Nakhmen and Etty, recently arrived immigrants, visit. Benjamin and Nakhmen reminisce about their boyhood shtetl, and Nakhmen talks about how hard he is working and how he misses home, including some of the religious rituals he never sees anymore. The act ends with the two couples hearing the wailing of a neighboring woman whose tubercular husband has just died, leaving her with five children.[75]

Little dramatic action occurs in this first act. The characters are introduced with broad strokes. The audience understands that Rosa and Benjamin love each other and have material ambitions; that Harris and Hinda bicker constantly but have an effective and content partnership; that Etty and Nakhmen are glad to be in America but are shocked by the lack of community feeling; that Jacob both preys on people's fears and provides an important service at a time when death seemed very near. The conversation between Harris and Benjamin about the nature of women is intended as comic byplay, but it also sets up a frequent theme of Yiddish drama, the difference, not to say war, between the sexes.

The second act takes place eight years later. Benjamin and Rosa had Jakey and Alice in rapid succession eight and seven years ago, respectively. Rosa is intensely anxious about the children, much to the amusement of Hinda, who now has six children of her own and advises Rosa not to worry so much. Benjamin has recently lost his job, leaving the Gutmans in debt and behind on their rent and life insurance payments. Etty and Nakhmen still have no children, much to Etty's despair. Upon running into Jacob at the Gutmans' home, Etty and Nakhmen agree to take him in as a boarder. When Benjamin comes home from work, Rosa criticizes him for not earning enough money to provide for their household, and Benjamin admonishes her for not having dinner ready after his long, hard day at work, exclaiming, "Modern woman, delicate lady. . . and this was once my working woman." Harris stops by and reminds Rosa that she needs to consider how hard Benjamin works. In a fit of desperate anger, she tears up the life insurance policy they can no longer afford. When Alice comes down with a fever, Benjamin shouts, "Rosa, what a hard life! What's the use of living, anyway?" and collapses on the table.[76]

The difficulties of immigrant life, which would have been all too familiar to the audience at the National Roof Garden Theater, are starkly evident in this act. Benjamin was out of work because of strikes and layoffs, not due to anything within his control, and without any kind of financial safety net, the family swiftly fell on hard times. Ironically, Harris and Hinda, the couple portrayed earlier as having the fewest resources, are now on somewhat more stable ground because their children have begun to work and contribute to the family expenses. One of *Birth Control or Race Suicide*'s veiled discussions of birth control takes place within this context. Benjamin says to Harris, "A boy of thirteen and you already think of sending him for work. To confound his little head with worries about the future, oy, what kind of life is this? For this we have children. . . ." Harris replies that Benjamin thinks too much, advising him, "You don't have to be wiser than the next man; you have to go with nature. Whatever happens to everyone is good enough for me as well." For many during the early 1900s, this homely advice was so obvious as to foreclose further discussion; were they so different from their predecessors that they should think about, let alone take steps to prevent, bringing children into the world? Certainly Etty, who longs for children, does not want to hear her friend complaining about the travails of childbirth and motherhood. Etty replies that "a child is the only bit of happiness, the only small consolation, that a worker has."[77]

The most direct discussion of birth control in act 2 comes during a conversation between Rosa and Hinda. Sympathizing with Etty's plight, Hinda sighs, "One woman wants a child and can't have one, while others can have children and don't want to—they do all kinds of things to avoid having children. They want to be Yankees." Rosa asks if she thinks that is a crime. When Hinda emphatically says yes, Rosa disagrees, "because conditions these days don't allow us to have a lot of children; we can't give them what they need." Taken aback, Hinda responds that Rosa is like a sister to her but "You're a sinner. . . .I'm telling you, you must do as God commanded, as people are supposed to behave. Remember, God will punish you." The play clearly associates family limitation with the impious behavior of the "Yankees," an uncomfortable concept for Jewish immigrants struggling to strike a balance between tradition and modernity. It also introduces an explicitly religious perspective on the issue of birth control, with Hinda assuming that it is a crime not to submit to God's will in this matter. However, the play also acknowledges the capriciousness of God's will, which grants children to some but not to others.[78]

By the time the third act of *Birth Control or Race Suicide* begins, another year has passed. Benjamin is now a permanent invalid who has had some sort of nervous breakdown. Rosa calls in a specialist, who prescribes sleeping pills and several months of rest at a resort, which the Gutmans cannot afford. She tries to speak more kindly to Benjamin, and both of them agree that "the conditions are so bad that even the best person couldn't control himself." As if to prove this point, Etty has become involved with her boarder, the insurance agent Jacob, and they are discovered by Nakhmen during a visit to the Gutmans' home. A relationship between a boarder and the man or woman of the home was another stock plot development of Yiddish theater.[79] Nakhmen is sad and hurt but hears Etty out when she tearfully explains that such a thing would never have happened if they had been able to have children.

In act 3, the issue of birth control comes up when the doctor is questioning Benjamin. After hearing that the Gutmans have been married for nine years and have only two children, he asks if they have "interfered with nature." Benjamin explains that they "did what many other workers do these days." The doctor responds vehemently that nature punishes those who try to fool her with illness, weakness, and insanity—all of Benjamin's symptoms. Distressed, Benjamin says that what leads to sickness is the inability to provide for the children he already has. The doctor acknowledges there is some truth in what Benjamin says but adds that he also knows many poor workers who cheerfully have six or seven children and make do. Benjamin retorts that if anything is unnatural and sinful, it is the prospect of sending children to work under terrible conditions that will cause them to ask their parents why they were born. Disagreeing, the doctor tries to calm Benjamin down by reminding him about all the people who desperately want children but cannot have them. He insists that in addition to taking the sleeping pills and rubbing his body with cold water, Benjamin must start "living naturally." At this point, both Benjamin and Rosa have explained their motivations for having only two children. Other characters have acknowledged that their rationales make sense. However, their point of view is not the one supported by the play, which presents in Hinda and Harris the poor but content family with as many children as nature or God intended, in Etty and Nakhmen the sad couple whose lives together have been destroyed by childlessness, and in the doctor an authority figure who has the last and negative word on the subject of birth control.[80]

The brief concluding act of the play takes place one year later. Benjamin has broken down completely. Rosa fears she pushed him over the edge by suggesting she go to work, to which he reacted with shame and sorrow. When Etty, now married to Jacob and the mother of a son, comes to visit the Gutmans, she is relieved that Nakhmen does not seem to bear a grudge about how things worked out. As Etty, Nakhmen, Harris, and Hinda stand by helplessly and watch their friend rave about how the angry world wants to kill him, the doctor tells Rosa that Benjamin must be institutionalized. When Rosa tries to help Benjamin, he hollers, "Away from me, you sinner. I won't allow myself to be misled by you anymore. You made me sin against God and He punished me for it." Rosa leaves the room in tears, and the others try to comfort and calm Benjamin. As the men in white coats come for Benjamin, he turns to his children, clutches his chest, and falls down, dead.[81]

The swift and tragic conclusion of Birth Control or Race Suicide leaves little doubt as to the consequences of contraception for the Gutman family. The illness, weakness, and insanity that the doctor predicted have triumphed over Benjamin. His references to Rosa and to himself as sinners can only refer to the "sin" of limiting their family.[82] Despite Kalmanowitz's inclusion of a variety of positive arguments for birth control, there can be little question that at least in this play, he sees contraception in a negative light. The title *Birth Control or Race Suicide* apparently refers not so much to concerns among eugenic thinkers like Theodore Roosevelt that the "right" (i.e., native-born, white, middle-class, Protestant Americans) people were not having enough children but to beliefs held by at least some American Jews that to use birth control was to commit a kind of self-murder. The fact that the play was produced in a major Yiddish theater suggests that this perspective on birth control resonated with at least some portion of the American Jewish community.

Unlike *Birth Control or Race Suicide*, which for all its heightened emotions is a more or less realistic play that dutifully allows for some ambivalence, *A Woman's Duty in Birth Control* is a melodrama with an unmistakable attitude toward birth control. Produced in Chicago in late November 1916, *A Woman's Duty in Birth Control* by Samuel B. Grossman was almost certainly written in reaction to Margaret Sanger's birth control clinic in Brownsville, which made national headlines. It is possible that Grossman's far more vehement presentation was a response heightened by the fact that women's access to safe, inexpensive, medically supervised contraception was clearly imminent, even if the birth control movement had suffered a temporary setback with the closing of the Brownsville clinic. *A Woman's Duty in Birth Control* not only uncompromisingly condemns birth control but also can be read as denouncing women in terms approaching misogynist.

The cast of characters in *A Woman's Duty in Birth Control* includes Louis Goldman, an insurance agent, and Esther, his wife; Lilly, Esther's younger cousin, and Willie Sheynblum, her fiancé; Mary, the Goldman's maid; Dr. Edward Miller, their family physician; and Madame Charlotta Fuchs, their neighbor. In the first act, however, none of these characters appear. Instead, the entire first act is devoted to a debate between the Angel of Death, also called the Devil, and the Angel of Life. The fantasia sequence that contains the confrontation between the male Devil and the female Angel of Life includes some bizarre elements for a play written for a Yiddish-speaking Jewish audience. The piece begins with the tolling of church bells. The Devil is described as wearing a hat of thorns, his companions dressed in "black dominoes" and armed with blades. The unmistakable Christian imagery here may represent another argument against American Jews' use of birth control: Christians are encouraging Jews to have fewer children out of anti-Semitic motives, rather than concern for women's health or autonomy or families' economic well-being. The Angel of Life is depicted in a gauzy costume, wearing a diamond tiara adorned by a star, also not a Jewish image.[83]

When the Devil and the Angel of Life meet, they argue about the worth of people on earth, with the Devil condemning women as traitors and men as cheaters and the Angel insisting that men are successful providers and women are faithful wives and mothers. The Devil thinks that the modern woman, in order to prevent slavery to hearth and home, avoids having children. The Angel counters that every living thing on earth wants only to protect and sustain life but concedes the Devil's point that death seems to have an upper hand throughout the world in these times when war rages throughout the world and husbands and wives might "try to exterminate . . . with various violent acts and medicinal herbs" their unborn children.[84]

It seems evident from this first act of A Woman's Duty in Birth Control that the context of World War I was important to Grossman, who may have felt that at a time when human life seemed so cheap, it was the work of the devil to prevent any new life. He apparently also had a clear vision of gender roles that would support bringing new life into the world. If all men were dependable providers and all women were devoted to the "sacred purpose of having and raising children" as they should be, there would never be any reason to thwart God's plan for the world. The Devil raises inconvenient questions about how God's plan could include the current carnage of war or the refusal of women to become slaves to their bodies and homes, but it is the Angel who gets the last word before the main action of the play begins, intoning, "Begone you miserable death and make room for life." Even before the main characters are introduced, the perspective of the play is already clear from the association of the Angel of Life with motherhood and the association of the Devil with death in all its modern manifestations, including total war and contraception.[85]

Act 2 of A Woman's Duty in Birth Control begins the more ordinary dramatic action. Esther and Louis Goldman are a comfortable Jewish couple who can afford a nice home with tasteful furniture and a maid. Esther, in conversation on the telephone with the doctor, reveals that she owes him money for something she begs him not to tell her husband about. When Madame Fuchs comes to visit, it becomes apparent that she advised Esther to have an abortion rather than to risk losing her husband's love by sacrificing her youth, good looks, and free time to motherhood. Esther is also visited by her cousin Lily and her fiancé Willie, who come to get some advice. They are concerned about how expensive everything is, but they are eager to get married and start a family. The doctor comes to collect what is owed him. He brings a document for Louis to sign affirming that he authorized the operation (abortion) the doctor performed on Esther, but Esther is horrified at the thought of telling Louis what she has done. Madame Fuchs is still there, and it turns out she and Dr. Miller were once married. He is very angry that she was the one who convinced Esther to have the abortion, yelling, "One woman talks another into committing such a crime against her own self. And you still call yourself a woman?" When Louis comes home from work, he happily tells Esther that he is about to get a raise, which will be helpful when they have a baby. He notices that Esther does not look well and insists on calling the doctor, despite her objections. The act ends with both Dr. Miller and Madame Fuchs returning to the Goldmans' home despite the lateness of the hour.[86]

This very long act is full of material relevant to the broader debate over birth control. Grossman, however, immediately stacks the decks by equating birth control with abortion, a crucial distinction that virtually all birth control activists drew. They did not support abortion; they supported prevention of unwanted pregnancies. As one activist explained, the idea was to "*prescribe* contraception in order to *proscribe* abortion."[87] The association of contraception with abortion extended beyond this one Yiddish play and was an invidious one that birth control activists, consumers, and distributors had to work hard to overcome. In a *Medical Woman's Journal* article, the Hull House doctor Rachelle Yarros flatly dismissed the idea that birth control would lead to abortion; in fact, contraception would greatly reduce the incidence of abortion, which she and other activists variously characterized as illicit, immoral, and dangerous.[88] Part of the achievement of birth control activists during the 1920s was the fairly successful separation of contraception from abortion in the mind of the public, a necessary accomplishment if birth control was to win popular support.

By creating Esther, a character who has gone so far as to have an abortion rather than risk losing her husband's love, Grossman ensures that there can be little sympathy for her. Esther's tortured reasoning for taking such drastic action when she knows that her husband wants children—she fears he will no longer love her when she loses her youth and pretty shape and focuses on their children—has been indoctrinated into her by the sinister neighbor, Madame Fuchs. Esther's guilt is compounded by the ease with which Lily discusses her similar fears with Willie, who soothes her and promises to be as good to her after they are married and have children as he has been before.

This play is thus not a discussion of birth control at all; it is the indictment of a woman who deserves to suffer for committing the crime of having an abortion and the condemnation of wives for not trusting in their husbands' love. The engaged Willie, divorced Dr. Miller, and married Louis all reject the idea that motherhood diminishes the love of husbands and wives. Louis says, "An honest man loves his wife and remains faithful to her his whole life; only a coarse, ignorant person is looking for a woman's attractive body, rather than her soul. Such a person doesn't understand the . . . holiness, the greatness of woman." Esther has not trusted in this ideal, and now she bitterly regrets her actions. There is no way to know how audiences responded to this play, but as this act comes to a close, there is little doubt that they are meant to denounce Esther and to reject Madame Fuchs's vision of the conditional nature of the love between husbands and wives. By equating contraception with abortion, Grossman allows no uncertainly as to his opinion of birth control.[89]

The third act of A Woman's Duty in Birth Control picks up just after the second left off. The doctor privately tells Louis to keep Esther calm because "she is presently in a delicate condition" but says no more and leaves. Louis reassures her that the doctor said she was healthy but too nervous. Esther cries out that she is not guilty of anything but loving him too much. Puzzled and assuming they are both talking about a pregnancy, Louis replies, "Guilty?! Every girl should get married for precisely that holy purpose: to become a mother." This sends Esther into further paroxysms of guilty sobbing, and when he embraces her, Louis discovers the document awaiting his signature so that Dr. Miller cannot be blamed for having performed the abortion. Louis furiously demands to know if the deed has already been done, and upon Esther's confession, he calls her a murderer, throws her to the floor, and says their marriage is over.[90]

Although there is some comic relief in the earlier part of act 3 as Esther, Louis, and Dr. Miller speak at cross purposes, the focus is on the confrontation between Esther and Louis when her actions are discovered. Louis is genuinely horrified, unable to believe that Esther ever thought he could understand her actions. The entire rest of the scene supports this perspective on what Esther has done. The only defense she offers is that she thought that he would no longer love her when she became a mother. She says that her intentions were good and reminds Louis that she risked her life out of love for him. She urges him to give her a chance to rectify her mistake. Louis responds angrily that even an animal "instinctively senses her sacred duty to carry and give birth to her children." Countering Esther's accusation that he must never have loved her at all if he can turn against her so easily, he says that he always worked hard for her out of love, despite difficult conditions, because he wanted so much to support a nice home and build a loving family. Now he sees his love was misplaced; he rejects her utterly and leaves their home.[91]

The play presents Louis not only as the deeply wronged husband but also as someone who did all the things a man should do: love his wife, provide for her, and look forward to a family. Esther, on the other hand, is depicted through Louis's bitter speech as an unnatural, perverted wife and woman. Their confrontation refers back to the exchange between the Devil and the Angel of Life in act 1, in which the Angel set out the roles and responsibilities of men and the Devil retorted that women were traitors and liars. If Esther is supposed to represent a "modern woman" here, then "modern woman" is a deeply depraved figure that proves the Devil was right about women. This misogynist message may or may not have been Grossman's intended state-ment, but given the negative characterization of Madame Fuchs as well, it is impossible to disregard.

In the final act of *A Woman's Duty in Birth Control*, Willie and Lily return to the Goldmans' home and squabble again but ultimately reconcile. Madame Fuchs enters, supporting a drunk Louis, who reels back off stage while Esther confronts her neighbor. Esther blames the other woman for giv-ing her "devilish advice" and throws Madame Fuchs out. Dr. Miller calls to say he is returning, and Louis gets out his gun to make the doctor pay for his deed. When the doctor comes in, Louis asks him what he thinks about women who have abortions. The doctor responds that they should be subject to death. However, he denies that the doctors who perform abortions should be similarly punished, because if one doctor will not do it, another will. This hypocrisy is too much for Louis, who brandishes the gun and wrestles with Dr. Miller. The doctor overpowers Louis and explains that even though he never got his own wish for "a quiet, peaceful family life," he has ensured that Louis and Esther will have just that. When Esther came to him, he recog-nized the malicious hand of his own former wife and only pretended to per-form the abortion so Esther would not go elsewhere for the procedure. He proudly announces that Esther will shortly become a mother. The play ends with both Esther and Louis gratefully grasping Dr. Miller's hands and a cho-rus of angels appearing on stage to sing hymns of praise.[92]

The surprising turn of events in this brief final act results in a superficially happy ending, but one that underlines the frailty and ignorance, if not out-right wickedness, of women. The reappearance of Lily and Willie, obviously foils for Esther and Louis, is centered around a quarrel that Willie and even Lily agree was all her fault. Extracting Lily's promise that she will "be a good girl," Willie is satisfied because he has regained the appropriate male mastery. During Esther's final confrontation with Madame Fuchs, there is yet another indictment of the "modern woman" when Madame Fuchs laughs and says Esther is old-fashioned and should be like "modern women [who] have a good laugh and thank God that their husbands want to leave them." As far as the doctor is concerned, Esther's inexperience and naïveté were all to the good, since they enabled him to fool her into thinking he had done as she asked and she then never realized she was still pregnant. As a result of his actions, Esther is an "honest and proper wife" who now knows "the duties of a woman: not to fight against life because life is eternal." To the modern reader, the overwhelming arrogance of the doctor, who manipulated his patient on the assumption that she did not know her own mind and body or understand her own interests or responsibilities, seems extremely problematic. But to at least some in the audience in 1916, the denouement of this play may have seemed like the perfect resolution. No crime against God or nature has been committed, the husband and wife have not only reconciled but are expecting a child, the male authority figure has prevailed, the evil influence has been exorcized, and all is right with the world.[93]

It is difficult to know exactly what Kalmanowitz and Grossman hoped to accomplish by writing these plays. Analysis of *Birth Control or Race Suicide* and *A Woman's Duty in Birth Control* out of context might lead to the conclusion that the American Jewish community generally opposed birth control. Certainly these two texts offer a negative perspective that was popular enough to justify the production of the plays and to attract audiences to the Yiddish theater in New York and Chicago. However, the plays cannot bear the burden of proof that most American Jews resisted birth control, either in 1916 or later. Multiple other sources demonstrate that the American Jewish community came to support the birth control movement, despite a few later incidents such as a synagogue in the Bronx refusing to allow Margaret Sanger to speak, leading to the rabbi's resignation.[94] Corners of opposition remained but were uncharacteristic of American Jewry as a whole.

It is also difficult to know much about the composition of the audience or to gauge whether Yiddish theatergoers tended to be more or less conservative in their views, although *Birth Control or Race Suicide* clearly appeals to an audience sensitive to economic challenges faced by the working class. The biographical entry on Samuel B. Grossman in Zalmen Zylbercweig's magisterial compendium *Leksikon fun Yidishn Teater* (*Lexicon of the Yiddish Theater*) does not even mention *A Woman's Duty in Birth Control*; it focuses entirely on Grossman's career as a minor actor on the Yiddish stage and gives no indication that he ever wrote any plays. The much longer entry on Kalmanowitz, a successful writer who also worked on a few early Yiddish films, merely lists *Birth Control or Race Suicide* by date, with none of the extended comments provided for his most significant work.[95] There is no evidence that either of the two plays were ever revived, although it was not that unusual for Yiddish plays to be quickly written and performed and equally as quickly forgotten.[96] It is even remotely possible that given the restrictive legal environment of the time, writing negative plays about birth control was the only way to introduce the subject into the Yiddish theater, although the level of vitriol in *A Woman's Duty in Birth Control*, at least, makes that scenario unlikely.

One way to explain the discrepancy between the negative attitudes toward birth control found in the Yiddish plays and the larger body of evidence supporting positive American Jewish attitudes is to consider the time frame. The issue of family limitation was not new in 1916—indeed, there is extensive discussion of it in rabbinic literature—but the availability of diaphragms to working-class women through birth control clinics was innovative and may have precipitated the expressions of hostility in the plays without necessarily reflecting an American Jewish consensus on the subject. Given the religious ramifications of birth control and the contemporaneous growth of Jewish denominationalism, there never was such a consensus. The events of the 1920s and 1930s illustrate quite clearly, though, that most American Jews used contraception regardless of the opinions of their religious authorities. Another way to explain the discrepancy is to note the association of birth control with modernity, especially in *A Woman's Duty in Birth Control*. The bewildering and rapid proliferation of technologies like birth control may have seemed threatening to Jews facing the dislocations of immigration and modernization, threatening enough that they welcomed cultural expressions of discomfort even when they did not actually practice resistance in their own lives.

Kalmanowitz's and Grossman's plays thus exemplify the huge range of opinion on most matters that characterized the American Jewish community of the early twentieth century. Even those who supported birth control came to the cause from numerous motives: economic necessity, feminist ideas about women's autonomy, eugenics, growing interest in companionate marriage, and Marxist analysis of family function, just to name a few. It is hardly surprising to find some ambivalence toward contraception even among a generally supportive ethnic/religious group. *Birth Control or Race Suicide* and *A Woman's Duty in Birth Control* are useful reminders of the rich, sometimes contradictory texture of American Jewish life and culture during the early twentieth century.

Conclusion

When Kate Simon was growing up in the Bronx during the 1910s, she and her friends, all of them children of immigrants, vaguely noticed the frequent presence of a Dr. James, who came to visit their mothers and left them resting briefly in bed. Only later did Simon discover that Dr. James had "dedicated himself to poor immigrant women for whom there was no sex information, no birth control clinics, nothing but knitting needles." Simon's own mother had thirteen abortions in Dr. James's safe hands, and she claimed that this was not the neighborhood record among women who were so determined to improve their families' lives by having fewer children that they repeatedly resorted to desperate measures.⁹⁷ By the time Rose Janofsky, born in Boston to immigrant parents, got married during the mid-1930s, such drastic, dangerous, and illegal measures were no longer necessary for women willing to educate themselves. Janosfky's friends took her to a birth control clinic where the doctor "told me all the things I should know, and she fitted me for a diaphragm."⁹⁸ Within a generation, the birth control movement had utterly transformed women's lives.

Jewish women participated in every phase of the transformation. Whether middle- or working-class, they supported the cause in large numbers. They rarely rejected motherhood, highly valued by most of them as a vital part of their roles as Jewish women, but they did seek to control it and thus shape their own lives and those of their families. Some saw their birth control decisions as purely private matters, but legal restrictions and contentious public debate encouraged many to view contraception as a public matter that required action outside the home. From native-born, middle-class, English-speaking American Jews to immigrant, working-class, Yiddish-speaking American Jews, the community debated the issue publicly as far as the law would allow.

Arguments on all sides stemmed from a cluster of social, economic, and religious attitudes, some especially Jewish, some particularly feminist, some specifically radical. They all politicized and publicized the private realm of sexuality. For Jewish women this may not have seemed so unusual, since so many were accustomed to—or at least exposed to—politicizing other supposedly private or domestic matters through such activism as kosher meat riots. The radical roots of the early birth control movement also underlined the feminist nature of a cause that encouraged women to see themselves as entitled to the control their own bodies. Judaism, which traditionally both celebrated and regulated (married) sexuality, proved fertile ground for birth control adoption and activism within the American Jewish community. Important pockets of resistance persisted, and the early movement remained constrained by legalities, but the shifting demographic profile of the American Jewish community indicated the extent to which contraception achieved legitimacy.

Of the many feminist causes taken up by American Jewish women at the turn of the century, birth control most obviously bridged the public and private. Nothing could be more personal to women than the right to control reproduction. The practical interests of Jewish families in general and Jewish women in particular were both well-served by involvement in the birth control movement. Because they were involved in both radical politics and feminism, Jewish women were well-placed to play key roles in some of the central developments of the early birth control movement and thus spark a multifaceted debate within the American Jewish community. The later 1920s and 1930s would see the continuing and expanding role of Jewish women as activists, consumers, and professionals who worked to bring birth control into the mainstream.

3

"We United with Our Sisters of Other Faiths in Petitioning for Peace"

Jewish Women, Peace Activism, and Acculturation

> How shall we retain in our group life the real value in our Jewish
> heritage; how shall we enrich our personalities by a full realization
> of these social and cultural values and how shall we so enriched
> integrate our lives into the common life about us?
> —Fanny Brin, ca. mid-1920s[1]

In 1924, the National Council of Jewish Women's (NCJW) national president
rebuked Minneapolis section president Fanny Brin for attending a Women's
International League for Peace and Freedom (WILPF) meeting in Washington, D.C. Brin, also the national chair of NCJW's Committee on Peace and
Arbitration, responded that she had gone as an active WILPF member rather
than in any official NCJW capacity. She and a growing number of other
NCJW members firmly believed NCJW should in fact affiliate with WILPF
in order to demonstrate Jewish women's serious commitment to peace.[2] She
saw no contradiction between her leadership roles in Jewish and non-Jewish women's organizations and urged the two groups to align themselves,
lending an official imprimatur to what was already a significant overlap in
membership and devotion to the growing peace movement of the 1920s. She
hoped that her own activism would set an example for other American Jewish women to follow.

As the histories of American Jewish women in the suffrage and birth
control movements illustrate, Jewish women's social activism crossed class
boundaries. The cause of peace so dear to Brin's heart also attracted women
activists from various backgrounds, in part by foregrounding gender identity
in an explicitly women's peace movement. That Jewish texts and traditions
encompassed multiple rationales for seeking peace only increased the enormous appeal of the movement for many Jewish women. Agitating for peace
carried the additional benefit of simultaneously fighting against the anti-
Semitism that threatened Jews worldwide.[3] Peace work therefore linked Jewish women both to an international Jewish community sensitive to the special threats war posed to Jews and to women worldwide who believed that

Fanny and Arthur Brin
with their children Rachel,
Howard, and Charles, 1922.
Courtesy of Judith Brin
Ingber

they were uniquely qualified to put an end to violence. Both working and middle-class Jewish women felt these responsibilities acutely. Middle-class Jewish women were especially likely also to see in peace a cause that would allow them to acculturate into the gendered conventions of American women's organizations. Few Jewish women became peace activists with such consciously instrumental motivations, but many perceived that their acceptance and prominence in the peace movement endowed them with greater power within the American Jewish community as well. The feminism—sometimes latent, sometimes explicit—at the heart of the women's peace movement catapulted significant numbers of Jewish women into new political realms.

Brin's early years planted the seeds for the powerhouse activist and role model she was to become for thousands of such American Jewish women. She was born in 1884 in Romania and brought to the United States as an infant by her parents, John and Antoinette Friedman Fligelman. She grew up in Minneapolis, graduating Phi Beta Kappa from the University of Minnesota in 1906, teaching English for several years, and joining the Peripatetics, an elite women's study club in Minneapolis for Jewish college graduates. By the time she married Arthur Brin in 1913, she was already active in the suffrage movement and the Minneapolis NCJW section. She also wrote articles for the local press on such subjects as "Russian Bureaucracy and the Jews," demonstrating her ongoing concern about the situation of Jews around the world. After the First World War ended and the Nineteenth Amendment finally passed, she joined the local peace movement, directing disarmament activities in Minneapolis in 1921. Later in life Brin identified women's rights, world peace, Judaism, and democracy as her four lifelong priorities, and the roles she played in NCJW, culminating in the national presidency from 1932 to 1938, gave her ample opportunity to work for these causes.[4]

As the mother of three children, Brin acknowledged that none of her activism would have been possible without an extremely supportive husband, financial stability, and domestic help.[5] Indeed, one of the reasons for the heavily middle-class composition of many women's social movements outside the labor movement was the "leisure" time that middle-class status conferred. The life of a clubwoman, as politically engaged women like Fanny Brin were sometimes called with admiration and sometimes with only slightly veiled contempt, more closely resembled that of the executive director of a modern-day NGO than of that mythological creature, the simple middle-class housewife.[6] As national chair of NCJW's Committee on Peace and Arbitration, Brin read voraciously on the subject of war and peace, participated in multiple study groups, monitored the press, sent letters to the editor, attended the meetings and set the policies of the many local, national, and international organizations to which she belonged, wrote articles for NCJW and other publications, collected and digested regular reports from nearly one hundred NCJW sections, sustained a voluminous correspondence with Jewish women and peace activists all over the country, and traveled constantly. During one year of her NCJW presidency, she spent February and March visiting sections in Omaha, Denver, Colorado Springs, Los Angeles, San Diego, Oakland, and San Francisco, then in May traveled to Terra Haute, Indianapolis, Cleveland, and Cincinnati, and in October went to Chicago, Schenectady, and Asbury Park. This list does not include two extended stints at NCJW's executive offices in New York or travel for any other reasons that year. When she was home, she oversaw her children's Jewish education and lit candles on Friday nights but also attended the symphony as part of her Shabbat relaxation.[7]

Brin described the post-suffrage woman's movement as one "not of rights but of responsibilities" and spent a lifetime trying to live up to those responsibilities. Identified as one of the ten most influential clubwomen in America in 1934, she devoted herself first and foremost to the cause of peace.[8] In doing so, she was one of many American women who saw their primary role following enfranchisement as making sure that gender equality would change the international power structure and, especially through maternalist thinking, socialize both men and women against war. As a Jewish woman observing the travails of Jewish communities worldwide, Brin felt this mandate especially keenly. Her firm sense of the consonance of her Jewish, female, and American identities permeated her life and formed the basis of her activism. The experiences she and other American Jewish women had in the peace movement illustrate the bridges that gender and maternalism built between American Jewish identity and women's culture of activism. Like the birth control movement, though in a somewhat more collective sense, the peace movement served as an important arena for American Jewish women consciously committed to drawing on their religious, ethnic, and cultural values and to demonstrating the possibility of acculturation to American social mores.

A Brief History of the Women's Peace Movement

The history of the peace movement in the United States is a long and varied one that did not begin only, as is often imagined, after World War I. Peace organizations with nineteenth-century roots included the Universal Peace Union, the Intercollegiate Peace Association, the World Peace Foundation, and the Church Peace Union. These groups generally shared a belief in the world's moral progress as administered by a rational elite who could use scientific knowledge to develop alternatives to war. Smaller scale peace organizations, such as the New York and Chicago Peace Societies, encouraged markedly more participation by women. Women were committed to many of the same goals as men but also tended to develop more humanitarian positions focused on population support and the disadvantaged rather than elite leadership alone.[9]

Following the carnage of World War I, peace groups sprang up all over the world. These groups constituted a movement rather than a political party or single organization. As such, the peace movement did not require formal affiliation and expanded beyond a finite group of leaders and organizations. The movement affected a broad swath of people with common attitudes, with or without common activities. Even people who disapproved on principle of pacifism were influenced by the ideas of the peace movement. After the war, the broad peace movement, though diverse, generally subscribed to at least three beliefs: war was the fault of a small group of military leaders and arms dealers; moral education created the best path to peace; permanent international institutions could prevent and end war.[10]

Many women entered the peace movement as a natural extension of their suffrage activities. For both British and American suffragists, at the heart of the suffrage campaign lay the idea that political power should be based on moral rather than physical force, a belief that provided a natural segue into peace work. American women finally got the right to vote just as the new world order after World War I offered them an international forum for political participation. Women's organizations commonly treated peace as an arena particularly suitable for women, who could not advance any kind of personal, social, domestic, or political agenda under the threat or conditions of war. Preexisting large women's organizations such as the International Council of Women (ICW) began to pour resources into their peace departments, arguing that war was inherently masculine and thus women could best support alternatives.[11]

Separate women's peace organizations emerged from widespread ideas about gender difference and women's solidarity. Before the United States entered the war, a 1915 meeting called by Hull House founder Jane Addams had already resulted in the Woman's Peace Party. Groups like this one believed themselves to be more committed to both nonviolence and social and economic justice than male and mixed-sex groups, which emphasized international institutions and law. Peace work expressed a widely felt conviction that women differed fundamentally from men in their commitments to preserve human life, provide every person with the highest quality of life, and resolve conflicts without severing relationships or resorting to violence. The Woman's Peace Party became the U.S. division of WILPF after the war. The organization favored any move toward world peace, economic and political justice, and arms reduction. The WILPF lobbied Congress, circulated petitions, convened conferences, staged demonstrations, and formulated legal alternatives to war.[12]

There were other significant American women's peace groups as well. Some women thought WILPF did not go far enough. The Woman's Peace Society, established in 1919, believed that lobbying for arms reduction was inadequate and resisted all war, insisting on complete and universal disarmament though educational campaigns and lobbying. The group also opposed compulsory military training, a position most of the other American peace organizations came to share. The most absolutist women's organization was the Women's Peace Union (WPU), founded in 1921, which worked to secure a constitutional amendment outlawing war and organized nonviolent resistance actions. The WPU members signed a pledge not to aid or sanction any war, participate in relief work, or contribute any labor to wartime society. The largest women's peace group was the National

Committee on the Cause and Cure of War (NCCCW), created by the former suffragist leader Carrie Chapman Catt in 1924 as a coalition group of women's organizations interested in peace work. The NCCCW adopted no ideologically rigid stance but supported internationalist efforts such as the League of Nations, World Court, and disarmament conferences. It convened regular "roundtables" of member delegates for intensive discussions of foreign policy and peace education and drew up recommendations for practical steps toward world peace.[13]

All four of the major American women's peace groups emphasized education about international affairs for voting women, relied on feminist networks, and often preferred working only with women. They deployed suffrage strategies and tactics in the service of a peace movement that appealed to an even broader swath of women in the United States and worldwide. These women's peace groups achieved undeniable prominence. During the 1920s, Frederick Libby, the leader of the National Council for Prevention of War (NCPW), estimated that women constituted two-thirds of Americans in the peace movement.[14]

Definitions related to the peace movement remained untidy throughout the interwar period. Prior to America's involvement in World War I, "pacifist" generally meant someone committed to international peace through cooperation, but after 1917 it typically denoted a more absolutist stance against war. Pacifists who refused to serve in the armed forces could be and were imprisoned. Following the war, "pacifist" might mean a foreign policy isolationist, a liberal pacifist who opposed war but could sometimes admit its defensive necessity, or an absolutist pacifist who opposed all war under any circumstances. These positions reflected, in part, Addams's distinction between older ideals of peace, which appealed to a moral sensibility or conviction, and newer ideals of peace, which promoted international institutions and preventive action. Both, she felt, were necessary. Further distinctions among women in the peace movement appeared as international conditions changed during the 1920s and 1930s. Some peace activists, for instance, differentiated between wars undertaken by a single country and those fought collectively by an international force, the latter serving the interests of world peace and justice. Others distinguished absolutist pacifism, which utterly condemned all war in every time and place and for whatever reason, from liberal pacifism, or what some scholars have called "pacific-ism," which occasionally admitted the necessity of defensive war or the use of force to prevent larger scale war if all other avenues had been exhausted.[15] These distinctions would become critical during the 1930s for Jews in the peace movement worldwide.

American Jewish Women's Early Peace Activities

The Spanish-American War provided the first major opportunity for American women to make their voices heard in foreign policy. Politically active women typically condemned masculine warmongering, cast themselves as protectors of Cuba's women and children, and insisted that the world would be better off if women voted. Sadie Jacobs, a Jewish student at Randolph-Macon College, summed up the opinion of many American women in her 1898 oration on "Demands of Civilization" when she argued that the United States should never be drawn into war unless its interests were directly involved. Many women, however, including the prominent suffragist Elizabeth Cady Stanton, believed United States interests were involved and supported the Spanish-American War.[16] American Jewish women differed among themselves. The recently founded NCJW made public statements supporting the war, but NCJW's first president Hannah Greenebaum Solomon said in 1898 that "it was our hope that the voice of the majority of the women of our land might assist in averting the dread calamity . . . we united with our sisters of other faiths in petitioning for peace. Not through war are the great questions of the universe to be decided."[17] Once the fighting started, NCJW members contributed to the war effort in their local communities, but NCJW also joined other American women's groups in publicizing the 1899 international conference on world peace held at the Hague. Even from its earliest years, NCJW found that peace worked as a bridge issue allying the Jewish women's group with other women's organizations such as the National Council of Women or the General Federation of Women's Clubs.[18]

During the years between the Spanish-American War and the First World War, Jewish women continued to gravitate toward the peace movement. In a 1904 address delivered from the pulpit of Temple Israel in St. Louis, still a rarity for women in public Jewish life, Solomon argued that part of the religious mission of women was to promote world peace. She pointed out that as an already transnational religious group, Jews had a special interest in seeking international cooperation. Jewish women, in particular, should participate in the increasingly successful ventures that united women worldwide to work for peace. The suffragist and National Consumers' League president Maud Nathan addressed a New York crowd of thousands in 1907 to proclaim war too expensive in both human and monetary cost to be part of the new century. Both Solomon and Nathan played instrumental roles in the establishment of NCJW's Committee on Peace and Arbitration in 1908.[19]

Nathan and Solomon also became part of a small but influential group of American Jewish women who regularly traveled abroad to attend meetings of the ICW, sponsor of numerous peace resolutions, and the International Woman Suffrage Alliance (IWSA), which focused more narrowly on enfranchisement but nonetheless saw peace as an international women's issue and a necessary condition for women's political equality.[20] Sadie American, another influential NCJW founder, went to the ICW Congress in 1899, and both American and Solomon attended the 1904 ICW Congress. There they met with other prominent Jewish activists, including Aletta Jacobs, a pioneering Dutch doctor, suffragist, pacifist, and birth control advocate; Constance Rothschild, Lady Battersea, a British activist working to curb the "white slavery" ensnaring immigrant Jewish girls; and Bertha Pappenheim, founder of the German Jüdischer Frauenbund. These international encounters led to the establishment of the World Council of Jewish Women, which at its founding represented more than a million women worldwide. Solomon reported learning a great deal from the 1904 meeting, but she also noted encountering definite anti-Semitism, a problem that continually haunted Jewish women in the peace movement.[21]

The Hungarian feminist Rosika Schwimmer's visits to America further strengthened the international connections among Jewish women interested in peace. Many American Jewish women were inspired by Schwimmer, who achieved great prominence in the United States before later being discredited as a radical. Both the American and the Jewish press covered Schwimmer's 1914 lecture tour. Her speeches were well received by general and Jewish audiences alike, though Schwimmer herself was perturbed to find that some of the strongest American advocates of peace, such as Henry Ford, had no compunction about expressing anti-Semitism as well.[22] The *American Hebrew*, a mainstream Jewish periodical, referred to her as "the most democratic person in the world" and approved of her insistence that "the mission of the women in Israel is peace." In December 1914, Schwimmer spoke at New York's Temple Emanu-El at a joint meeting of NCJW and the Eastern Council of Reform Rabbis. She argued that women's maternal instincts led to their natural abhorrence of war, pointing out that women were supposedly denied the vote because men were their guardians, but men were not protecting women and their homes when they went to war.[23]

One of Schwimmer's greatest contributions was her assumption of a symbiotic relationship between peace and suffrage, reflecting a broader feminist viewpoint. She contended that women of peace could have no real influence as long as they had no voice in making law. Many American suffragists took up this theme as well, including Nathan, who argued forcefully that "nations are plunged into cruel wars without the protest of the women being heard." Like the link between suffrage and birth control, the connection between suffrage and the peace movement predated the Nineteenth Amendment but tightened as women began to test and exert their new political power. The nineteenth-century women's movement had encompassed multiple issues, including peace, which meant that even women's organizations that originally opposed suffrage, like the Women's Christian Temperance Union (WCTU), advocated peace as an means of bringing an end to violence against women. Once the WCTU changed its position on suffrage under Frances Willard's leadership during the 1880s, peace became even more important, and from the turn of the century on, the international WCTU'S Department of Peace and Arbitration highlighted the links among religion, suffrage, and peace. The program for the National Suffrage Bazaar held at Madison Square Garden in December 1900 included a "Peace and Arbitration Pageant," illustrating the long-standing ties between peace and suffrage. Complementary lines of suffrage and peace debate became increasingly common. At a 1915 Carnegie Hall speech, Schwimmer posed the question of why women of peace had so little influence in a belligerent world. She explained, "The women have preached and preached . . . but you have to have law to enforce these things, and the women have no voice in making the laws." Since peace could be accomplished only through the cooperation of existing institutions and organizations, women must gain the vote and a role in public affairs in order to bring their different moral priorities, including peace, to the world of international relations.[24]

The Challenge of the Great War

As war broke out in Europe and threatened to draw in the United States as well, American Jewish women began to express their opinions on war and peace with ever louder voices. No one was surprised when the notorious anarchist Emma Goldman made her feelings clear by publishing *Preparedness, The Road to Universal Slaughter*, just as no one would have been surprised by the prominent radical Rose Pastor Stokes's private 1914 letter condemning "that stupendous slaughter-house" and the "unthinkable madness" of the war in Europe. Yet even practical progressives like Lillian Wald, founder of the Henry Street Settlement, and Women's Trade Union League's leader Rose Schneiderman were gratified by the large turnout of Jewish women at the 1914 antiwar parade they helped to plan.[25]

Though Jewish identity did not mean much to Wald personally, she nonetheless remained tightly connected to the Jewish community by virtue of the location of the Henry Street Settlement on the Lower East Side, home to hundreds of thousands of immigrants. Wald shared Jane Addams's conviction that women could and should make a special contribution to the world in promoting peace as a moral alternative. She made the Henry Street Settlement an important address for peace activism, holding up the inter-ethnic cooperation so in evidence at the settlement house as a model for international cooperation. She explained the links between neighborhood-based work among such immigrants and her constantly expanding social activism: "Experience in one small East Side section . . . has led to . . . widening circles, until our community relationships have come to include the city, the state, the national government, and the world at large." Wald feared that the war would end the hard-fought reforms to which she had dedicated her life, and she used her status as a nationally prominent reformer to work tirelessly for peace. The parade she helped organize sent 1,200 women dressed in black and white marching down Fifth Avenue. The Henry Street Settlement hosted a series of roundtable conversations about the war and terms of possible peace settlements. Wald focused especially on the campaigns of the American Union Against Militarism. Also supported by important Jewish

Lillian D. Wald. Courtesy
of the Jacob Rader Marcus
Center of the American
Jewish Archives

community leaders like rabbis Stephen Wise and Judah Magnes, the American Union Against Militarism resisted preparedness and the draft and eventually tried to protect wartime civil liberties.[26]

The American Jewish community was divided in its response to the war, reflecting the complications of personal politics. Writing in the socialist newspaper *Der Fraynd*, Adela Kean Zametkin assumed that "the war has given women the best opportunities to demonstrate that she is also a human being," but she wondered "whether the chance for the women is worth all the horrible sacrifices." Some Jewish women found that maintaining their commitments to both peace and other causes, such as Zionism, was virtually impossible in a world at war. Henrietta Szold and Jessie Sampter, two of the most prominent Zionist women in America, joined a pacifist group called the People's Council for Peace and Democracy but were pressured into resigning by other members of the American Zionist leadership, including Louis Brandeis, who regretted the war but saw in it an opportunity to transform the map of the Middle East. Others, like suffragist Caroline Katzenstein, saw peace activism as complementary to their long-standing political commitments. Katzenstein worked closely with Alice Paul and others to convince Congresswoman Jeanette Rankin, whom Katzenstein knew well from the Montana suffrage campaign, to vote against the United States' entry into the war.[27]

While many Jewish radicals agreed that the slaughter in Europe could only be seen as tragic, some believed that the conflict was a necessary cataclysm that would end war forever. The members of Marie Ganz's anarchist circle in New York fought bitterly over the most appropriate reaction. At first Ganz felt, "I was against war, against this war and all wars, and appeals to patriotism would never change me." As a Russian Jewish immigrant and an anarchist, Ganz was also not inclined to support any alliance with the czar, but after the Russian Revolution, she began to believe that war had overthrown tyranny and might therefore not be completely unacceptable. Similarly, Rose Pastor Stokes, on the path toward increasingly doctrinaire communism, resigned from the Woman's Peace Party in March 1917 because she claimed to believe in the U.S's stated mission to use war to end war.[28]

Less politically radical Jewish women also changed their attitudes toward the war as it continued. In 1916, Hannah Greenebaum Solomon had backed Woodrow Wilson's presidential campaign because he promised to keep the United States out of the war. She found the militarist aspects of his inauguration very disappointing. That same year, NCJW's national president Jane Harris advised NCJW not to join the Women's Department for National Preparedness because such work would not mesh with it's peace agenda.[29] Once the United States entered the war in 1917, however, plenty of NCJW members supported the war effort, resigning themselves to reality. Sophie Weil Brown had saved all the peace literature that came her way, but now she ran liberty bond campaigns and gave patriotic talks in movie theaters in her Georgia hometown.[30] As Ernestine Dreyfuss, who succeeded Harris as NCJW's national president, explained:

> It appears that Peace cannot be secured to the world through education no matter how persistent and serious is the consideration given to the subject. Through the months of this war and particularly lately, we are constrained to give no expression to this sentiment and we can only pray that we may be permitted to keep Peace before us as an attainable ideal and use every influence that we can command to make it realized and permanent.[31]

This statement hints at the political repression and limitations on free speech that so marred the country's war years. It is entirely possible that the patriotism of NCJW members was aroused during the war and that many of them believed the United States should be involved, but it was also in their best interests to proclaim their patriotism loudly. Those American Jews who did not do so were excoriated by some elements of an American Jewish community still unsure of its welcome and security in the land of the free and the home of the brave.

So successful were activists with interests in both peace and suffrage in linking the two causes that when, after the United States entered the war, Carrie Chapman Catt made the difficult but pragmatic decision to offer the National American Woman's Suffrage Association's (NAWSA) help with the war effort, storms of protest erupted. Pacifist and well-known vocational educator Elsie Borg Goldsmith and other Jewish women angrily signed a denunciation of this policy as carried out in New York. Suffragists with strong commitments to peace understood the practical ramifications of cooperating with the government—newly widespread support for enfranchisement—but that did not make them any happier about what they saw as compromising their principles. If a major goal of suffrage was for women to use the vote to achieve world peace, then supporting the war effort seemed both craven and counterproductive.[32]

The aftermath of the armistice seemed to vindicate the decision of Catt, Maud Nathan, and other suffragists to support the war effort. President Wilson finally endorsed enfranchisement, and the final years of the suffrage campaign took on an air of inevitability, at least from suffragists' point of view. In January 1919 Alice Goldmark Brandeis, Supreme Court Justice Louis

Brandeis's wife, invited Catt to speak about "The Redirection of Women's Energies Under Peace" at the American Women's Victory Dinner and Conference. Brandeis, Catt, and many other activist women saw the postwar era as one of opportunity. Especially after the Nineteenth Amendment passed, significant numbers of suffragists became committed to the idea that the most important thing they would do with their hard-won votes would be to put an end to war. Even suffragists who had carefully avoided painting a picture of men as inherently antagonistic to women just because of sex differences now blamed men for warmongering and posited newly enfranchised women's moral superiority as the basis for bringing an end to war. Many, though not all, women interested in peace opted to work through separate women's peace organizations as a natural extension of their rhetoric blaming men and masculinity for the absence of peace in the world.[33]

Not all former suffragists automatically transformed themselves into peace activists. At the National Woman's Party (NWP) victory convention in February 1921, Alice Paul, herself a pacifist, nonetheless stifled debates on peace, birth control, and racism in the women's movement in a successful maneuver to keep NWP's focus on the issue of equal rights. She could not stop individual NWP supporters from devoting some of their time and energy to peace—Rebecca Hourwich Reyher, for example, became an increasingly prominent pacifist—but she could direct the organization she headed to avoid the distractions of any cause other than narrowly defined feminist agitation for equal rights.[34]

Only a small proportion of former suffragists affiliated with NWP, and peace appealed to large numbers of women as the most important issue of the post-suffrage era. Most Jewish women with political interests fell into the latter category. Ray Morris David, the superintendent of the Denver Jewish Aid Society and an appointed member of the Colorado State Board of Pardons, had supported suffrage from the 1890s forward and, in the wake of federal enfranchisement, became a delegate to the Children's World Peace Movement. Gertrude Weil, a suffrage leader in North Carolina, frequently addressed the members of a Raleigh Jewish women's group, urging them as voting citizens to add their voices to those clamoring for peace. During the 1920s the NCJW's New York section devoted regular meetings to political topics such as "Woman and the Vote" and "Symposium on the World's Greatest Need," the latter a major peace program that included talks from such peace luminaries as Anna Garlin Spencer, a minister and former suffragist, and NCJW's own national president Constance Sporborg. The links between suffrage and peace, usually predicated on ideas about women's moral superiority, remained pertinent throughout the interwar years.[35]

Because birth control and peace were among the most important social movements of the post-suffrage era, there was an effort to link them as well. The neo-Malthusian perspective so critical to the birth control movement took it for granted that population reduction worldwide would lead to peace, blaming overpopulation and the high cost of raising children as major sources of international aggression. The forward to Margaret Sanger's 1920 book *Woman and the New Race* connected "the possibility of abolishing from the world the desolating scourge of war" to the "wise limitation of the human output."[36] However, even with its focus on sexual expression and radical politics tamped down to some degree after 1920, the birth control movement still seemed too radical, vulgar, or simply uninteresting to some former suffragists. By contrast, peace became an almost mainstream cause that many Jewish women with political interests and social consciences could espouse and indeed already had embraced.

Women, Peace, and the American Jewish Community

Jewish identity, whether defined in religious, ethnic, cultural, or ethical terms, clearly played a significant role in Jewish women's peace activism. Also related was the distinctive internationalism they developed following the disastrous effects of World War I on Jewish communities in Europe. American Jewish women, living in relative safety, tried to help other Jews being persecuted worldwide by working to prevent future violence. They drew liberally on both Jewish and maternalist ideals of peace. Even before the war, a speaker at the 1912 NCJW Triennial meeting had called on Jewish women to exert their special powers as mothers and Jews to "supplant the war system of nations by the system of peace, arbitration, and law." Articles in the Jewish press underlined this point, exhorting the "new woman" to teach her children about the evils of bloodshed and the importance of loving all human beings.[37]

The American Jewish community offered a great deal of support for peace work, which led Jewish women to cooperate more fully with male peace activists than some other American women pacifists, although Jewish women typically valued the independence of women's peace work as well. Before the United States' entry into World War I, many working-class Jewish women applauded New York's congressman Meyer London and the labor lawyer Morris Hillquit's participation in a December 1915 Socialist Party delegation to President Wilson to persuade him to join a conference of neutral nations. Just after the United States declared war, Judah Magnes, a rabbi whose unrepentant pacifism ultimately led to the loss of his pulpit position, spoke at the First American Conference for Democracy and Terms of Peace. In this speech, entered into the Congressional Record in June 1917, Magnes referenced both American and Jewish imagery to argue that ordinary people would blame leaders for this misguided war, which must end as swiftly and peaceably as possible.[38]

Following the armistice, many individual Jewish men achieved great prominence in the peace movement. In 1921, the Chicago attorney Salmon O. Levinson founded the American Committee for the Outlawry of War, which proposed international legislative alternatives to war. Throughout the following decade, Jewish men developed many of the most serious proposals for achieving world peace. Max Green's 1924 *The Problem of Universal Peace and the Key to Its Solution* suggested a Federated States of the World on the model of the U.S. government, with every nation in the world represented in a bicameral legislature and eligible to bring international disputes before a Supreme Court. No armed forces would be necessary when no nation would dare defy international law.[39]

The Bok American Peace Award, named after the *Ladies' Home Journal* editor Edward Bok, ran a competition to elicit further proposals along this line. Many entrants were Jewish. Samuel Fleischman's 1925 submission suggested the creation of a new World Conference, which would differ from the League of Nations. Instead of forcing countries to settle their differences through peaceful methods, the World Conference would work to eliminate all distrust and friction between nations, thereby eliminating the causes of war. M. A. Borochow's idea was an International Peace Fund, which would compensate all injured national parties through funds assessed from all member nations, making even defensive war too expensive to justify. Along similar lines, Israel Matz pushed for a law making it illegal for any person or corporation to make a profit out of war, thereby reducing what he believed was the major motivation for armed conflict.[40] Although in retrospect these proposals seem hopelessly naive, especially given the fact that the United States had not even joined the League of Nations, they all attracted publicity and were frequently referenced by activists across the spectrum of the peace movement, including Jewish women who took pride in the fact that these authors were Jewish.

Among those active in the peace movement were many rabbis, who exerted a great deal of influence in the Jewish community. Peace groups acknowledged the vital role clergy could play. In the run-up to the July 1922 No More War Demonstration in New York, WPU called upon all clergy-men to devote special sermons to peace, suggesting that ministers discuss the Sermon on the Mount and rabbis discuss the famous passage in Isaiah prophesying a day when the nations "shall beat their swords into plowshares and their spears into pruning hooks."[41] Certain rabbis, often those known for socially progressive views on other issues, labored long and hard for the cause of peace. Louis Mann of Chicago's Temple Sinai, Stephen Wise of New York's Free Synagogue, and Edward Israel of Baltimore's Temple Har Sinai, among others, became strong rabbinic voices for peace during the 1920s and early 1930s. The participation of male religious leaders in peace work aroused even greater interest in the American Jewish community at large, which in turn brought more Jewish women into the movement. As a member of a Jewish women's group in Chicago explained in a report on Mann's 1923 Armistice Day denunciation of war, it behooved them all to "rejoice that the peace movement has found such a fearless, inspired leader" within the American Jewish community.[42]

The American Jewish man most prominently associated with pacifism was probably Abraham Cronbach, a faculty member at Hebrew Union College, the Reform movement's rabbinical seminary, whose unwavering passion for peace had gotten him fired from his pulpit during World War I. In 1926 he set up the Peace Heroes' Memorial Society, headquartered in Cincinnati where he lived, to honor nonmilitary heroes who died in service, elevating firemen, policemen, and women who died in childbirth above soldiers whose deaths were in vain. With the support of the Reform movement, Cronbach published *The Jewish Peace Book for Home and School* in 1932. He drew on Jewish teachings to make the case that Judaism is a religion of peace and does not countenance war. For example, he retold the biblical story in Genesis of Abraham and Lot's decision to separate when Lot wanted his own land. Cronbach highlighted Abraham's understanding that many things were more precious than land or material wealth. Selfish, grasping Lot ended up fleeing Sodom and losing most of his family, while Abraham ended up speaking to God, lover of peace. Cronbach concluded that nations should, like Abraham, yield land and riches to save lives and preserve peace.[43]

The Reform movement's Central Conference of American Rabbis (CCAR) dealt with questions about peace throughout the interwar period. Not all the members approved of Cronbach's pacifism, and they expressed considerable ambivalence toward the "Pledge for Jewish Pacifists" that he circulated among his fellow Reform rabbis in 1924. David Goldberg of Temple Israel in Brockton, Massachusetts, signed the pledge and published it in his synagogue's newsletter, but Solomon Bazell of Altoona, Pennsylvania's Temple Beth Israel, though supportive of Jewish pacifism in spirit, declined to sign the pledge because of its position on civil disobedience. Morris Faber refused the pledge because he did not think any movement should be called Jewish unless it was strictly religious in nature, adding that Jewish sources contained a multitude of approaches to war and peace that could not be reduced to pacifism.[44]

The issue of the Jewish perspective on peace became central to CCAR proceedings. At the 1925 CCAR convention, the Committee on Cooperation with National Organizations recommended supporting NCPW. The Committee on International Peace, suggesting that peace required practical action, agreed to develop a resolution for the CCAR to consider.[45] The following year, the CCAR approved a statement that grounded peace in religious values and Jewish history.

> The CCAR in Annual Convention assembled, confidently affirms the vision and the wisdom in the assertion of the ancient prophets of Israel that the ultimate aim of mankind is peace. . . . The passing years emphasize for us the conviction that peace is not only a religious ideal, but also a fundamental necessity conditioning the very life of nations. . . . May our beloved country head the world in fostering "the will to peace" among the nations of the earth through recognition of the prophetic truth that "righteousness exalteth a nation."[46]

The statement went on to urge the United States to advocate arms reduction, join the World Court, oppose compulsory military training and object to glorification of the military. A few years later, the same committee noted with approval that many Reform congregations held special services on Armistice and Memorial Days and Chanukah, usually at the instigation of the temple sisterhoods that comprised the National Federation of Temple Sisterhoods (NFTS).[47]

The NFTS worked closely with congregations and rabbis to make sure that peace remained on the Jewish communal agenda. One of NFTS's most visible projects was a commissioned book by Rabbi Roland Gittelsohn, *The Jew Looks at War and Peace*. This book served as a serious study guide for synagogue sisterhoods and religious schools and also included a lengthy list of contacts for more information and resources. Congregations and groups outside the Reform movement used it as well. Gittelsohn dealt with a wide array of issues relating to Jews and peace, arguing that organized religion should denounce war and remain pacifist even in the face of violence. He provided detailed information about government military spending and prioritized disarmament as the best means to prevent further warfare. Many of Gittelsohn's recommendations targeted women. He cited the Greek play *Lysistrata* as an example of the power women have to stop war and pointed out that "Men have been seeking peace for eternity without finding it. The search must now rest in the hands of women." As mothers, religious educators, and civic activists, all Jewish women could be moral forces for peace.[48]

Jewish women worldwide took this responsibility seriously. At the 1923 meeting of the World Council of Jewish Women, the first held after the war, the international body of delegates passed a resolution affirming that "the mission of Israel is peace, and its watchword 'Shalom'" and committing to "zealously devote ourselves to struggle to this end until mankind is healed and reconciled." A similar resolution passed in 1929 when the noted peace activist Estelle Sternberger was serving as the executive secretary of the council.[49] Jewish women's groups consistently positioned peace as a religious issue, using Jewish texts to support their statements. Even the least ritually observant Jewish women typically drew on religious themes in explaining their attitudes. Fanny Brin argued that the values of democracy—individual freedom, the people as a source of authority, the importance of education, a sense of accountability, and social consciousness—were all rooted in Judaism, which even in ancient Israel had restricted the power of the monarchy and limited the possibility of war. Brin delivered hundreds of peace speeches as NCJW president and as an active WILPF member and NCCCW delegate. Her NCJW addresses incorporated Jewish content, as when she used the repetitive rhetorical form of the Yom Kippur prayer service confessional to make the case for peace:

> We repent . . . that we sent some 12,000,000 young men to their death. . . . We repent that we caused 8,000,000 women to be widowed. . . . We repent that we caused 5,000,000 children to be orphaned. . . . We repent that we squandered 250,000,000,000 billions of dollars, one-half the total wealth of nations, on this madness of mutual destruction.[50]

Perhaps because of the centrality of Judaism to their peace work, remarkably few Jewish women denied their religious identity, even in the face of the kind of prejudice that might hurt their cause. Anti-Semites both outside and inside the peace movement pointed to a dangerous tradition of Jewish radicalism, but even women for whom religion was less important than gender or class still typically identified themselves as Jewish. Hannah Greenebaum Solomon's attitude served as an inspiration for several generations of Jewish women activists. As one admirer described her, "She has always been outspokenly Jewish. She has never flinched in the presence of her non-Jewish friends and co-workers." From her adolescence, when Solomon and her sister were the first Jewish members of the Chicago Women's Club, to her old age, when she continued to insist, "It is important to be a vital part of the community where you live," Solomon embodied her conviction that it was not only possible but desirable for Jewish women to be fully integrated into the American community. Yet she also believed that such integration should not preclude a special interest in Jewish affairs and a commitment to working with Jewish women. When she was honored in 1937 by an international radio broadcast, an impressive roster of both Jewish and non-Jewish women, including speakers in London, Stockholm, Geneva, Toronto, and Prague, spoke about "Women's Place in World Problems Today." At Solomon's funeral in 1942, Brin summed up the contributions of one of the elder stateswomen of Jewish women's activism, declaring, "She taught us that we, as Jewish women, must know our heroic past and our great traditions, in order that we might better serve ourselves, our own people, and our country."[51]

The prominence of Jewish women like Solomon in the peace movement encouraged others to take themselves seriously as both Jews and political actors. A New Mexico resident, Flora Spiegelberg, took it upon herself to compose "The Ten Commandments of World Peace," using the biblical model to outline an American program for pacifism. Resolutions passed by synagogue sisterhoods pledged their patriotism as Americans, emphasized their peacemaking opportunities as women and mothers, and acknowledged their traditional responsibilities as Jews for bringing an end to war.[52]

Non-Jewish leaders, too, recognized the outsized presence of Jewish women in the peace movement. In her skit "Mars Takes a Sabbatical," Carrie Chapman Catt introduced a line of historical women who approved of women's modern-day attempts to abolish war. She had the biblical figure of Deborah, the only woman judge of ancient Israel, say "Were I living now, I'd join one of the great groups of Jewish women and . . . help them to make war impossible."[53] That Catt singled out this Old Testament figure, who could have served as a role model or symbol for Christian women as well, and explicitly linked her to Jewish women demonstrates her acknowledgment of Jewish women's significance in the peace movement.

Multiple Motivations for Jewish Women's Peace Work

A combination of factors lay behind Jewish women's engagement with the peace movement in addition to the Jewish identity, though understood in multiple ways, that provided such significant motivation. For some, class identity was most important, with socialism and the labor movement providing a path toward peace work. Feminist claims that women had a special interest in supporting and promoting peace also proved appealing. These rationales were inextricably linked for many activists, who often did not distinguish between their identities as women and as Jews.

Working-class American Jewish women belonged to a variety of groups, some of which, like the Socialist Party, supported certain formulations of international cooperation and world peace, though always in service of the overriding demand for political, economic, and social transformation. The ladies auxiliary group of the socialist Workmen's Circle pressed for peace and encouraged its members to join WILPF during the 1920s. However, domestic duties made it difficult for married women to attend evening meetings, and there were always far more men than women active in the Workmen's Circle. Single working women often found that their interests lay elsewhere and turned to other groups more explicitly concerned with women's unique needs, which may or may not have included peace. Jewish working women of any family status typically prioritized workplace justice and industrial feminism, with their local concerns serving as the main engine for their collective action. Although working women's concern with labor issues did not preclude an interest in peace, their multiple commitments made them less likely to foreground it. The labor organizer Jennie Matyas, for example, identified herself as a pacifist, but in practical terms, her union activities left her little time to agitate for peace as a separate issue. She believed socialist overthrow of class structure, which pitted workers against employers, to be a more pressing concern than nations fighting each other.[54]

Working-class Jewish women's relationships to peace illustrated the delicate nature of the alliances in the broadly defined women's movement of the first decades of the twentieth century. Transnational organizations like WILPF successfully mobilized women worldwide around peace, but doing so required papering over cracks created not just by nationalist consciousness but also by class. Working-class women, especially political radicals, cast a jaundiced eye on the promises of universal sisterhood. Many of them agreed that peace was a worthy cause but not one more important than economic equity. Still, Jewish women workers never absented themselves from the peace movement. The union organizer Rose Pesotta called on workers to refuse to fight in any imperialist war and warned that capitalists saw them as disposable weapons in a fight for economic dominance. This kind of trenchant socialist critique also appeared prominently in the student activism of the 1930s, when many working-class Jewish students rejected the class system they believed shaped higher education and led directly to war.[55]

American Jewish women also drew liberally on maternalist ideals when working for peace. Lillian Wald's conviction that mothers could make a special contribution by promoting peace as a moral alternative appealed to women across class, ethnic, and religious boundaries. Given the strength of maternalism as a theme, goal, and raison d'être of many forms of women's activism, it was possible for women of any background to share the conviction that motherhood led inexorably to pacifism. As the former suffragist Caroline Katzenstein wrote, "We women, because we are the mothers of the race, know perhaps better than men the true value of life, and it is up to us to show that war and the causes that lead to it can be abolished."[56] Framing the issue as an appeal to mothers made it a message that all women could presumably subscribe to.

The pervasive theme of motherhood in women's peace work reflected a form of difference feminism. Women's capacity for motherhood, unique to women, therefore gave them a moral advantage in envisioning peace. A similar element of women's peace work that appealed to many feminists was the promise of a universal sisterhood that would redeem the word from its wicked (masculine) ways. Like wartime sexual violence, which women pacifists linked to militarism, and the responsibility of female citizenship, maternalism offered women a justification for organizing separately from men to work for peace. The WPU lobbyist Frieda Langer Lazarus, who agitated for peace in the United States and abroad, believed that even the most committed men were far more likely to compromise their pacifism than were women.[57]

Women of diverse backgrounds also saw in peace a women's issue that would erase—or at least diminish—the ethnic, religious, and national differences that might otherwise divide them. The women's movement sounded this bell particularly loudly in the aftermath of World War I. At the 1920 IWSA meeting in Geneva, the first after the armistice, IWSA leaders pointed with pride to the German, French, and British women working together for women's political rights and for peace.[58] Jewish women from varied religious and class backgrounds generally shared the traditional Jewish value of prizing motherhood and family and enthusiastically embraced the cooperative dimensions of women's peace work.

For many Jewish women, the ideological underpinnings of both maternalism and Jewishness combined to provide a unique peace calling. After suffrage and the end of the war, one NCJW speaker exhorted her audience to combine their Jewish and female identities through peace work:

Not long ago we were interested in the rights of women—now we talk of the responsibilities of women. . . . And if we have greater responsibilities as women and as mothers, what shall we say of our responsibilities as Jewish mothers? We have a great heritage. We must know it and understand it.[59]

As Fanny Brin explained Jewish women's role, "One can say of the entrance of women into public life at this time of social change as did Mordecai of Esther when she was taken into the household of the King, 'Who knows but that you have come into power for such an hour as this?'"[60] The reference to the biblical book of Esther, one of the few named for a woman, was not lost on an audience of Jewish women who believed that striving for peace was their heritage of old.

Maternalism formed an ideology common to both American identity and Jewish identity. American women deployed ideas about motherhood to extend their spheres of activity outward from the household into reform, and Jewish women in NCJW, NFTS, and other organizations used similar tactics to justify the increasingly public nature of their own communal work. Because maternalism reaffirmed gender roles, it offered Jewish women a way to acculturate within a familiar framework. They did not have to abandon traditional ethnic or religious Jewish ideas about the centrality of motherhood in order to move into the arenas now occupied by other American women engaged in reform. Maternalism even exerted a cross-class appeal for Jewish women, as it implied a public role that many working-class Jewish women were already accustomed to and often unwilling to abandon, especially if they were politically engaged. The centrality of Jewishness to their peace work meant that few Jewish women denied their religious identity, even in the face of the kind of prejudice that might hurt their cause. As a result, Jewish women's activism allowed for a fruitful combination of their Jewish and gender identities in a women's movement that at least purported to put aside any differences that would compromise the goal of world peace.

Peace Activism and the Specter of Anti-Semitism during the 1920s

The postwar decade saw a flowering of opportunities for Jewish women to join the burgeoning peace movement. Some informed themselves about international affairs and then took action on their own, as did a former suffragist, Jennie Loitman Barron. She had no official sponsor for her public lectures in Boston protesting the 1921–1922 congressional appropriations for the army and navy. But she pointed out that the monies involved could build 148,000 homes and that arms limitations would allow all nations to spend their money more wisely on cities, schools, and domestic improvements. Other Jewish women joined women's peace organizations or became involved with the peace work of other women's organizations, as did Marion Misch, a Jewish communal leader from Providence who chaired the Peace and Arbitration Committee of the Rhode Island State Federation of Women's Clubs in 1919–1920. Still other Jewish women felt most comfortable working through NCJW and NFTS, which increasingly made peace a priority during the 1920s. Both NCJW and NFTS embraced the emerging version of World War I as the consequence of pro-British propaganda, greedy arms manufacturers, and myths of neutrality. This stance put them right in line with a cynical and disgruntled American public, which questioned the need for the United States to become involved in problems overseas.[61]

Unfortunately, as Maud Nathan discovered at the 1920 IWSA meeting in Geneva, a narrative about "merchants of death" allowed ample opportunity for a number of official speakers to refer to "Jew Profiteers" as the source of the recent misery. Nathan first tried privately to convince the speakers to retract their statements but then decided to protest publicly. She used statistics to demonstrate how widespread profiteering was and how unfair it was to single out any one group for blame. Her message that prejudice and discrimination would not lead to world peace seemed well received by the IWSA audience, but Nathan saw the incident as a harbinger of continued and growing anti-Semitism on the world stage. Other American Jewish women had similar experiences abroad. When the WTUL leader Rose Schneiderman traveled to the Third International Congress of Trade Union Women in 1923, she was distressed by the anti-Semitic handbills she saw in Germany en route to Vienna and even more disturbed by the popular acceptance of such blatant prejudice.[62]

Despite the continuing shadow cast by anti-Semitism, future Jewish leaders of the peace movement served important apprenticeships during the early 1920s. In a 1923 article, Fanny Brin explained that women must take on the responsibility of educating the public, especially men, not to fight. She believed every woman should belong to some peace organization and that Jewish women especially should concern themselves with peace, since Jews suffered most in times of war. The following year she became chair of NCJW's Committee on Peace and Arbitration and then national NCJW president later in the decade. In 1924 Frieda Langer Lazarus signed the WPU Pledge and then became the only Jewish member of the WPU Working Committee, lobbying against war in Washington, D.C. As Gertrude Weil, an emerging leader in the women's peace movement in North Carolina, explained in an Armistice Day letter to the editor:

> Some of us took seriously and literally the statement that was current during the war that we were fighting a war to end wars. . . . That the hideous cruelties and barbarities of that war should never be repeated. . . . Surely

war is grimly real enough—ask any ex-doughboy. May not peace be made just as real?[63]

The two most influential women's peace organizations during the 1920s, NCCCW and WILPF, attracted significant Jewish membership. NCJW was one of the first members of NCCCW, and various sections sent numerous representatives to NCCCW events. After attending the 1927 NCCCW round-table, Augusta Rothschild reported back to the Baltimore NCJW that had sponsored her participation. Nine hundred delegates representing nine organizations with a combined membership of ten million women had attended. The assistant secretary of state delivered a keynote address about the proposed Kellogg-Briand pact to rule out war as an instrument of international relations. The conference consensus was that the only good policy was to sign a truly international agreement, not just a bi- or trilateral one. The NCCCW founder Carrie Chapman Catt enjoyed a particularly strong relationship with NCJW. She addressed the 1923 NCJW Triennial meeting on "War or Peace" and frequently referred to NCJW peace resolutions as models of intelligent activism. She considered Brin one of the most competent and influential peace workers in the United States, and the two women sustained a lively correspondence.[64]

Like NCCCW, WILPF also attracted both individual Jewish women and Jewish women's organizations. Some branches of WILPF, especially in densely Jewish areas, were led by Jewish women. Rose K. Edelman, the long-serving president of WILPF's Brooklyn branch, worked with the national organization to recruit Jewish women teachers and also spoke frequently to Jewish audiences ranging from the Jersey City section of NCJW to the women's auxiliary of a yeshiva in Brooklyn. Setty Swartz Kuhn, a WILPF member, welcomed an international delegation of peace activists to her Cincinnati home in 1924 and coordinated the response to the local American Legion's opposition to the visit. In 1929 the United Order of True Sisters, a national Jewish group with 12,000 members, voted to affiliate with WILPF.[65]

The widespread interest of Jewish women was not lost on WILPF leaders at home or abroad. During a countrywide lecture tour in 1924, the WILPF international secretary Gertrude Baer, Jewish herself, commented, "Always whenever approached have the Jewish groups willingly and enthusiastically shown their sympathy."[66] WILPF encouraged Jewish women's membership by passing a resolution condemning anti-Semitism at its 1924 International Congress and distributing the pamphlet *Anti-Semitism, an Aftermath of the War* for discussion. At the 1926 WILPF meeting in Dublin, Baer and her colleagues Lida Heymann and Anita Augsburg, the heads of the German women's peace movement, were already warning anyone who would listen about the potential threat of the fascism and anti-Semitism promoted by a would-be demagogue named Adolf Hitler.[67]

These measures became even more necessary as opponents of the peace movement tried to play on anti-Semitism by emphasizing the prominence of Jewish individuals and organizations in peace work. After attending the 1922 ICW meeting at the Hague, the NCJW member Seraphine Pisko reported that European women's "unfortunate prejudices" were palpable but hastened to add that she hoped more regular contact with Jewish women would ultimately weaken these prejudices. Instead, the situation worsened throughout the 1920s, when charges of radicalism leveled at peace groups often conflated Judaism and communism and, for good measure, referenced the notorious forgery *Protocols of the Elders of Zion* as evidence of a vast Jewish conspiracy behind the peace movement. As Catt disapprovingly commented in 1924, "Such terrifying tales are being told to women about the Bolsheviki and the Jews and a super-state ruled by them that women are afraid even to pass resolutions in favor of any peace movement."[68]

Clearly, not all pacifists were socialists, much less Bolsheviks, whose ideas about world peace had more to do with revolutionary class warfare than international relations, but some Red-baiting of even middle-class peace activists proved an effective strategy for opponents of the peace movement during the 1920s. For Rosika Schwimmer, already under attack for her radical beliefs but still acceptable enough to be published in the mainstream *B'nai B'rith Magazine*, Jewish women's peace activism was in itself not only so brave as to defuse accusations of Jewish cowardice but also significant in a gendered sense:

> I am always slightly amused when indignant fighters against the contemptuous generalization that Jews are cowards, burst into a recital of "heroic actions" of Jewish soldiers. It isn't my business to defend "Jewish courage" yet I always feel provoked to ask: "is that all you have to disprove the stupid generalization? And what about the courage of Jewish women?" When moral courage once will clearly be recognized as superior to mere physical bravery the record of Jewish women's courage will balance if not outweigh the evidential value of Jewish military acts.[69]

Jewish pacifists constantly faced stereotypes of Jews as cowardly, weak, and disloyal to their country, but the anti-Semitism so apparent inside and outside the peace movement did not discourage Jewish women from acting on their principles.

Jewish Women's Organizations and Peace

As a result of these problems with anti-Semitism in the broader peace and women's movements, a significant number of Jewish women chose to direct their peace work through Jewish organizations, regardless of the good will of NCCCW and WILPF. The NCJW, the Reform movement's NFTS, and the Conservative movement's Women's League of the United Synagogue all became major players in the peace movement. It is not surprising that these were the Jewish women's organizations most committed to peace, since they were also home to the American Jewish women most interested in using American associational life to demonstrate their acculturation. The mainly middle-class women who belonged to these organizations were proud to be Jewish but emphasized the interests and priorities, like peace, that they shared with other women. From its earliest years NCJW had successfully positioned itself as the primary representative of middle-class Jewish women. It was now the organization approached by both the suffrage and birth control movements when they were seeking the most effective ways to gain Jewish women's support. The NFTS was also especially successful as a representative Jewish women's organization because Reform Judaism's liberal practice and theology seemed more American to women's organizations than other denominations. More recent immigrants or more ritually observant Jewish women were less likely to see the peace movement as a stage for the performance of American identity, although the members of the Conservative movement's Women's League made a special point of combining tradition and modernity.[70]

Founded in 1913 to enlarge women's public responsibilities in Judaism and the synagogue, NFTS brought together thousands of synagogue sisterhood members across the United States. Within a decade, NFTS had become a cooperating organization of the National Council for Limitation of Armaments, later NCPW. President Hattie Wiesenfield stated emphatically that NFTS steered clear of politics but saw peace as a humanitarian rather than a political cause, especially for mothers who suffered the most during wartime. By 1925 NFTS had a standing national committee on peace and made regular contributions to NCCCW and NCPW. Local sisterhoods took up issues such as U.S. membership in the Permanent Court of International Justice and forwarded resolutions to their political representatives, as did the sisterhood of Oheb Shalom, Gertrude Weil's Goldsboro's congregation in North Carolina in 1925. In 1926 the sisterhood of Temple Emanu-El in New York participated in "Peace Week," hosting an interfaith meeting at which Lillian Wald delivered the keynote address.[71]

There may have been some lingering discomfort among NFTS members about expanding their religious mission into public affairs. The Pennsylvania Federation of Temple Sisterhoods invited Maud Nathan to speak to the 1926 biennial meeting on "Women in Public Life" to address these concerns. However, the same meeting also hosted a forum on "What Shall Be the Contribution of the Jewish Women for World Peace," and there does not seem to have been much resistance to continuing peace work. The following year, NFTS passed resolutions supporting international disarmament and arbitration, urging the elimination of compulsory military training, endorsing the Traffic in Arms Conference treaty restrictions on chemical and germ warfare, and recommending America's entry into the World Court. NFTS forwarded these resolutions to the U.S. Senate. By 1929 NFTS's Committee on International Peace had brushed aside any previous claims to apolitical behavior, forcefully denouncing the rejection of Rosika Schwimmer's citizenship petition. To those who questioned the need for NFTS to take positions on these issues, Jennie Kubie, chairman of the Committee on International Peace, explained, "We, as Jewish women, have, I feel, a distinct duty in this work. For Peace has always been the prayer and the hope of our People, and Peace is truly our mission."[72]

The Conservative movement's Women's League shared these sentiments, becoming involved with peace work immediately upon its 1918 establishment to perpetuate traditional Judaism in the home, synagogue, and community. In 1924 the American Peace Committee awarded the Bok Peace Award to the Women's League for its peace education efforts. The Women's League and NFTS cooperated on programs that would educate Jewish women beyond their own membership. For example, New York's Central Synagogue sisterhood sponsored a peace poster contest. The winning design—the biblical image of a lion lying down with a lamb—was available to other Jewish women's groups for three-quarters of one cent to be sold for one cent each and the profits used for peace work.[73]

Because the Women's League's founding mission focused on preserving traditional Judaism in the face of constant threats from assimilation, there were members who resisted taking any kind of stand on peace issues, concerned that the patriotism of the Women's League was at stake and that it was not their place to dictate to politicians or policymakers. At the 1927 Women's League convention, a resolution condemning military training in schools did not pass for this reason. Another resolution, this one not to support any future wars, passed only after delegate Dorothy Prussian, who was also an active WPU member, told the group "that if our belief in God as Jewish women, daughters of Israel, meant anything, it had to mean the repudiation of war. . . . [We hear] a lot about the importance of preserving traditional Judaism. In three minutes of another war, nothing would be left of traditional Judaism." Well aware of the catastrophic destruction World War I had brought to Jewish communities all over Europe, the members of the Women's League ultimately agreed that promoting peace would further, not distract from, their core purpose.[74]

Of all the Jewish women's groups involved in peace work, NCJW became the exemplar of the movement of many American women's organizations toward serious engagement with international affairs and world peace. Its leaders urged members to join other women in working for peace. In 1917 Gertrude Feibleman, chair of the Committee on Peace and Arbitration, acknowledged the difficulties of promoting pacifism during wartime but expressed the hope that Jewish women would ultimately be able to persuade the world of the righteousness of the cause. As soon as the war ended, the national NCJW office asked all local sections to create a Committee on Peace and Arbitration if they did not already have one and to adopt pro-League of Nations resolutions.[75]

Local sections began their own peace initiatives. The Staten Island section sponsored a peace medal to be awarded to a member of every eighth- and twelfth-grade class who publicized peace at his or her school. The Cincinnati section ran an essay contest in its religious schools on the topic of "What Can the Boys and Girls of Today do to Avert the Wars of Tomorrow?" The Philadelphia section held a "Peace Tableaux" program with readings, tableaux, and demonstrations of international dancing to promote international cultural appreciation. This program was described in *The Jewish Woman*, NCJW's national magazine, as a model that other sections could emulate. In 1922 NCJW resolved that "war should be abolished and should be outlawed by international agreement."[76]

Not every member of NCJW was even mildly pacifist. The organization's former president Rebekah Kohut, for one, tartly said later that "pacifism against a monster was a suicidal attitude which favored the monster."[77] At first the national NCJW proceeded with some caution toward expanding its peace work. When in 1924 Fanny Brin encouraged NCJW to send a letter to President Coolidge protesting the idea of a Mobilization Day, she was rebuffed by national officers who worried about repercussions, especially since the War Department was then monitoring women's organizations for disloyalty. By supporting America's entry into the League of Nations and the World Court and working on disarmament issues, however, NCJW had already attracted attention. That the organization was associated in the public arena with peace work became all too clear when it appeared on the

infamous "Spider Web Chart" in 1924 that linked it with other such supposedly dangerous and subversive groups as WILPF.[78] Yet as an organization,
on both local and national levels NCJW became increasingly committed to
peace. This development was due especially to the growing influence of Brin,
who moved into the national presidency after heading the Committee on
Peace and Arbitration, and Estelle Sternberger, editor of *The Jewish Woman*
and author of several books about peace.

Both Sternberger and Brin used *The Jewish Woman* magazine to reach a
wide audience. In 1926 Sternberger editorialized in favor of the joining the
World Court, a step she felt was necessary to make the United States a force
for preventing another war. She admitted that such a move might still allow
the United States to otherwise maintain its isolationist stance but hoped that
it would bring the country into "close partnership in the mission of international peace." Brin's Committee on Peace and Arbitration reports educated
readers about pressing international issues and outlined practical programs
for carrying out peace work. Writing about the Kellogg-Briand pact, she
reminded NCJW members that they were among twelve million American
women working to gain favorable public opinion. She recommended readings
for every local section's peace committee chair, including WILPF bulletins and
NCPW publications. Brin urged each section to hear a report on peace work
at every meeting and encouraged all of them to pass and publicize resolutions
supporting the Kellogg-Briand treaty. Under Brin and Sternberger's leadership, even the National Council of Jewish Juniors created a peace committee,
proudly proclaiming itself "the only Jewish youth group who has dedicated
itself to peace." These efforts paid off on the international Jewish women's
scene as well. When the World Council of Jewish Women met in Hamburg
in 1929, the international cooperation of Jewish women for the cause of world
peace was one of the few issues all present could agree to support.[79]

One of the reasons that NCJW achieved such prominence in the larger
American peace movement was the organization's long-standing ties to the
larger American women's movement. From its founding in 1893, NCJW had
been connected to other women's groups. At NCJW's 1896 convention in
New York, Mary Lowe Dickinson, the National Council of Women's president, addressed the group and spoke of Jewish women like biblical figures
Miriam and Deborah who did good in the wider world. As a matter of
course, NCJW's New York section was invited by other women's groups to
join the May 1907 celebration of the upcoming Hague Conference on international peace.[80]

NCJW representatives regularly appeared on the programs of the conventions of women's and peace groups. The national NCJW president Rose

Brenner served on the program committee on the 1923 National Council of Women biennial meeting. The Minneapolis NCJW section joined eighteen other city organizations to observe No More War Day on July 6, 1924.[81] At a statewide peace rally in Kentucky, Laura Slaughter Ottenheimer, chairman of NCJW's Committee on Civic and Communal Affairs, delivered the keynote address:

> When our preachers and priests and rabbis, when our inspired super-beings, the poets, painters and sculptors and dramatists, pay tribute to the hero for peace as he has to the hero for war; when the public shall become educated to treat with valor the citizen who will give up a lucrative position to fill an office of responsibility for his city or state; when intelligent pageants will take the place of drills, then everyone will labor for peace, and peace will be forever ours.[82]

Her smooth interpolation of rabbis into the list of religious authorities demonstrated the extent to which Jewish women's peace work was increasingly taken for granted. By the time NCPW's Florence Brewer Boeckel wrote "Women in International Affairs" for a special 1929 issue of the *Annals of the American Academy of Political and Social Science*, her inclusion of NCJW as a prominent example of the great activism of American women's organizations in international affairs seemed only natural.[83]

Some Jewish women purposefully chose to work for peace through either a general women's peace organization or a Jewish women's group; others, such as Brin, who remained active in WILPF and NCCCW even while ascending to the national NCJW presidency, took many simultaneous paths toward peace work. Jennie Franklin Purvin's experiences shed some light on how Jewish women's commitment to peace played out over time and fluctuated depending on circumstance and context. Purvin maintained a consistent interest in peace amid her many other activities. In 1923 she went to a peace meeting at a private home, attended a community-wide peace dinner at Merton Hall, and gave a speech at the Association for Peace Education, a Chicago group that included rabbis and other local Jewish leaders on its board. Purvin addressed the group as a representative of the Chicago Woman's Aid, another Jewish women's organization in which she was very active. The Chicago Woman's Aid staged a series of peace events during the 1920s, and by 1929 Purvin not only represented the Chicago Woman's Aid in its peace programs but had also become a member of the speakers bureau run by the Chicago branch of WILPF. She did not have the highest opinion of the WILPF women, commenting later in her diary that they were "delightful women with complete laissez faire methods," but she continued to work with them.[84]

In her religious life, too, Purvin found plentiful outlets for her interests in peace. She heard prominent rabbis like Cleveland's Abba Hillel Silver and Chicago's Louis Mann deliver peace sermons and found it difficult to understand how any of her fellow American Jews could still believe in war.[85] Purvin found that Jewish identity was bound up with her peace work. She wrote in 1930 after a busy decade in the peace movement:

> There is no flag on earth which does not float over some part of Judaism. . . . There is no corner of the globe in which the fortune of the Jew is not the fortune of every other Jew. Thus does it behoove us to make the most of all the ability we may possess, to establish lasting peace on earth. . . . It is our mission, as Jews, as citizens of America, to promote the doctrine of peace.[86]

Purvin's experiences demonstrate the ways in which Jewish women's communal and religious life supported the peace movement. Her reference to both Jewish and American identity also illustrates the complex social and political identities developed by Jewish women engaged in peace work. For many Jewish women, involvement in peace work allowed them not only to pursue a cause they passionately believed in but also to do so in an organic fusion of identities and affiliations.

Conclusion

The 1920s seemed full of promise to peace activists of all stripes. The Washington Conference of 1922, which limited the naval arms race and established some international security agreements, and the Kellogg-Briand Pact of 1928, which outlawed war as an instrument of international relations, promised a brighter future. American peace workers and internationalists remained frustrated by the U.S.'s refusal to join the League of Nations or the World Court, but campaigns to change that policy proved to be important rallying points for a variety of peace groups. Ever-increasing numbers of American Jewish women informed themselves about international affairs, joined one of the major women's peace organizations like WILPF, and became involved with the peace departments of large women's organizations like the League of Women Voters. They looked to Jewish international role models such as Aletta Jacobs, Rosa Manus, and Gertrude Baer, leaders of the women's peace movement in Europe, for inspiration.[87] Due to continuing strains of anti-Semitism in the peace movement, many felt most comfortable working through NCJW and NFTS, both of which made peace a priority.

Throughout the 1920s and early 1930s, Jewish activists developed close working relationships and deep friendships with non-Jewish women in the peace movement. Both the Jewish community as a whole and a network of socially progressive American women encouraged Jewish women's peace activism in all its variety. Maternalism, feminism, Jewishness, and a growing conviction that the United States could play a special role in the world provided strong motivations for the growing numbers of American Jewish women active in peace work. All these convictions would face serious challenges in the years ahead.

4

"They Have Been the Pioneers"

American Jewish Women and the Mainstreaming of Birth Control

It is no more p   ...   flow of contraceptive knowledge
than to stem the tides of the oceans that wash the shore.[1]
—Dr. Hannah Mayer Stone, 1937

In April 1929, the police raided the Birth Control Clinical Research Bureau
(BCCRB) in New York, then under Dr. Hannah Mayer Stone's direction. An
anonymous tip had resulted in an undercover sting operation. Posing as a
patient, Mary McNamara, a policewoman, gave a family and medical history,
underwent a physical exam, and was prescribed a diaphragm and shown
how to use it. The "patient" returned to the clinic for her follow-up appointment with Stone and then came back a few days later with a team that confiscated medical supplies and patient records. Stone and four other doctors and
nurses were arrested and sent to the police station in a paddy wagon. The
trial received a great deal of attention in the press and also led to the panic-
stricken phone calls of hundreds of women to Morris Ernst, Stone's Jewish
attorney, who assured them that the seizure of their medical records was only
temporary. Doctors' outrage at this breach of patient confidentiality helped
bring the weight of the medical establishment to bear on the case, and the
judge at the preliminary hearing ended up dismissing all the charges when
a bevy of experts testified that there were medical indications for prescribing contraception to the policewoman, meaning that no one's actions were
illegal. Ironically, McNamara later came to the clinic as a legitimate patient.[2]

As the birth control movement gained traction from the early 1920s on,
activists negotiated a minefield of legal obstacles, hostility to women's leadership, and deeply divided public opinion. Virtually every clinic that opened
soon boasted a full client list, demonstrating the dire need among poor
women, in particular, for contraceptive services. Still, opposition to wom-
en's public activism around what seemed to many to be the most private of
issues continued. American Jewish women, who saw their family sizes drop
sharply during the first decades of the twentieth century, clearly made use of
the steady expansion of access to contraception.[3] Yet many did not confine

Dr. Hannah Mayer Stone.
Courtesy of the Library of
Congress

themselves to using birth control as a means of gaining personal autonomy
or as a strategy for their own families' social mobility. They saw themselves as
part of a movement of great social significance and supported it in a variety
of ways. As individuals they played key roles in birth control organizations
as editors, administrators, lecturers, donors, and fund-raisers. They contributed to clinics as doctors, nurses, lay volunteers, and board members. And as
members of Jewish women's organizations, they helped fund clinics, encourage public discussion of the issue within the American Jewish community,
and counter concerns about the relationship of birth control to religion and
to the popular but, to many Jews, potentially disturbing eugenics movement.
Regardless of their path toward engagement, participation in the mainstreaming of the birth control movement encouraged them to rethink what was possible for them as women and as Jews living through rapid social change.

   Hannah Mayer Stone, a daughter of immigrants who became a pediatri-
cian, occupied a special place in the birth control movement of the 1920s and
1930s. Margaret Sanger hired her to replace the first director of the BCCRB
in New York. As a result of her new position, Stone was denied privileges
at New York's Lying-In Hospital and excluded from the New York Academy
of Medicine. During her first year on the job, Stone provided contraceptive

advice to more than 1,600 women, keeping comprehensive records that she presented in 1925 at the Sixth International Neo-Malthusian and Birth Control Conference to an audience of more than 1,000 doctors.[4]

With Sanger's encouragement and despite a difficult legal climate, Stone produced numerous papers and pamphlets, contributing greatly to the clinical research on birth control methods and clinic clients. Her writings included *Contraceptive Methods of Choice* (1926), *Therapeutic Contraception* (1928), *Contraception and Mental Hygiene* (1933, with Henriette Hart), and *Birth Control: A Practical Survey* (1937).[5] She frequently spoke about birth control, delivering talks to all kinds of audiences on techniques, sociological perspectives, the so-called safe period of the menstrual cycle, planned pregnancies, and impotence. Back at home at the BCCRB, Stone used three-dimensional models of the pelvis and reproductive system to teach women about their bodies. She interpreted the legally required medical indication for birth control broadly, including women's desire for spacing their children as well as their physical problems as factors in prescribing contraception. She and her husband, the urologist Abraham Stone, together pioneered marital counseling, blaming social conditions rather than individual dysfunctions for sex problems. In 1935 they published the well-received *A Marriage Manual*, which was translated into several languages worldwide. The Stones lectured together on marriage and sex topics and always answered audience questions about both conception and contraception.[6]

Stone was a beloved figure in the birth control movement, described by one observer as a "small, slim, charming woman." Other Jewish women doctors wrote to her often. Sarah Marcus, for example, a staff physician at the Maternal Health Association of Cleveland, kept up a chatty correspondence full of matters both personal and professional. Sanger, a notoriously prickly woman who sometimes viewed her most competent allies as threats to her leadership, never felt that way about Stone. She "loved Hannah Stone," Sanger's son recalled, "I don't think Mother and Hannah Stone ever had a cross word."[7] Stone and Sanger's successful collaboration was all the more remarkable because it survived what could have been an extremely uncomfortable conflict. When Sanger opened a birth control clinic in Harlem in 1930, she appointed Stone as medical director. Stone ran the Harlem clinic much as she ran the BCCRB, but she was frustrated by what she perceived as the disinterest of the staff in taking instruction on contraceptive techniques and the relatively high failure rate of the clinic patients to use birth control correctly. Community members in Harlem, in turn, found Stone insensitive and insisted that the clinic add African American staff. Stone immediately agreed to and acted on this suggestion, but Sanger still found it prudent to bring in a representative from the Rosenwald Fund that paid for the clinic to assess the situation. The observer found no fault in Stone and attributed the tension at the clinic to racial misunderstanding, but Sanger replaced Stone nonetheless, appointing Marie Levinson Warner, another Jewish doctor. African American doctors, nurses, and social workers worked smoothly with Warner, and there were no further problems. Stone lost no status in Sanger's eyes and continued to play a central role in both the national and international birth control movement.[8]

When Stone died suddenly in 1941, she was greatly mourned. Two hundred fifty people attended her funeral at the Free Synagogue, presided over by the long-standing birth control advocate Rabbi Sidney Goldstein, and Sanger served as one of the honorary pallbearers. Condolence letters came pouring in from birth control activists everywhere, including many of the Jewish women for whom she had been a role model. Warner, Stone's replacement at the Harlem clinic, wrote, "I, who was associated with her from the 'early days' of the birth control movement am deeply moved at the loss of my 'teacher' in birth control." Dr. Cheri Appel, one of Stone's former assistants at the BCCRB, similarly wrote, "We needn't tell you of the sincere affection we had for Dr. Hannah as an individual and as a person."[9] Stone's Labor Temple colleague, the historian Will Durant, eulogized her at a special memorial service, declaring

> [We] will not think of her as the fearless crusader, facing contumely and jail in a once unpopular cause, and by her quiet courage and imperturbable courtesy, winning battle after battle in the war of liberation for the women of America; but we will picture her as she sat before us in her home, dressed with the simplicity of a stoic Matron, her features recalling the Sephardic Aristocracy; calm in every emergency; not raising her voice in argument nor complaint.[10]

The references in Durant's memorial to Stone's courageous activism, magnetic personality, and Jewish identity illustrate the multiple perspectives from which her colleagues appreciated her unique gifts. She was eulogized by periodicals as divergent as the *New York Times* and the Yiddish Labor Zionist *Die Pionern Froy* (*The Pioneer Woman*), further demonstrating her prominence in both the birth control and the Jewish communities for whom her work was so beneficial and meaningful.[11]

Stone exemplified the Jewish women who were so central to the birth control movement. Nearly all women advocates for birth control believed that independent facilities free of the organized control of American medicine should distribute birth control, though they disagreed about the degree of professional training necessary. The clinics that resulted from this innovative thinking offered unique opportunities to Jewish women as consumers, activists, and doctors. Working-class and middle-class Jewish women alike, especially those living in urban areas, increasingly enjoyed access to contraception, which allowed them to shape their families as they desired. Because disseminating birth control information and distributing contraceptive devices only gradually became legal, clinics were largely privately funded and operated by networks of birth control volunteers. Both the American Birth Control League (ABCL) and the Voluntary Parenthood League (VPL) knew that Jewish women could be depended upon to offer support. Jewish women's organizations like the Chicago Woman's Aid and the National Council for Jewish Women (NCJW) became essential activist partners. An important cadre of Jewish women doctors turned to birth control clinics as places where they could practice medicine, conduct research, and contribute to a cause they virtually all believed in. Although there was a robust Jewish religious debate over birth control, and the relationship between birth control and eugenics troubled some, overall American Jews took advantage of expanding contraceptive opportunities and supported the movement. The generally positive relationship between the American Jewish community and the birth control movement enhanced the central roles American Jewish women played in bringing contraception into the mainstream during the 1920s and 1930s.

The Clinic Movement

The demographic shift to smaller families signaled the ongoing significance of birth control to the American Jewish community during the interwar period. Demonstrating their eagerness to catch up to the new family model of a modern society, Jewish families experienced a reduction in fertility between 1920 and 1940 that was two times that of the native-born white population. The Depression led to postponed marriages and fewer children, but the birth control movement enabled the drop in fertility to take place, with the general birthrate falling from 21.3 births per 1,000 people in 1930 to 18.4 in 1933. Jewish women gave birth to 69 babies per 100 born to white women in the general population. They often delayed their firstborn, lengthened the spacing between childbirths, and had only two or three children. Class differentials affected Jewish women's fertility rates. A 1938 study of Buffalo showed that the poorest Jewish families still had the most children, though the average Jewish family had only 2.49 children. Still, family size was shrinking among the Jewish working class as well as the middle class there, due at least in part to the dissemination of birth control information by Buffalo unions and the influence of Jewish social workers who steered poor Jewish women to clinics if they requested guidance. Clinic doctors in Newark, New Jersey, during the late 1920s and early 1930s noted that Jewish women of all class backgrounds had the lowest number of pregnancies.[12]

The growing number of clinics across the United States facilitated Jewish women's increasing control over their fertility. As clinics rapidly expanded in number and size, birth control moved further into the mainstream. This was exactly the outcome that Margaret Sanger and Mary Ware Dennett had hoped for when they dedicated many of the resources of ABCL and VPL to clinics. During the 1920 and 1930s, there were three major types of facilities: hospital clinics controlled by doctors, state health department clinics that also provided basic medical care, and voluntary clinics run by lay people and staffed by doctors and nurses. Most clinics were associated with either ABCL or VPL, but not all. ABCL required associated facilities to pay one-fourth of their fees to the national organization, so some clinics, like the Maternal Health Association of Cleveland where Sarah Marcus worked, opted to remain independent. Even to clinics that did not choose formal affiliation, ABCL was willing to provide samples of medical records forms, supply requisitions, follow-up letters to patients, referral forms, and monthly reports.[13]

The ABCL recommended readings for doctors but also suggested that they secure specialized training. This training was necessary because few American doctors knew much about the use of the diaphragms that all the clinics prescribed, usually in conjunction with spermicidal jelly. Invented in 1842 by a German gynecologist, the Mensinga diaphragm was a rubber ring with springs. Diaphragms were in wide use in European birth control facilities and proved more effective than cervical caps. As they required individual fittings by trained professionals, however, clinic doctors and patients alike needed to learn how to use them. Diaphragms presented challenges to poor women without privacy and running water, but they were the most effective method then available, and they put control of contraception in the hands of women.[14]

Birth control clinics spread rapidly, growing in number from 39 in 1929 to 232 in 1935, with 26 in the New York City area alone. There were legal problems with some of these clinics, as Sanger's short-lived 1916 clinic in Brownsville foreshadowed. Even in states like Illinois, where doctors could legally disseminate birth control, the state commissioner of health would not allow a public clinic at Hull House. Instead, the Illinois Birth Control League opened private clinics. From 1924 to 1932, 8 clinics served 22,871 women in the state. The proliferation of clinics meant that multiple segments of the population could be reached. When Sanger opened the Harlem clinic in 1930, for instance, during its five years of existence it served thousands of African American women who might otherwise have had no place to go for gynecological exams and contraception.[15]

Most clinics operated along similar lines. Staff ideally included a doctor, social worker, and secretary. The secretary, often a volunteer activist, charted the personal, economic, and social history of the patient. The doctor took a medical history, performed a gynecological exam, and, if indicated, fitted the patient for a diaphragm and taught her how to use it. Patients were supposed to come back six weeks later for a follow-up visit and every three months thereafter. The social worker coordinated the follow-up appointments and made home visits to delinquents. The ideal clinic consisted of a reception room, playroom for children, interview room, and examination room.[16] The fact that a playroom was often provided indicated the prevalence of women who already had children coming to the clinics to seek help with future family planning. Collection of patient data allowed staff to conduct research into the demography of the patients. One such study estimated that fewer than 10 percent of clinic patients had never used a contraceptive before. Condoms, withdrawal, and douches were most common, but these methods showed a high failure rate. Of the first 500 cases at the Illinois Birth Control League clinic in Chicago, those women had already had 1,766 pregnancies, 164 abortions, and 197 miscarriages, the presumption being that many of these latter were "induced miscarriages."[17] Clinic patients generally wanted not to prevent conception altogether but to space childbirth according to their medical, social, and economic needs.

Many Jewish women who came to birth control clinics already practiced contraception and were merely seeking the most reliable form. Of the 112 Jewish women seen at the Bureau for Contraceptive Advice in Baltimore in 1933, only 6 had never used birth control before. Ninety-five percent of the Jewish women, most of them foreign-born, in a 1934 survey had used birth control before coming to a New York clinic, 40 percent of them right after marriage and another 40 percent before a second pregnancy. Even before receiving special training at the clinic in the use of contraceptive devices, these women had found other birth control methods approximately 75 percent effective. Another study by the same authors showed in 1935 that 45 percent of Jewish couples used birth control right after marriage and 87 percent before a second pregnancy, most of them relying on either withdrawal or condoms before the women were fitted for diaphragms at clinics. They were also far more likely to plan their pregnancies than their Protestant or Catholic counterparts.[18] The resulting decline in family size was seen by Jewish parents and observers alike as a sign of Americanization.[19] Smaller families improved chances for upward economic mobility and enabled the creation of child-centered homes on the American middle-class model.

Jewish Women's Organizations and the Birth Control Movement

The demonstrable interest of so many Jewish women in safe and effective contraception was evident not only in the large number who went to clinics but also in the widespread support of Jewish women's organizations for the birth control movement. A 1931 *Birth Control Review* article argued that the best way to reach women who most needed birth control information and contraceptive materials was to work with charitable and communal organizations. The author cited the Maternal Aid Society, a Jewish agency for prenatal care on New York's Lower East Side, as an example of a community agency that, when approached by ABCL, readily agreed to include birth control information among its programs for poor neighborhood women.[20] By 1931 there was nothing particularly innovative about this working relationship, but the fact that an article in *Birth Control Review* used a Jewish organization as an example of best practices suggests the extent to which significant numbers of Jewish women's organizations had become very closely tied to the birth control movement.

In some places, Jewish women's organizations served as major providers of birth control services. In Atlanta, the Jewish Social Service League funded a clinic at Grady Memorial Hospital that provided contraception to both white and African American patients. A group of Jewish women raised private funds and worked with the Jewish Welfare Fund of Detroit to open the Mothers Clinic for Family Regulation in 1926, the only birth control clinic between New York and Chicago at the time. Elsie Kohut Sulzberger, NCJW leader Rebekah Kohut's stepdaughter, served as president, and a range of women from various elements of the Jewish community helped staff the clinic, fund-raise, and secure the cooperation of the Jewish Social Service Bureau and the Jewish Centers Association. Only 10 percent of the clients were Jewish; the clinic served the entire Detroit community, including, albeit with separate hours, a significant African American clientele.[21]

Birth control clinics attracted all kinds of Jewish communal interests. Local networking widened circles of Jewish support; at a clinic in Little Rock, Arkansas, the volunteer receptionist Raida Cohn Pfeifer also served on the executive committee and brought her mother, sister, brother-in-law, and mother-in-law onto the board. The annual reports of clinics all over the country included rabbis' names on list of trustees or advisory council members. Cooperation with Jewish social services was common. In Chicago, the Jewish Social Service Bureau offered sex education classes for both birth control and improved marital relations. Starting in 1926, families were referred for sex hygiene services for multiple reasons, from poverty to the mental deficiency of parents or children to illness to a history of abortions. In every case, both the husband and the wife had to agree to accept the services. Both received full medical exams, and then a woman doctor fit the wife for a diaphragm and taught her about contraception. After a few years, the Jewish Social Service Bureau began to provide these services even to newly married couples. As a result of such institutional cooperation, Jewish communal professionals became invaluable to the birth control movement. In this role, Harry H. Lurie, director of the Bureau of Jewish Social Research, spoke about "Child Welfare and Birth Control: What the White House Conference Left Out" at the 1931 ABCL annual meeting.[22]

Across the United States, a variety of Jewish women's organizations supported clinics and even broke the law when they felt communal interests would be better served by the birth control movement than current legislation restricting contraception. The accomplishments of the Jewish women's organizations served not only the Jewish community but the larger community as well, as in Atlanta and Detroit. When the Chicago Woman's Aid, an elite Jewish women's philanthropic group, began to consider whether to support the opening of a clinic, the question first came before the group's Public Health Committee, which sent Irma G. Byfield to a 1923 speech Margaret Sanger delivered in Chicago about the morality of birth control. After Byfield reported favorably on Sanger's speech and on the birth control efforts of local Jewish doctors like Rachelle Yarros and Olga Ginzburg, the Chicago Woman's Aid enthusiastically agreed that supporting a clinic, both by raising funds and providing volunteers, would be a natural extension of its mission to work as Jewish women to improve the general community. In 1927 the Chicago Woman's Aid established a clinic in the Jewish People's Institute building. The Jewish women's group maintained its support for local access to contraception over a long period and in 1940 sponsored another clinic at the Jewish Social Service Bureau.[23]

Other Jewish women's organizations also participated in the birth control movement. In 1933, the Reform movement's National Federation of Temple Sisterhoods (NFTS) passed a resolution endorsing the legislative effort to exempt medical professionals from laws regulating the sending of birth control information and devices through the mail. Members of Bas Lomeda, an association of Jewish women college graduates in Minneapolis, invited the executive secretary of the Minnesota Birth Control League to address them on "Birth Control: Its Contribution to a New Social Order." At the February 1935 "Birth Control Comes of Age" dinner in Washington, D.C., one of the greetings read aloud came from Fanny Brin, the national president of NCJW.[24]

By then, both the national NCJW and local NCJW sections had become important supporters of the birth control movement. In 1931 NCJW passed an official resolution demanding the legalization of disseminating contraception through the mail, which the national body then asked each section to affirm. Like most other sections, the Baltimore NCJW required little discussion time and voted overwhelmingly in favor of the resolution. Local NCJW sections often worked closely with the relevant state birth control associations. In New Jersey in 1932, representatives from the New Jersey Birth Control League addressed both the Newark and Jersey City NCJWs , which then supported the Maternal Health Center in Newark, the first clinic in New Jersey. A mix of local and national decisions went into NCJW's birth control policies. In 1933 the New York NCJW's legislative committee undertook an intensive study of proposals related to birth control but waited for both local board approval and national NCJW recommendations before making definite policy statements. By 1938 NCJW appeared on a list of national women's organizations that reliably lobbied in favor of birth control bills. At the Triennial convention that year, NCJW proclaimed that it stood for "the principle of birth control information and urge[d] cooperation whenever possible."[25]

Local NCJW sections moved beyond offering resolutions. When the New York NCJW began to support birth control clinics, terms such as "Maternal Health Clinic" were the preferred euphemisms and remained the nomenclature even after most of the legal barriers had been removed. In February 1931, ABCL approached the New York NCJW with a request to open such a clinic in Council House, the NCJW-sponsored settlement house. NCJW's chair of the Health Work Committee reported that several clinics had been opened in similar community centers, and the section agreed that as long as there would be no expense to NCJW, ABCL could go ahead. The Brooklyn NCJW played a more active role in the Mother's Health Bureau it sponsored, working with the United Jewish Aid Societies to provide both funding and volunteer staff and eventually opening a second clinic in Coney Island. By the mid-1930s, all the New York–area birth control clinics associated with NCJW operated on similar lines. They were typically staffed by a doctor paid by ABCL and a nurse paid at least in part by NCJW. The NCJW tried to increase financial support as the Depression worsened and the need grew greater, insisting of their clients that the clinics were "of utmost importance not only to their economic but to their marital happiness." The New York NCJW sections maintained support for birth control clinics for a sustained period. Not until 1944 did the Brooklyn NCJW turn over the three clinics it sponsored to the Kings County Committee for Planned Parenthood, which by then was following Planned Parenthood's attempts to professionalize birth control by removing clinics from the voluntary sector.[26]

Of all the NCJWs involved in birth control, the St. Paul section earned recognition both inside and outside the Jewish community as one of the most important and innovative. A close look at the St. Paul NCJW activities illuminates the involvement of Jewish women's organizations in the movement as a whole and the way that the Depression contributed to the further mainstreaming of birth control. The St. Paul NCJW president Irma Cain Firestone, a Vassar graduate and former suffragist, provided the initial impetus. At the May 24, 1932, board meeting, the minutes recorded, "Our president presented the need of a Birth Control Clinic to meet some very urgent cases under the Jewish Welfare. Discussion followed as to the advisability of interesting outside groups or carry out this work quietly because of the immediate need." The board decided to work with a Jewish Welfare Fund representative and provide financial support for a clinic. In August, the board allotted $100 to pay for a doctor's services and supplies. The St. Paul section also joined the Minnesota Birth Control League to solicit advice and information.[27] A Minnesota Birth Control League representative explained that the diaphragms for the clinics would need to come from a Chicago supplier and would cost forty cents each, with a 2 percent discount for cash payment. The spermicidal gel that birth control clinic staff would prescribe along with the diaphragms was available from a local medical supply company for thirty cents a tube. These prosaic details revealed the dubious legality of various contraceptive techniques. Spermicidal gel, often officially labeled as something else, was locally available because there might be other uses for it, but diaphragms clearly designed as contraceptive devices had to be imported— quietly and preferably with cash payment—from another state.[28]

By January 1933, the St. Paul Mothers' Service Clinic was up and running. The local Jewish women most likely to go there were working-class women who, like Mrs. Bobronsky, with her eight children and "domestic difficulties," or Mrs. Wolf, with her five children and "drunk man," sought desperately to avoid further pregnancies. However, the St. Paul NCJW board also discreetly encouraged its largely middle-class members to take care of their own needs at the clinic as well. The board drafted a letter to all the Jewish doctors in St. Paul and Minneapolis, informing them about the clinic and suggesting that they either buy their supplies through the clinic if they wished to provide contraception at their private offices or send women who could not afford to pay to the clinic. This missive elicited a friendly warning from a local Jewish doctor that the letter should be rescinded so as not to implicate any physician in suspect activities. It would be better for women to be referred to the clinic through other channels. The board agreed but expressed its indignation at the repressive legal environment by sending a telegram to the Minnesota senators asking them to vote the pending birth control bill out of committee and into Congress.[29]

The St. Paul NCJW board continued to appropriate money for the clinic, but not until November 1933 was the Mothers' Service Clinic mentioned in the regular membership meetings, though presumably at least some of the members knew about the birth control activities of the board. NCJW provided three dollars per patient in addition to supplies at the clinic. The majority of women listed as non-paying clients had Jewish names, but the client base was certainly not all Jewish. NCJW continuously monitored the legal status of its own activities and was reassured to hear from the Minnesota Birth Control League in January 1934 that state law now allowed dissemination of birth control information to women with physical or mental health reasons not to have any more children.[30] At this point, the St. Paul NCJW began to publicize the work it was doing. In a published report to NCJW's North Central Interstate Conference, a St. Paul correspondent wrote:

> St. Paul Section has been justly proud of their Mothers' Aid Work. They have been the pioneers in sponsoring this Birth Control Education in St. Paul. Through the Jewish Family Welfare, the names of women whose health or economic situation warrant this service are secured. A trained volunteer worker makes the contact, acquaints them with the Mothers' Aid Service and arranges for their instruction, which is given them by a physician.[31]

A separate birth control committee made regular reports to St. Paul NCJW meetings and also circulated petitions urging President Roosevelt and the Minnesota congressional delegation to support pending federal birth control bills.

The success of NCJW's Mothers' Service Clinic encouraged the Minnesota Birth Control League to open its own clinic in St. Paul in May 1935. The St. Paul NCJW contributed $25 and then, after several months of discussion, decided to turn its clinic over to the Minnesota Birth Control League as well, citing the more professional environment that would result from salaried employees. It is likely that the need to provide a steady roster of volunteers as well as continuously increasing funding to the clinic put a real strain on St. Paul NCJW's resources, especially as the Depression worsened.

The opportunity to relinquish financial responsibility was too appealing to decline. The St. Paul NCJW retained a relationship with the clinic, however, regularly inviting representatives from the Minnesota Birth Control League to meetings to deliver updates in person. The Jewish women's organization continued to send substantial donations to the clinic, which was now serving a wider constituency than before as befit its move away from denominational auspices.[32] Through their activism in the birth control movement, the NCJW members had not only brought something of real value to the Jewish women of St. Paul and surrounding areas but had also cemented their role in the larger community.

The Variety of Jewish Women's Birth Control Activities

The growth of the birth control movement during the 1920s and 1930s offered Jewish women opportunities for all kinds of activism even if they did not primarily express their support through work in Jewish women's organizations. For example, as a prominent peace activist and former suffrage leader, Gertrude Weil seemed like the obvious communal leader for ABCL to approach about establishing a North Carolina birth control association. The ABCL president Eleanor Dwight Jones assumed that Weil would agree with her that poor mothers throughout the state needed birth control information, and since North Carolina had no laws against disseminating contraceptive devices, Jones hoped Weil could help persuade social service agencies to do so. At the time Jones contacted her in 1930, Weil was skeptical about the prospects of a statewide birth control association, but not long thereafter Weil wrote to Margaret Sanger to express her interest and to invite her to speak in Goldsboro. Sanger could not come to North Carolina any time soon, but she suggested other speakers and encouraged Weil to take up the work. Weil eventually played an important role in the establishment of the North Carolina Maternal Health League in 1935 and remained on the board of directors for many years. Under her direction, the North Carolina Maternal Health League focused on the gap between state and federal aid recipients who most needed birth control information and the "better class" who always had greater access to scientific knowledge.[33]

Rather than joining a board of directors or lobbying for legislation, Lenore Guttmacher decided that her birth control work would take the shape of volunteering at a clinic. While her husband Alan, later the president of Planned Parenthood of America, completed his medical internship at Johns Hopkins, Guttmacher began to take notice of the difference that class and race made to the accessibility of contraception. She became the first volunteer to work directly with clients at the Baltimore Bureau for Contraceptive Advice that Bessie Moses opened in 1927. As there were no laws in Maryland against contraception, the Baltimore clinic was free to offer information and fit women for diaphragms. Guttmacher introduced clients to basic information about their reproductive systems, helped them undress, and prepared them for their exams by the doctors, who in Moses's clinic were all women.[34]

Some Jewish women primarily expressed their interest in birth control through financial support rather than direct action. When Augusta Rosenwald, the wife of Sears Roebuck magnate Julius Rosenwald, made a sizable donation to VPL in 1923, she announced, "I consider it a more intelligent use of money to help people to get out of trouble than to provide them with relief when they are in the midst of suffering. No babies should be looked upon as trouble," Rosenwald explained, but that attitude was an inevitable consequence of too many babies too soon and could be remedied by intelligent use of birth control. Similar sentiments were expressed by the prominent philanthropist and socialite Adelaide Wolff Kahn, who helped sponsor the "Birth Control Comes of Age" dinner that Sanger held in February 1935.[35]

Few American Jewish women could match Rosenwald or Kahn's financial resources, but many worked as activists in the larger community. Jean Brandeis Tachau, Louis Brandeis's niece, served as the first president of the Kentucky Birth Control League. Bertha Beitman Herzog, Lenore Schwab Black, and Helen Schwab Hillman took a stand by becoming founding members of the Maternal Health Association of Cleveland in 1928, along with the prominent rabbi Abba Hillel Silver. In Philadelphia, Marguerite Goldsmith joined a group of birth control supporters who established the Maternal Health Center and worked to change state law so that contraceptive information would be more accessible. Commitments such as these were often long-standing, lasting even past the mid-1930s successes of the birth control movement in removing legal barriers to the dissemination of birth control. Irma Cain Firestone, the moving force behind the St. Paul NCJW's pioneering clinic during the early 1930s, served as president of Planned Parenthood of St. Paul from 1946 to 1947.[36]

In addition to offering Jewish women venues for public expression and volunteer activism, the birth control movement also offered them opportunities for professional accomplishment all the more satisfying for being motivated by activism. Stella Bloch Hanau began working in the circulation department of *Birth Control Review* and eventually moved up to assume the editorship from 1929 to 1933.[37] The lawyer Harriet Pilpel got her start by working with Sanger's counsel, Morris Ernst, on birth control cases and became one of the most renowned reproductive rights attorneys of the twentieth century. For Pilpel, the cause was at once personal and political. She later said:

> Birth control and the freedom of women to choose whether or not to have children was of burning interest to me. This may have been partly because I always wanted to have a career and children, but if I had no control over when I had the children it wouldn't have been possible for me to plan my career.[38]

Florence Rose's experiences provide one of the best examples of a Jewish woman who made her career in the birth control movement. At a meeting of former activists in 1957, Rose recalled being inspired by one of Sanger's speeches in 1930 and determining to work for her and a cause she believed in. She wrote saying she had heard that Sanger was having trouble finding a good assistant and offered herself. From the start, Rose hoped that birth control would offer both a career and a calling. Twenty-eight at the time, she wrote, "I am still young enough to be shaped into a really valuable assistant to some executive in a position that I can regard as lifelong. I look upon my job as a man would. I want it to be one that will hold my interest, enlist my sympathy, and draw me towards a worthy goal."[39] Sanger hired her immediately, and Rose became a trusted companion and important part of the movement. Her obvious competence led to an expansion of duties beyond the secretarial. During the summer of 1933 Rose went on a national lecture tour to spread support for legislation then pending in Congress, giving speech after speech in support of declassifying birth control as obscenity. She was well received nearly everywhere she went. A Seattle newspaper described her as "small, slender, and essentially feminine . . . not the type one pictures as a leader in a great crusade . . . but her always alert face glows with all the fire of a pioneer who will give all to a cause she believes worthy." During this lecture tour, as in her work in New York, one of Rose's special responsibilities was to reach out to Jewish groups.[40]

After returning to New York, Rose threw herself so feverishly into birth control work that she suffered something of a breakdown. In 1935 Sanger encouraged her to work less and spend more time outdoors, but even her reminders of the great successes Rose had already achieved could not stave off Rose's deepening depression. In August 1935 Rose requested an extended leave of absence. Sanger was preparing to go to India in any case, so she suggested Rose spend the next six months resting in Arizona and agreed to pay her $50 a month during her convalescence. The period of relaxation worked, and by the following March Rose was back in New York, visiting old friends like Judge Anna Moscowitz Kross, one of the first Jewish women on the bench in New York, to brief her on upcoming court cases related to birth control.[41]

As was the case with other Jewish birth control activists and professionals, Rose remained committed to the cause even after the eventual legal victories of the mid-1930s. During the late 1930s, she took on new duties and helped coordinate the regional educational activities of the BCCRB. She traveled to Asia to help plan public health conferences there and was temporarily trapped in Shanghai during the 1937 Japanese invasion. Her friend Sara Levine had just moved to Los Angeles with Sanger's former secretary Anna Lifshitz to work for birth control, and the correspondence among these friends and co-workers illustrated the matter-of-fact ways in which activist and Jewish identity meshed in their lives. In a December 1937 letter, for instance, Levine complained about the western regional director of the birth control organization and told Rose she was sorry to miss the Chanukah party Rose's mother hosted every year. When Rose told her that she was making plans to come West herself, Levine responded, "I hope you will get down to my house for a real good jewish [sic] meal." After a series of natural disasters in California in 1938, Rose immediately wrote to make sure her friends were safe. "I'll bet you and Anna must feel like veterans of some kind," Rose exclaimed. "She escaping an earthquake, you a flood—oh yeah, and me a war! Nice job, this birth control job—I'll bet no insurance accident company would take us if they knew we just attract trouble!"[42] Rose also maintained a far-flung correspondence with the network of women doctors, many of them Jewish, who ran clinics all over the country and became central figures in the gradual mainstreaming of birth control in America.

Jewish Women Doctors in the Birth Control Movement

Though they have received little credit for it, Jewish women played a significant role as activists for birth control at both the grassroots and leadership levels, both inside and outside the American Jewish community. What has been even less noted by historians is how prominent they also were as distributors and disseminators of birth control, although in a 1930 survey of birth control clinics, the author Caroline Hadley Robinson commented, "The Jewish physicians in the United States have done more to aid organized clinics than any other body of people."[43] A significant cadre of Jewish women doctors staffed birth control clinics throughout the United States. Bessie Moses in Baltimore; Elizabeth Kleinman and Lucile Lord-Heinstein in

Boston; Anna Samuelson in the Bronx; Evelyn Berg in Brooklyn; Olga Ginzburg and Rachelle Yarros in Chicago; Sarah Marcus in Cleveland; Nadine Kavinoky and Rochelle Seletz in Los Angeles; Esther Cohen and Golda Nobel in Philadelphia; Hannah Stone, Marie Warner, Cheri Appel, Anna Spiegelman, Naomi Yarmolinsky, and Lena Levine in New York; Hannah Seitzwick-Robbins in Trenton; and dozens of others were crucial activists. These Jewish women directed clinics, promoted sex hygiene and often marriage counseling in their communities, advocated for relaxation of anti-birth control statutes in their states, wrote books about contraception, worked to overturn restrictive legislation, advised policy makers, and, most importantly, served as the human face of the movement for many thousands of women. They also became internationally known birth control researchers. At the Seventh International Birth Control Conference in Zurich in 1930, for example, Kavinoky, Stone, and Yarros all addressed large audiences on scientific and social aspects of contraception.[44]

The Jewish women physicians who became birth control pioneers operated within the larger context of women in American medicine. During the mid-nineteenth century, efforts to raise the standards of medical education led to a series of conflicts over the best practices and to the establishment of numerous medical schools, making it easier in general to obtain a degree. These fluid professional standards eased women's access to medical education during the late nineteenth century. Meanwhile, developments in medicine and technology reduced the need for physical strength that earlier practitioners had insisted was so important. The growing use of anesthesia meant that it was difficult for doctors to continue claiming that they had to be strong men. Most important were the changes in women's roles from the mid-nineteenth century on. Although domestic ideology and gender norms continued to shape women's lives, the expansion of higher education for women and the movement of women into the professions, especially those which, like medicine, could be linked to women's traditional roles as nurturers and caretakers, encouraged hundreds of women to seek medical degrees.[45]

Many of the first generation of American women physicians received at least some of their training abroad. Not until 1893 did Johns Hopkins University, under intense pressure from a wealthy group of female donors, become the first major medical school to admit women. A sizable number of women continued to earn their degrees at women's medical schools such as the New England Female Medical College and the Woman's Medical College of Pennsylvania, but coeducational medical schools increased in number and prestige at the turn of the century. By 1900 there were more than 7,000 female doctors in America, and they faced many challenges. The American Medical Association refused to admit women as members until 1915. Like other turn-of-the-century professional women, doctors struggled to maintain a balance between work and family. During the last quarter of the nineteenth century, 25–30 percent of women doctors were married. During the first quarter of the twentieth century, 30–40 percent of women were married. These numbers meant that doctors were among the women professionals most likely to have both careers and families at a time when many female college graduates remained single by either choice or circumstance.[46]

Despite the great strides that women physicians made at the turn of the century, by the 1920s they were already losing ground. In 1902 there were 1,280 female medical students, but there were only 992 in 1926 even though women's college attendance rose sharply during that same period. The number of women doctors declined in both percentage of physicians and absolute numbers after peaking at 6 percent of the national total in 1910. In 1925 the big medical schools informally adopted a quota of approximately 5 percent for admitting women. A 1913 article in *American Hebrew* pointed out that women could go to medical school, if not vote, and noted the growing number of Jewish women doctors, but their opportunities were restricted by discrimination against both women and Jews in the medical profession.[47]

The Medical Women's National Association endorsed birth control in 1928, nearly a decade before the American Medical Association did.[48] Since public opinion generally confined women doctors to the treatment of women, the association of female physicians with the birth control movement even before 1928 was hardly surprising. Not all agreed, as some in the first few generations of women physicians had been unpleasantly startled by the large number of middle-class patients who assumed that female doctors' main role was to perform abortions.[49] It became critical for birth control doctors to differentiate abortion sharply from contraception. Still, the birth control movement offered women major professional opportunities as practitioners and, perhaps even more importantly, researchers and administrators. Female doctors supported birth control out of both personal conviction and professional interests.

There may have been a natural affinity of some female physicians for women's reproductive health, but there was another important reason Jewish women doctors became so involved in birth control work, especially in the freestanding clinics promoted by both ABCL and VPL. Many of them faced such intense double discrimination as Jews and as women that they found it nearly impossible to obtain positions within the established medical framework of hospitals or even private practices. Indeed, a major motivation for the proliferation of Jewish hospitals during the late 1800s and early 1900s was the anti-Semitism that prevented Jews from receiving thorough medical training. As one veteran of campaigns to build Jewish hospitals in Newark and Pittsburgh sarcastically wrote in 1924, "I know how much opportunity Jewish physicians have in non-Jewish hospitals . . . there is a definite need in the Jewish community."[50] However, many of the Jewish hospital boards were not too eager to allow women to take up positions that should "rightfully" belong to Jewish men. Sarah Marcus's experiences were typical. She always believed she was turned down both for medical school and then for internships because she was Jewish. Marcus eventually did graduate from medical school and worked for a doctor who dispensed pessaries and contraceptive suppositories. This experience enabled her to join the Maternal Health Association of Cleveland clinic staff in 1930, whereupon she lost her admitting privileges at several area hospitals.[51]

When Marcus first began to practice, she did not know much about diaphragms, so she went to New York to observe the work of one of the ABCL birth control clinics. She ultimately became the head of the Department of Obstetrics and Gynecology at Women's Hospital of Cleveland, and women doctors from other parts of the state came to her in turn for birth control training. Several generations of Jewish women in Cleveland availed themselves of Marcus's medical advice.[52] Through the Women's Hospital of Cleveland and the Maternal Health Association, Marcus offered not only contraceptive services but also marriage and sex counseling, which she believed necessary to prevent "the development of domestic friction and disharmony." While pregnant herself in 1935, she wrote an article on "The Planned Family as a Social Constructive Measure" that identified birth control as the pinnacle of public health work.[53]

There was nothing particularly new about viewing birth control as a public health concern, but Marcus's views became more popular during the Depression as the birthrate dropped steeply in response to the national economic crisis. The growing acceptance of this perspective delighted doctors like Rachelle Yarros, by the 1930s something of an elder stateswoman among Jewish physicians involved in birth control. Yarros first made her mark as a founder of the American Social Hygiene Association in 1914 and was convinced long before the Depression that birth control, along with sex hygiene, ought to be seen as a public health concern. She publicized these views in her roles as a professor at the College of Physicians and Surgeons of Chicago and as Supervisor of Education for Women at the Illinois Department of Public Health. Yarros was a popular speaker in spite of her strong—and controversial—advocacy of sex education for adolescents, and she lectured widely on social hygiene, reproductive biology, venereal disease, and male/female relationships.[54]

As a doctor in residence at Hull House, Yarros became a staunch birth control advocate because of the high rate of abortions she saw in the immigrant communities around her. Decrying the illegality of prescribing birth control, she wrote in 1916, "No matter what your ideas of the sacredness of human life and the criminality of performing abortions, your heart aches while you send a woman out of your office, knowing that she is surely going to a quack."[55] In 1923 Yarros revitalized the Illinois Birth Control League and began to run her own clinic along the lines of Marie Stopes's London clinic. Gaining the support of prominent backers and a wide swath of the Chicago community, the Illinois Birth Control League opened five more clinics over the next ten years. Yarros continued to contend that birth control should decrease the abortion rate and argued that the modern recognition that abstinence was not conducive to adult well-being made the need for contraception obvious. She sided with Mary Ware Dennett in the debate over legal strategies, preferring the repeal of all obscenity laws and open access to contraceptive information rather than the passage of doctors-only bills. In 1935 Yarros appeared before the Committee on the Social Security Act to argue that birth control should be part of the social security plan so that not just privileged women with access to birth control could have lower mortality rates and healthier children. She pointed out that the birthrate was highest among already overburdened, unemployed people and urged the committee to incorporate contraceptive advice into any social welfare legislation.[56]

Marcus and Yarros operated somewhat independently of either Sanger's ABCL or Dennett's VPL. Both of them nonetheless benefited from and provided mentorship to other female doctors, especially the Jewish women who could not secure hospital affiliations and relied instead on the thriving professional network within birth control clinics. As the condolence letters in the wake of Hannah Stone's untimely death indicated, one of her major roles in the birth control movement had been to mentor other women doctors, many of them Jewish. Cheri Appel first went to the BCCRB to obtain contraception for herself, but Stone quickly recruited her, and Appel joined the clinic's medical team in 1931 while maintaining her part-time private practice. Like other clinic doctors, Appel performed gynecological exams and took case histories, spending about an hour with each patient to teach her how to use a diaphragm. Many of her patients had previously had abortions. Appel believed that birth control would prevent such actions in the future, but she still found that some of her Italian patients' priests blamed her as a Jewish woman for leading gullible women into sin. On Stone's recommendation,

Appel became the staff physician at a new birth control clinic in Westches-
ter County. Though Appel did not like Sanger and claimed that none of the
staff did, she nonetheless took Stone's advice and accompanied Sanger on a
1934 trip to Russia to assess the state of contraception there. Appel was more
politically radical than some of the other clinic doctors. She started an International Workers of the World birth control clinic independent of ABCL. As
she put it, "I felt that I was doing, making a contribution. It was a place where
women could come and feel free to talk about sexual things, where they had
no other place to go."[57]

Two of Stone's other protégés, Marie Levinson Warner and Lena Levine,
agreed. Warner had flourished at the Harlem clinic. While working there, she
wrote a report titled "Birth Control and the Negro" that compared the patient
composition of the Harlem clinic with that of the more established Recreation Rooms and Settlement clinic on the Lower East Side. Warner noted
that 37 percent of the Harlem patients were Jewish, as opposed to 15 percent of the Lower East Side patients, despite the fact that the Lower East Side
housed a significantly larger Jewish population. She concluded that by the
early 1930s the Lower East Side women had already been using diaphragms
for years and required fewer clinic visits, while some of the Jewish women
in Harlem had not had access to birth control before the clinic opened and
required more intensive care and more frequent appointments. After the
Harlem clinic closed, Warner continued to work at the Recreation Rooms
and Settlement Clinic and also became medical director of the clinic at Jewish Memorial Hospital.[58] Levine had attended medical school in New York
with Appel, where they were among the twenty-five women in a class of four
hundred. Of those twenty-five women, only six received any kind of training in contraception. Levine worked closely with both Sanger and Stone and
became Abraham Stone's professional partner after Hannah Stone's death.
She directed the Marriage Counseling Service at the BCCRB, later renamed
the Margaret Sanger Bureau, and eventually became the medical director of
all the New York City Planned Parenthood clinics. She gave speeches to Jewish groups praising traditional Jewish ideas about compatibility in marriage
partners and urging rabbis to offer premarital counseling to young couples.[59]

Jewish women doctors outside New York also achieved prominence in
the movement. Nadine Kavinoky was an early disciple of Sanger and friend
of Stone who opened a clinic in Los Angeles and, as a representative of the
local health department, ultimately became associated with eighteen out
of the thirty-three Los Angeles birth control clinics. She taught contraceptive practice to medical students and frequently delivered public lectures on
birth control. She clashed repeatedly with local birth control activists, many

Dr. Bessie Louise Moses.
Courtesy of the Planned
Parenthood of Maryland
Collection, University of
Baltimore

of whom in California tended to side with Dennett and deplore Kavinoky's insistence on a doctors-only bill. Kavinoky felt so strongly about birth control as privileged information that should be restricted to a doctor/patient exchange that she resigned from any clinic where nurses began to disseminate contraceptive advice along with the doctors.[60] On the other side of the country, Bessie Moses ran the Bureau for Contraceptive Advice in Baltimore to great acclaim. Against all advice and in the face of some threats, she welcomed African American women into the clinic, though at different hours than white women.[61] In Boston, Elizabeth Kleinman parlayed her experiences lecturing for the Birth Control League of Massachusetts into a staff appointment at the Mother's Health Office. When applying for the job in 1932 she summarized her experience, providing a valuable example of the impressive qualifications many Jewish women brought to their birth control work:

> I am a graduate of the New York Medical College of 1918, serving my internship at Bellevue Hospital and having besides three years training at other hospitals. I served one year abroad with the Serbian army and also studied at the University of Vienna for a short period. I hold three state licenses, N.Y., Conn. and Mass. I have been in practice here 6 ½ years at

present I am on the staff (medical) of the New England Hospital. I am a member of the N. England Woman's Medical, Mass. Med. Society and Greater Boston med. Society. I have been in the birth Control movement from the beginning. I have also been lecturing thru-out Mass. for the league here.[62]

One of Kleinman's birth control colleagues in Massachusetts was Lucile Lord-Heinstein. Her mother, a staunch suffragist and feminist, insisted that she attend medical school. Lord-Heinstein received her medical degree from Tufts in 1927. She contracted tuberculosis and did not immediately start to practice, but when she recovered her health, she began to work at a birth control clinic in Brookline. The Brookline clinic was next door to a police station, but there was no trouble. At the time she began working at the clinic, Lord-Heinstein was completely inexperienced. She only encountered diaphragms once she got there, as contraception had not been part of her medical school curriculum. She learned quickly, aided by a Conference on Contraceptive Research and Clinical Practice in New York that the Birth Control League of Massachusetts sent her to in 1936. She even developed her own techniques to help women whose repeated pregnancies and deliveries had led to so much internal damage that they could not insert a standard diaphragm.[63]

Ignoring the warnings of a lawyer who was a family friend, Lord-Heinstein founded a Mother's Health Office in Salem, which served married women referred by their doctors. This clinic was raided by police after the 1938 Massachusetts Superior Court decision that closed down all birth control clinics in the state, but Lord-Heinstein continued to lecture to a variety of women's groups, explaining the importance of contraceptive information and clinics. During her trial, she demonstrated the use of various teaching models and contraceptive devices to the court. She emphasized that birth control was entirely distinct from abortion and testified that she did not even know how to perform an abortion. Both the initial court and the appeals court ruled against Lord-Heinstein and the birth control movement in Massachusetts, but the Birth Control League of Massachusetts paid her $100 fine, and she continued to engage in birth control work. Lord-Heinstein explained later, "I continued to break the law, oh I certainly did. . . . I was thoroughly convinced with [every] cell in my body, and I would stand there with my fist raised, that this was good medicine."[64]

The spotlight shone brightest on doctors in the birth control movement, but nurses played a pivotal role as well. Elizabeth Cohen Arnold, the daughter of Jewish immigrants in Trenton, New Jersey, graduated from the

Englewood Hospital School of Nursing in 1929. Like Lord-Heinstein, she learned nothing about contraception during her medical training, but she took a job at the Maternity Center Association in New York, where her work in prenatal care and maternal mortality prevention helped connect her to the birth control network. The Maternity Center Association staff had to promise not to give out contraceptive advice or refer patients to birth control clinics, so Arnold would walk her patients to the nearby corner of Sixteenth Street and Sixth Avenue and tell them that they could be helped down the block at the brownstone with the BCCRB sign. Frustrated that few nurses knew about contraception, Arnold also thought "birth control" was not the best term. For her, "you're not really trying to control birth. . . . I felt that you are trying to help people have babies when they could have them, afford to have them, and want to have them." She stayed involved in the movement for decades, in 1956 accepting an appointment as a supervisor at a Planned Parenthood clinic. For Arnold, as for all the Jewish women medical professionals, the birth control movement provided an arena for a satisfying blend of professional achievement and political activism.[65]

The Fight to Decriminalize Birth Control

The male medical establishment generally remained suspicious of contraception; those male doctors who did support birth control often tried to take over the movement.[66] However, public opinion increasingly accepted birth control, which thanks in large part to women doctors found a new legitimacy during the 1930s. In 1932 the *Medical Woman's Journal* began to plan for an exhibit at the upcoming World's Fair in Chicago and compiled a list of birth control books and pamphlets written by women, illustrating how unobjectionable birth control had become in the public sphere.[67] A number of polls demonstrated steadily growing support for contraception, especially for married couples obtaining advice from doctors. In 1936 a *Fortune* survey found that 63 percent of the population supported the teaching and practice of birth control, and a 1938 *Ladies Home Journal* poll showed 79 percent of American women supported contraception. The people surveyed explained their positive attitudes toward birth control with a variety of rationales, from concerns about preserving mothers' and children's health to anxieties about family income in difficult economic times.[68] The work of the National Committee on Federal Legislation for Birth Control (NCFLBC), which Margaret Sanger founded in 1929 to pressure Congress and educate the public, was paying off in terms of public opinion, if not successful legislation.

Jewish women confronted the continuing legal obstacles to birth control as doctors, patients, and activists. As the primary lawyer for Sanger, Mary Ware Dennett, and the birth control movement in New York during the late 1920s and 1930s, Morris Ernst kept a sharp eye out for possible test cases like the 1929 clinic raid that had temporarily sent Hannah Stone and her co-workers to jail. Virtually all activists agreed that it was necessary to secure federal birth control legislation rather than deal with the inconsistent patchwork of state laws. In the hopes of garnering the medical profession's support, Sanger's NCFLBC pushed for "doctors-only" legislation that would prevent other professionals from distributing contraception through social welfare and private programs. She wrote to Rabbi Stephen Wise in 1931 to ask him to use his political contacts to garner support for a birth control bill about to go before Congress, which he agreed to do. Dennett continued to disagree with this medical model, believing women should be able to obtain birth control on demand in multiple venues. She also contacted Wise, sending him a copy of a letter she had written explaining the limitations of Sanger's approach. Was it fair, Dennett asked, for a woman to go to jail or pay a hefty fine for sending her sister the same detailed instructions and contraceptive literature that she herself had legally received from her own physician?[69]

By the mid-1930s the majority of Americans favored legalizing contraception, but inconsistent laws and court rulings had not caught up to popular opinion. In 1938 Ernst denounced the laws still on the books in Massachusetts that had recently led to the enforced closure of all birth control clinics in the state. The medical personnel at the clinics had all been charged with crimes as well. Lucile Lord-Heinstein, the Jewish physician in charge of the Salem clinic, fell prey to the raids in her state. As in New York a decade earlier, a stooge patient came to the clinic and was prescribed a diaphragm. A week later, four police officers stormed into the clinic, shut it down, and confiscated equipment and medical records. Lord-Heinstein had been expecting a raid, so she quickly threw a number of diaphragms and the contents of the clinic's cash register into her doctor's bag and went down to the police station without resistance. She and the other clinic workers were arrested but not jailed.[70] Sanger, Stone, and other nationally prominent activists spoke out in defense of all the Massachusetts clinics. Stone especially condemned the seizure of patient records in the Salem raid as a breach of doctor/patient confidentiality. Journalists across the United States denounced the enforced closure of the Massachusetts clinics. The renowned columnist and birth control advocate Dorothy Dunbar Bromley wrote in disgust that apparently "Little will be done in a State that cradled American liberty to save the lives and promote the well being of over-burdened mothers."[71] Lord-Heinstein's trial came just after the American Medical Association finally approved contraception in 1937. She was not convicted but remained disturbed for years by the fact that she had a police record, which she eventually moved to seal in 1976 when she was seventy-three years old.[72]

Congressional approval of changes to existing legal restrictions on contraception proved difficult to secure. A series of hearings during the early 1930s provided activists with multiple opportunities to state their case but also with multiple opportunities for failure to get their legislative program through Congress. The press covered the activities of NCFLBC in depth. A January 1934 *Time* article, "Birth Controllers on Parade," took an amused but generally supportive tone in describing recent hearings on Capitol Hill. The heavy involvement of Katharine Houghton Hepburn, mother of the actress and one of Sanger's most important lieutenants, naturally attracted attention, though she refused to have her photograph taken. The activists pointed out that contraception was already in wide use and that continuing to prohibit shipping of birth control information and supplies would not change social reality. Testifying as a spokesman for religion, Rabbi Edward Israel of Baltimore commented sardonically, "If you members of the committee think birth control is immoral, then pass a law that will drive contraceptives out of every home in the nation." Israel was trying to point out the absurdity of federal laws that allowed the use but not the distribution of contraception.[73]

The January 1934 hearings included testimony from both birth control supporters and opponents, many of whom prefaced their remarks by stating how many children they had. Representative John Camillus Lehr of Michigan responded to Israel's sarcastic comment that he had six children and had never had a contraceptive in his home; Hepburn retorted that she, too, had given birth to six children. Referring to President Franklin Delano Roosevelt's "Forgotten Man" speech, Sanger demanded to know why the "forgotten woman" could obtain free lunches for her children but "can do nothing for her own most pressing problems." Oft-repeated arguments about race suicide also appeared at the hearings. The radio personality Father Charles Coughlin complained that undesirable groups were having too many children, and the middle-class white women who came to testify would be better off staying home and having larger families. A birth control advocate dismissed Coughlin's statement, saying "Father Coughlin doesn't care how much the children suffer on earth, so long as they are prepared to pick up their little harps and sing Hallelujah."[74]

The activists did not get very far with the January House subcommittee hearings, but they launched an even bigger effort a few months later. The 1934 hearings before a Senate judiciary subcommittee brought Jewish women from numerous backgrounds into the halls of government. The NCJW and the Federation of Jewish Women's Organizations of Greater New York, collectively representing nearly 150,000 Jewish women, appeared alongside the Central Conference of American Rabbis (CCAR) and the United Synagogue of America on the list of legislative sponsors. Rose Heiman Halpern, the Brownsville mother who had been one of the first patients at Sanger's original clinic in 1916, arrived as a witness. Mrs. Mark Lansburgh, the NCJW legislative representative, also testified on behalf of amending the criminal code of the United States to allow dissemination of birth control information through the mail. Lansburgh cited the case of one of her fellow NCJW officers, who was "crippled because of the birth of a child, after the doctor had told her she should not become pregnant again but failed to give her contraceptive information."[75]

Few of the Jewish speakers made specific Jewish arguments in favor of birth control at these hearings. However, the presence of so many social service professionals who worked within the Jewish community, such as Jacob Billikopf of the Federation of Jewish Charities of Philadelphia and Harry L. Lurie of the Bureau of Jewish Social Research in New York, illustrated the significant role Jewish communal workers played in the entire field of social welfare in the United States during the interwar years. No one questioned their presence at the hearings or the ways in which their depth of Jewish communal experience qualified them to speak about social issues.[76]

Despite the best efforts of NCFLBC, the judiciary rather than the legislative branch of government finally reconstructed the law to allow contraception. In 1932 Sanger first had a Japanese colleague send her a package of diaphragms, which U.S. customs officials promptly confiscated, and then took Ernst's advice and had another package sent to Stone instead, who as a doctor would make a better test case for medical exemption. Customs officials duly seized this package as well and then charged Stone with violating the prohibition against importing contraceptive devices. Ernst successfully defended Stone in the U.S. District Court, which ruled in 1935 that tariff prohibitions did not apply to the importation of contraceptives for legitimate medical purposes. The government appealed, but the federal appeals court upheld the original decision. The higher court ruled that the Comstock Act was never designed to prevent the importation through the mail of devices that conscientious doctors could use on their patients' behalf. They advised that contraceptives also no longer fit into the classification of illegal imports because birth control was no longer as immoral or unsafe as it had been considered at the time the Comstock laws went into effect in 1873. The resolution of *United States v. One Package* in 1936, in which Stone was the central figure, was a critical victory for the birth control movement in general and Sanger in particular, as the court ruling focused on doctors.[77]

Once the 1936 decision removed federal restriction on sending birth control materials through the mail and declassified birth control as obscenity, there was little need remaining for NCFLBC.[78] In 1939 ABCL, BCCRB, and the National Committee on Maternal Health combined to form the Birth Control Federation of America. The new entity had primarily male leadership, despite its roots in organizations largely founded and headed by women. The philanthropists Albert and Mary Lasker gave the Birth Control Federation of America $25,000 for four years if two matching gifts could be found. The success of this capitalization led to an even bigger organization, renamed the Planned Parenthood Federation of America in 1942.[79]

The women doctors who ran birth control clinics continued to publish studies of their patient populations, and by the time the Birth Control Federation of America was established, these studies illustrated how much had changed. In a 1940 study Marie Warner, then medical director of two New York clinics, included the usual tables showing the reasons patients requested contraception, duration of marriage and age of couples at time of consultation, frequency of marital intercourse, previous fertility, family size, and contraceptive methods used before consultation. The five hundred cases Warner analyzed were disproportionally Jewish, hardly surprising since one of the clinics she ran was at Jewish Memorial Hospital and the other at a Jewish settlement house. But the most striking indication of how much the birth control movement had changed came in Warner's matter-of-fact table showing the marital status of the women at the time of consultation. One hundred thirty-two unmarried women requested birth control; of those, 93 were engaged, but 39 were completely "unattached." The single women constituted only 7.2 percent of the whole, but similar clinic studies of fifteen years earlier would never have included information about unmarried women seeking birth control. All but the most radical activists had made a point of emphasizing that birth control was for married women. Further changes in American social norms of sexuality could be seen in the number of women who admitted to premarital sex, 9.2 percent of the married women and 38 percent of the engaged women. These numbers reflected the major shifts in sexual behavior between the first generation of clinic patients in the early 1920s and their counterparts fifteen to twenty years later. The fact that the *Journal of the American Medical Association*, which less than fifteen years earlier had refused to carry Stone's similar clinical analysis of contraception, published Warner's piece also indicated attitudinal changes within the medical profession.[80]

Religion and Birth Control

While changes in medical attitudes toward contraception were critical to growing social acceptance of birth control, it was equally important for the movement to confront the major social force of religion. It was not clear at first what position organized religion would take, but activists knew that technological innovation in the past had led to religious denunciation and fully expected similar attitudes toward the highly charged issue of contraception. At clinics, intake interviews included questions about religious affiliation so that activists and health care personnel could get a sense of popular religious thinking. Some religious perspectives did not denounce the limitation of family size to protect a mother's health or even a family's economic well-being, but there was a persistent religious insistence that the method should be "natural" abstinence rather than "artificial" contraception.[81] Birth control advocates understood this distinction and planned an educational campaign to promote the morality of birth control. The entire religious discussion took place within the context of married couples' use of contraception; if birth control had any chance of winning respectability and general acceptance, it would have to be perceived as far removed from free love or premarital sex. The social hygiene pioneer Rachelle Yarros, arguing that birth control allowed for a "single standard of morals for both men and women," also appealed to a religious audience by contending that birth control would reduce the incidence of men seeking sexual fulfillment outside their marriages.[82]

Because religion maintained significant influence on people's private lives, the birth control movement never underestimated its importance. A 1930s ABCL pamphlet titled *The Churches and Birth Control* explained:

> The attitude of religion is perhaps the focal point of the whole Birth Control situation. It is easy to point out the bearing of Birth Control on child labor, unemployment, poverty, overcrowding, war. But the motivation towards action must spring from a fervent belief in the rightness of the movement.[83]

The pamphlet included endorsements from a variety of clergymen, including a few rabbis. When *The Nation* published a special birth control issue in January 1932, many of the articles referred to the potentially fraught relationship between contraception and religion, with contributors insisting that birth control was of great spiritual value and reflected the spiritual evolution of the human race beyond the merely physical reproductive relationships of earlier ages.[84]

Roman Catholics remained the most vociferous religious opponents of birth control, though the theological proscription developed at least in part in response to the birth control movement and not in advance of it. The lead editorial in *The Nation's* 1932 special birth control issue stated the case in stark terms: "In America the chief enemy is, of course, the Catholic church." Margaret Sanger's longer article, "The Pope's Position on Birth Control," argued that Catholic teaching on birth control was "illogical, not in accord with science, and definitely against social welfare and race improvement." She sharply criticized Pope Pius XI's recent encyclical "Of Chaste Marriage" for, on the one hand, allowing marital intercourse even in cases of sterility, pregnancy, and women's menopause and, on the other hand, asserting that marital intercourse was only for procreation. Characterizing the Catholic attitude toward birth control as one "conditioned by a disapproval of human enjoyment and an apparent relishing of the theory that suffering is good for our souls," she invited the pope to "hear true stories from Catholic, Protestant, and Jewish women which I should think would be enough to shake sense into the head of any man."[85]

The historian Kathleen Tobin-Schlesinger has argued that Sanger knew she could not fight Protestants, since they could provide the mainstream support she needed, and did not fight Jews, since there were too few of them to matter, so she made Roman Catholicism the religious bogey instead. She relied on Protestant anti-Catholicism to draw religious support to her cause, which she positioned as one of freedom and personal morality. A master tactician, Sanger welcomed Jewish support for birth control but was cautious about publicizing it too much for fear of anti-Semitism. She had good reason for concern. In 1931 the Missouri Synod Lutherans condemned those in favor of birth control by labeling them unmarried, Jewish, "camp followers." Chronic American anti-Semitism made widespread Jewish support for birth control something of a mixed blessing for activist leaders. Despite employing a series of Jewish women as editors and running frequent articles on religion and birth control, *Birth Control Review* only rarely published articles about Jews or Judaism and birth control.[86] The absence is all the more notable given the widespread acknowledgment of both Sanger and Dennett's circles that Jewish women were absolutely critical to the movement as clinic clients, doctors, and activists.

Unsurprisingly, considerable debate over birth control continued within the American Jewish community. Rabbis Stephen Wise, Sidney Goldstein, and Edward Israel offered sustained support. Wise admitted that "Birth Control can hardly be said to be sanctioned by the teachings of the Jewish religion" but insisted that in the modern world, rabbis had the right to alter such teachings based on the tenet that "the religion of Israel holds human life to be sacred."[87] At congressional hearings in 1931, Goldstein pointed out that as the biblical injunction to "go forth and multiply" was commanded at a time when there were hardly any people in the world, the obligation did not apply unrestrainedly in the very different world of the twentieth century. During additional hearings the next year, Israel spoke out against forms of "dogmatic religion" that had always opposed scientific progress, citing heliocentrism and evolution as additional examples.[88] Israel wrote in *Birth Control Review*, "Birth control becomes for the modern religionist, not only a permissible code of conduct but a divine mandate."[89]

Wise, Goldstein, and Israel were all liberal rabbis with progressive political views, however, and they could not speak for American Jewry as a whole. An example of a very different attitude toward birth control came from Rabbi I. L. Bril, who wrote in 1932:

> I am not so sure that those who preach and practice birth control are actuated altogether by unselfish motives. The desire for ease, for greater luxuries is very often the motivating reason for not wanting children. Many women prefer a dog or cat to a child. Very many marriages go on the rocks because they are childless, because the wife refused to have children.[90]

Even though there was no religious content to this particular critique, also notable for the focus on women, that did not mean there was no Jewish argument to be made against birth control. When Sanger's assistant Florence Rose met with Rabbi Moses D. Abels, until recently the president of the Brooklyn Association of Rabbis, in February 1936, he brought her numerous Talmudic citations to help build a religious argument for the cause. She was gratified to find that he personally supported contraception. However, Abels also explained to Rose that the Brooklyn Association of Rabbis would never endorse birth control because there were too many Jewish reasons not to support it. The high priority Judaism traditionally placed on children and family life was reason enough for some rabbis, Orthodox, Conservative, and Reform alike, to oppose easing restrictions on contraception. In Jewish legal terms, birth control was also suspect because of the welter of traditional Jewish laws and customs surrounding sexuality and childbirth. Taking a position on birth control would cause great dissension and also get at least some of the rabbis into trouble with their own congregations.[91]

The first major Jewish religious group to wrestle at length with the question of Judaism's position on birth control was the CCAR, the American rabbinical association of Reform Judaism. Although there was dissent within the

CCAR as well, the fact that the organization represented only one denomination of Judaism made discussion and action at least possible. In 1926 the National Catholic Welfare Association approached the CCAR to ask for support in protesting legal changes that might allow birth control information and contraceptive devices to be sent through the mail.[92] The question came before the CCAR's Commission on Social Justice, which concluded that "the traditional religious points of view ought certainly to receive consideration" but only as one of many factors, which should also include "social health . . . national welfare . . . economic exigencies and . . . moral considerations." The commission recommended that discussion of such an important issue should be energetically pursued by those in the pulpit and in the press in order to ascertain whether birth control was really in the best interests of the nation in general and American Jewry in particular.[93]

Although unwilling to join the National Catholic Welfare Association in its protests, most commission members agreed that oral advice, given directly by doctors and perhaps social workers to patients and clients, was sufficient for dissemination of birth control information and therefore that amendment of current laws relating to the mail was unnecessary. Some CCAR dissenters pointed out that this approach assumed that all women had access to private medical care, while others insisted that the CCAR should take absolutely no stand until the issue of birth control could be thoroughly analyzed from a religious perspective. The group ultimately decided to wait until the following year's convention, at which Rabbi Jacob Lauterbach would present the detailed paper he had prepared on the subject.[94] Lauterbach, a professor of Talmud at Hebrew Union College in Cincinnati, had received his intensive, traditional Jewish education and ordination in European seminaries before coming to the United States in 1903 and was widely recognized as the most halakhically expert member of the CCAR. His opinion, based on learned readings of traditional rabbinic sources, was necessary if the Reform movement, the most liberal Jewish denomination, wanted to put forth a position on birth control that had any chance of being accepted as legitimate by American Jews with a greater allegiance to Jewish law and custom.

There was general agreement at the 1927 CCAR convention that birth control was a major halakhic issue with important religious implications, but the issue remained under the purview of the Commission on Social Justice rather than the CCAR group that issued Jewish legal decisions.[95] Still, Lauterbach's comprehensive Jewish legal analysis was presented to the CCAR in 1927 and was published in full in the *CCAR Yearbook* for maximum exposure. Lauterbach approached the issue of birth control from a legalistic perspective, first establishing the tenet that marital sexual relations that could not lead to pregnancy, as in the case of a pregnant or postmenopausal woman, were absolutely permitted by Jewish law. This meant that the proscription against "spilling of seed" implied masturbation or sexual perversion rather than normal sexual intercourse between husband and wife, which in itself could be quite varied according to the Talmud, though some medieval rabbinic authorities had imposed additional limitations. Lauterbach went on to explore Talmudic sources that seemed actually to mandate certain forms of contraception in particular circumstances and discussed in great detail the relative merits of douching and inserting some kind of absorbent material either before or after sexual relations. As he put it, "When there is danger of harm resulting to the unborn child or the child already born, all teachers agree that it is obligatory to take the precaution of using a contraceptive." Some of the rabbinic authorities he cited went further in allowing contraceptives in cases where harm might come to the mother as well.[96]

Although the biblical injunction to be fruitful and multiply might seem to have been of paramount importance, Talmudic sources explained that this commandment was incumbent only upon men, as God never commanded people to do something that would put their lives in as much danger as childbirth entailed for women. Men obviously required women to fulfill the commandment, but there was rabbinic discussion about how many children were halakhically necessary—the consensus was two, but there was a debate whether two boys or a boy and a girl would suffice—and thus the concept of spacing or limiting children, though not preventing them altogether, had a firm basis in Jewish law. Lauterbach traced the growing aversion to contraception that had developed in more recent Jewish legal sources but demonstrated that even the most disapproving rabbinic authorities did not deny the legality of birth control under a variety of circumstances.[97]

Lauterbach's responsum received a great deal of attention and ultimately served as the basis of the Conservative movement's Rabbinical Assembly's decisions about birth control as well as those of his own Reform movement. It also illustrated the ways in which an intellectual exercise could be affected by contemporary circumstance. For the most part, Lauterbach confined his analysis to the legal precedents in Talmudic and rabbinic sources. He presented conflicting evidence where necessary and drew the kinds of conclusions common to responsa literature. In one telling paragraph, however, contemporary social ideology crept into the analysis. Lauterbach concluded that contraceptives were not only allowed but actually required in situations when childbirth would harm either mother or potential child. He added:

Neither can I see any difference between protecting a child from the danger of being deprived of the nourishment of its mother's milk, and protecting the already born children of the family from the harm which might come to them due to the competition of a larger number of sisters and brothers. For the care and the comfort which the parents can give to their children already born, will certainly be less if there be added to the family other children claiming attention, care and comfort.[98]

At no point in the Talmudic or rabbinic sources that he discussed did the rights of children to caring, comfortable homes make an appearance. This rhetoric seems more akin to Progressive Era ideas about children and protected childhood than the rabbinic sources about dangers to mother and child. Interestingly, Lauterbach did not make the point that as the most up-to-date contraceptive devices, diaphragms were preferable according to Jewish law as well as science because they did not create a barrier to the male organ as condoms did.

Despite Lauterbach's thorough legal analysis, which clearly demonstrated flexibility, albeit limited, of even the most traditional Jewish attitudes toward contraception, the Commission on Social Justice was not yet ready to make a statement. At its 1929 convention, the CCAR "urge[d] the recognition of the importance of the control of parenthood as one of the methods of coping with social problems" but delayed a formal statement or vote yet again due to concerns about appearing to undermine "the holiness and crucial importance of domestic relations" in Judaism.[99] The obvious reluctance of even the most liberal rabbinical association to take a stand on an issue that many of its individual members had already publicly supported illustrated the danger the CCAR felt it would face in appearing too radical. The CCAR may also have feared that endorsing birth control would create a rift between its members and the rabbis of the other denominations of Judaism.

Ultimately, the CCAR condoned birth control. In a 1930 "Message of Social Justice," the CCAR stated:

Birth is one of the many forces of nature which like steam, air, gravitation, electricity, and chemical valence, succumb to human control as civilization progresses. Where the intelligent regulation of birth can avert suffering and degradation, the voice of mercy speaks. That voice should not go unheeded. It went not unheeded among the sages of the Jewish past.[100]

By connecting this very modern decision with the "sages of the Jewish past," the CCAR was offering an additional comment on its own decision, which was based at least as much on contemporary concerns and economic conditions as on Jewish legal precedent. But there continued to be dissent within the CCAR, particularly from rabbis who feared that the official endorsement of birth control was tantamount to endorsing the sexual licentiousness of the modern age.[101]

The CCAR decision, followed shortly by the endorsement of Conservative Judaism's Rabbinical Assembly, meant that a positive attitude toward contraception became part of many American Jews' thinking. By the time Sidney Goldstein wrote *The Meaning of Marriage and the Foundations of the Family* in 1942, he could position birth control as just one of many modern changes to the structure, organization, and function of family life. Goldstein included an entire chapter on contraception, reminding his readers that having children was a fundamental Jewish value but that "unrestrained and reckless reproduction" was not a Jewish ethic. Assuming marital use, Goldstein explained that birth control would reduce child mortality, protect mothers' health, save families from economic distress, maintain a balance between supply and demand of labor, and remove overpopulation as a cause of war.[102] None of these arguments moved Orthodox rabbinic opinion on birth control, however, as none were religious arguments. Sidney Hoenig's competing volume, *Jewish Family Life: The Duty of the Woman*, distributed by the Union of Orthodox Jewish Congregations, concluded that barring exceptional circumstances overseen by rabbinic authorities, "The Jewish religion does not permit direct birth control. Mechanical means to avoid contraception are allowed the woman only in cases where childbirth might endanger her life." Hoenig explained that the family purity laws observed by traditional Jewish couples themselves "provide essential periods of protection for the Jewish woman from excessive births, since she understands the rhythmic sense of birth control and may be guided by it."[103] The Orthodox Jewish position did allow for some use of birth control, particularly in instances of threats to women's health, which differentiated it significantly from the Roman Catholic approach. Married couples could consult with Orthodox rabbis and gain approval to use contraception for a variety of reasons, but each case was more of a temporary exemption than a blanket permission. Birth control remained controversial when viewed from a strictly halakhic perspective. How many American Jews maintained that perspective can best be surmised by the marked decrease in Jewish childbirth rates.

Birth Control, Eugenics, and Jews

For Jews interested in birth control, one of the difficulties that consistently arose was the fluid but ever-present link between birth control and eugenics.[104] In an intellectual environment steeped in what were then respectable, even conventional, ideas about scientific racism, it was hardly surprising that a eugenics movement contemporaneously emerged that was devoted to improving the world by improving the people in it. During the early twentieth century, eugenics developed both a positive mode, that is, that the best people should have the most children, and a negative mode, that is, that the fertility of inferior groups should be restricted. The heart of the matter, of course, was who made the decisions about which groups were superior or inferior. One observer, commenting on the success of birth control clinics run by Jewish social service agencies, praised the eugenic outcome of healthier Jewish women and children, remarking "To the race that is clever and strong shall be given the privilege of profiting by eugenics to become yet more strong and clever."[105]

Many American Jews cast a suspicious eye on any such categorization, however, because even eugenicists who cited Jews as examples of how well eugenics could work sometimes did so with anti-Semitic overtones. Before World War I, the British physician Caleb W. Saleeby explained that a cultural emphasis on motherhood and the low incidence of alcohol abuse had been good for the Jewish community, but the real reason why Jews had survived as long as they had was due to the continuous persecution that had left only the strongest and "best" Jews alive to reproduce. Saleeby did not explicitly draw the conclusion that persecution had been good for the Jews, but that did not make his thinking any more palatable to the Jewish community. Other eugenicists were even less circumspect. Raymond Pearl, a biologist at Johns Hopkins University, insisted on Jewish racial distinctiveness. He openly favored quotas for Jewish students at Ivy League universities and feared that Jews would take over the world unless their numbers were reduced. Pearl's ideas met with considerable resistance from those who insisted that culture, not nature, made Jews distinctive, but it was Pearl who played a major role in the birth control movement by carrying out a series of important fertility studies.[106]

Margaret Sanger did not set Jewish concerns to rest when she used eastern European Jewry as an example of overpopulation.[107] Even from her earliest days of birth control activism, Sanger encountered repeated accusations of anti-Semitism as well as racism.[108] At the 1917 trial resulting from her arrest at the Brownsville clinic, at least one witness claimed that she had heard Sanger making disparaging remarks about Jews, but another witness disputed this claim.[109] Sanger always denied harboring any form of anti-Semitism and certainly worked very closely with innumerable Jewish women, but she embraced eugenics throughout her decades of activism, arguing that she, like religious and scientific leaders across a wide spectrum, was primarily concerned with the quality of life and believed that birth control was the way to achieve a higher quality of life for the world at large. She undoubtedly advocated positive rather than negative eugenics, but the distinction was not enough to satisfy her critics. For Sanger, however, the field of eugenics was so prestigious that borrowing its language helped make birth control more acceptable to a larger audience of both public health advocates and feminist activists.[110]

The link between birth control and eugenics continued to provide a mutually supportive environment for both movements during the 1920s and 1930s. As far as the public—and even the law—was concerned, there was often little distinction. During the 1936 *United States v. One Package* federal court case, the defense asked doctors to confirm the hereditary nature of a number of diseases and then added eugenics and poor heredity to the list of other reasons—including poverty, mental deficiency, and anatomical weakness—that birth control was in the best interests not only of the patient but also of society.[111]

Some American Jews supported eugenics as a means of strengthening a small, presumably weak minority. At an address at the 1925 Neo-Malthusian Conference, Rabbi Stephen Wise said that he thought birth control was "supremely important as an item in the eugenic program," but he cautioned that "the eugenic program is not Messianic" and that alone it could not promote "the ideals of human justice and human decency and human brotherliness in the life of the world."[112] Rabbi Sidney Goldstein served as an even more enthusiastic bridge between birth control and eugenics. At the ABCL convention in January 1933, Goldstein publicly urged state-mandated sterilization of people with "serious hereditary defects."[113] Even after the Nuremberg Laws were passed in Germany, a development that left many American Jews finding the line between birth control and eugenics impossibly thin, Goldstein continued to lend legitimacy to eugenics in the United States by appearing on the program of the American Eugenics Society annual meeting in May 1936. He was chairman of the CCAR's Commission on Social Justice at the time but apparently saw no contradiction in these commitments.[114]

For every Goldstein, there was a Dr. Rachelle Yarros who energetically fought against linking birth control and eugenics, despite their common interest in promoting healthier babies. Yarros faulted eugenicists for paying attention only to heredity and not to environment, writing "They talk of improving the human race as if environment and conditions of life and work had no effect on human character."[115] As a Hull House doctor, she daily witnessed the successes of immigrants and their children, people whom the eugenics movement might dismiss as inferior. At the 1934 ABCL conference, Yarros resisted the idea that during a depression the middle and upper classes were threatened by a working class with a higher fertility rate. Although she was an early, prominent, and active supporter of birth control, she did not believe that quality of character was tied to class status. "I hope this conference won't stress the privileged classes," Yarros urged, adding, "we don't know who they are, and if we know now, we probably won't five years from now."[116] Given the economic turmoil of the times, Sanger conceded this point, but eugenics did not just disappear from birth control rhetoric.[117]

As the historian Cathy Moran Hajo argues, birth control activists typically judged fitness by a combination of biological and environmental factors, with most of the patients labeled "unfit" due to poverty and illness rather than heredity, religion, or race. Sanger stated clearly in 1934, "If by 'unfit' is meant the physical or mental defects of a human being, that is an admirable gesture, but if 'unfit' refers to races or religions, then that is another matter which I frankly deplore." Because clinics were sites of voluntary contraception for patients who chose to practice birth control, viewing them as sites of forced eugenics is problematic. Clinics had the power to withhold birth control but not to force it.[118] During the late 1930s, though, Sanger was still using the language of eugenics to justify birth control as a means of building "for the future a better, stronger, more healthy race . . . a race worthy to carry on the tradition of our pioneering forefathers whose courage and stamina started the nation on its upward path."[119] Given events in Nazi Germany, the idea of a superior race left many American Jews wary of eugenics. Still, Jewish women kept their own interests at the forefront and enthusiastically continued to support and practice birth control even if they rejected some of the ideas that traveled along with the movement.

Conclusion

For all the Jewish women active in the birth control movement, their involvement signaled a disruption of a public/private distinction that in terms of reproduction had been shaky from the start. While sexuality, childbearing, and contraception seemed on the surface to be the most private of matters, in fact the public spheres of law, religion, and custom had continuously regulated women's bodies. Reproduction was social as well as physical, with meaning for the community and state as well as the individual and family. The Jewish—whether halakhic, cultural, or merely traditional—aspects of birth control decisions also affected a majority of those women interested in having children while protecting themselves and raising healthy families within a Jewish community still set apart by a combination of choice and exclusion. Although the liberal denominations of Judaism were the most aggressive in redefining the public need for private contraceptive decisions within a Jewish value system, even the most traditionally observant American Jews enjoyed some flexibility for making individual family planning decisions based on a combination of rabbinic strictures and personal needs. As birth control consumers, activists, and professionals, American Jewish women simultaneously occupied public and private spaces and redefined them on the basis of claims to women's autonomy, the role of the family in the community, and the potential for synchronicity among religion, traditional culture, and technology.

The 1936 federal court decision involving Hannah Stone permanently altered the birth control movement, paving the way for the creation of the Birth Control Federation of America and ultimately Planned Parenthood. Battles remained to be fought, especially over the kinds of state laws that shut down Lucile Lord-Heinstein's Salem, Massachusetts, clinic in 1938. Five years after that raid, the Jewish periodical *The Reconstructionist* was still reporting on legislative initiatives in Massachusetts that would allow doctors to prescribe birth control devices to married women with medical indications, illustrating both the continuing legal restraints on contraception in some state and the ongoing American Jewish interest in birth control.[120] By then demographic evidence pointed to overwhelming Jewish acceptance—or at least use—of contraception for family limitation. Jewish women had adopted birth control for their own purposes in large number; Jewish women doctors had made important contributions to the movement and had used it as a vehicle for professional advancement; and Jewish activists had successfully expanded the accessibility of contraception in a variety of settings. The birth control movement did not simply disappear—indeed, not until the 1972 *Eisenstadt v. Baird* Supreme Court decision was contraception for unmarried women protected under a right to privacy—–but the tone became less urgent by the late 1930s, even as the movement gradually expanded to include a larger category of reproductive rights than had earlier been the case. Jewish women remained involved in the movement, but many found it possible to claim victory and turn their attention to the darkening clouds on the threatening horizon of international affairs.

5

"Where the Yellow Star Is"

American Jewish Women, the Peace Movement, and
Jewish Identity during the 1930s and World War II

Most of us who are pacifists are overburdened with the feeling that
time is running away from us.
—Rebecca Hourwich Reyher, 1938[1]

In 1937, Rebecca Hourwich Reyher joined the "Flying Caravan" of delegates
sent to South America by the People's Mandate Committee (PMC). The purpose of this delegation was to arouse sentiment for a petition demanding that
governments renounce war and to secure ratification of treaties approved
at the Inter-American Court for the Maintenance of Peace that had met in
Buenos Aires the previous December. There was a great deal of publicity for
the PMC delegation, greeted everywhere with shouts of "Viva la Paz!" During the Rio de Janeiro stop, Reyher and the other delegates addressed the
Women's Club and called on the foreign minister. The delegation also met
with President Getúlio Vargas, who assured them that the treaties would be
ratified, and then attended a reception tendered in their honor by the U.S.
ambassador. Reyher believed in the value of this work but noted dryly that
the apparently peaceful Rio harbor was full of battleships. She traveled to
South America for PMC rather than as a representative of any Jewish organization and was treated there no differently, but Reyher was identified
as Jewish in much of the press coverage. Commenting that the delegation
received an enthusiastic reception in Venezuela, she also reported that forty-
six communists had recently been deported from the country in order, it
was explained to her, to "keep the Jews out of here." For Reyher, the Flying
Caravan experience highlighted the growing difficulties of sustaining pacifist
convictions in a world on the brink of a war in which Jews would clearly be
in grave danger as Jews.[2]

The daughter of socialist, agnostic parents, and someone who had never
been particularly connected to the American Jewish community, Reyher
discovered that she was beginning to feel a Jewish solidarity new to her. She

Rebecca Hourwich Reyher.
Courtesy of the Schlesinger
Library, Radcliffe Institute,
Harvard University

embodied the complicated personal politics of American Jewish pacifist women during the 1930s, and she became a prominent, if reluctant, example of the phenomenon of newly awakened Jewish identity. Her suffrage and peace activism had not taken place within a Jewish context, but in the face of the obvious threat during the Hitler era, Reyher felt that "I must take my side where the yellow star is . . . when Jews were being persecuted it was certainly the obligation of anybody who was remotely connected with being a Jew, whether they were religious or not, to do something about it."[3] As a well-connected, well-traveled journalist and activist with an international outlook, Reyher learned of the atrocities taking place in Europe even earlier and more thoroughly than many other American Jews, although a great deal of information was readily available to all Americans.[4] To her own surprise, Reyher found herself not so much renouncing her pacifism as rethinking a Jewish identity she had not previously cared much about. She even reconsidered her former ambivalence toward Zionism, coming to believe that in the wake of Nazism, the establishment of a national Jewish homeland was both essential and justified.[5] Reyher remained deeply involved in the peace movement in the face of increasingly threatening world events during the late 1930s, but disillusionment with universalist ideals that seemed divorced from reality tempered her convictions.

Reyher's participation in the PMC peace mission was only the latest in a series of activist endeavors that stretched back to her adolescence. Both her father, the prominent economist and presidential advisor Isaac Hourwich, and her mother, Lisa Jaffe Hourwich, who had harbored dreams of becoming a lawyer, pushed all their children to strive for as much education as possible and to use their knowledge in the wider world. As a high school student in Washington, D.C., during the early 1910s, Reyher read Jane Addams's autobiography and was inspired to do "something dramatic" with her life. She first tried emulating Addams by volunteering at a settlement house, but she found the work uninspiring and instead became a suffrage street speaker and organizer. After finishing high school, she went to New York, and joined the Feminist Alliance, which further sparked her lifelong concern with women who combined career and marriage. Following the failed 1915 New York suffrage referendum, Reyher attended the University of Chicago, where she remained politically engaged and demonstrated an interest in peace by becoming president of the University Women's Peace Society. In early 1917, Mabel Vernon drew her into Alice Paul's inner circle, and Reyher left college to picket the White House, organize a successful southern suffrage publicity tour, run the National Woman's Party's (NWP) New York headquarters, and organize NWP's Massachusetts suffrage campaign during the final push for the Nineteenth Amendment.[6]

Reyher and Vernon, a pacifist Quaker who became Reyher's dear friend and confidante, were troubled by Paul's single-minded focus on the Equal Rights Amendment following the suffrage victory. Together they turned their attention to peace work, though Reyher, already married to the author Ferdinand Reyher, had a daughter and spent much of the 1920s supporting herself as a writer rather than devoting herself full time to activism as Vernon did. Still, Reyher developed into a staunch pacifist and became a major spokesperson for peace by the 1930s. She and Vernon worked especially closely on PMC, which originated in 1936 as a Women's International League for Peace and Freedom (WILPF) campaign to collect fifty million signatures worldwide to demand that governments renounce war. Prominent Jewish women like Lillian Wald and Frieda Schiff Warburg were also involved with PMC, which eventually became an independent movement, and there was also some support in the organized American Jewish community. Staff members of the American Jewish Committee signed the petition, even though their employer took no official position, and National Council of Jewish Women (NCJW) sections around the country helped collect signatures.[7]

The involvement of some American Jewish women in PMC's signature campaign was one of their last major collective peace endeavors. During the years leading up to the Second World War, virtually all Jewish pacifists like Reyher, men as well as women, faced the challenge of concrete threats to their abstract ideals of peace.[8] The dilemmas they faced must be seen in light of the varied reactions of all Americans, not just Jews, to Nazism. However, a special focus on Jewish women is important because the extensive literature on the American Jewish response to the Holocaust has been slow to include any kind of gender analysis or even to see women as subjects.[9] The major bodies claiming to represent American Jewry, such as the American Jewish Committee, American Jewish Congress, and B'nai B'rith, rarely gave women a seat at the table, which partially explains why NCJW carried out much of its work in the context of the women's movement instead. The crisis confronting Jewish women became a problem for peace groups in general, which had complex responses of their own that need to be integrated into any understanding of larger American attitudes to events at home and overseas during the 1930s.

Eventually most Jewish women in the peace movement faced an agonizing choice between their religious/ethnic/cultural identities and their political beliefs. Should they hold fast to their ideals? Would standing by peace or demanding action against Hitler be most faithful to their understanding of Jewish identity? What part should their roles as women and mothers play in their actions? Would Jewish defection from the peace movement heighten anti-Semitism and make Jews scapegoats for a war that was already victimizing them? What would happen to their committed peace work based on universalist ideals if they now acknowledged a very particularist threat? Ultimately, decades of committed peace activism at home and abroad, meaningful friendships, and synthesis of gender and religious/ethnic identity could not withstand what most American Jewish women considered betrayal of the highest ideals of peace and the existential threat to the survival of Jews and Judaism. Even activists who had never given much thought to their Jewish identities found that in the age of Nazism and in the face of near silence from both world powers and their own colleagues in the peace movement, their activism could not help but become tied to Jewishness as never before.

Before the Darkness

At the beginning of the 1930s, American Jewish women seemed poised to become even more involved in the peace movement. An external audit of NCJW in 1930 found that 91 percent of the more than ninety sections, representing more than 50,000 women, ran regular peace programs. Eleven sections reported that peace work was their most important activity. As one example, at the 1931 twenty-fifth anniversary commemoration of Charleston's NCJW section, the entire community celebrated NCJW's local peace work, which included running a peace study group, supporting legislation leading to peace, bringing "goodwill programs" to the public schools, and staging peace events every November around Armistice Day. As another, NCJW's Minneapolis section wrote to President Hoover in 1931 to call for a special Senate session to approve World Court protocols. When Fanny Brin hosted a 1932 regional NCJW conference at her Minneapolis home, the NCJW founder Hannah Greenebaum Solomon addressed the members on "The Expanding Universe," and the group discussed alternatives to war. On the national level, NCJW cooperated with the National Committee on the Cause and Cure of War (NCCCW) to collect signatures for a petition urging another disarmament conference. On an international level, when the International Council of Women (ICW) formed a Peace and Disarmament Committee in 1931, based in Geneva, the World Council of Jewish Women became a charter member. At the 1932 NCJW Triennial in Detroit, delegates from more than two hundred cities voted in favor of a policy change resulting in a greater focus on national legislation and vocational guidance, reflecting the impact of the Depression. NCJW also

Standing from *left* to *right*, Fanny Brin, Jane Addams, Hannah Greenebaum Solomon, and Elsa Levi at a NCJW meeting in Chicago, 1934. Courtesy of Judith Brin Ingber

voted to reorganize itself and abolish all former departments in favor of a more centralized administrative structure. However, so many NCJW members deemed the cause of peace critically important that the Department of Peace remained intact.[10]

As had been the case during the 1920s, the activist environment of many American Jewish women continued to forge connections among causes. Individuals participated in multiple social movements simultaneously. For example, Lillian Cantor Dawson, a former suffragist teaching in Pittsburgh, lost her job during the Depression. She first used her involuntary leisure time to attend a WILPF conference at the Hague and then went to Palestine to spend time with "that superb pacifist" Henrietta Szold, the founder of Hadassah. Back in the United States, she became increasingly involved with WILPF while also starting a Workmen's Circle social service bureau in New York, which for nine dollars a month covered a whole family's complete medical expenses, including the birth control services available at the clinic. Jewish women's organizations moved smoothly from one kind of activism to another as well. In 1935 NCJW's Baltimore section sent official representatives to hear Margaret Sanger and Katharine Houghton Hepburn address Baltimore women on birth control; worked hard to get every single Baltimore NCJW member's signature on the PMC petition; and invited WILPF executive director Dorothy Detzer to address a regular meeting.[11]

Most notable was the continuing cooperation and joint activism of Jewish women's organizations and women's peace groups. The Jersey City NCJW section and Brooklyn Hadassah chapter both requested WILPF speakers to attend their meetings and run special study groups of peace-related issues such as disarmament. A list of organizational WILPF members in New York State included ten lodges of the United Order of True Sisters, one of many Jewish groups on the list despite the fact that WILPF did not always attend to Jewish sensibilities. One WILPF fund-raising letter asked members for donations "when you are making your Easter offerings." Individual Jewish women who became interested in peace contacted WILPF and NCCCW for further information. Both organizations published suggestions for engaging in peace work, listing Jewish organizations like the National Federation of Temple Sisterhoods (NFTS) and NCJW as important providers of information about international affairs and local peace activism.[12]

Formal Jewish religious life, especially among the more liberal denominations, also supported peace strongly during the early 1930s. A number of rabbis used their pulpits to promote peace. In 1930 Joseph Kornfeld delivered a widely reprinted lecture on peace that called the prophet Isaiah "first among the world's statesmen to foretell Universal Peace." He cited the famous verse from Isaiah, "Nation shall not lift up sword against nation, neither shall they learn war any more" and compared it to the Kellogg-Briand Pact. Roland Gittelsohn frequently preached disarmament during his sermons, arguing that the world was too small to fight in or over. In an eloquent discourse on "More Human Bondage," he reminded his congregation that during the binding of Isaac in Genesis, the angel called out, "Abraham, Abraham" to stop the father from sacrificing his son. Gittelsohn offered the interpretation that the angel's first "Abraham" referred to the situation at hand with Isaac, but the second "Abraham" stood as a promise for all time that there should be no more human sacrifice. "Have we stopped sacrificing human life?" asked Gittelsohn in concluding his sermon. Only world peace could fulfill the angel's words, and it was up to the Jews to see that they came to pass. At a time when anti-Semitism was on the rise, the willingness of American Jews to take public positions on a potentially controversial matter demonstrated the ease with which Judaism meshed with peace.[13]

The specific issue around which peace activists of all kinds coalesced during the early 1930s was disarmament, especially after an international disarmament conference was called in Geneva in 1932.[14] NCJW cooperated with NCCCW on an educational campaign aimed at getting the United States to join the World Court before the conference. NCJW also collected signatures for NCCCW's petition to the conference, using special beige paper to keep track of the Jewish signatories. The World Council of Jewish Women collected more than eight million signatures on a disarmament petition presented at the Geneva Conference, and even more Jewish women were represented in the petitions submitted by other women's peace groups like WILPF and the International Woman Suffrage Alliance (IWSA).[15]

The most prominent American Jewish woman at the 1932 Geneva Conference was Frieda Langer Lazarus, who had signed the Women's Peace Union (WPU) pledge in 1924 and since 1928 had been lobbying in Washington, D.C., to make sure that a constitutional amendment outlawing war stayed on the congressional calendar. The daughter of immigrants and a member of the Ethical Culture Society, Lazarus was also a frequent speaker during WPU's weekly radio broadcasts on WEVD, the Eugene Victor Debs radio station. She put aside all other commitments and spent several months in Geneva during the disarmament conference in early 1932. The WPU so valued her political acumen and skills that the organization contributed to her child care and household expenses while she was away. As a WPU representative, Lazarus lobbied for a program of immediate and total disarmament and the outlawry of war, believing that only government action could truly end war. The WPU plan included immediate cessation of all military recruitment, arms manufactures, and military appropriations, with a deadline of no more than a year for the disposal of all war matériel. To further publicize these goals, Lazarus rented an electric sign to flash "Total Disarmament Now" outside the WPU office, much to the annoyance of the Geneva police. The WPU's absolutist position did not sit well with other women's peace groups, including WILPF, which offered its own platform to the conference, and Lazarus mistrusted mixed gender peace groups, which she thought prone to compromise. Lazarus herself never wavered in her commitment to immediate and total disarmament and remained an absolutist throughout the decade.[16]

Jewish Attitudes toward Peace in Dangerous Times

The Jewish roots of peace work extended so far and so deep that even the darkening clouds of the 1930s did not immediately or completely destroy them. The growing student antiwar movement provided one arena for Jewish women's activism as the decade progressed. In February 1933, undergraduates at the Oxford Union upheld a resolution not to fight for England under any circumstances. In the United States the Oxford Pledge was rephrased to "refuse support for any war that the United States government might conduct." Absolutist pacifists were dissatisfied with this pledge, since the option of supporting wars *not* conducted by the United States government was left open, but the effect was to draw student socialists, who opposed national wars but not necessarily class warfare, into the campus antiwar campaigns. Across the country, peace rallies during the 1934/35 academic year attracted half a million students, approximately half the undergraduate population in the United States. In 1935 polls showed that 81 percent of students opposed taking up arms overseas. Campuses with significant Jewish populations, such as Brooklyn College and Temple University, staged peace strikes involving many thousands of students.[17]

On April 12, 1935, 175,000 students participated in the nationwide Students Strike Against War. At 150 schools, students left classes and marched in protest. In New York, 30,000 students were involved, including rabbinical students at the Jewish Theological Seminary. At City College, then predominantly Jewish and working-class, 1,544 students took the American version of the Oxford Pledge, while 2,200 Hunter College students, forced off campus by the administration, staged their own protest at another location. At Hunter College, the "Jewish Girls' Radcliffe," which by some estimates was 75 percent Jewish during the 1930s, students Beatrice Schapiro, Millie Futterman, Theresa Levin, and Lillian Dropkin, among others, were suspended for their roles in planning and carrying out peace strikes. The president of

Hunter eventually bowed to public outcry and reinstated the students, but he forcibly disbanded all the campus peace groups. The following year even more students from campuses all over the United States rallied for peace, with a substantial number of them explicitly rejecting a class system that shaped autocratic forms of higher education as well as leading to war. The historian Eileen Eagen has suggested that the anti-Semitism so prevalent on many college campuses contributed to administration and some faculty's harsh opposition to the student peace movement.[18]

Throughout this period, Estelle Sternberger, then executive director of World Peaceways, argued that social scientists were wrong to conclude that war was necessary to stimulate culture and creativity. She pointed to the rich cultural heritage of the Jews, who only rarely over the past 1,800 years had taken up arms except in immediate self-defense. In a 1935 *New York World-Telegram* profile, Sternberger advocated strongly for "bloodless wars" like the boycott of German goods rather than "barbarous" actual war. She believed that the virulent anti-Semitism in Hitler's Germany and elsewhere offered people worldwide a chance to embrace peace by abjuring prejudice. As she explained to the reporter, "If men stop hating the Jew, they will stop hating men of every group." The result, she believed, would be universal and lasting peace.[19]

Members of the rabbinate were not so sure. Although the Central Conference of American Rabbis (CCAR) was on record in many ways as supporting peace, the events of the 1930s reawakened serious discussion of Judaism's attitude to war and peace. The issue came to a head at the 1935 CCAR convention. The Committee on International Peace recommended a resolution opposing all war and encouraging Jews to refuse to bear arms. A lengthy debate followed. A small number of the Reform rabbis present, mostly those with strong pacifist credentials, supported the resolution as presented. Philip Bernstein baldly stated, "I for one would infinitely rather countenance an injustice rather than go out and kill somebody. I am a pacifist and I would like this Conference to renounce war." Several others concurred, and Rabbi Markowitz pointed out that "if there is one group in Israel which should stand fearlessly and unequivocally by an ideal, it is a conference of rabbis." But even Markowitz felt that the small number of people at the convention made it undesirable to impose the will of the few on the many. Those present agreed that moral persuasion, not executive decisions, should shape the CCAR's actions.[20]

Other CCAR members objected strongly to the resolution on ideological rather than procedural grounds. Frederick Cohn worried that the clause recommending conscientious objection was unpatriotic. Rabbi Singer agreed, countering that the American public was sure to denounce strongly a resolution that could be interpreted as unconstitutional, un-American, and perhaps even cowardly. He, like several other delegates, wanted to amend the resolution to support peace but promised that "should an invasion come to our shores, all of us will arise as one man in defense of our country." Most of the rabbis present, even those who supported a statement against war, assumed that if the United States were attacked, countless American Jews would immediately take up arms in defense of their country anyway, rendering the resolution as written meaningless. As Rabbi Feldman put it, "Let us attempt to prevent war as we prevent fire but when a fire breaks out in our home, we do not run away and let the thing burn down without resistance." The discussion led to a majority consensus that as long as the CCAR would support individuals who engaged in conscientious objection, there was no need to recommend such a path to all American Jews and ample justification for not doing so, given the still insecure position of American Jewry.[21] There was a definite undercurrent of fear of the anti-Semitism that a pacifist statement might engender during these parlous times.

Regardless of the earlier positions the CCAR had taken in identifying Judaism with peace, some members strongly objected to any blanket statements rejecting war. Rabbi Joseph L. Baron commented that "religion demands that we pursue an aggressive policy of justice for our fellow men as well as for ourselves," which meant that Judaism could condone offensive as well as defensive war in some cases. Several rabbis called for further study of the fundamental Jewish attitude toward war before making any major public statement. Though Rabbi Luchs made an impassioned plea that "war is a denial of religion," the delegates voted to commission scholarly studies of Judaism vis-à-vis war and peace and to circulate future resolutions on the subject more broadly before taking action.[22]

When the CCAR ultimately did adopt a resolution in 1937, it bore little resemblance to the one proposed two years earlier. The 1937 resolution stated that because Jews loved their country, they wanted the United States to lead the world to peace, which should be defined as active international cooperation, not merely the absence of war. The resolution went on to state that American Jews were not extremists committed to nonresistance and that they believed in both the right of nations to defend their existence and righteous wars, although it was hard to judge righteous causes in an age of propaganda.[23] The adopted resolution, far weaker in content and import than the earlier version, reflected the opinions of both a wider swath of American Jewry and, in all likelihood, the worsening conditions in Europe.

Despite the watered-down CCAR peace resolution, some American rabbis and many American Jewish organizations continued to proclaim the Jewish commitment to peace. Philip Bernstein, chairman of the CCAR Commission on International Peace, brought the Jewish perspective to the national stage when he addressed President Roosevelt as part of a peace delegation. He called "attention to the stand which has been taken by leading Jewish organizations in favor of the building up of an enduring world peace and the substitution of peace machinery for the present race in armaments."[24] A 1938 National Council for Prevention of War (NCPW) list of allied organizations still included NCJW, NFTS, CCAR, the Rabbinical Assembly of America, the United Synagogue of America, the Women's League of the United Synagogue of America, and the Women's Branch of the Union of Orthodox Jewish Congregations. As late as 1937, the Texas State Federation of Temple Sisterhoods made a donation to NCPW and called on the United States to exert world leadership in international cooperation, demilitarization of education, and international cooperation. Resolving that "of all who should speak the word for peace, women—mothers, sisters, wives—should be the first," the group reaffirmed that peace was commanded by God and the prophets, offering religious justifications for what they acknowledged might be their unpopular position. David de Sola Pool, a prominent Orthodox rabbi in New York, spoke at the December 1938 War Resisters League (WRL) dinner despite the fact that the organization refused to identify Jews as the most in need of the more open refugee policy it supported. Even after the United States entered the war, a few Jewish pacifists continued to argue vehemently that Judaism signified peace, as did Abraham Cronbach and Henry Slonimsky at a 1943 conference on Science, Philosophy, and Religion at Columbia University.[25]

American Jewish Women, Peace, and the World Crisis

Although Jewish women's interest in peace work remained strong, world events necessarily affected their activism, especially the rise of Hitler and the obvious threat that Nazism presented to Jews. Jennie Franklin Purvin, the Chicago social reformer, continued to go to peace meetings and to attend peace sermons, but unease about Germany began to creep into her diary. At a dinner party in 1932, Purvin found her inner circle discussing the impact of Hitler's rise to power. One friend said "things will go bad with Jews in Germany when Hitler is in . . . they have earned it by trying to be too German." The following year, she was elected to the board of WILPF's Chicago branch but went to an anti-Hitler mass meeting even though WILPF refused to sponsor the event. Purvin came to believe the proposed boycott of German goods would be the "only efficacious thing." Throughout 1933, her diary entries became longer and more political. In October she wrote that the best way to help the German Jews was to "[make] our problems that of other oppressed groups there and by not shouting about it."[26]

For much of the decade, Jewish women peace activists adopted this approach, continuing to work for peace while keeping a wary eye on events unfolding in Europe and sometimes shifting their attitudes or activities as circumstances seemed to demand. Individual Jewish women found it easier to maintain their pacifism, as their decisions carried less political weight than those of organizations. The labor organizer Rose Pesotta stepped up the pace of her peace work and, as a representative of the Keep America Out of War Committee, addressed audiences like the Youth Congress Against the War and the Madison House settlement in Boston. Jane Evans, executive director of NFTS, recognized Hitler as a serious threat but believed, "There are many ways to struggle against evil other than to slaughter a person who disagrees with you." As an individual, not as NFTS staff, Evans even contributed to Abraham Cronbach's goodwill fund for Germans, something NCJW's executive director Marion Miller refused to do in no uncertain terms.[27]

Jewish women's organizations did not immediately or conclusively back away from long-standing commitments to peace. In New York, the Federation of Jewish Women's Organizations sponsored a talk by Mayor LaGuardia on the importance of fighting Hitlerism. Yet both the 1935 and 1936 annual meetings of the Federation of Jewish Women's Organizations highlighted peace programming, including sessions on "The Peace Movement Today at Home and Abroad" and "What Makes for Peace" with speakers from the Women's Arbitration Council. The NFTS continued to ally with other peace groups while also supporting campaigns to make sure that large department stores like Macy's stopped buying, selling, or displaying German merchandise. In 1936 the sisterhood of Oheb Shalom, a Newark synagogue, inaugurated a new annual meeting devoted to peace. As late as 1940, a group of Jewish women in Woodridge, New York, formed a new peace organization and contacted WILPF for help with literature and speakers. As an *American Hebrew* article stated in 1934, it was "quite in keeping with any program for the prevention of war to take action and a decisive stand against the intolerable conditions" in Germany.[28] No one knew what lay ahead.

NCJW's activities during this period demonstrate how difficult it was to walk the fine line between demanding action against Hitler and denouncing the possibility of war. NCJW sections in some cities became even more active in peace work during the 1930s. The Cincinnati section started a Peace Library and worked with local synagogue sisterhoods to convene a new monthly peace study group. NCJW's Fresno, California, section co-sponsored mass community peace meetings and encouraged members to take

their children to movies that "express[ed] Anti-War sentiment instead of pictures glorifying war."[29]

In Fresno, as in other places, NCJW members used drama to illustrate
issues related to peace, acting out scenes based on Roland Gittelsohn's book
The Jew Looks at War and Peace during the November 1937 meeting. "The
Peace Clinic," a skit written and directed by Palisades, New Jersey, NCJW
members, dramatized a series of encounters between worried female patients
and "Dr. Peace." Dr. Peace counseled his patients that neutrality was the best
preventive medicine, advised against military training for boys, touted the
advantages of the League of Nations, diagnosed the State Department as
lacking in funds and staff, and guaranteed that the United States was in no
danger of attack. Dr. Peace concluded by telling the nurse that "I do hope
our patients follow the instructions given them. Then instead of continuing
to be a dream, Peace will some day become a reality." The NCJW section in
Camden, New Jersey, staged a similar play, "The Education of a Sceptic," [*sic*]
set at a NCCCW conference. The eponymous skeptic, Tillie, complains that
fourteen years of NCCCW meetings have not accomplished anything and
that "the world is crashing about our ears and all we do is sit here and talk."
The other delegates agree that the condition of the world is grave indeed, but
they argue that the United States cannot afford to ignore the rest of the world
and that it is women's special responsibility to agitate for peace. These home-
grown skits were not without playfulness—Tillie suggests devoting a session
to the hat styles on display at the conference—but they all demonstrated
ongoing interest in and commitment to peace among NCJW members. They
also reflected the deepening concern about the appropriate Jewish reaction
to world events.[30]

On the national level, NCJW supported the boycott of German goods.
Fanny Brin, as NCJW's national president, did not believe a boycott would
change German behavior, but she promoted it anyway in the hope that some
Germans would be persuaded to revolt. NCJW expected local sections to follow the national office's lead in backing the boycott but also warned them not
to protest the situation in Germany "indiscriminately," fearful of a backlash.
Brin, who had access to a series of confidential Jewish Telegraphic Agency
reports on the situation in Germany and the backstage maneuvering of
various Jewish organizations, put together a committee to increase Jewish
women's knowledge of their own history so that they could fight prejudice
more effectively. In 1935 the committee issued *Anti-Semitism: A Study Outline* for members who hoped to gain an understanding of what was happening in the world. Unlike most American Jewish groups, NCJW also urged the
United States to withdraw from the 1936 Olympics. However, after decades

of prominent peace work, NCJW found it very difficult to change course. As late as 1941, NCJW still officially supported neutrality and alternatives to war.[31]

NCJW's dilemma was hardly surprising. The events of the 1930s posed a serious threat to peace activists everywhere. As not only economic but political relations deteriorated and shadows of fascism deepened, and as Hitler and Mussolini gained power and trumpeted their expansionist ambitions, ambivalence over issues of war and peace concomitantly grew. Gauging the shifting attitudes toward peace, which to many worldwide had seemed the only possible option following the carnage of the Great War, some observers commented that many groups were genuinely interested in peace but few were actually pacifist, especially in the United States. Though understating pacifist passions following the war, the writer Marie Syrkin claimed in the Labor Zionist Alliance's journal *Jewish Frontier* that war had never really become inconceivable except to uninfluential, small groups of absolutist pacifists. Sonia Hyman, writing under the sponsorship of the Communist League for Industrial Democracy, explained that as long as governments acted against the interest of the people they purported to represent, peace was, at best, merely the absence of war rather than a planned, positive force that would yield both global security and economic justice. Rose Rees, a former Minneapolis NCJW president, believed strongly in the ultimate necessity of peace in the modern world but feared that state actors would never willingly limit their own sovereignty in the ways necessary to assure peace.[32]

The real shift among people involved with the peace movement was not so much admitting ambivalence toward peace as newly acknowledging the appropriateness of that ambivalence given the current circumstances. The Baltimore attorney and former suffragist Rose Zetzer sadly wrote to a friend, "We cannot fool ourselves into believing that we can abolish war in our own generation."[33] Both Jewish and non-Jewish peace activists struggled to come to terms with the state of the world. By 1939 many prominent pacifists had recanted, including the journalist Dorothy Thompson and the national YMCA director Sherwood Eddy. After decades of leadership in the peace movement, the international WILPF secretary Emily Greene Balch came to see Hitler as a new and different kind of threat that had to be stopped. WILPF leaders in Europe like Lida Heymann, Anita Augspurg, and Gertrude Baer miserably agreed that, as Heymann put it, "Fascism and national socialism *today* can be destroyed only through means which are capable of impressing the brutal men. . . . Such means are the means of brute force. From repeated experiences we women pacifists in Europe have come to recognize this."[34]

Heymann refused to renounce her beliefs completely, but it was clear that Baer and other Jewish peace leaders, all fugitives from Nazism, had been forced to face the difficulties not only of retaining pacifist convictions in the face of totalitarianism but also of reconciling the increasingly obvious tensions between Jewish identity and peace work. The choices confronting American Jewish peace activists were painful. One the one hand, as Estelle Sternberger explained in a speech, "If we remain silent in the face of the perverted doctrines of Hitlerism, we stamp ourselves as traitors of the race." On the other hand, as another Jewish peace worker put it, many Jewish women still believed strongly that their "natural female role of helping the culture survive might lead to peace."[35] The difficult decisions led some former contributors to peace organizations to stop supporting their former causes. The executive director of WILPF's New York branch informed the state board in 1936 that "Several large contributions we had expected were not forthcoming, due to (1) disagreement with our policies and (2) the growing feeling, especially among Jews, that Hitler can only be crushed by another war for Democracy against fascism." Frieda Schiff Warburg, a major PMC donor, wrote in early 1938 that she could no longer in good conscience fund a movement that she now believed was wrong to work against a war that would eventually be necessary to fight.[36]

For a while, American Jewish pacifists tried to follow the guidance of the activist Herman Bernstein, who encouraged all religious voices to take a stand for peace and against Hitler, who could only bring war. Ultimately, however, most of even the staunchest pacifists admitted the unique nature of the situation. Rabbi Stephen Wise, who in a 1932 speech had summed up his pacifism by stating "I would as little support a war to crush Hitlerism as a war for strengthening Jewish claims in Palestine," became the major representative of American Jewry trying to convince Roosevelt not only to enter the war but also to save Jewish lives through Zionism. Wise also criticized American peace leaders for their inaction, privately denouncing his frequent correspondent Frederick J. Libby, head of NCPW, for never saying "one word against Hitlerism and Hitler's anti-Jewish furer [sic]." Hebrew University's chancellor Judah Magnes, who had been excoriated for his pacifism during World War I, compared his agonizing abandonment of pacifism in the face of Nazism to a change in religion. In an October 1939 speech in Jerusalem, he said, "It is, with one's eyes open, accepting a lower belief, the belief that the taking up of arms though never righteous, is inevitable at this juncture, now that the war has been unleashed. This is apostasy from the pacifist faith."[37]

Jewish women who had been dedicated to peace for years felt deep disappointment that the peace movement could not offer a viable response to the targeted persecution of Jews. Sadie Cohen spoke for many when she wrote, "Must we Jewish women speak for ourselves when our souls are so burdened? Can we not expect those by whose side we have labored in the cause of World Peace to speak for us in our direst need?"[38] At the 1935 international WILPF meeting, the social worker Lillian Cantor Dawson and others tried to introduce a resolution condemning Hitler's actions. When officials would not entertain the motion, more than one hundred delegates, Jews and non-Jews, walked out. Dawson "just could not believe that the world should stand by and let Hitler happen. But at the same time I thought war was the greatest scourge of mankind. It was, of course, a difficult personal decision for me." Ultimately, Dawson felt compelled to support any measure, even war, that might save her fellow Jews.[39]

As a result of what they perceived as indifference to the special crisis faced by the Jews, Jewish women like Dawson found their religious and ethnic heritage newly meaningful to them during the 1930s. Unlike her sister Maud Nathan, the former anti-suffragist Annie Nathan Meyer rarely incorporated her Jewishness into her public persona for most of her adult life. During the 1930s, though, Meyer began to publish short stories with Jewish content for the first time, a development that did not go unnoticed by the friends and acquaintances who wrote to her about it. Katharine Asher Engel, a future NCJW national president, described herself as a "playgirl" until Hitler's clear threat to Jews propelled her into social work in the Jewish community, including refugee assistance through NCJW. In San Francisco, the civic activist Lucile Koshland put her own changing attitude in blunt terms, recalling, "People talk about the foul-weather Jews—you know, I was one of those. The more Hitler activities appeared on the horizon the more Jewish-conscious I became." On a tour of the Midwest in 1939, the Hadassah fund-raiser Rose Bender noticed that "a number of the women who are going to be the most active members . . . have only recently become aware of the fact that they are Jews. They are converts to Zionism because of Hitler."[40]

As Brenner's comments suggested, not just Judaism in general but Zionism in particular became more important to a large number of American Jews during this time of crisis, when it was clear that the Jews of Europe desperately needed a refuge. NCJW endorsed unrestricted Jewish immigration to Palestine and development of a Jewish state as per the 1917 Balfour Declaration. Even the previously anti-Zionist Reform movement officially changed its position on Palestine, though still not endorsing political Zionism, when issuing the Columbus Platform in 1937.[41] Because the organized American Jewish community had so many links to Jewish organizations abroad and so many American Jews had relatives in Europe, information about conditions there flowed even more freely than through the not-very-interested American press. The news—all bad—moved large numbers of women toward acknowledging and embracing their Judaism more than ever before.

Women's Peace Groups and the Winds of Change

Events abroad forced even the most resolute peace activists to reassess their commitments, with the Nazi treatment of Jews occasioning deep soul-searching. American Jewish women uneasily and then with growing panic waited as the outright condemnation they expected from their co-workers in the peace movement failed to appear. As Jennie Franklin Purvin wrote in her diary of Jews worldwide, "We *are* different," and she hoped her non-Jewish allies in the peace movement would understand this truth as well.[42]

Purvin and countless others like her were doomed to disappointment. Numerous pacifist women protested Nazi treatment of Jews, but of all the women's peace organizations, only NCCCW worked steadily for Jewish rights and attempted to secure refugee status in the United States for Jews fleeing Europe. Many American feminists, especially those involved with ICW and IWSA, had a well-developed internationalist perspective but were unwilling to take positions on national issues that might derail work on behalf of women. They had stayed out of the Irish question before World War I, for example, and they were not about to embroil themselves in German affairs now. Even the National Consumers' League, led for decades by Maud Nathan, refused on these grounds to participate in the 1930s boycott of German goods. Influential American women heavily involved in international organizations traveled a great deal, recognizing and even fighting anti-Semitism abroad. Many of their European feminist friends and colleagues were Jewish, so they heard about anti-Semitism firsthand from trusted sources. They could also see that events in Europe, especially in Germany, were curtailing the activities of international women's groups. Still, these activist American women were reluctant to address the issue of anti-Semitism at home by either acknowledging its existence in the United States, including within women's organizations, or by raising awareness of the situation in Europe.[43]

Carrie Chapman Catt was a major exception to the careful silence preserved by most activist women, an irony given the tenor of some of her xenophobic remarks during her suffrage career. During a post–World War I trip through Hungary, Austria, Czechoslovakia, and Germany in the company of her beloved Jewish IWSA colleague Rosa Manus, Catt had seen European anti-Semitism firsthand. Over the next decade Manus continued to correspond with her about anti-Semitism, but Catt remained hopeful that women's organizations could ameliorate the problem. Before Hitler came to power, she wrote to a German IWSA colleague, "You have some splendid leaders in Germany and I still think that Germany may prove to be the world's most fearless leader in the establishment of permanent peace." As soon as the Nazis took control, however, Catt became a tireless worker for Jewish rights. She and Manus attended the International Congress of Women in Chicago in 1933 and consulted there with an international group of Jewish women deeply concerned about Hitler's rise to power. Catt praised those German women's groups that dissolved rather than expel Jewish members; she also served as a sort of one-woman clearing house for information about Jewish peace activists who were forced into exile. After hearing James McDonald, head of the Foreign Policy Association, report on his recent fact-finding trip to Germany, Catt advised Manus to tell her brother-in-law to leave Germany because "worse things may happen . . . than have yet come." Much to her frustration, Catt found that not all her correspondents believed the bad news. Evelyn Riley Nicholson of the Women's Foreign Missionary Society wrote that her German contacts denied the published reports of Jewish persecution, and she urged Catt to expend her energy fighting incipient militarism in the United States instead. Catt sent back a strongly worded letter imploring Nicholson not to believe her duped contacts or Nazi propaganda. "As a matter of fact," Catt emphasized, "There has never been anything in the modern world to compare with the scheme of the Hitlerites toward the Jews."[44]

In 1933 Catt circulated a petition condemning German anti-Semitism. She secured the signatures of more than nine thousand non-Jewish women and sent the petition to the State Department. Nearly every notable woman in America responded positively to Catt's request. As Charlotte Perkins Gilman, not previously known for philo-Semitism, wrote, "Of course I am glad to add my name to the Committee of Women protesting against German cruelty and injustice to Jews. . . . How could anyone refuse?"[45] For her efforts, Catt was awarded the American Hebrew Medal. Eleanor Roosevelt presented the medal to Catt, who proclaimed at the ceremony, "It is my earnest hope that Non-Jews, everywhere, will comprehend the significance of the stupendous problems created by the recent happenings in Germany." She pointed out that Christians and Jews shared ideas about universal justice, rights, and peace, commenting, "I have long believed that the Jews, being the only people scattered among all the nations, have a peculiar and distinct call to leadership against war." Catt kept up her efforts throughout the 1930s. She joined former NCJW president Rebekah Kohut and others on a Committee of Ten to secure the signatures of one hundred distinguished women on a letter to President Roosevelt protesting the rigid interpretation of immigration quotas. She sent a telegram to the State Department protesting the events of Kristallnacht in November 1938, and the NCCCW she had founded worked steadily to loosen immigration quotas in order to admit more Jewish refugees to the United States.[46]

Other American women's peace groups found the murky waters of the 1930s more difficult to navigate. In 1936 WPU inserted into its membership pledge a statement "against every form of racial violence in thought, speech, or deed" but did little to help Jewish refugees or condemn Nazi anti-Semitism outright.[47] As in other women's organizations, ambivalence toward Jews and Judaism sometimes played a role in WPU's activities. The same year that WPU's executive director Tracy Mygatt pushed through the reworded membership pledge, she also wrote to a colleague that she was concerned about the overwhelmingly Jewish membership of WPU in New York.

> Perhaps you have more of our kind out in Chicago, but here we're certainly few and far between. Not that I don't enthusiastically love and enjoy my Jewish comrades. Don't think that for an instant. But I'd like to feel that Americans, too, from that apocryphal Mayflower, were standing up for the right.

Mygatt hastened to add that she was, of course, free of "race prejudice," but the fact that she did not see the Jewish WPU members as "our kind" or even as Americans reflected the deep, perhaps unconscious prejudices that shaped reactions to persecution of Jews abroad.[48]

It was this kind of prejudice, sometimes even more blatantly and publicly displayed, that Maud Nathan reacted to in an April 1936 letter written to (though not published by) *The Nation*. Nathan wrote to protest the pro-Nazi German-American League, which had officially announced that its goal was to fight the "Moscow-directed madness of the Red-world menace and its Jewish bacillus carriers." She urged that the German-American League not be granted a charter or any kind of recognition and hoped her audience would agree that embracing Nazism was not necessary in order to fight communism. Pointing out that "the Jews have been in America since the landing of Columbus," she criticized the German-American League for casting aspersions on the patriotism of American Jews and scornfully encouraged "those Germans who wish to be led by the nose by an Austrian degenerate" to go to Germany and see how they liked it there.[49] Both Mygatt's concern about the WPU being too Jewish and Nathan's spirited defense of American

Jews as Americans reveal the tensions and prejudices underlying women's peace organizations' reactions to the challenges that faced them.

A close examination of the checkered relationship of Jewish women to WILPF provides insight into the links among pacifism, Jewish and female identity, and anti-Semitism. WILPF was particularly important because although the anti-radicalism of the 1920s prevented it from ever becoming a truly mass movement, the organization was extremely well connected and exerted real power at the federal level. The national headquarters were strategically located in Washington, D.C., where an executive board with strong central powers generally made all national policy decisions. Each state and local branch of WILPF enjoyed a certain degree of autonomy, but part of the membership dues went to the national office, which left much of the smaller scale fund-raising to the branches. State and local branches varied considerably in constituency, but those areas with significant Jewish populations always produced WILPF branches with disproportionately high Jewish membership, particularly in New York and Chicago. As WILPF's executive director Dorothy Detzer explained, WILPF consistently took stands against the "degradation of religious or political persecution," intervening during the early 1930s, for example, at the highest levels of government and commerce to ensure that no slave labor would be used in a proposed dam to be built in Abyssinia.[50] Jewish members could hardly be blamed for expecting WILPF to take the high moral ground when other kinds of threats presented themselves as well.

From 1932 on, WILPF faced a policy crisis, with some members insisting that only detached neutrality would ensure American non-involvement in war and other members promoting American involvement in international affairs to prevent aggression. WILPF leaders considered adopting an agenda that would distinguish between aggressor and victim, condemning the aggressor, but the organization ultimately rejected this "neutrality revision." Still, in early 1933 the U.S. WILPF branches collectively sent statements to German consulates and to international WILPF headquarters to protest Nazi treatment of Jews. In April WILPF's international executive board passed a resolution stating that "the special laws treating Jewish citizens as an inferior class . . . are degrading not just to Jews but to humanity," a development that Estelle Sternberger approvingly publicized to a large Jewish readership in *B'nai B'rith Magazine*. Both Detzer and Emily Greene Balch personally visited the German ambassador to the United States and were disgusted by his denial of any persecution at a time when reports of anti-Semitic actions were in wide circulation and when German women's groups that refused to expel Jewish members had been forcibly disbanded.[51]

Estelle M. Sternberger
delivering a radio broad-
cast. Courtesy of the Jacob
Rader Marcus Center
of the American Jewish
Archives

There were other examples of WILPF's denunciation of Nazism and cooperation with the organized American Jewish community. Right after Hitler
came to power, WILPF participated in the March 7, 1934, "The Case of Civilization Against Hitlerism" mass meeting at Madison Square Garden and also
cooperated in such Jewish communal protests as the American Jewish Congress's May 10, 1934, demonstration against Nazism. There does not seem to
have been much controversy within WILPF over these actions, and the New
York State branch also publicized a list of Hitler's anti-Semitic decrees in an
attempt to educate its members about the Nazi threat.[52]

The "Jewish problem" weighed heavily on every level of WILPF, albeit
sometimes in disguise. Though in 1933 the Minnesota branch decried the
Nazi policies that forced Gertrude Baer and other Jewish WILPF leaders to
flee, the meeting minutes referred to them as "highly cultured pacifists" and
made no mention of the Jewishness that was the real reason for their forced
flight. The following year, the national WILPF *Programs and Policies* was a
bit more forthcoming, proclaiming its "opposition to dictatorship and tyranny" and urging members to help "Jewish, pacifist, and all other victims
of these policies." By 1938 the Minnesota branch was officially expressing
its sympathy to Jews and pressuring the British government to allow Jewish
immigration to Palestine as a means to prevent war. Throughout this period,

Jewish women continued to serve the branch in leadership roles. Fanny Brin gave a talk on "Peace, a Condition of Survival" at the annual meeting of the Minnesota branch in December 1934. Nevertheless, in response to the growing complications of world events, the number of Jewish WILPF members began to drop in Minnesota just as it did elsewhere.[53]

WILPF was a peace group, not a Jewish advocacy group, and it declined to join the boycott against German goods. The 1934 WILPF platform condemned "German persecutions on grounds of race and political opinion" but believed that any boycott must be a step toward war. The national office pointed out to one of its members in the Bronx that pacifists and other Germans were also suffering under the Nazi regime, not Jews alone. That member, Mrs. J. X. Cohen, worried about the growing gap between the national organization's policy and the local members' "constantly growing feeling . . . that our National organization has not been sufficiently outspoken in condemning the twentieth-century inquisition known as Hitlerism." The Bronx members, almost all of whom were Jewish, were pleased that WILPF participated in the Madison Square Garden meeting but did not think that this was enough. They dedicated their WILPF branch to providing as much information as possible about conditions in Germany and held a series of open meetings to publicize eyewitness accounts of "Nazi madness and its workings." These public education campaigns paid the additional dividend of increased membership in the Bronx chapter. Yet greater numbers of members did not indicate greater support for WILPF policies. Mrs. Cohen wrote in the annual report of the Bronx branch in March 1934, "The constant reiteration on the part of some of our liberals of the Versailles Treaty as an excuse for Hitlerism makes one think of saying of a criminal who kills and persecutes and violates all inherent human rights, 'The poor dear has had such a bad bringing up.'"[54]

There was no specific mention of Jews in the annual report, but it was evident that local and national WILPF policies were headed toward a collision course. As conditions worsened in Germany, the New York State branch of WILPF began to have even more trouble fund-raising than had already followed on the heels of the Depression. A number of large donors, several of them Jewish women, withdrew their financial support from WILPF, which remained committed to neutrality and condemned the idea of collective security as a fatal step down the path to war. The executive director of this branch blamed dwindling support on "the growing feeling, especially among Jews, that Hitler can only be crushed by another war for Democracy against fascism." WILPF chapters in other parts of the country did not face these internal tensions to the same degree, but they were palpable in New York and other large cities. In 1938 Detzer, a major player on the foreign policy scene in D.C., reminded branches that they could take up questions with the national organization but should not make public statements of dissent.[55]

The heavily Jewish membership of so many of the troublesome branches also brought WILPF into direct confrontation with the anti-Semitism, in all of its shades, of many of its members. When WILPF began to compile a pamphlet on religion and peace in 1938, leaders at the top levels discussed how many Jewish clergy and leaders should be represented. There was agreement that some Jewish voices were necessary, "inasmuch as our membership includes so many Jewish people," but there was also a concern that many WILPF members "wouldn't care to subscribe to a publication which was predominantly Jewish."[56] For all its progressive pronouncements on peace and policy, WILPF was no more immune to the prejudices of the day than any other segment of American society.

Given WILPF's cautious response to any explicitly Jewish issue, it was not surprising that collective security organizations, even communist ones like the American League for Peace and Democracy, made inroads into WILPF's constituency. Both organizations condemned war and worked for peace, but WILPF's insistence on absolute neutrality did not allow for the leeway that the American League had to denounce, in the most forceful terms, particular actions taken by particular governments against particular people. Many American Jews found this stance appealing, as the American League harshly criticized Nazi policies toward Jews. WILPF not only disagreed with the American League's collective security platform, it also decried the American League's habit, sometimes violent, of breaking up pro-Nazi meetings. In 1938 WILPF's national board voted to cut all ties with the American League for Peace and Democracy, displeasing many Jewish members, who would rather have cooperated with communists than back away from denouncing Nazism in the strongest possible terms.[57]

New York City eventually provided a testing ground for Jewish women's loyalties and for the limits of peace organizations' responses. The year 1938 became one of WILPF showdowns. In April, the Brooklyn branch recommended opposing neutrality and supporting the boycott of German goods, positions in direct opposition to national WILPF policy. In describing this rebellion to Detzer, the New York State branch's executive director Lyn Smith listed only one or two Jewish women, such as longtime Brooklyn branch leader Rose K. Edelman, who could still be depended upon. Smith tried to rein in the seven hundred members of the Brooklyn branch but was afraid they would all be lost to the American League for Peace and Democracy if the national office did not take swift action. Detzer responded that at national meetings, too, the issue of "separating the Jewish question from the larger minority problems" was a recurring one. Tired of dealing with what she saw as a relatively minor issue in the context of a world on the brink of another war, she even wrote to Smith—ironically, to be sure—that "for the first time in my life I am beginning to feel a little anti-Semitic!" When WILPF did not amend its national policies to reflect concerns about Nazi persecution of the Jews, disaffection in the New York branches boiled over. The leaders and most members of both the Brooklyn and Bronx branches resigned. The Brooklyn branch survived, albeit in greatly reduced numbers and influence, but 140 of 150 Bronx members left WILPF and the branch effectively ceased to function.[58]

The events in New York, though indicative of the difficulties Jewish women in the peace movement faced as their universalist pacifism came into conflict with their particular concerns about the status of European Jewry, do not tell the whole story of WILPF and the Jewish question during this period. While remaining firmly committed to keeping the United States out of a war that looked increasingly inevitable, WILPF did gradually join other peace organizations in addressing anti-Semitism at home and abroad. In 1938, just as the Bronx and Brooklyn WILPF branches were falling apart, Detzer lobbied Congress to pass an emergency refugee act for European Jews even if they would present a "threat to the labor movement." She personally joined Peter Bergson's Emergency Committee to Save the Jews, though she could offer no solution to the problem of where rescued Jews could go. Detzer and the national WILPF president Hannah Clothier Hull wrote to President Roosevelt suggesting that the United States loosen quotas so that Jewish refugees could escape to safety. National, state, and local publications circulated readings lists recommended by WILPF's newly appointed National Committee on Anti-Semitic Trends, listing such works as J. X. Cohen's *Toward Fair Play for Jewish Workers* and M. S. Sheehy's *The Pope Condemns Anti-Semitism*. These activities helped WILPF retain the loyalty of some Jewish women. A small group of Jewish women activists, including Jane Evans, Sarah Lifton, Stella Moos, Mercedes Randall, Meta Riseman, and Eda White remained WILPF members throughout the war, even though their commitments usually put them at odds with their friends, neighbors, and family members.[59]

During the Storm

Despite strained relations, American Jewish women sustained ties to the peace movement. Both WILPF and NCCCW representatives participated in NCJW's 1938 Triennial meeting in Pittsburgh. In 1939 WILPF endorsed passage of the Wagner-Rogers bill to admit 20,000 Jewish refugee children to the United States; the same year WILPF also supported mandatory neutrality and anti-draft legislation.⁶⁰ Once war broke out in Europe, all the women's peace groups struggled to formulate a response. NCJW issued a statement that the job of groups devoted to peace had now become laying the foundation for a new postwar world order, hopefully by keeping the United States out of the war and in a position to oversee the eventual peace. WILPF carefully considered whether to join a protest meeting against Nazi cruelties in Poland, wholeheartedly condemning the atrocities but fearing any action that might foment further hatred and militarization. The tattered remains of the Brooklyn branch of WILPF gave up all pretense of conforming to the organization's national policies and focused only on refugee aid and support for the humanitarian work of the American Friends Service Committee abroad. By 1940 NCCCW allowed for the possibility that the United States could best serve a higher purpose by fighting Hitler.⁶¹

Although some pacifists had a history of working to strengthen American ties with Asia and knew something of the threat posed by Japan, Pearl Harbor nonetheless caught many peace activists off guard. Jennie Franklin Purvin ruefully wrote in her diary on December 7, 1941, "Got the first news on Japan bombing of Manila and Hawaii. Pres. Roosevelt is a child of fortune—he does not need to declare war—Japan has done it for him."⁶² At emergency meetings held just after the attack, both WILPF and NCJW attempted to come to terms with the new reality. WILPF reaffirmed its core belief that "war remains the final infamy" but also emphasized its policy of supporting the democratic process and the decisions of duly elected representatives of the people. NCJW suffered almost immediate anti-Semitic criticism that its peace work had contributed to the U.S.'s lack of preparedness for attack but chose not to respond to such allegations. Instead, NCJW, like WILPF, shifted focus to planning for world reorganization after the war's end.⁶³ As chairman of NCJW's recently renamed Committee on International Relations and Peace, Fanny Brin issued a statement just after Pearl Harbor expressing disappointment with the failure of the peace movement to prevent catastrophe.

> We must never forget the lessons we have learned, that isolation does not protect us, that it breaks down when we need it most; that when it breaks down, it ends in intervention; that we can only avoid intervention by setting up agencies which make possible collective action. We must learn and teach the lesson of cooperation and search for the form it must take.⁶⁴

Jennie Kubie, the longtime chair of NFTS's Peace Committee, wrote in a similar vein in January 1942 and, like Brin, refused to give up hope and called for intelligent postwar planning.⁶⁵

The mood of the American people was hardly conducive to peace work in the aftermath of the United States' entry into the war. The peace movement split into several loose groups. A small minority continued to believe in absolute pacifism, represented by such groups as the WRL. A larger group of liberal pacifists urged the United States to fight a limited defensive war and to develop plans for a just and lasting peace based on sounder principles and more powerful international institutions than had developed following the First World War. Still other pacifists felt they had no choice but to abandon their convictions, at least temporarily. Neither absolutist nor liberal pacifism seemed much concerned with the plight of Jews in Europe. American Jews were horrified by the scale of destruction so evident in the world war, but they also saw America's entry into battle as an opportunity to save Jews in Europe. They were disillusioned by the continued lack of interest among many pacifists in singling out the Jewish case as unique and worried about the accusations of isolationists like Charles Lindbergh that Jews were responsible for drawing the United States into the war. In 1942 Rabbi Stephen Wise advised the CCAR to withdraw from the National Peace Conference, which was preparing to suggest terms for a negotiated peace settlement with Germany as preferable to continuing to fight.[66]

Jewish women aligned themselves with all the strands of wartime pacifism. Frieda Langer Lazarus became an important figure in the WRL, which pushed for an immediate armistice and generous peace terms for all the belligerent nations. Believing that the war was the biggest problem facing mankind, Lazarus gave up all her other commitments, including her previous work on behalf of the Equal Rights Amendment, in order to devote her full attention to supporting conscientious objectors through the WRL. She worked with colleagues like Esther Eichel who never wavered in their commitment to absolutist pacifism. Eichel, whose husband was imprisoned during both world wars for conscientious objection, continued to resist war by supporting the families of other imprisoned conscientious objectors. Throughout the war and despite deep disapproval from other American Jews, she protested abuses, offered moral support, picketed prisons, and held support group meetings to promote pacifist ideals.[67]

Other pacifist Jewish women chose a different tack. Rebecca Hourwich Reyher reluctantly admitted the necessity of a defensive war but would not participate in traditional war work. Instead, she joined the efforts of the Dominican Republic Settlement Association to help refugees. Reyher explained, "Hitler was rampant. I wanted to do something against him." For her, working with the nominally nonsectarian Dominican Republic Settlement Association—even though most refugees and board members were

Jewish and the American Jewish Joint Distribution Committee provided most of the funding—satisfied her desire to work in a peaceful manner to do good in the world.[68]

Reyher also tried to restrain the intensity of the hatred many American Jews felt toward the Germans. She wrote a pamphlet titled *There Must Be No Bitterness* to encourage American Jews not to fall into the trap of a hatred that could only lead to more war. "Today," she pointed out, American hatred is "directed against the Germans, but tomorrow [it] may be directed against Jews, Catholics, Negroes and other minorities." She believed that as victims of persecution, Jews had a special obligation to show the world how vindictiveness would destroy any future hopes of world peace. Jewish women pacifists outside the large Jewish women's organizations felt some skepticism about their ability to hold fast to their former principles of peace. Reyher was not surprised that NCJW declined to distribute *There Must Be No Bitterness*. She was "convinced that the Jewish organizations seem to feel that violent hatred against the Germans is frank reaction to atrocities committed against the Jews and any other feeling is treachery to the Jews."[69] Fierce expressions of Jewish loyalty and solidarity swept American Jews in much the same way as fierce expressions of patriotism swept the country as a whole. In both cases, Reyher felt, to suggest any kind of dissent from mainstream thinking was treacherous.

Peace organizations of all stripes suffered from the disapprobation, and sometimes outright hatred, of an American public committed to "the good war." Few of the women's peace groups could withstand the pressure. WPU was moribund by 1940. In 1943 NCCCW, the largest women's peace group in the United States, became the Women's Action Committee for Victory and Lasting Peace, with Brin as a vice-chairman.[70] Losing members daily, WILPF began to grant the crisis of European Jewry a more central position as news of the death camps reached the United States. In April 1943, Jewish board member Mercedes Randall wrote an open letter to WILPF members detailing that

> Thousands upon thousands of Jews have been packed into sealed, lime-strewn cattle cars, with no food, water, or elementary conveniences, and shunted off to die standing. Records tells of "scientific" extermination centers, asphyxiation trucks, gas-chambers, machine-gunning into self-dug graves, introduction of air bubbles into veins. Innumerable Jews have vanished completely with no record at all. Thousands of Jewish mothers and fathers, assuming they survive, will never know what became of their children, or children know who their parents were.[71]

In a year-end publication that December, Dorothy Detzer wrote that "the responsibilities for this hideous program rests squarely on Hitler and his party" but also confessed that "by our failure to act to save these trapped people, we cooperate with Hitler's program of extermination and by this 'sin of omission' are guilty with him."[72] No WILPF member could later claim not to know what was happening.

WILPF finally acknowledged the enormity of the crimes being committed against the Jews, but the organization also worried that the literature on Jewish persecution available in the United States was so inflammatory that all it accomplished was to arouse a fighting spirit and hatred of Germans. To counteract these tendencies, WILPF authorized a pamphlet to lay out the facts without rancor and to suggest rescue efforts without vindictiveness. Randall wrote *The Voice of Thy Brother's Blood* in 1944 with the cooperation of the American Jewish Congress, American Jewish Committee, World Jewish Congress, and Joint Distribution Committee, all of which gave her free access to their files.[73] The pamphlet, which reached hundreds of thousands of Americans, enumerated Nazi atrocities in no uncertain terms and harshly criticized United States refugee policy, but it reflected its origins by trying not to, as an earlier WILPF statement put it, "spread hatred or endanger the chance of mediation or truce."[74]

Rosika Schwimmer, who had been discredited as a radical during the interwar period and needled both Jewish and non-Jewish women's groups throughout those years, wrote to Randall complimenting her on her work in arousing awareness of refugees. However, Schwimmer added, she had been writing about Jewish refugees for a decade, "and the W.I.L. looked the other way; and my appeal remained the cry in the wilderness."[75] American Jewish groups of all kinds emphasized that experience had taught them that they could and should rely mostly on their own efforts to save their own people. At the 1943 NCJW Triennial meeting in Chicago, Katharine Asher Engel said:

> I need not tell you of the critical and crucial position of the Jews in the world of today. I cannot sufficiently emphasize to you that whatever happens to any minority in any country immediately reacts upon you, who are also a minority group. . . . Every thinking Jew is confronted with the responsibility of all minority problems. From this chaos and heartbreak, we must all work together for a common unity of purpose.[76]

Whereas twenty years earlier an NCJW speaker might well have elaborated at great length Jewish women's peace-loving ties to other women at home and abroad, during this time of crisis Jewish identity rather than female or maternal identity took precedence. It was not primarily as women but as Jews that NCJW members could and should reach out to their sister Jews and all those in danger as persecuted minorities throughout the world.

At different times the pendulum swung between Jewish and gender identity, though neither was ever absent from the thinking of most Jewish women concerned with peace. The Rosh HaShanah greetings from NCJW in 1944 captured this blend of identity, with two former NCJW presidents, both of whom were nationally prominent in the peace movement as well, expressing their hopes for the upcoming year. Brin wrote:

> The year ahead is a year of decision. What we decide in the coming months will largely determine whether or not we can build a world free from the curse of war. As women who have had the privilege of training and of the ballot, we are accountable for what is done and what is left undone. One can only devoutly pray that no woman will rest from her responsibility. May God grant that we do not fail.

Nearly twenty-five years after suffrage, Brin continued to link American women's privileged position as voters to their ability to create the world they wanted to live in, a world of peace. Constance Sporborg, who had led the women's delegation to the Pan-American conference in 1938, stated:

> Let us hope that mankind will profit by the spiritual instruments the Jews, over five thousand years ago, contributed to the evolution of the human race and which may yet help to fortify civilization after the tragic setback of this decade. May the spirit of peace hover over the coming year.

Her focus on the religious and historical gifts of Jews to civilization was meant to arouse the readers' pride in their Jewish heritage. Taken together, the messages illustrate the ways in which all components of their identity motivated so many Jewish women to strive for peace under even the most difficult circumstances until peace, or at least the avoidance of war, posed a stark threat to Jewish survival.[77]

A few Jewish stalwarts remained peace activists. Rabbi Arthur Lelyveld, who had edited the leftist *Spectator* while a student at Columbia in the early 1930s, served as president of the Jewish Peace Fellowship from 1941 to 1943 and as secretary of the Joint Rabbinical Committee on Conscientious Objection. Abraham Cronbach continued firm in his conviction that "of all the outrages committed against the Jews by Hitler, none is more calamitous than this—he has banished from the hearts of many Jews the will to peace."

He often worked with Jane Evans, the executive secretary of NFTS, whose personal pacifism did not reflect the position of her employer. Esther Eichel believed that the most important thing she could do in opposition to "the great war machine" was support those who refused to fight. In October 1945, for instance, she picketed the White House and the Department of Justice on behalf of still imprisoned conscientious observers, who did not have the court system on their side.[78]

It would be unrealistic to expect most Jewish women's peace activism to continue during and after the war as if nothing had happened. Some felt deeply betrayed by others in the peace movement, while even more no longer believed that pacifism could resolve issues of the magnitude of Nazism and the Holocaust. Formerly liberal pacifists like Brin often developed an even more passionate belief that international institutions were the means of achieving lasting world peace. Brin chaired a meeting for women's groups considering the United Nations charter and attended the San Francisco conference where the charter was signed as a representative of both NCJW and the Women's Action Committee for Victory and Lasting Peace. She served as one of the sponsors for a 1947 dinner honoring Carrie Chapman Catt, a dear colleague in the peace movement, and remained a member of WILPF all her life.[79]

Brin was not alone in her continuing, albeit transformed, interest in peace, but for the most part, the issue of peace quietly slipped off Jewish women's agenda. The entire peace movement was seriously weakened by World War II, and in the anti-communist climate of the late 1940s and early 1950s, pacifism was a dangerous cause to embrace publicly. Many of the histories of NCJW on both the national and the local level barely mention peace, and an organization that had been on the radical edge during the 1920s and early 1930s became quite politically conservative during the 1950s. NFTS became significantly less concerned with national politics as suburbanization realigned Reform, Conservative, and Orthodox Jewish denominationalism during the postwar era. Not until the Vietnam War again brought issues of pacifism and conscientious objection to the forefront did the major American Jewish religious, communal, and philanthropic organizations again take up issues of Judaism and peace.

Conclusion

The experiences of American Jewish women in the peace movement during the 1930s demonstrate that their Jewish identity became more, not less, integral to their lives, despite the fact that peace work had successfully functioned in part as a form of Americanization. Their dilemma was at once unique and representative of the many other American ethnic and immigrant groups continuously renegotiating their identities. Jewish women did not renounce altogether the gender solidarity or acculturation efforts inherent in their activism, but their priorities changed. Even if Jewish women had not worked mostly through Jewish organizations before (though many did), or even if they had not previously articulated Jewish rationales for activism (though many did) because they had seen feminism or maternalism as their motivation, the question of what it meant to be a Jewish peace activist became impossible to ignore. The response to Nazism altered the direction of Jewish women's path toward Americanization away from universalist ideals of peace and toward the particular protection of Jewish rights. The maternalism that had undergirded many Jewish women's peace activism similarly shifted to focus on their role in preserving Jewish life. The larger peace movement understandably made no such moves, making conflict and disillusionment nearly inevitable. In the face of particular threats to Jewish survival and the apparent silence of their activist colleagues, Jewish women did not so much abandon their internationalist ideals as gradually and painfully redirect them to Jewish identity rather than universal peace.

For several decades, identity politics had carved out a unique political space for American Jewish women, one that generated a distinctive activist sensibility shaped by ideas about both Jewish responsibilities and gender roles. During the 1930s the murderous disarray of world politics led them to redefine their political mobilization. However, Jewish women who ultimately retreated from peace work did not thereby abandon the path toward Americanization. Ironically, nothing was more American or patriotic than joining the war effort, even if the motive for doing so was to defend Jewish interests. Similarly, their gendered focus on protecting the world by promoting peace as women transmuted into a focus on protecting Jews by accepting a mandate to defeat Hitler. Both perspectives assumed that they had a special part to play on the world stage. While the events of the 1930s required a reevaluation of what it meant to be Americans, Jews, and women, Jewish women remained unwaveringly committed to advancing the causes they believed in, even when changing realities forced them to renegotiate their activism in light of their personal identities.

To think of others is as natural to the Jewish woman as to breathe.
—Belle Lindner Israels Moskowitz, 1917[1]

I stood for Jewish interests, Jewish thought, Jewish feeling quite as
much as I stood for the broader and more universal outlook on life.
—Maud Nathan, 1933[2]

When Fanny Brin rose from her seat of honor at the Speakers' Table and
stepped up to the podium at the closing session of the Woman's Centennial
Congress in November 1940, she stood there as a representative of American women. Her longtime colleague and friend Carrie Chapman Catt had
convened the Woman's Centennial Congress to assess "how far women have
progressed in the past century and how today they may best continue this
forward movement." Hundreds of women, including Eleanor Roosevelt,
Margaret Mead, Pearl Buck, and foreign dignitaries, convened at the Hotel
Commodore in New York to hear reports on women's achievements in economic and social welfare, government and politics, ethical and religious values, and world peace and international relations. They celebrated one hundred American women in careers that had not been open to them a century
earlier, when women could not even be seated as delegates to the 1840 World
Anti-Slavery Convention in London. With war already raging in Europe, the
participants in the Woman's Centennial Congress resolved "to work for the
progressive securing of freedom, social justice and peace for all people."[3]

Brin, identified in the press coverage as the former president of the
National Council of Jewish Women, embodied the activists attending the
Woman's Centennial Congress, women who called attention to what was
wrong in the world and worked to make it right. American Jewish women
could take pride in the prominent role played by one of their own, someone
who had spent decades explaining how her Jewishness shaped and motivated
her activism. Brin was not alone: suffrage and peace activists Maud Nathan,
Constance Sporborg, and Gertrude Weil; labor leaders Pauline Newman,
Rose Schneiderman, and Fannia Cohen; birth control advocate Nadine Kavinoky; political radical Rosika Schwimmer; and Zionists Tamar de Sola Pool,

Julia Dushkin, and Emily Solis-Cohen all attended the Woman's Centennial Congress as well, many at the special invitation of Catt and the organizing committee. They represented thousands upon thousands of American Jewish women who, like them, had spent the past fifty years engaged in activism that had resulted in significant social, legal, educational, and civic change.[4]

Over a period of several decades and several generations, American Jewish women of diverse class, national, and religious backgrounds embraced the exuberance of large-scale social movements that promised to grant them political authority and citizenship, enhance their power over their own bodies and families, and expand their roles in international relations through the promotion of peace. Though Jewish identity constantly fluctuated, many women held fast to their own ideas of what it meant to be Jewish. Jewishness often shaped their political commitments to secular causes. Each individual crafted her own identity as an American, Jew, and woman, and American Jewish women's experiences fused these divergent dimensions of identity. That fusion helps explain Jewish women's prominence not only in Jewish movements like Zionism and Jewish-inflected movements like labor activism but also in American women's social movements.

As the preceding chapters illustrate, *Ballots, Babies, and Banners of Peace* seeks to contribute to the ever-broadening story of American feminism as a diverse movement. Any analysis that attempts to explain the complexity of movements oriented to women must acknowledge the great differences among them. This history of American Jewish women's participation in the suffrage, birth control, and peace movements aligns with earlier critiques of women's history as too focused on middle-class, white, Protestant women and also explores the important differences among Jewish women, whose ideas about gender, Jewish identity, and activism were shaped by their varied class, ethnic, religious, national, and ideological backgrounds.[5] At the same time, Jewish women also shared interests among themselves and with other women that led to remarkable activist success.

The suffrage movement has been criticized as a relatively conservative, homogenous movement. Although there is some truth to that characterization, the engaged presence of Jewish women as well as other marginalized groups such as African American and working-class women challenged early feminism to expand ideas about what equal citizenship would mean for women. Similarly, opponents and some historians of the birth control movement have seen it as a form of social control. However, the eagerness with which both working-class and middle-class Jewish women availed themselves of contraception and participated in the movement to make birth control legal and accessible requires an acknowledgment of the agency all these women demonstrated in making the best decisions possible for themselves and their families. In the wake of the bloody twentieth century, the peace movement is sometimes seen as hopelessly quixotic, a dismissal due in part to the dominance of presumably powerless women in peace work. But early twentieth-century women were savvy and practical activists, and Jewish women in the movement demonstrated that they were fully capable of acting on their own interests.

American Jewish women's participation in nonsectarian women's social movements raises intriguing possibilities for understanding the processes of acculturation and the shift of ethnic and immigrant groups from the margins toward the center during the early twentieth century. While both Jewish women and men generally sought some integration into mainstream American society, their paths to acculturation often diverged, due in part to gender differences. The similarity of women's gender roles across all kinds of boundaries of ethnicity, religion, class, and even race—particularly the common valorization of motherhood—offered Jewish women opportunities for social integration less available to Jewish men, who first had to overcome stereotypes of effeminacy that may have dogged their efforts to take on attributes of American manhood. Native-born white men who still commanded the power structure of early twentieth-century America saw little need to accommodate immigrant men, let alone Jewish men of suspect masculinity, by expanding access into their bastions of male privilege.

This is not to say that differences of class and national origins played no role. Native-born American Jews or Jewish immigrants who came from central and western European countries where Victorian values held sway had fewer changes in gender roles to negotiate. The continuity of such roles probably eased the transition to American middle-class family and economic structures. By contrast, the public economic roles that many eastern European Jewish women played prior to immigration required adjustment in an American society only gradually coming to grips with an expansion of women's activities at the turn of the century. Similarly, the ideal of men devoted to intellectual pursuits and the study of Torah rather than economic responsibility, while never describing more than a minority of eastern European Jews, nonetheless affected traditional understandings of men's roles that seemed unacceptable in a New World that assumed men would—and should—be the breadwinners. As a result, gender formed an important element of the culture clashes that faced all immigrant Jews in America and sometimes served to differentiate new Jewish arrivals from their more established, American-born, second-, third- or fourth-generation Jewish counterparts.[6]

The realignment of gender roles, which moved toward a middle-class set of norms while still allowing for a somewhat unconventional public space for

Jewish women's political expression, thus helped form the American Jewish community throughout the period of mass migration and then consolidation following restrictive immigration legislation. Feminist activism, far from endangering acculturation, in fact facilitated it for Jewish women through participation in American women's associational life. Despite persistent anti-Semitism, only rarely did Jewish women feel it necessary to abjure Jewish identity as participants in American social movements. Jewish women instead deployed a strategic range of engagements with both women's movements and Jewish identity that offered a level of complementarity. Their notable participation in the great women's movements of suffrage, birth control, and peace not only helped shape early twentieth-century feminism but also laid the groundwork for the further development of feminism in later decades.

Whether native-born or immigrant, working or middle class, urban or rural, Jewish or Catholic or Protestant, American women who embraced feminist causes shared values and goals related to improving women's status. Social movements enriched their lives and increased their sense of autonomy. Though in retrospect the gendered nature of activism during the early twentieth century may seem limiting, most women developed strong commitments to the idea that their power to effect change in the world stemmed from gender difference, not in spite of it.

The suffrage and birth control and especially the peace movements proved expansive enough to admit specifically Jewish arguments and political identities as well. American Jewish women saw no reason to disregard their Jewishness when they entered these movements. On the contrary, their Jewishness enhanced both their own activism and the contributions they could make to the larger movements. Ultimately they also brought their feminist interests to bear on their Jewish communal life, as Jewish suffragists did when they demanded greater representation in the synagogue, or as Jewish birth control activists did when they examined the relationship of Jewish law to contraception, or as Jewish peace activists did when they called on biblical texts about peace and pointed out the special interest of a diasporic group in ending war. These activist Jewish women set the stage for the expansion of women's roles in the Jewish community as well as in American society more generally. Even though these goals were not fully realized in the prewar era, an important process of education, reevaluation of women's status in the Jewish community, and politicization was launched by Jewish women activists.

Americans have always claimed that they are free to reinvent their identities and to fashion themselves as they wish. Jewish women did not necessarily have to present themselves as Jewish or even give much thought to what

Jewish identity might mean to them. But it is telling that very few denied being Jewish. They became activists in such numbers because Jewishness shaped their understanding of politics and gender and impelled them to activism regardless of possible constraints of class position or prejudice. And when Jewishness writ large increasingly came under attack during the 1930s, Jewish identity became more rather than less important to them just at the moment when it might have made more practical sense to deny it altogether. For women who had always viewed even nonsectarian causes like birth control and peace as implicitly reflective of Jewish concerns, the transition was comparatively smooth. But for those who had not seen much of a connection between the Jewish dimensions of their identity and their political work in the past, the new importance Jewish identity acquired during the years leading up to World War II required a rethinking of the relationship between their political activism and Jewishness. Jewishness moved to the forefront of their consciousness, where it would remain for the rest of the crucial decade of war and peace.

Although relatively few women activists observed the letter of Jewish law, the diaries, memoirs, speeches, and correspondence of suffragists, pacifists, and birth control activists, as well as the organizational records produced by groups such as NCJW and NFTS, bear significant witness to the central importance of Jewish identity. Again and again American Jewish women cited their upbringing in a culture of concern for other Jews and the wider world as primary factors in their political activism. Jewish values of community and *tzedakah*, usually translated as "charity" but more accurately understood as "righteous justice," provided ample Jewish justification for women's activism.[7]

American Jewish women of the early twentieth century bequeathed this legacy of activism to their daughters, granddaughters, and great-granddaughters. As political activism and then feminism flourished anew in the postwar era, a striking number of American Jewish women continued to operate on the cutting edge of social movements. The struggle of Jewish women to balance their feminist and Jewish commitments remained complex and continuously complicated the changes they made to both Jewish life and broader social institutions. Yet they all could draw on a Jewish heritage of concern for community, commitment to social justice, willingness to confront powerful institutions, and empathy for the oppressed. Like their predecessors, the Jewish women activists of the 1960s and 1970s and beyond brought Jewish insights to the women's movement and feminist insights to Jewish life, enriching both and transforming a world they believed they could make a better place.

ABBREVIATIONS USED IN NOTES AND BIBLIOGRAPHY

AJA	American Jewish Archives Center (Cincinnati)
AJHS	American Jewish Historical Society (New York)
HML	Harvard Medical Library in the Francis A. Countway Library of Medicine (Boston)
HSP	Historical Society of Pennsylvania (Philadelphia)
JHSUM	Jewish Historical Society of the Upper Midwest, University of Minnesota (Minneapolis)
JMM	Jewish Museum of Maryland (Baltimore)
MHS	Minnesota Historical Society (St. Paul)
PJAC	Philadelphia Jewish Archives Center, Special Collections, Temple University Libraries (Philadelphia)
NCOA	North Carolina Office of Archives and History of the North Carolina Department of Cultural Resources (Raleigh)
NYPL	New York Public Library, Manuscripts and Archives Division, Astor, Lenox and Tilden Foundations (New York)
RHC	Rose Heiman Halpern Collection (In possession of Victor Garlin)
SCPC	Swarthmore College Peace Collection, Swarthmore College (Swarthmore, PA)
SL	Schlesinger Library on the History of American Women, Harvard University (Cambridge, MA)
SSC	Sophia Smith Collection, Smith College (Northampton, MA)
SWHA	Social Welfare History Archives, University of Minnesota (Minneapolis)
UMJA	Upper Midwest Jewish Archives, University of Minnesota (Minneapolis)
YIVO	YIVO Institute for Jewish Research (New York)

NOTES TO INTRODUCTION

1. *Papers of the Jewish Women's Congress Held at Chicago*, 5.
2. 1926 Jennie Franklin Purvin diary, Box 2278e, Jennie Franklin Purvin Papers, MS 502, AJA.
3. August 23, September 24, 1890, Jennie Franklin diary, Box 2278e, Purvin Papers, MS 502, AJA. For more on Purvin's adolescence, see Klapper, *Jewish Girls Coming of Age in America, 1860–1920*.
4. Poem, ca. 1916, Box 2278L, Folder "NCJW–Chicago Section," Purvin Papers, MS 502, AJA.
5. *Annual Report of the Illinois Birth Control League*, 1926, Box 5, Folder 25, Margaret Sanger Research Bureau Records, MS 320, SSC.
6. Program for the National Council of Women Biennial Session, Decatur, Illinois, October 29–November 3, 1923, Box 2278L, Folder "NCJW–Chicago Section," Purvin Papers, MS 502, AJA.
7. The history of women and social movements provides a rich field for exploring questions of identity politics and gender. In African American women's history, for instance, scholars have illustrated the ways in which the intersection of race, class, and gender during the early twentieth century yielded a commitment to activism among African American women that encompassed education, civil rights, religious reform, and anti-lynching agitation. For examples of such work, see Darlene Clark Hine, *Hine Sight: Black Women and the Reconstruction of American History* (Bloomington: Indiana University Press, 1996) and "African American Women and Their Communities in the Twentieth Century: The Foundation and Future of Black Women's Studies," *Black Women, Gender, and Families Journal* 1 (Spring 2007): 1–23; Evelyn Brooks Higginbotham, *Righteous Discontent: The Women's Movement in the Black Baptist Church, 1880–1920* (Cambridge, MA: Harvard University Press, 1993) and "Clubwomen and Electoral Politics in the 1920s" in Ann D. Gordon, ed., *African American Women and the Vote, 1837–1965* (Amherst: University of Massachusetts Press, 1997); and Glenda Gilmore, *Gender and Jim Crow: Women and the Politics of White Supremacy in North Carolina, 1896–1920* (Chapel Hill: University of North Carolina Press, 1996).
8. Scholars have explored working-class Jewish women's involvement in the labor movement to great effect, but it is now time to explore a fuller range of Jewish women's turn-of-the-century activism, especially that of middle-class women. For important examples of studies of working-class Jewish women that are also foundational for American labor history, see Kessler-Harris, "Where Are the Organized Women Workers?" and "Organizing the Unorganizable"; Glenn, *Daughters of the Shtetl*; and Orleck, "We Are That Mythical Thing Called the Public" and *Common Sense and a Little Fire*. By way of comparison to Catholic women's activism, see Cummings, *New Women of the Old Faith*; Guglielmo, *Living the Revolution*; Petit, "Organized Catholic Womanhood"; and Skok, "The Historiography of Catholic Laywomen and Progressive Era Reform."
9. For overviews of the enormous literature on the Progressive Era, see Diner, *A Very Different Age*; Flanagan, *America Reformed*; Gould, *America in the Progressive Era*; McGerr, *A Fierce Discontent*; and Rodgers, *Atlantic Crossings*. Scholarship on women and reform during the Progressive Era is too vast to cite in full here. Exemplary works include Flanagan, *Seeing With Their Hearts*; Frankel and Dye, eds., *Gender, Class, Race, and Reform in the Progressive Era*; Ginzberg, *Women and the Work of Benevolence*; Muncy, *Creating a Female Dominion in American Reform*; Scott, *Natural Allies*; and Sklar, *Florence Kelley and the Nation's Work*.
10. Major histories of the WCTU include Bordin, *Woman and Temperance*; Epstein, *The Politics of Domesticity*; and Tyrell, *Woman's World/Woman's Empire*. For the first major study of Jews and Prohibition, see Davis, *Jews and Booze*.
11. Classic works from the rich literature on the Jewish labor movement include Brandes, "From Sweatshop to Stability"; Davidowicz, "The Jewishness of the Jewish Labor

Movement in the United States"; Epstein, *Jewish Labor in the United States*; Hardman, "The Jewish Labor Movement in the United States"; Perlman, "Jewish-American Unionism"; and Rischin, "The Jewish Labor Movement in the United States." More recent work includes Green, *Jewish Workers in the Modern Diaspora*; Kosak, *Cultures of Opposition*; and Michels, *A Fire in Their Hearts*. (On Jewish women and labor, see n. 8.) Major works on Zionism in America include Cohen, *The Americanization of Zionism*; Gal, *David Ben Gurion and the American Alignment for a Jewish State*; Raider, *The Emergence of American Zionism*; and Urofsky, *American Zionism from Herzl to the Holocaust*. Reinharz and Raider, *American Jewish Women and the Zionist Enterprise*, collects both documents and recent scholarship on women and Zionism. (On Hadassah, the Zionist women's organization, see n. 27.)

12. This interpretation follows Cott, *The Grounding of Modern Feminism*.

13. General histories of the American suffrage movement include Buechler, *Women's Movements in the United States*; DuBois, *Harriot Stanton Blatch and the Winning of Woman Suffrage*; Flexner, *Century of Struggle*; Mead, *How the Vote Was Won*; Wheeler, *One Woman, One Vote*. (For further references, see chap. 1.)

14. General histories of the American birth control movement include Engelman, *A History of the Birth Control Movement in America*; Gordon, *Woman's Body, Woman's Right* and *The Moral Property of Women*; Kennedy, *Birth Control in America*; McCann, *Birth Control Politics in the United States*; and Reed, *The Birth Control Movement and American Society*. (For further references, see chaps. 2 and 4.)

15. General histories of the American peace movement include Chatfield, *The American Peace Movement*; Curti, *Peace or War*; Howlett, ed., *History of the American Peace Movement, 1890–2000*; Patterson, "An Interpretation of the American Peace Movement"; and Wittner, *Rebels Against War*. For general studies of American women and peace activism, see Alonso, *Peace as a Women's Issue* and Zeiger, "Finding a Cure for War." (For further references, see chaps. 3 and 5.)

16. For more on this transition, see Anderson, *After Suffrage*.

17. Historians have never bought into the "doldrums" thesis, though the popular narrative about modern feminism beginning with the 1963 publication of Betty Friedan's *The Feminine Mystique* has been difficult to overcome. See Scharf and Jensen, eds., *Decades of Discontent*; Rupp, *Survival in the Doldrums*; and Meyerowitz, ed., *Not June Cleaver* for challenges to the idea that there was little activism during the decades between suffrage and second-wave feminism. In *The Grounding of Modern Feminism*, Cott argues that suffrage was the preliminary stage and enabler of feminism, not a goal that once achieved left women disinterested in political activism until the 1960s.

18. On ERA activism, see Anderson, *After Suffrage*; Butler, *Two Paths to Equality*; and Wilson, *The Women's Joint Congressional Committee and the Politics of Maternalism*. On industrial feminism, see Cobble, *The Other Women's Movement*; Orleck, *Common Sense and a Little Fire*; and Pastorello, *A Power Among Them*.

19. This book is part of a growing literature on the diversity of feminism. For a recent collection of exemplary work, see Hewitt, ed., *No Permanent Waves*, which not only contests the periodization of the history of feminism but also points to the foundational, if too often unacknowledged, role played by a variety of groups beyond the most visible white, middle-class women. Despite its capacious view of feminist history, *No Permanent Waves* is more interested in race and class than ethnic diversity and pays relatively little attention to religion.

20. Standard works on turn-of-the-century American women's social movements that make no or minimal reference to Jewish women include Alonso, *Peace as a Women's Issue*; Bolt, *Sisterhood Questioned*; Buechler, *Women's Movements in the United States*; Buhle, *Women and American Socialism*; Chesler, *Woman of Valor*; Cohen, *When the Old Left Was Young*; D'Itri, *Cross Currents in the International Women's Movement*; DuBois, *Harriot Stanton*

Blatch and the Winning of Woman Suffrage; Gordon, *Woman's Body, Woman's Right*; Kennedy, *Birth Control in America*; Mead, *How the Vote Was Won*; Reed, *The Birth Control Movement and American Society*; Steinson, *American Women's Activism in World War I*; Tone, *Devices and Desires*; and Wheeler, ed., *One Woman, One Vote*.

21. Otherwise fine older histories of American Jews that generally fail to consider women or incorporate gender analysis include Cassedy, *To the Other Shore*; Feingold, *Zion in America*; Gurock, *When Harlem Was Jewish*; Karp, ed., *Golden Door to America*; Rischin, *The Promised City*; and Sorin, *The Prophetic Minority*. The exemplary case is Howe's *World of Our Fathers*, which prompted Seller, "Putting Women into American Jewish History" and Weinberg, *The World of Our Mothers*.

22. Overviews of American Jewish women's history include Antler, *The Journey Home;* Diner and Benderly, *Her Works Praise Her*; and Nadell, ed., *American Jewish Women's History*.

23. Sarna, *American Judaism*, 375.

24. On this Jewish renewal, see Sarna, *A Great Awakening*.

25. For an overview of second-generation American Jews, see Moore, *At Home in America*.

26. The best recent comparison of the various waves of Jewish immigrants is Diner, *The Jews of the United States*. On immigrant Yiddish culture, see Kosak, *Cultures of Opposition* and Michels, *A Fire in Their Hearts*.

27. Major work on NCJW includes Rogow, *Gone to Another Meeting*; Elwell, "The Founding and Early Programs of the National Council of Jewish Women"; Ginsburg, "From Club Women to Progressive Philanthropists"; Golomb, "The 1893 Congress of Jewish Women"; Korelitz, "'A Magnificent Piece of Work'"; Kuzmack, *Woman's Cause*; and McCune, "*The Whole Wide World Without Limits*". Hadassah, founded in 1912, became an even larger Jewish women's organization, but since during the interwar years it focused on health, welfare, and education in Palestine, Hadassah activities do not come under the purview of this book. Hadassah scholarship is flourishing; for two recent studies, see Katzman-Yungman, *American Women Zionists and the Rebirth of Israel* and Simmons, *Hadassah and the Zionist Project*.

28. Misch, "How Jewish is the Council of Jewish Women?" *Jewish Tribune and Hebrew Standard*, November 2, 1923; Horvitz, "Marion Misch," 31; Irwin, *Angels and Amazons*, 430.

29. Women's associational life served multiple functions for all American women. See Clemens, "Securing Political Returns to Social Capital"; Rupp and Taylor, "Forging Feminist Identity in an International Movement"; and Scott, *Natural Allies*. Kuzmack, *Woman's Cause*, explores these issues for Jewish clubwomen in England and the United States. McCune, "*The Whole Wide World Without Limits*", focuses on American Jewish women's organizations' participation in reconstruction efforts in Europe following World War I.

30. See Hyman, *Gender and Assimilation in Modern Jewish History*.

31. (On women's social movements, see n. 20.) Standard works on immigrant Jewish women include Glenn, *Daughters of the Shtetl*; Pratt, "Transitions in Judaism"; Reinharz and Raider, eds., *American Jewish Women and the Zionist Enterprise*; Seller, "Defining Socialist Womanhood"; and Weinberg, *The World of Our Mothers*. There are also numerous comparisons to Italian immigrant women, as in Coser, Anker, and Perrin, *Women of Courage*; Ewen, *Immigrant Women in the Land of Dollars*; Friedman-Kasaba, *Memories of Migration*; and Smith, *Family Connections*. Literature on middle-class Jewish women encompasses reform but mostly within the American Jewish community. See Hyman, "The Jewish Body Politic"; Wenger, "Jewish Women of the Club"; Albert, "Not Quite a 'Quiet Revolution'"; and NCJW citations above. Exceptions to the overlooking of American Jewish women in larger social movements have mostly to do with suffrage. See Jeanne Abrams, *Jewish Women Pioneering the Frontier Trail*; Ruth Abrams, "Jewish Women in the International Woman Suffrage Alliance"; and Lerner, "Jewish Involvement in the New York City Suffrage Movement." On Jews and whiteness, see especially Brodkin, *How the Jews Became White Folks* and Goldstein, *The Price of Whiteness*.

32. Dye, *As Equals and As Sisters* remains a classic study of the WTUL. For a foundational study of how difficult it was to prioritize gender identity, see Rupp, *World of Women*. Rupp notes in passing the prominence of some Jewish women and the anti-Semitism many of them encountered but does not follow up on the significance of either of these features of international women's organizing.

33. Maternalism is an important element of gender history, especially in work on the origins of the welfare state. See Gordon, ed., *Women, the State, and Welfare*; Koven and Michel, eds., *Mothers of a New World*; Ladd-Taylor, *Mother-Work*; Muncy, *Creating a Female Dominion in American Reform*; and Skocpol, *Protecting Mothers and Soldiers*. These authors disagree on some matters. For example, Gordon finds considerable elitism in maternalism while Skopcol suggests common notions of motherhood could cut across class difference. However, all acknowledge the centrality of motherhood to the development of social policy and reform.

34. The debate over communalism and dispersionism, previously expressed as a critique of the tendency toward hagiography, filiopietism, and insularity within immigration history, took on new life in the field following the 2008 Biennial Scholars' Conference on American Jewish history. The keynote speaker, David Hollinger, who subsequently published a slightly revised version of his remarks, suggested that a move toward dispersionist history might aid in better integrating American Jewish history into U.S. history. While receptive to the valuable points Hollinger raised about Jews and modernity and eager to see American Jewish history and its concerns taken as more central to U.S. history, most of the scholars who responded in an *American Jewish History* forum expressed some doubts about the usefulness of this bifurcation. Hollinger clearly did not mean that there was no overlap between approaches, but the range of not only the historiography but also the history of American Jews nonetheless problematizes the formula. For Hollinger's remarks, reactions by Diner, Kraut, Michels, and Hyman, and Hollinger's response, see *American Jewish History* 95 (March 2009).

35. For an overview of American anti-Semitism, see Dinnerstein, *Antisemitism in America*.

36. Lerner began to explore these issues in "American Feminism and the Jewish Question."

NOTES TO CHAPTER 1

1. Nathan, New York, to community rabbis, New York, April 23, 1917, Reel 2, Volume 6, Maud Nathan Papers, M-83, SL.

2. Unidentified clipping, May 12, 1911, Reel 1, Volume 2, M-83, Nathan Papers, SL.

3. Nathan, *Once Upon a Time and Today*, 49. For more on Nathan, see Antler, *The Journey Home*, chap. 2.

4. Mononson, "The Lady and the Tiger," 100. For more on the CL and its longtime executive director, see Sklar, *Florence Kelley and the Nation's Work*.

5. Nathan, *Once Upon a Time and Today*, 112–113; Nathan, "The Wage Earner and the Ballot," *Political Equality Series* 3 (1908): 71–73, History of Women Microfilm Reel 948, SL; Nathan, "The Suffrage Convention," undated *New York Sun* clipping, Reel 1, Volume 2, M-83, Nathan Papers, SL.

6. Nathan, *Once Upon a Time and Today*, 182–185, 187; "Maud Nathan," *The Woman's Journal*, March 14, 1908; "Women Don't Like It, But Will Parade," *Evening Globe*, May 4, 1911, Reel 1, Volume 2, M-83, Nathan Papers, SL.

7. Nathan, *Justice and the Expediency of Woman Suffrage*; "Mrs. Nathan Gave Talk," *Greenwich News*, September 17, 1909. The classic study of the justice and expediency tropes is Kraditor, *The Ideas of the Woman Suffrage Movement*.

8. Nathan, "Jewesses in the Suffrage Movement," *American Hebrew*, March 29, 1912. British Jewish suffragists made similar arguments. See Davis, *Some Reasons Why the Jew Should Desire Woman Suffrage*.

9. See Dubois, *Feminism and Suffrage*, for the standard account of the movement through 1869. The enlarged edition of Flexner's classic *Century of Struggle* remains valuable. Starting in the 1990s there was an explosion of suffrage scholarship, some of it collected in the essays in Wheeler, *One Woman, One Vote*. For now-standard works on the movement after 1890, see Buechler, *Women's Movements in the United States*; Cott, *The Grounding of Modern Feminism*; DuBois, *Harriot Stanton Blatch and the Winning of Woman Suffrage*; Graham, *Woman Suffrage and the New Democracy*; Lumsden, *Rampant Women*; and Mead, *How the Vote Was Won*. For more on Rose, see Doress-Worters, ed., *Mistress of Herself* and Kolmerten, *The American Life of Ernestine L. Rose*.

10. Ginzberg provides a good overview of this period in *Elizabeth Cady Stanton*.

11. Graham, *Woman Suffrage and the New Democracy*, argues for the significance of this period to building a mass movement, despite few concrete achievements.

12. For a contemporary take, see Beard, "The Legislative Influence of Unenfranchised Women," 55. Classic scholarship on this issue includes Baker, "The Domestication of Politics" and McGerr, "Political Style and Women's Power." On suffrage and race, see Newman, *White Women's Rights*.

13. On women's clubs and suffrage, see Flanagan, *Seeing With Their Hearts* and Scott, *Natural Allies*. Sneider, *Suffragists in an Imperial Age*, 6ff, cogently analyzes the shifting state and federal strategies.

14. On suffrage rhetoric, see Sharer, *Vote and Voice*. For the connections between suffrage and citizenship, see Bredbenner, *A Nationality of Her Own*.

15. On southern suffrage, see Green, *Southern Strategies* and Wheeler, *New Women of the New South*. For a partisan contemporary biography of Catt, see Peck, *Carrie Chapman Catt*. More scholarly analyses include Fowler, *Carrie Catt* and Van Voris, *Carrie Chapman Catt*. For her own account, see Catt and Shuler, *Woman Suffrage and Politics*.

16. Standard works on Paul and NWP include Adams and Keene, *Alice Paul and the Suffrage Campaign*; Ford, *Iron-Jawed Angels*; and Lunardini, *From Equal Suffrage to Equal Rights*. For firsthand accounts, see Irwin, *The Story of the Woman's Party* and Katzenstein, *Lifting the Curtain*.

17. Alonso, "Suffragists for Peace During the Interwar Years" explores the challenges World War I posed to suffragists. All the literature cited in n. 9 deals with the campaign's final years.

18. This inhospitality was not unique to the American suffrage movement and continued to be an issue in feminism. See Bolt, *Sisterhood Questioned*.

19. Personal conversation with Irma Cain Firestone's granddaughter, Judith Brin Ingber, St. Paul, Minnesota, June 19, 2008; Fligelman, "Mother Was Shocked," 630–635.

20. Albert, "Not Quite a 'Quiet Revolution,'" 70–71; Lord-Heinstein, "How I Became A Suffragist," January 25, 1951, Box 1, Folder 2; untitled article on Lord-Heinstein by Suzanne Bailey, 1976, Box 1, Folder 1, Lucile Lord-Heinstein Papers, MC 310, SL.

21. Kohut, *My Portion*, 72–73; "Leaders of All Faiths Plan Jubilee for Rebekah Kohut," *New York Post*, October 28, 1935. For more on Kohut, see Antler, *The Journey Home*, chap. 2. Recent scholarship criticizes suffragists sharply for their conservative, even reactionary views on race in particular. As an example, see Amidon, "Carrie Chapman Catt and the Evolutionary Politics of Sex and Race."

22. Miriam Allen De Ford, "In the Streets," 2–30.

23. Ida Blair, Caroline Duer, Anne Cochran, and Elisabeth Strange, New York, to Oppenheim, New York, March 11, 1915; Nathan, Troy, New York, to Oppenheim, New York, October 9, 1915; Beatrice Forbes-Robertson Hale, New York, to Oppenheim, New York, May 1, 1917, Amy Schwartz Oppenheim Papers, MS 116, SSC.

24. On the controversial nature of public elements of the campaign, see Ford, *Iron-Jawed Angels*; Lumsden, *Rampant Women*; and McCammon, "Out of the Parlors and Into the Streets."

25. Tribute to Barron, Box 1, Folder 1, Jennie Loitman Barron Papers, MC 410, SL. Sharer, *Vote and Voice*, points out that both the suffrage and anti-suffrage movements staged plays to make their cases. Friedl, *On to Victory*, collects some of the most popular suffrage plays.

26. "Sixth of Open-Air Rallies Held for Suffrage," *Framingham News*, July 19, 1915.

27. Fligelman, "Mother Was Shocked," 630–635; Kohut, *My Portion*, 252.

28. Litman, *Ray Frank Litman*, 56–57; "Work of a Woman Rabbi," *San Francisco Bulletin*, November 15, 1895. On the anti-suffrage movement, see Goodier, "The Other Woman's Movement"; Marshall, *Splintered Sisterhood*; and Thurner, "Better Citizens Without the Ballot."

29. "Annie Nathan Meyer, Wife and Mother, Opposes Woman Suffrage," *American Hebrew*, June 12, 1914. For more on Meyer, see Antler, *The Journey Home*, chap. 2.

30. Meyer, typescript of *It's Been Fun*, Box 8, Folder 6; clipping of review of *The Dominant Sex*, *New Yorker Staats Zeitung*, April 9, 1911, Box 1, Folder 3, Annie Nathan Meyer Papers, MS 7, AJA. There are several extant versions of Meyer's autobiography *It's Been Fun*; this and subsequent citations refer to the typescript as specified above.

31. Goodier, "The Other Woman's Movement," 117; Nathan, "Carranza for Antis," *New Republic*, September 30, 1916.

32. Dodge, New York, to Meyer, New York, December 26, 1916, Box 1, Folder 1, Meyer Papers, MS 7, AJA. Marshall, *Splintered Sisterhood*, points out that women who opposed suffrage did not necessarily oppose women's public activities and often had a great deal of reform experience.

33. Golomb, "The 1893 Congress of Jewish Women," 55–56; Lerner, "American Feminism and the Jewish Question," 316–317. See Goldstein, *The Price of Whiteness* for more on the fluid contours of American Jewish racial identity during the early twentieth century.

34. Ginzberg, *Elizabeth Cady Stanton*, 135–136; Gage quoted in Sneider, *Suffragists in an Imperial Age*, 57–58.

35. Stanton, *Eighty Years and More*, 381.

36. Kuzmack, *Woman's Cause*, 39; Rogow, *Gone to Another Meeting*, 81–82.

37. Kern, *Mrs. Stanton's Bible*, 66, 168, 157–158.

38. Kern, *Mrs. Stanton's Bible*, 208; Equal Suffrage Association of North Carolina, "The So-Called 'Woman's Bible,'" ca. 1896, Box 56, Folder 2, Gertrude Weil Papers, NCOA.

39. DuBois, *Harriot Stanton Blatch and the Winning of Woman Suffrage*, 41, 148–149; Catt's testimony at suffrage hearing, April 20, 1917, Box 5, Folder 1, Carrie Chapman Catt Papers, NYPL; Lerner, "American Feminism and the Jewish Question," 308–309; Vernon, "Speaker for Suffrage and Petitioner for Peace," 157; Belmont, "Jewish Women in Public Affairs."

40. On the international women's movement, see Berkovitch, *From Motherhood to Citizenship*; D'Itri, *Cross Currents in the International Women's Movement*; DuBois, "Woman Suffrage Around the World"; Holton, "'To Educate Women into Rebellion'"; International Council of Women, *Women in a Changing World*; Rupp, *Worlds of Women*; Rupp and Taylor, "Forging Feminist Identity in an International Movement"; and Tyrell, *Woman's World/Women's Empire*.

41. Abrams, "Jewish Women in the International Woman Suffrage Alliance, 1899–1926," 2; Jacobs, *Memories*, 59–60, 76.

42. Jacobs, Amsterdam, to Solomon, Chicago, January 21, 1900, Hannah Greenebaum Solomon scrapbook, Box X-172, AJA; Jacobs, St. Moritz, to Schwimmer, January 1, 1906, in Bosch and Kloosterman, eds., *Politics and Friendship*, 66; Peck, *Carrie Chapman Catt*, 161.

43. Kuzmack, *Woman's Cause*, 75; Solomon, *Fabric of My Life*, 120–124; Nathan, "Women and Internationalism in Europe," *Independent*, October 23, 1913.

44. Quoted in Van Voris, *Carrie Chapman Catt*, 110.

45. Solomons, *How We Won the Vote in California*, 7–21; Silver, "Selina Solomons and Her Quest for the Sixth Star," 305–308.

46. DuBois, *Harriot Stanton Blatch and the Winning of Woman Suffrage*, 92–93.

47. DuBois, *Harriot Stanton Blatch and the Winning of Woman Suffrage*, 94–95; Lerner, "Jewish Involvement in the New York City Suffrage Movement," 444–447; Nathan, "Jewesses in the Suffrage Movement," *American Hebrew*, March 29, 1912. Dye's study of the WTUL, *As Equals and As Sisters*, remains an important study of the tensions between gender and class interests, which affected both Schneiderman's career and her ability to prioritize cross-class alliances through the WTUL. See also Schneiderman, *All for One* and Antler, *The Journey Home*, chap. 3.

48. "It Took Nerve to be a Suffragette Then," *Philadelphia Record*, August 22, 1945; Schneiderman quoted in Kuzmack, *Woman's Cause*, 142; Orleck, *Common Sense and a Little Fire*, 91–95; DuBois, *Harriot Stanton Blatch and the Winning of Woman Suffrage*, 135.

49. DuBois, *Harriot Stanton Blatch and the Winning of Woman Suffrage*, 117–119; Seiler, "On the Soapbox," 28.

50. Quoted in Van Voris, *Carrie Chapman Catt*, 71.

51. Bolt, *Sisterhood Questioned?*, 29–30; Adickes, *To Be Young Was Very Heaven*, 53. See also DuBois, "Woman Suffrage and the Left" and the relevant essays in Miller, *Race, Ethnicity, and Gender in Early Twentieth-Century American Socialism*.

52. Buhle, *Women and American Socialism*, 218; Conger-Kaneko, "What Will Woman Suffrage Conventions do for the Working Woman?" in Keetley and Pettegrew, eds., *Public Women, Public Words*, 170.

53. Goldman, "The Tragedy of Woman's Emancipation," in Keetley and Pettegrew, eds., *Public Women, Public Words*, 16; Goldman, "Woman Suffrage," in *Anarchism and Other Essays*, 201. For more on Goldman, see Adickes, *To Be Young Was Very Heaven*; Antler, *The Journey Home*, chap. 3; Chalberg, *Emma Goldman*; Drinnon, *Rebel in Paradise*; Falk, *Love, Anarchy, and Emma Goldman*; and Wexler, *Emma Goldman*.

54. Lemlich, "Relieving Working Women of the Burdens and Responsibility of Life," n.d., History of Women Microfilm Reel 950, SL; "Jennie Matyas and the I.L.G.W.U.," 65–67.

55. Orleck, *Common Sense and a Little Fire*, 42; Newman, Philadelphia, to Schneiderman, New York, September 14, 1911, Box 5, Folder 77; Newman, "On Woman Suffrage," Box 1, Folder 4, Newman Papers, MS 324, SL; Newman, "The Twentieth-Century Trade Union Woman: Vehicle for Social Change," 15, 48–49.

56. Orleck, *Common Sense and A Little Fire*, 96–97.

57. Quoted in Sorin, *The Prophetic Minority*, 138.

58. Basch, introduction to Malkiel, *The Diary of a Shirtwaist Striker*, 59–60; Buhle, *Women and American Socialism*, 233–234.

59. Abrams, *Jewish Women Pioneering the Frontier Trail*, 45, 170–172, 184; Solomons, *How We Won the Vote in California*, 3–4. For more on Solomons's suffrage play, see Friedl's introduction in *On To Victory*.

60. Mead, *How the Vote Was Won*, 160–161; Abrams, *Jewish Women Pioneering the Frontier Trail*, 149–150.

61. "Women to Men," *Woman Voter*, 1912, quoted in De Ford, "In the Streets," 48.

62. Van Voris, *Carrie Chapman Catt*, 134. On the "winning plan," see also the literature cited in n. 9.

63. "Suffragists Raise $105,619 at Rally," *NYTimes*, November 7, 1914; Abrams, "Jewish Women in the International Woman Suffrage Alliance," 20; Harriet Payne, Corning, New York, to Weil, Goldsboro, North Carolina, July 16, 1915, Box 18, Folder 14, Weil Papers, NCOA; "Suffragists at Theatres," *NYTimes*, October 28, 1915.

64. Ratner diary, October 29, November 1–3, 1915; Ratner, Brooklyn, to Mrs. H, November 1915, Berta Ratner Rosenbluth Papers, A/R8132, SL.

65. DuBois, *Harriot Stanton Blatch and the Winning of Woman Suffrage*, 178–179; Lerner, "Jewish Involvement in the New York City Suffrage Movement," 443.

66. Kuzmack, *Woman's Cause*, 152–153.

67. On this change, see Daniels, "Building a Winning Coalition."

68. "The Nail," in Haskell, *The Banner Bearers*, 114–138.

69. "Big Suffrage Rally at Marion Friday," *New Bedford Times*, August 11, 1918.

70. Weil, Goldsboro, North Carolina, to Brinson, Washington, D.C., May 18, 1919, Box 54, Folder 1, Weil Papers, NCOA. At a moment when Jewish whiteness was arguably still in flux, both Weil and Brinson clearly saw Weil as white. See Goldstein, *The Price of Whiteness;* Green, *Southern Strategies;*and Taylor, "The Woman Suffrage Movement in North Carolina" for further context.

71. Weil, Northampton, Massachusetts, to Mina Weil, Goldsboro, North Carolina, November 4, 1900, Box 8, Folder 11; NAWSA materials, Box 53, Folders 2–3; Mina Weil, Goldsboro, North Carolina, to Weil, Fayetteville, North Carolina, May 6, 1914, Weil Papers, NCOA; Scott, "Gertrude Weil and Her Times."

72. Catt, New York, to Weil, Goldsboro, North Carolina, April 1, 1918; Walter Clark, Raleigh, to Weil, Goldsboro, April 4, 1918; Catt, New York, to Weil, Goldsboro, May 6, 1918, Box 53, Folder 1; Mrs. Abrams to Weil, Goldsboro, January 15, 1919, Box 19, Folder 4; Weil, Goldsboro, to Equal Suffrage League of North Carolina, August 3, 1920, Box 54, Folder 1, Weil Papers, NCOA.

73. Untitled clipping from *Jewish Exponent*, June 10, 1955; unidentified clipping, July 21, 1955; untitled clipping from *Philadelphia Inquirer*, August 14, 1955, in Caroline Katzenstein Papers, ACC 1246, PJAC; "Conversations with Alice Paul," 60–61.

74. See Newman, *White Women's Rights*.

75. Katzenstein, *Lifting the Curtain*, 55–57, 33–34; *Philadelphia Life Insurance Company Bulletin* (December 1922) in Katzenstein Papers, ACC 1246, PJAC. For more on the popularity of suffrage consumer goods, see Finnegan, *Selling Suffrage*.

76. Katzenstein, *Lifting the Curtain*, 161, 309–310, 322–323.

77. Irwin, *The Story of the Woman's Party*, 181.

78. Crockin speech on the history of the League of Women Voters in Baltimore, 1946, Box 2, Folder 28, Sadie Jacobs Crockin Collection, MS 95, JMM.

79. See, for example, Nathan, *Once Upon a Time and Today* and Kohut, *My Portion*, 248.

80. See literature cited in nn. 9 and 16 for more on the NAWSA/NWP split.

81. Kettler, "Behind Bars," 1–34. For more on suffrage prisoners, see Lumsden, *Rampant Women* and Stevens, *Jailed for Freedom*.

82. Adams and Keene, *Alice Paul and the American Suffrage Campaign*, 119, 245; Vernon, "Speaker for Suffrage and Petitioner for Peace," 155; Reyher, "Search and Struggle for Equality and Independence," 90.

83. Oral history of Reyher by Peat, 67–69, SL; Vernon, "Speaker for Suffrage and Petitioner for Peace," 152–153; Reyher, "Search and Struggle for Equality and Independence," 57–64. For more on Reyher, see Ford, *Iron-Jawed Angels*, which is dedicated to her.

84. Vernon, "Speaker for Suffrage and Peace," 153; Reyher, "Search and Struggle for Equality and Independence," 75, 84, 66; "Malone to Open Suffrage Battle," *Boston American*, March 3, 1918.

85. Reyher, "Search and Struggle for Equality and Independence," 96, 113; Vernon, "Speaker for Suffrage and Peace," 168.

86. See Alonso, "Suffragists for Peace During the Interwar Years, 1914–1941," 243–262.

87. Oppenheim, New York to Mrs. A. Brannan, New York, June 1917, Oppenheim Papers, SSC.

88. See Kuzmack, *Woman's Cause* and Rogow, *Gone to Another Meeting;* "An Appreciation," in NCJW–Minneapolis Section, "History of Minneapolis Section," SC-8736, AJA.

89. Abrams, *Jewish Women Pioneering the Frontier Trail*, 51–54.

90. Blumberg, "Sophie Weil Brown," 14; State Questionnaires, 1915, Box 3, Folders 3–5, Catt Papers, NYPL; Kuzmack, *Woman's Cause*, 1; Abrams, "Jewish Women in the International Woman Suffrage Alliance," 213; Davis, *Some Reasons Why the Jew Should Desire Woman Suffrage*.

91. Kohut, *My Portion*, 214.

92. "Atlanta Social," 36; Wenger, "Jewish Women of the Club," 311–333.

93. Quoted in Rogow, *Gone to Another Meeting*, 78.

94. NCJW–Charleston Section Minutes, February 24, 1908, Box 1, Folder 2, NCJW–Charleston Section Papers, MS 414, AJA; NCJW–Minneapolis Section Minutes, January 3, 1914, Viola Hoffman Hymes Papers, 146.F.9.9(B), MHS; Ginsburg, "From Club Women to Progressive Philanthropists," 67; NCJW–New York Section *Year Book*, 1915–1916 (5676), 99.

95. "The Jewish Woman and the Suffrage Movement," *American Hebrew*, February 5, 1915.

96. History of the NCJW–Jamaica Section, 1957, Box 1, Folder "Affiliate Organizations," Federation of Jewish Women's Organization Papers, I-208, AJHS.

97. Quoted in Rogow, *Gone to Another Meeting*, 79; see also McCune, "*The Whole Wide World Without Limits*," 72–73.

98. Rogow, *Gone to Another Meeting*, 79–80; Benjamin quoted in Abrams, *Jewish Women Pioneering the Frontier Trail*, 68.

99. *Twenty-Fifth Anniversary Celebration and Annual Meeting of NCJW–New York Section, May 6, 1918*, Box 65, Folder 7, NCJW Papers, I-469, AJHS.

100. McCune, "*The Whole Wide World Without Limits*," 71–74.

101. Quoted in Lerner "Jewish Involvement in the New York City Suffrage Movement," 456.

102. Lerner, "Jewish Involvement in the New York City Suffrage Movement," 456–458.

103. R. C. Beadle for the Men's League for Woman Suffrage, New York, to Wise, New York, March 7, 1913, Box 69, Reel 74-48, Stephen S. Wise Papers, P-134, AJHS; "Louis D. Brandeis Brings Women In," *Woman's Journal and Suffrage News*, July 3, 1915; London, "Woman Suffrage," speech to House of Representatives, September 24, 1917, Box 1, Folder 1, Suffrage Collection, MS 447, SSC.

104. Cohen's statement in *Living Witness*, New York State Woman Suffrage Party pamphlet, Box 7, Folder 3, Ethel Eyre Valentine Dreier Papers, SSC.

105. Program for "An Evening Devoted to the Discussion of Woman Suffrage," March 14, 1915, Reel 2, Volume 6, Nathan Papers, M-83, SL; Katzenstein, *Lifting the Curtain*, 129; Solomons, *How We Won the Vote in California*, 35–36.

106. McCune, "*The Whole Wide World Without Limits*," 223, n. 74; Abrams, "Jewish Women in the International Woman Suffrage Alliance," 223–224.

107. Duniway, Portland, to Louise and Stephen S. Wise, September 18, 1913; Anna Howard Shaw, New York, to Wise, New York, December 5, 1911, Box 69, Reel 74-48, Wise Papers, P-134, AJHS. On Wise, see Urofsky, *A Voice that Spoke for Justice*.

108. Wise, "Woman and Democracy," 140, 142, 144, 157.

109. "Mrs. Nathan on Suffrage Issue," *New Haven Union*, October 25, 1912; "Jews Besiege Theatre to Hear Suffrage Plea," *Philadelphia Record*, November 1915, Reel 2, Volume 6, Nathan Papers, M-83, SL.

110. "Democracy as Miss Wald Sees It"; "Home and the Vote According to Mrs. Kohut," *American Hebrew*, September 10, 1915.

111. *American Hebrew*, June 19, 1914.

112. "Mrs. Seligman Defines Woman's Sphere"; "Miss Lauterbach Prefers Man-Made Mandates," *American Hebrew*, September 10, 1915.

113. "Democracy and Feminism as Viewed by Mrs. Annie Nathan Meyer," *American Hebrew*, September 10, 1915. For more on the relationship between suffrage and feminism, see Cott, *The Grounding of Modern Feminism* and DuBois, *Feminism and Suffrage*.

114. "Democracy as Miss Wald Sees It"; "Home and the Vote According to Mrs. Kohut"; "Only Women Can Understand Women's Woes, Says Mrs. Einstein"; "Strong Statistics by Mrs. Nathan," *American Hebrew*, September 10, 1915.

115. "Jewesses as Suffragettes," *American Hebrew*, May 10, 1912; Rabinovitz, "Deborah, the First Suffragette," *American Hebrew*, September 13, 1912; "Feminism Among Wives," *American*

Hebrew, October 30, 1914; "Editorial," *American Hebrew*, October 29, 1915; Seligman, "Versatility of Jewish Women," *American Hebrew*, September 14, 1917.

116. For more on the American Yiddish press, see Michels, *A Fire in Their Hearts*. On *Forverts* in particular, see Manor, *Forward*.

117. L.V. to *Forverts*, in Metzker, *A Bintel Brief*, 94–95.

118. Seller, "Defining Socialist Womanhood," 416–438; Seller, "World of Our Mothers," 95–118; Rojanski, "Socialist Ideology, Traditional Rhetoric," 329–348.

119. "The Struggle for Women's Rights in the World," *Der Fraynd*, December 1914; Luria, "The Last Conquests on the Suffrage Front," *Der Fraynd*, June–July 1919, trans. Asya Vaisman (AV hereafter).

120. "From the Women's World," *Di Froyen Velt*, April 1913; "From the Women's World," *Di Froyen Velt*, November 1913, trans. AV.

121. "From the Women's World," *Di Froyen Velt*, June 1913; "From the Women's World," *Di Froyen Velt*, August 1913, trans. AV.

122. "From the Women's World," *Di Froyen Velt*, July 1913, trans. AV.

123. Mary Oettinger, Kinston, North Carolina, to Weil, Goldsboro, August 21, 1920, Box 19, Folder 5; L.J.H. Mewborn, Saulston, North Carolina, to Weil, Goldsboro, August 26, 1920, Box 19, Folder 5; Catt, New York, to Weil, Goldsboro, December 28, 1920, Box 3, Folder 1, Weil Papers, NCOA.

124. Leinenweber, "The Class and Ethnic Basis of New York City Socialism," 33. See Anderson, *After Suffrage*, for more on women in party politics following ratification.

125. Cott, *The Grounding of Modern Feminism*, 85–86; Anderson, *After Suffrage*; Wilson, *The Women's Joint Congressional Committee and the Politics of Maternalism*, 2–3, 6.

126. For more on LWV, see Young, *In the Public Interest* and Stuhler, *For the Public Record*.

127. Purvin, "The Illinois League of Women Voters"; *Chicago Women's Aid Bulletin* 7 (January 1924): 20; "Chelsea Woman Represents State," *Chelsea Evening Record*, April 15, 1921; Abrams, *Jewish Women Pioneering the Frontier Trail*, 166–167; Litman, *Ray Frank Litman*, 165; Meyer, typescript of *It's Been Fun*, 224, AJA.

128. On NWP post-suffrage, see Butler, *Two Paths to Equality* and Lunardini, *From Equal Suffrage to Equal Rights*.

129. Reyher, "Search and Struggle for Equality and Independence," 102.

130. Rogow, *Gone to Another Meeting*, 83–84; McCune, "*The Whole Wide World Without Limit*," 124–125.

131. See, for example, Juanita B. Edwards, New York, to Newman, New York, April 17, 1939, Box 8, Folder 136, Newman Papers, MC 324, SL; Reyher, "Search and Struggle for Equality and Independence," 115.

132. On international feminist struggles, see Berkovitch, *From Motherhood to Citizenship* and Rupp, *Worlds of Women*.

133. Reyher travel diary, October 22, November 14, November 15, November 17, 1929, Series: Diaries, Journals, Engagement Calendars, Folder "Palestine Trip 1928–1929," Rebecca Hourwich Reyher Papers, MC 562, SL; Kuhn travel diary, November 14, 1929, Box 4, Folder 1, Setty Swartz Kuhn Papers, MS 173, AJA.

134. Bettman, untitled, undated essay about women, Box 2, Folder 10, Iphigene Bettman Papers, MS 667, AJA.

135. Quoted in McCune, "Creating a Place for Women in a Socialist Brotherhood," 597–598.

136. Lifshitz, "Is Woman Suffrage Failing?"; Stokes, "Is Woman Suffrage Failing?"; Schneiderman, "Is Woman Suffrage Failing?" in Keetley and Pettegrew, eds., *Public Women, Public Words*, 263–266.

137. Quoted in Wenger, "Jewish Women of the Club," 326–327.

138. "Woman Suffrage Adopted by Jewish Congregation Here," *Union Bulletin*, January 1921; quoted in Horvitz, "Marion L. Misch," 33.

139. Wolf, Wolf, and Feibel, "History of the Council, 1895–1965," SC-1961, AJA; Sporborg, "President's Message," 17.

NOTES TO CHAPTER 2

1. "Statement of Rose Halpern, New York City," in *Birth Control: Hearings before a Subcommittee of the Committee on the Judiciary*, 65.
2. "Mrs. Sanger's Aid is Found Guilty," *NYTimes*, January 9, 1917; Garlin, "Rose Halpern"; Chesler, *Woman of Valor*, 159. Rosenbaum, "'A Call To Action,'" is the only recent scholarly treatment of the Brownsville Jewish mothers and the clinic.
3. For more on contraception prior to the twentieth-century birth control movement, see Brodie, *Contraception and Abortion in Nineteenth-Century America*; Lefkowitz, *Rereading Sex*; and Tone, "Black Market Birth Control" and *Devices and Desires*.
4. Zelizer, *Pricing the Priceless Child*, explores this transition in economic thinking about children.
5. See Hyman, *Gender and Assimilation in Modern Jewish History*, especially chaps. 3 and 4.
6. The standard (though not historical) works on Jewish law and birth control are Feldman, *Birth Control in Jewish Law* and Millen, *Women, Birth, and Death in Jewish Law and Practice*.
7. For the eastern European background of Jewish fertility rates, see Freeze, *Jewish Marriage and Divorce in Imperial Russia*, 54ff.
8. Garlin, "Rose Halpern."
9. Anne Kennedy, New York, to Halpern, New York, March 13, 1925; Halpern, New York, to Sanger, March 21(?), 1931; Sanger, Washington, D.C., to Halpern, New York, April 23, 1932; Halpern, New York, to Sanger, Washington, D.C., February 21, 1934; Sanger, Washington, D.C., to Halpern, New York, February 25, 1934, RHC; "Statement of Rose Halpern," 65; Herrick, "Senators Hear Mother Tell How Birth Data Saved Her," *Chicago Daily Tribune*, March 2, 1934; Sanger, Tucson, to Halpern, New York, December 29, 1937, RHC; Chesler, *Woman of Valor*, 467.
10. For more on Jewish fertility rates in the United States, see Robison and Starr, *Jewish Population Studies* and chaps. 2, 4.
11. Frank, "Housewives, Socialists, and the Politics of Food," 273–279; Lerner, "American Feminism and the Jewish Question, 1890–1940," 320. On the relationship between socialism and suffrage, see chap. 1 and Buhle, *Women and American Socialism*.
12. Quoted in Chesler, *Woman of Valor*, 127.
13. Jensen, "The Evolution of Margaret Sanger's 'Family Limitation' Pamphlet," 551.
14. See Cott, *The Grounding of Modern Feminism* and Anderson, *After Suffrage*.
15. Chesler, *Woman of Valor*, 324.
16. The fertility rate is the average number of children born per woman during her lifetime. Woloch, *Women and the American Experience*, 606.
17. For more on abortion before its outright criminalization, see Mohr, *Abortion in America* and Brodie, *Contraception and Abortion in Nineteenth-Century America*.
18. For more on the market in contraceptive devices and the impact of technology, see Tone, *Devices and Desires*, especially chaps. 7 and 8.
19. Major works on the history of the birth control movement in America include Chen, *The Sex Side of Life*; Chesler, *Woman of Valor*; Engelman, *A History of Birth Control in America*; Gordon, *Woman's Body, Woman's Right* and *The Moral Property of Women*; Kennedy, *Birth Control in America*; McCann, *Birth Control Politics in the United States*; and Reed, *The Birth Control Movement and American Society*.
20. For more on the clinic movement and women's retention of local control, see chap. 4 and Hajo, *Birth Control on Main Street*, especially 98–99. This periodization of the birth control movement follows Ray and Gosling, "American Physicians and Birth Control, 1936–1947," 399. For more on Dickinson and the Committee for Maternal Health, see

especially Reed, *The Birth Control Movement and American Society* and Engelman, *A History of Birth Control in America.*

21. Burns, *The Moral Veto*, 4; Hornell, "Changing Social Attitudes and Interests," 415.
22. For a contemporary perspective on this "cultural complex" of radical reforms, see Vreeland, "Birth Control and Social Change," 1.
23. Abraham Stone, "A Green Old Age: A Tribute to Dr. Ben Zion Liber," March 13, 1955, Box 11, Folder 63, Stone Papers, H MS c 157, HML. For more on the Stones, see chap. 4.
24. Tone, *Devices and Desires*, 82.
25. On the radical milieu in New York, see Adickes, *To Be Young Was Very Heaven* and Fishbein, *Rebels in Bohemia.*
26. "Big Meeting Moves for Birth Control," *NYTimes*, May 27, 1915.
27. For more on doctors and birth control, see Rosen, "Federal Expansion, Fertility Control, and Physicians in the United States," 53–73.
28. Haslett, "Hull House and the Birth Control Movement," 268; Yarros, "Some Practical Aspects of Birth Control," 189.
29. Yarros, "Some Practical Aspects of Birth-Control," 188–190; *Journal of the American Medical Association*, Chicago, to Robert L. Dickinson, New York, December 13, 1927, Box 12, Folder 28, Stone Papers, H MS c 157 HML. Gender bias probably played a role in the fact that the letter was addressed to Dickinson, who merely contributed the introduction to an article that Hannah Stone wrote herself.
30. "Mrs. Stokes to Address the Jewish Council," *Brooklyn Eagle*, December 18, 1915.
31. The best biography is Falk, *Love, Anarchy, and Emma Goldman.*
32. Adickes, *To Be Young Was Very Heaven*, 127.
33. For example, see *Mother Earth* 2 (August 1907); Goldman, "The Hypocrisy of Puritanism," in *Anarchism and Other Essays*, 175–178.
34. Drinnon, *Rebel in Paradise*, 167–169; Goldman, *Living My Life*, vol. 2, 552–554. This autobiography is famously problematic but a valuable source nonetheless.
35. Goldman, Chicago, to Sanger, New York, December 17, 1915, Margaret Sanger Papers, Manuscript Division, Library of Congress, "From Haven to Home," www.loc.gov/exhibits/haventohome/haven-home.html.
36. Sanger, *Margaret Sanger*, 196.
37. Benjamin L. Reitman to Norman Himes, quoted in Gordon, *The Moral Property of Women*, 145–146.
38. Adickes, *To Be Young Was Very Heaven*, 134; Henrietta Moscowitz Voorsanger's autobiography, 312–313, Elkan and Henrietta Voorsanger Papers, MS 256, AJA; Meyer, "Birth Control Policy, Practice, and Prohibition in the 1930s," 63.
39. Leonard Abbott, New York, April 27, 1916, for the Birth Control Committee, Box 1, Folder 8, Rose Pastor Stokes Papers, MS 573, Sterling Library, Yale University, microfilm reel 3213/1 at AJA.
40. *Yiddishes Tageblat* clippings, Box 6, Folder 2; Goldman, New York, to Stokes, New York, October 17, 1916, Box 2, Folder 40, Stokes Papers, MS 573, Sterling Library, Yale University, microfilm reels 3217/5 and 3214/2 at AJA. For more on Stokes, see her unfinished autobiography, Stokes and Sterlings, eds., "*I Belong to the Working Class*" and Zipser, *Fire and Grace.*
41. May 5, 1916, speech typescript annotated in Stokes's hand, Box 6, Folder 22, Stokes Papers, MS 573, Sterling Library, Yale University, microfilm reel 3217/5 at AJA.
42. Stokes, *The Woman Who Wouldn't*, 29.
43. Sanger, New York, to Stokes, New York, November 22 and December 4, 1917, Box 3, Folder 88, Stokes Papers, MS 573, Sterling Library, Yale University, microfilm reel 3215/3 at AJA.
44. Chesler, *Woman of Valor*, 163. Sanger's departure from the radical roots of birth control has engendered criticism from historians of the movement, particularly Kennedy, *Birth Control in America* and Gordon, *The Moral Property of Women.* Reed, *The Birth Control*

Movement and American Society; McCann, *Birth Control Politics in the United States;* and Engelman, *A History of the Birth Control Movement in America* are more sympathetic to her pragmatism.

45. Helene, San Francisco, to her mother, Rypin, 1890?, in Kula, Assorodobraj-Kula, and Kula, eds., *Writing Home,* trans. Josephine Wtulich, 491.

46. Morgan, Watkins, and Ewbank, "Generating Americans," 96, 113–114. The study cautions that although the drop in fertility rate was real and significant, first- and second-generation immigrants were contemporaneous.

47. Watkins and Danzi, "Women's Gossip and Social Change," 479.

48. Fannie Shapiro is the pseudonym used in Kramer and Masur, eds., *Jewish Grandmothers,* 13–14; Weinberg, *The World of Our Mothers,* 220–221; Watkins and Danzi, "Women's Gossip and Social Change," 480–481. A 1936 expose of fraudulent contraceptive products lamented the number of women whose lives had been ruined by the corruption of a contraceptive market that could only be improved by legalization of birth control. See Palmer and Greenberg, *Facts and Frauds in Woman's Hygiene.*

49. Of 1,053 induced abortions reported to the Maternal Health Center in Newark in a 1925 study, which included Jewish women in proportion to their share of the general population, 469 had been performed by doctors, 121 by midwives, and 463 by the patients themselves. Sanger, *Biological and Medical Aspects of Contraception,* 66.

50. Sarah Rothman is the pseudonym used in Kramer and Masur, *Jewish Grandmothers,* 28; Weinberg, *The World of Our Mothers,* 210, 219–221; Watkins and Danzi, "Women's Gossip and Social Change," 480.

51. Watkins and Danzi, "Women's Gossip and Social Change," 480; Kramer and Masur, *Jewish Grandmothers,* 133; Voorsanger, Milwaukee, to Sanger, Tucson, December 8, 1941, Box 13, Folder 2, Florence Rose Papers, MS 134, SSC.

52. Tone, *Devices and Desires,* 35. For more on Dennett and Sanger, see Chen, *The Sex Side of Life.* For a contemporary take on the conflict between them, see Benjamin, "Lobbying for Birth Control," 52.

53. Hajo, *Birth Control on Main Street,* 23; Chesler, *Woman of Valor,* 153–156; Rosenbaum, "'A Call to Action'"; "Birth Controllers Up Early for Trial," *NYTimes,* January 5, 1917.

54. "Report of the Woman's Committee of One Hundred Meeting," January 1917, Box 1, Folder 11, Stokes Papers, MS 573, Sterling Library, Yale University, microfilm reel 3213/1 at AJA; Tone, *Devices and Desires,* 106–108.

55. Dennett explained the VPL's approach in *Birth Control Laws* and *Who's Obscene?*

56. "A Special Message to the Council, Contributors, and Friends of the Voluntary Parenthood League," November 18, 1921, Document 20 from Melissa Doak and Rachel Burger, eds., "How Did the Debate Between Margaret Sanger and Mary Ware Dennett Shape the Movement to Legalize Birth Control?" *Women and Social Movements in the United States, 1600–2000,* www.womhist.alexanderstreet.com.

57. *Principles and Aims of the American Birth Control League,* ca. 1921, Box 5, Folder 1, Margaret Sanger Research Bureau (MSRB hereafter) Records, MS 320, SSC; Chesler, *Woman of Valor,* 148–149.

58. American Jewish Autobiographies #42, RG 102, YIVO; Isaacson, Merrick, New York, to Abraham Stone, New York, September 8, 1941, Box 12, Folder 50, Stone Papers, H MS c 157, HML.

59. Ray and Gosling, "American Physicians and Birth Control," 403.

60. Stone, "Report of the Clinical Research Department of the American Birth Control League," 1925, Box 12, Folder 27, Stone Papers, H MS c 157, HML; Moses, *Fifth Report of the Bureau for Contraceptive Advice* (Baltimore), 1933, Box 5, Folder 19, MSRB Records, MS 320, SSC; Chesler, *Woman of Valor,* 153–155.

61. For an example of Israel's prominence in the birth control movement, see "Birth Controllers on Parade," *Time,* January 29, 1934. For an example of Wise's letters to legislators,

see Wise, New York, to Honorable John H. Conroy, Albany, March 6, 1923, Box 69, Reel 74-48, Stephen S. Wise Papers, P-134, AJHS.

62. Goldstein, "Birth Control as a Moral Issue," 210–216. For more on birth control and eugenics, see chap. 4.

63. Goldstein, "Birth Control as a Moral Issue," 217–220.

64. Joselit, *The Wonders of America*, 63–64.

65. *"Onvyzung"* ("Instructions,") Box 20, Folder 4, Rose Papers, M-134, SSC

66. As one example, see "The Question of Birth Control," *Forverts*, October 23, 1916. See also Seller, "Defining Socialist Womanhood," 433.

67. Liber, *Dos Geshlekhts Lebn*; Lederhandler, "Guides for the Perplexed," 339, n. 29; Zametkin, *Der Froys Handbuch*, 193–197.

68. Landes, *Geburts Kontrol*, 3, 7–8, 10, 12, trans. Sebastian Schulman (SS hereafter).

69. Landes, *Geburts Kontrol*, 16–17, 26–27, trans. SS.

70. Grossman, *Di Flikhten fun a Froy in Geburt Kontrol* (*A Woman's Duty in Birth Control*), copyrighted November 25, 1916, #438 in Lawrence Marwick Collection of Copyrighted Yiddish Plays, Library of Congress; Kalmanowitz, *Geburth Kontrol, oder, Rassen Zelbstmord* (*Birth Control or Race Suicide*) , copyrighted July 18, 1916, #506 in Lawrence Marwick Collection. The play titles will be abbreviated hereafter in the notes to *WD* and *BC*, respectively. There is some evidence of other 1916 Yiddish plays on the subject as well. See, for example, the poster for *The Great Question* by Zalmen Libin, which premiered at Philadelphia's Arch Street Theater on September 14, 1916, in Sandrow, *Vagabond Stars*, 153.

71. For examples, see Joselit, *The Wonders of America*, 64 and Lambert, "Unclean Lips," 81.

72. Histories of the American Yiddish theater include Burko, "The American Yiddish Theatre and Its Audience before World War I"; Howe, *World of Our Fathers*; Lifson, *The Yiddish Theatre in America*; Nahshon, *Yiddish Proletarian Theatre*; Rosenfeld, *Bright Star of Exile*; and Sandrow, *Vagabond Stars*.

73. By 1927 the number had already dropped to twenty-four Yiddish theaters in the entire United States, including eleven in New York and four in Chicago. Diner, *The Jews of the United States*, 242; Hapgood, *The Spirit of the Ghetto*, 122–123; Nahshon, "The Yiddish Theater in America"; Sandrow, *Vagabond Stars*, 286.

74. Advertisement for *BC*, July 16, 1916.

75. Translation of *BC* by Naomi S. Cohen. Kalmanowitz, *BC*, act 1.

76. Kalmanowitz, *BC*, act 2.

77. Kalmanowitz, *BC*, act 2.

78. Kalmanowitz, *BC*, act 2

79. Kalmanowitz, *BC*, act 3

80. Kalmanowitz, *BC*, act 3

81. Kalmanowitz, *BC*, act 4.

82. It is also possible that the sin referred to here has explicitly to do with condom use, the form of contraception most widely available prior to the establishment of a network of birth control clinics a few years later. Birth control activists promoted diaphragms at least in part because they allowed women to gain control of contraception. Within the Jewish community, diaphragms may also have been more palatable because they circumvented biblical strictures against men "spilling their seed" (Gen. 38:9–10), which made condom use problematic in Jewish legal terms and taboo even to many non-observant Jews.

83. Translation of *WD* by Naomi S. Cohen. Grossman, *WD*, act 1.

84. Grossman, *WD*, act 1.

85. Grossman, *WD*, act 1.

86. Grossman, *WD*, act 2.

87. Italics in original. Robinson, *Seventy Birth Control Clinics*, 42

88. See, for example, Yarros, "Birth Control and Its Relation to Health and Welfare."

89. Grossman, *WD*, act 2.

90. Grossman, *WD*, act 3.
91. Grossman, *WD*, act 3.
92. Grossman, *WD*, act 4.
93. Grossman, *WD*, act 4.
94. Chesler, *Woman of Valor*, 219.
95. "Samuel B. Grossman," 1:523 and "Harry Kalmanowitz," 4:3691 in Zylbercweig, *Leksikon fun Yidishn Teater.*
96. There is no evidence either of the two plays were ever revived. They do not appear on the lists of productions in Lifson, *The Yiddish Theatre in America*, 567–594, although they were not Yiddish Art Theatre, Artef, or Folksbeine Yiddish Theater productions to begin with.
97. Simon, *Bronx Primitive*, 69.
98. Cowan and Cowan, *Our Parents' Lives*, 170.

NOTES TO CHAPTER 3

1. Brin, "Jewish Education," ca. mid-1920s, Box 24, Folder 1, Fanny Fligelman Brin Papers, A.B58, MHS.
2. Brin, Minneapolis, to Rose Brenner, Brooklyn, June 6, 1924, Box 1, Folder 10, Brin Papers, A.B858, MHS.
3. With the important exception of Wilcock, *Pacifism and the Jews*, which includes virtually no information on women, there is very little historical literature on Judaism and peace.
4. Brin, "She Heard Another Drummer," 2, 4–5, 8; Brin, "Russian Bureaucracy and the Jews," undated but pre-1917, Box 24, Folder 3, Brin Papers, A.B58, MHS. For more on Brin, see Stuhler, "Fanny Brin."
5. Personal interview with Judith Brin Ingber, June 19, 2008.
6. On clubwomen, see Flanagan *Seeing With Their Hearts* and Scott, *Natural Allies*.
7. Brin, "Triennial Report, 1938, Pittsburgh," Folder NCJW 1928–1946, Viola Hoffman Hymes Papers, 146.F.9.9(B), MHS; Brin, "She Heard Another Drummer," 4.
8. Brin, "She Heard Another Drummer," 8; Schloff, "Fanny Fligelman Brin," 184–185.
9. Curti pioneered American peace history in *Peace or War*. For overviews, see Chatfield, *The American Peace Movement* and *For Peace and Justice*; DeBenedetti, *The Peace Reform in American History*; Howlett and Zeitzer, *The American Peace Movement*; Marchand, *The American Peace Movement and Social Reform*; and Wittner, *Rebels Against War*.
10. Eagen, *Class, Culture, and the Classroom*, 14–16; Patterson, "An Interpretation of the American Peace Movement," 29–30.
11. Alonso provides an important overview in *Peace as a Women's Issue*. See also Vellacott, "A Place for Pacifism and Transnationalism in Feminist Theory," 23. The connection between suffrage and pacifism formed part of a feminist complex that shaped the interwar international women's movement. See Cott, *The Grounding of Modern Feminism* and Rupp and Taylor, "Forming Feminist Identity in an International Movement."
12. Zeiger, "Finding a Cure for War," 69–86. On the Woman's Peace Party, see Costin, "Feminism, Pacifism, and the 1915 International Congress of Women"; Degen, *The History of the Woman's Peace Party*; and Schott, "The Woman's Peace Party and the Moral Basis for Women's Pacifism." On women's peace activism during World War I, see Early, *A World Without War* and Steinson, *American Women's Activism During World War I*. On WILPF, see Bussey and Tims, *Pioneers for Peace*; Catherine Foster, *Women for All Seasons*; Carrie Foster, *The Women and the Warriors*; Hensley, "Feminine Virtue and Feminist Fervor"; and Pois, "The U.S. Women's International League for Peace and Freedom and American Neutrality." Rupp, *Worlds of Women*, places WILPF within the framework of other international women's groups.
13. For more on the women's peace organizations, see Alonso, "Suffragists for Peace During the Interwar Years," 243–262 and *The Women's Peace Union and the Outlawry of War*.
14. Brown, *Setting a Course*, 66.

15. Chatfield, *For Peace and Justice*, 4; Addams, *Newer Ideals of Peace*, 1–6; Sternberger, *The Supreme Cause*, 123; Summy and Saunders, "Why Peace History?" 9.

16. Sneider, *Suffragists in an Imperial Age*, links suffragism to international relations. Jacobs, "Demands of Civilization," 1898, Box 1, Folder 9, Sadie Jacobs Crockin Collection, MS 95, JMM; Bolt, *Sisterhood Questioned?*, 19.

17. Solomon, "Our Problems," in *A Sheaf of Leaves*, 87.

18. Alonso, *Peace as a Woman's Issue*, 52–53. See Rogow, *Gone to Another Meeting* for more on these relationships.

19. Solomon, "The Religious Mission of Israel," in *A Sheaf of Leaves*, 125–126; "Peace Meetings Draw Thousands of Enthusiasts," *Seattle Post Intelligencer*, ca. 1907, Scrapbook Vol. III, Reel 1, Maud Nathan Papers, M-83, SL; Solomon, *Fabric of My Life*, 145; Rogow, *Gone to Another Meeting*, 178.

20. On the ICW and IWSA, see D'Itri, *Cross Currents in the International Women's Movement*, Rupp, *Worlds of Women*, and the ICW's organizational history, *Women in a Changing World*.

21. Kuzmack, *Woman's Cause*, 75; Solomon, *Fabric of My Life*, 120–124.

22. Wenger, "Radical Politics in a Reactionary Age," 69–70; Patterson, *The Search for Negotiated Peace*, 152. Schwimmer met Ford when she was lobbying him to support the "Peace Ship" that set out in 1915, carrying activists like Schwimmer and Jane Addams, who hoped to negotiate a peace settlement and end the war. On the ill-fated mission, see Kraft, *The Peace Ship* and Patterson, *The Search for Negotiated Peace*.

23. "Rosika Schwimmer Appeals to Jewish Women," *American Hebrew*, December 18, 1914; "Says Week's Halt Would End the War," *NYTimes*, December 8, 1914.

24. "Maud Nathan on Votes for Peace," *The Woman's Journal*, September 13, 1913; Alonso, *Peace as a Women's Issue*, 48–49; Program for National Suffrage Bazaar at Madison Square Garden, December 3–8, 1900, Box 3, Folder 6, Carrie Chapman Catt Papers, NYPL; "Boycott is Remedy of Woman for War," *NYTimes*, November 21, 1915; Schott, "The Women's Peace Party and the Moral Basis of Women's Pacifism," 21–22. On the WCTU, see Tyrell, *Woman's World/Woman's Empire*.

25. CDGA Emma Goldman, SCPC; Stokes, Stamford, Connecticut, to Butler Davenport, September 4, 1914, A/5874, SL; Alonso, *Peace as a Women's Issue*, 56–57. See Marsh, *Anarchist Women*, on radical women's reactions to the war.

26. On Wald's Jewish identity, see Feld, *Lillian Wald*. Wald, *Windows on Henry Street*, 10; Patterson, *The Search for Negotiated Peace*, 21–28, 188; Cook, "Female Support Networks and Political Activism," 414.

27. Zametkin, "Around the Women's World," *Der Fraynd*, March 1917, 7, trans. SS; McCune, "*The Whole Wide World Without Limits*," 52–53; Wilcock, *Pacifism and the Jews*, 45; "Conversations with Alice Paul," 161.

28. Ganz, *Rebels*, 264–268; Degan, *The History of the Woman's Peace Party*, 189. For more on Ganz, who ultimately renounced many of her anarchist beliefs, see Marsh, *Anarchist Women*. For more on Stokes, see Zipser, *Fire and Grace*.

29. Solomon, *Fabric of My Life*, 177–178; McCune, "The Whole Wide World Without Limits," 54–55.

30. Blumberg, "Sophie Weil Brown," 16–17.

31. Quoted in Campbell, *The First Fifty Years*, 47.

32. "Pilgrims for Peace to Visit Congress," *NYTimes*, February 9, 1917; Alonso, "Suffragists for Peace During the Interwar Years."

33. Brandeis to Catt, New York, January 24, 1919, SC-1305, AJA; Cott, *The Grounding of Modern Feminism*, 243.

34. "Political Mobilization," in Keetley and Pettegrew, eds., *Public Women, Public Words*, 228–229. On NWP after suffrage, see Lundardini, *From Equal Suffrage to Equal Rights*.

35. Abrams, *Jewish Women Pioneering the Frontier Trail*, 63–65; "Raleigh's Educational Program," 24–25; *Bulletin*, October 1925; *Bulletin*, February 1928. The *Bulletin* was published

by the New York NCJW section. October 1925 through May 1930 issues are in Box 79, Folder 1, NCJW Papers, I-469, AJHS.

36. Sanger, *Woman and the New Race*, viii. See also *Church and Society* 4 (February 1932), a special issue on "Voluntary Parenthood" with articles by Margaret Sanger and Hannah Mayer Stone, among others. This attitude remained salient well into World War II. As the sociologist Henry Pratt Fairchild stated in the *Annals of the Academy of Political and Social Science* in 1943, "If the question of worldwide birth control can be faced unemotionally, scientifically, and impartially, some adequate solution may eventually be found, and one great foundation stone of world peace be permanently laid." Fairchild, "Family Limitation and the War," 86.

37. NCJW, *Program of Work: Seventh Triennial Period, 1911–1914* , Box 1, Nearprint File–NCJW, AJA; "The Woman After the War," *Der Fraynd*, October 1917, trans. SS.

38. Patterson, *The Search for Negotiated Peace*, 184; Sternberger, *The Supreme Cause*, 8–9. For more on Magnes, see Szajkowski, "The Pacifism of Judah Magnes" and Wilcock, *Pacifism and the Jews*, chap. 2.

39. Alonso, *Peace as a Women's Issue*, 88; Green, *The Problem of Universal Peace and the Key to Its Solution*.

40. Fleischman, *A Plan for World Peace Based on a Permanent World Conference*; Borochow, *The M.A.B. Plan*; Bernstein, ed. *Can We Abolish War?*

41. WPU, New York, to members, July 6, 1932, Box 1, Folder "Correspondence 1921–1933," WPU Records, Acc. #44, M 95, NYPL.

42. *Chicago Woman's Aid Bulletin* 7 (December 1923): 11.

43. "Peace Heroes' Memorial Society Provisional Articles of Organization," Box 3, Folder 10, Abraham Cronbach Papers, MSS 9, AJA; Cronbach, *The Jewish Peace Book for Home and School*, 3–4. For more on Cronbach, see Wilcock, *Pacifism and the Jews*, chap. 6.

44. Goldberg, Brockton, Massachusetts, to Cronbach, Cincinnati, January 12, 1924, Box 2, Folder 11; Bazell, Altoona, Pennsylvania, to Cronbach, Cincinnati, January 29, 1924, Box 1, Folder 9; Faber, Tyler, Texas, to Cronbach, Cincinnati, January 17, 1924, Box 2, Folder 5, Cronbach Papers, MSS 9, AJA. Hebrew Union College reprimanded Cronbach for circulating the pledge in the first place, since the rabbinical seminary expected its faculty to remain apolitical. On Reform rabbis and pacifism, see Arian, "'Disciples of Aaron.'"

45. "Report of the Standing Committee on Cooperation with National Organizations" and "Report of the Standing Committee on International Peace," *CCAR Yearbook 1925*, 77, 106.

46. "Report of Special Committee on International Peace," *CCAR Yearbook 1926*, 74.

47. "Report of the Committee on International Peace," *CCAR Yearbook 1931*, 74. For more on NFTS, see Nadell and Simon, "Ladies of the Sisterhood."

48. Gittelsohn, *The Jew Looks at War and Peace*, 1–4.

49. *World Congress of Jewish Women, Vienna, May 6–11, 1923*, 129; "Women's World Conference in Hamburg," *American Hebrew*, June 14, 1929. On the World Council of Jewish Women, see Las, *Jewish Women in a Changing World*.

50. Brin, "Democracy in Jewish Heritage," ca. 1939, Box 24, Folder 1; Brin, "A Woman Looks At Disarmament," November 22, 1932, Box 22, Folder 1, Brin Papers, A.B858, MHS.

51. Waldstreicher, "Radicalism, Religion, Jewishness," 74; Jennie Franklin Purvin, "A Tribute to Hannah G. Solomon," February 3, 1933, Box 22780, Folder "Sinai Temple," Purvin Papers, MS 502, AJA; Untitled article by Sylvia Lehman about Solomon, 1936, in Stone, "Lifelong Volunteer in San Francisco," appendix 39a; "Women in 7 Lands Plead for Peace," *NYTimes*, January 12, 1937; Brin, eulogy for Solomon, 1942, Box 23, Folder 1, Brin Papers, A.B858, MHS.

52. Spiegelberg, "The Ten Commandments of World Peace," 1919, Flora Spiegelberg Papers, Microfilm reel 511, AJA. For an example of sisterhood actions, see "Resolution—Keneseth Israel and Rodef Shalom Sisterhoods," 1921, Series B5, Box 24, WILPF Collection, DG 043, SCPC. The combined membership of the two Philadelphia groups was 1,600 women.

53. Catt, "Mars Takes a Sabbatical," 1933, Box 4, Folder 1, Catt Papers, NYPL.
54. McCune, *"The Whole Wide World Without Limits,"* 175–176; McCune, "Creating a Place for Women in a Socialist Brotherhood," 585–588; "Jennie Matyas and the I.L.G.W.U," 63–64. See Buhle, *Women and Socialism,* for extended treatment of the relationship between women and the Left and Michels, *A Fire in Their Hearts* for a valuable discussion of Jewish socialism in America, though not one strong on gender analysis. On industrial feminism, see Cobble, *The Other Women's Movement* and Pastorello, *A Power Among Them*
55. Pesotta, "No More War," January 15, 1930, Box 1, Folder "General Correspondence, 1930–1933," Rose Pesotta Papers, NYPL; Eagen, *Class, Culture, and the Classroom,* 11–12.
56. Abrams, "Jewish Women in the International Woman Suffrage Alliance," 176; Caroline Katzenstein Papers, ACC #1246, PJAC. On maternalism and peace, see Ruddick, *Maternal Thinking.*
57. Rupp, "Constructing Internationalism," 1583–1585; Alonso, "Commentary," 50; Alonso, *The Women's Peace Union and the Outlawry of War,* 137.
58. See Bolt, *Sisterhood Questioned,* on these differences and D'Itri, *Cross Currents in the International Women's Movement,* on the postwar IWSA, 109ff.
59. Unidentified NCJW speech, ca. 1933, Box 23, Folder 3, Brin Papers, A.B858, MHS.
60. Unidentified Brin speech, ca. mid-1930s, Box 24, Folder 5, Brin Papers, A.B858, MHS.
61. Barron, "On Limitation of Armaments," Box 6, Folder 105, Jennie Loitman Barron Papers, MC 410, SL; Horvitz, "Marion L. Misch," 40; Spivak, ed., *The Price of Peace.*
62. Nathan, *Once Upon a Time and Today,* 273–275; Schneiderman, *All for One,* 168. See Rupp, *Worlds of Women* and Cooper, *Patriotic Pacifism,* for brief treatments of anti-Semitism in the international women's and peace movements, and see chap. 5 for a more extended discussion.
63. Brin, "Women and the Peace Movement"; Alonso, *The Women's Peace Union and the Outlawry of War,* 89; Weil, "Thoughts on Armistice Day," Undated, unidentified typescript of letter to the editor, Box 98, Folder 3, Gertrude Weil Papers, NCOA.
64. Report on NCCCW Conference, ca. 1927, 91.126.1, JMM; Solomon, *Fabric of My Life,* 211; Catt, "The Problem Stated," undated, Box 5, Folder 5, Catt Papers, NYPL.
65. List of Edelman's speaking engagements, Fall 1930, Series B3, Box 8, Folder 3; WILPF–New York State Branch Report, April 26, 1929, Series B3, Box 1, Folder 2, WILPF Collection, DG 043, SCPC; Kuhn's autobiography, Box 3, Folder 10, Setty Swartz Kuhn Papers, MS 173, AJA; Foster, *The Women and the Warriors,* 51–52.
66. WILPF–Massachusetts Branch Annual Report, 1924, Box 1, Folder 2, WILPF–Massachusetts Branch Records, 83-M23, SL.
67. Foster, *The Women and the Warriors,* 179–180; Detzer, *Appointment on the Hill,* 76–77.
68. Pisko, "Report of the Second Vice-President," *National Council of Jewish Women Tenth Triennial Convention,* 34; Catt, untitled essay about charges of communism against the peace movement, 1924, Box 3, Folder 8, Carrie Chapman Catt Papers, MS 31, SSC. On this forged but still damaging text, see Bronner, *A Rumor About the Jews* and Singerman, "The American Career of the *Protocols of the Elders of Zion.*"
69. Schwimmer, "Women Pioneers of a New International Order," 231.
70. On the Women's League, see *They Dared to Dream.*
71. Box 1, Volume 1, Women of Reform Judaism Papers, MS 73, AJA; Mrs. E.E. Eutsler, Goldsboro, to Senator F.W. Simmons, Washington, D.C., November 9, 1925, Box 82, Folder 1, Weil Papers, NCOA; "Three Groups Join in Peace Week Here," *NYTimes,* May 8, 1926.
72. Clipping from the *Courier,* February 1926, Carton 2, Folder 12, Bertha Sanford Gruenberg Papers, 837-69-31, SL; Cronbach, *The Quest for Peace,* 155–158; Report of the Committee on International Peace, *CCAR Yearbook, 1929,* 79; Kubie, New York, to NFTS members, April 22, 1931, Box 84, Folder 2, Weil Papers, NCOA.
73. Kubie, New York, to NFTS members, April 22, 1931, Box 84, Folder 2, Weil Papers, NCOA; *They Dared to Dream.*

74. Dorothy Prussian to Caroline Lexow Babcock, New York, ca. 1927, Box 1, Folder "Correspondence, 1921–1933," WPU Records, NYPL.

75. Feibleman, "Report of the Committee on Peace and Arbitration," *Official Report of the CJW Eighth Triennial Convention,* 241–242; NCJW–Baltimore Section Minutes, May 12, 1919, Box 17, Folder 635, NCJW–Baltimore Section Records, MS 124, JMM.

76. History of the Staten Island Section of NCJW, Box 1, Folder "Affiliate Organizations," Federation of Jewish Women's Organization Papers, I-208, AJHS; Wolf, Wolf, and Feibel, "History of the Council, 1895–1965," SC-1961, AJA; "Peace," 28; quoted in Catt, "The Problem Stated," Box 5, Folder 5, Catt Papers, NYPL.

77. Kohut, *More Yesterdays,* 107.

78. Sternberger, New York, to Brin, Minneapolis, August 11, 1924, Box 1, Folder 10, Brin Papers, A.B858, MHS; Rogow, *Gone to Another Meeting,* 178; Maxwell, "Spider Web Chart."

79. Sternberger, "Editorial," 20; Brin, "Peace," 16–17; National Council of Jewish Juniors, *War vs Youth,* 1; "Women's World Conference in Hamburg," *American Hebrew,* June 14, 1929; Las, *Jewish Women in a Changing World.*

80. *Proceedings of the First Convention of the NCJW,* 23–27; NCJW–New York Section, *Year Book 1906–1907 (5667),* 21.

81. Program for the National Council of Women Biennial Session, Decatur, Illinois, October 29–November 3, 1923, Box 2278L, Folder "NCJW–Chicago Section," Purvin Papers, MS 502, AJA; "The Golden Years," 12, box 1, Folder 2, NCJW–Minneapolis Section Papers, #0545, JHSUM.

82. "Council Speaker Urges Action for No More War," *American Hebrew,* September 15, 1922.

83. Boeckel, "Women in International Affairs," 231.

84. April 15, June 5, December 19, 1923, May 2, 1933, Jennie Franklin Purvin diaries, Box 2278e; Alice Boynton, Chicago, to Purvin, Chicago, May 17, 1929, Box 22780, Folder "World War One and Two," Purvin Papers, MS 502, AJA.

85. April 16, 1923, November 9, 1930, Purvin diaries, Box 2278e, Purvin Papers MS 502, AJA.

86. *Seventeenth Annual Report of the National Federation of Temple Sisterhoods, April 1930.*

87. On the LWV's peace activities, see Young, *In the Public Interest.* On the European peace movements, see Cooper, *Patriotic Pacifism.*

NOTES TO CHAPTER 4

1. "N.Y. to Help Birth Control Clinic Fight Here," *Boston Post,* August 9, 1937.

2. Stone, "The Birth Control Raid"; Ernst, *The Best is Yet . . . ,* 253; Engelman, *A History of Birth Control in America,* 157–158.

3. Due to the varying methods of fertility rate calculations used by social scientists and compilers of Jewish community statistics, it is difficult to assign an exact number to the decline in American Jewish family size. However, there is unanimous agreement that the drop was steeper and faster than that of other ethnic groups and that Jewish use of contraception provided the major explanatory factor. For a collection of Jewish community studies offering data on family size, see Robison, *Jewish Population Studies.* For examples of statistical calculations, see Jaffe, "Religious Differentials in the Net Reproduction Rate," which concludes that Jewish women's net reproductive rate declined by nearly a half between 1925 and 1935; and Greenberg, "The Reproduction Rate of the Families of the Jewish Studies at the University of Maryland," a case study contending that within a generation the average family size had declined by more than 50 percent.

4. Chesler, *Woman of Valor,* 278–279, 304–306.

5. Box 4, Folder 1, Margaret Sanger Research Bureau (MSRB hereafter) Records, MS 320, SSC; for an example of a legal warning, see Morris L. Ernst, New York, to Abraham Stone, New York, April 15, 1935, Box 10, Folder 16, Abraham Stone Papers, H MS c 157, HML.

6. Speech transcripts, Box 12, Folder 29; Hannah Stone, New York, to Ann Chou, Shanghai, December 16, 1935, Box 10, Folder 18, Stone Papers, H MS c 157, HML; Chesler, *Woman*

of Valor, 280, 361; review of Stone and Stone, *A Marriage Manual* in *NYTimes*, October 6, 1935; report of the annual meeting of the Birth Control Federation of America, New York, January 23-25, 1940, Box 5, Folder 11, MSRB Records, MS 320, SSC; Union Health Center Educational and Social Service Department Report for the First Six Months of 1940, Box 6, Folder 98, Pauline Newman Papers, MC 324, SL.

7. Genn, "Science Reveals Why Marriages Fail," *Philadelphia Public Ledger*, 1937; Marcus, Cleveland, to Abraham and Hannah Stone, New York, September 21, 1935, Box 10, folder 16, Stone Papers, H MS c 157, HML; transcript of Grant Sanger interview conducted by Ellen Chesler, August 1976, 26-27, Family Planning Oral History Project Records, OH-1, MC 223, SL.

8. McCann, introduction to *Birth Control Politics in the United States*; Document 14, "Advisory Council Meeting Minutes, 23 March 1932"; Document 15, "Hannah Stone, Medical Director of the Clinical Research Bureau, to Margaret Sanger, 27 March 1932"; Document 16, "M.D. Bousfield to Michael Davis, Rosenwald Fund, 9 April 1932"; Document 21, "Suggestions Approved by Mrs. Sanger: New Program for Harlem Branch, 18 October 1932"; Document 29, "Questions Asked After Lecture by Dr. Levinson [Warner] at New York Urban League, 26 January 1933," "What Perspectives did African American Advocates Bring tot he Birth Control Movement and How Did Those Perspectives Shape the History of the Harlem Branch Birth Control Clinic?" *Women and Social Movements in the United States, 1600-2000*, www.alexanderstreetpress.com.

9. "250 Attend Rites Here for Dr. Stone," *NYTimes*, July 14, 1941; Marie and Ben Warner, New York, to Abraham Stone, New York, July 11, 1941, Box 12, Folder 58; Cheri Appel and Benjamin Segal, New York, to Abraham Stone, New York, July 17, 1941, Box 12, Folder 44, Stone Papers, H MS c 157, HML.

10. Box 12, Folder 17, Florence Rose Papers, MS 134, SSC.

11. "Dr. Stone, Pioneer in Birth Control," *NYTimes*, July 11, 1941; H. Jaffe,"Dr. Hannah Mayer Stone," *Die Pionern Froy*, August 9, 1941.

12. Diner and Benderly, *Her Works Praise Her*, 330; Watkins and Danzi, "Women's Gossip and Social Change," 470, 479; Engelman, "A Study of Size of Families in the Jewish Population of Buffalo," 9-12, 29-32, 59-60; Stone and Hart, *Maternal Health and Conception*, 20-23.

13. Ray and Gosling, "American Physicians and Birth Control, 1936-1947," 402; Meyer, "Birth Control Policy, Practice, and Prohibition in the 1930s," 88; *How to Start a Contraceptive Center: Suggestions Offered by the American Birth Control League*, ca. 1934, Box 75, Folder 4, Gertrude Weil Papers, NCOA. All histories of birth control cover the clinic movement as a matter of course, but Hajo, *Birth Control on Main Street*, is especially valuable for its coverage of clinics outside New York.

14. Tone, *Devices and Desires*, 119, 56.

15. "Five Year's Progress"; Hajo, *Birth Control on Main Street*, 21; Haslett, "Hull House and the Birth Control Movement," 268; McCann, *Birth Control Politics in the United States*, 139-160.

16. Stone, *Report of the Clinical Research Department of the American Birth Control League for the Year of 1925*.

17. Stone, "Contraceptive Methods: A Clinical Survey," paper read at the Sixth International Neo-Malthusian and Birth Control Conference, March 29, 1925, in MSRB Records, Box 4, Folder 1, MS 320, SSC; Yarros, "Birth Control and Its Relation to Health and Welfare," 269-271.

18. Moses, *Fifth Report of the Bureau for Contraceptive Advice*, 1933, Box 5, Folder 19, MSRB Records, MS 320, SSC; Stix and Notestein, "Effectiveness of Birth Control," 68; Stix and Notestein, "Effectiveness of Birth Control: A Second Study," 164-165, 173.

19. See, for example, Yiddish Writers' Group of the Federal Writers' Project of the Works Progress Administration of the City of New York, *Yiddishe Familyes un Familye Krayz fun Nyu York (Jewish Families and Family Circles of New York)*, 72.

20. Nash, "Birth Control Clinics."

21. Hajo, *Birth Control on Main Street*, 34–35; Chesler, *Woman of Valor*, 228; *First Report of the Detroit Mothers Clinic for Family Regulation*, ca. 1928, Box 6, Folder 8, MSRB Records, MS 320, SSC. The Jewish population of Detroit never reached more than 4 percent of the general population, so the 10 percent of Jewish clients represented a disproportionate number of Jewish women using the birth control clinic. Bolkosky, *Harmony and Dissonance*, 141.

22. Hajo, *Birth Control on Main Street*, 79; Joselit, *The Wonders of America*, 68; Lurie, "Sex Hygiene and Family Life," 20–24; Invitation to ABCL Annual Meeting, January 15, 1931, Box 5, Folder 2, MSRB Records, MS 320, SSC.

23. *Chicago Woman's Aid Bulletin* 7 (December 1923): 11, Box 2278d, Jennie Franklin Purvin Papers, MS 502, AJA; Guthmann, *The Planned Parenthood Movement in Illinois*, 6.

24. *National Federation of Temple Sisterhoods Assembly Resolutions, 1913–1939*, 74, Box 12, Women of Reform Judaism Papers, MS 73, AJA; "Extension Planned" *Minneapolis Journal*, February 18, 1937; "Birth Control Comes of Age" materials, Box 17, Folder 4, Rose Papers, MS 134, SSC.

25. NCJW–Baltimore Section, Minutes, December 14, 1931, Box 17, Folder 640, NCJW–Baltimore Section Records, MS 124, JMM; "The Maternal Health Center: First Birth Control Clinic in New Jersey," ca. 1932, Box 6, Folder 4, MSRB Records, MS 320, SSC; NCJW–New York Section, Board Minutes, October 9, 1933, Box 3, folder 7; April 12, 1939, Box 4, Folder 1, NCJW Papers, I-469, AJHS; Benjamin, "Lobbying for Birth Control," 57. Previous histories of NCJW barely cover what became an important element of many local sections' work. See, for example, Rogow, *Gone to Another Meeting*, 143.

26. NCJW–New York Section, *Centennial Journal*, Box 3, Nearprint File–Special Topics: NCJW, AJA; NCJW–New York Section, Board Minutes, February 11, April 7, 1931, Box 3, Folder 6; Annual Report, May 1, 1936–December 31, 1936, Box 27, Folder 18, NCJW Papers, I-469, AJHS; NCJW–Brooklyn Section, *A History*, 11–12, 17.

27. NCJW–St. Paul Section, Board Minutes, May 24, 1932, NCJW–St. Paul Section Papers, #0546, UMJA.

28. Evelyn Friday, Minneaplis, to Helen Grodinsky, St. Paul, November 14, 1932, Box 25, Folder 4, Planned Parenthood of Minnesota Records, SW024, SWHA; For more on contraceptive supplies, see Tone, *Devices and Desires*.

29. Clinic records, Box 25, Folder 4, Planned Parenthood of Minnesota Records, SW024, SWHA; NCJW–St. Paul Section, Board Minutes, January 9, February 6, 1933, NCJW–St. Paul Section Papers, #0546, UMJA.

30. NCJW–St. Paul Section, Minutes, November 6, 1933, NCJW–St. Paul Section Papers, #0546, UMJA; Client List, Box 20, Folder 4; Dorothy B. Atkinson, Minneapolis, to Helen Grodinsky, St. Paul, January 22, 1934, Box 20, Folder 4, Planned Parenthood of Minnesota Records, SW024, SWHA.

31. *Bulletin*, North Central Interstate Conference of the NCJW, 1934, Box 8, Folder 5, NCJW–Minneapolis Section Papers, #0545, UMJA.

32. NCJW–St. Paul Section, Minutes, March 4, April 1, December 3, 1935, NCJW–St. Paul Section Papers, #0546, UMJA.

33. Jones, New York, to Weil, Goldsboro, November 19, 1930, Box 75, Folder 4; Sanger, Washington, D.C., to Weil, Goldsboro, May 13, 1932, Box 75, Folder 1; North Carolina Maternal Health League founding document, 1935, and other materials, Box 75, Folder 2, Weil Papers, NCOA. These sources do not mention the state's sterilization program, but there were connections between North Carolina's birth controllers and eugenicists. See Schoen, *Coercion and Choice*, and the section on eugenics below.

34. Transcript of interview of Lenore Guttmacher by James Reed for the Family Planning Oral History Project, 1974, 2–3, 6–8, Family Planning Oral History Project Records, OH-1/ MC 223, SL.

35. "Well Known Giver to Charity Says Prevention Better Than Relief," *Birth Control Herald*, December 21, 1923. "Birth Control's 21st," unidentified article, February 18, 1935, Box 2, Folder 1, MSRB Records, MS 320, SSC. *Birth Control Herald* was a VPL publication.

36. Dykemann, *Too Many People, Too Little Love*, 66; Meyer, "Birth Control Policy, Practice and Prohibition in the 1930s," 94–95; transcript of interview of Emily Mudd by James Reed for the Family Planning Oral History Project, 1974, 28–29, Family Planning Oral History Project Records, OH-1/MC 223, SL; Box 26, Folder 1, Planned Parenthood of Minnesota Records, SW024, SWHA.

37. Stella Bloch Hanau, New York, to Ira S. Wile, New York, December 12, 1928, Box 1, Folder 5, Ira S. Wile Papers, MS 173, SSC.

38. Transcript of meeting in honor of Sanger, June 18, 1957, Box 12, Folder 63, Stone Papers, H MS c 157, HML; quoted in Lambert, "'Unclean Lips,'" 95.

39. Transcript of meeting in honor of Sanger, June 18, 1957, Box 12, Folder 63, Stone Papers, H MS c 157, HML; Rose, Brooklyn, to Sanger, New York, July 2, 1930, Box 12, Folder 17, Rose Papers, MS 134, SSC.

40. "Birth Control Advocate Here," *Pocatello Tribune*, August 13, 1933; "Economic Woes Linked to Lack of Birth Control," *Seattle Daily Times*, August 25, 1933; Chesler, *Woman of Valor*, 290.

41. Rose to Sanger, August 31, 1935; Sanger to Rose, September 9, 1935, Box 10, Folder 2; Rose, New York, to Kross, New York, March 10, 1936, Box 7, Folder 20, Rose Papers, MS 134, SSC.

42. Levine, Los Angeles, to Rose, New York, December 6, 1937; Levine, Los Angeles, to Rose, New York, January 27, 1938; Rose, New York, to Levine, Los Angeles, April 1938, Box 7, Folder 22, Rose Papers, MS 134, SSC.

43. Robinson, *Seventy Birth Control Clinics*, 185.

44. Program for Seventh International Birth Control Conference, Zurich, September 1–5, 1930, Box 7, Folder 37, Stone Papers, H MS c 157, HML.

45. Abram, *"Send Us a Lady Physician,"* 60–62. Important histories of women in medicine include Morantz-Sanchez, *Sympathy and Science* and More, *Restoring the Balance*.

46. Abram, *"Send Us a Lady Physician,"* 100, 57, 102; More, *Restoring the Balance*, 24.

47. Morantz-Sanchez, *Sympathy and Science*, 234; Brown, *Setting a Course*, 157–158; "Jewish Women Doctors," *American Hebrew*, June 6, 1913.

48. More, *Restoring the Balance*, 164.

49. Morantz-Sanchez, *Sympathy and Science*, 230.

50. Jacob Billikopf to Morris Waldman, Detroit, October 30, 1924, Box 31, Folder 4, Jacob Billikopf Papers, MS 13, AJA. On Jewish hospitals in America, see Kraut and Kraut, *Covenant of Care*.

51. Transcript of Sarah Marcus interview conducted by Ellen Chesler, April 1976, 16–34, Family Planning Oral History Project Records, OH-1, MC 223, SL; Meyer, "Birth Control Policy, Practice, and Prohibition in the 1930s," 104–105; "'Yes I Can' Says Pioneer Woman Doctor," *Cleveland Jewish News*, June 25, 1971.

52. Meyer, "Birth Control Policy, Practice and Prohibition in the 1930s," 104–105; transcript of Sarah Marcus interview conducted by Chesler, 31. At the time of the interview, Marcus could not remember if she had an especially large Jewish practice, but Chesler's aunt, who lived in Cleveland, told her that many Jewish women had been eager to consult a Jewish woman doctor.

53. *Maternal Health Association Report of Fourth Year, March 1931–March 1932*, Box 6, Folder 3, MSRB Records, MS 320, SSC; Marcus, "The Planned Family as a Social Constructive Measure," February 12, 1935, Box 2, Folder 16, Family Planning Oral History Project Records, MC 223, SL; Marcus, Cleveland, to Abraham and Hannah Stone, New York, September 21, 1935, Box 10, Folder 16, Stone Papers, H MS c 157, HML.

54. Yarros, "Experiences of a Lecturer," 205–222; Haslett, "Hull House and the Birth Control Movement," 269–271, 263, 266.

55. Yarros, "Some Practical Aspects of Birth Control," 188.
56. Chesler, *Woman of Valor*, 226–227; Yarros, "Birth Control and Sex Hygiene," 4; "Statement of Dr. Rachelle Yarros, Hull House, Chicago" and "Supplementary Statement to the Committee on the Social Security Act, by Dr. Rachelle Yarros, Hull House, Chicago," *Social Security Online*, <www.ssaonline.us/history/pdf/s35yarros.pdf>.
57. Cheri Appel oral history, conducted by Ellen Chesler, 1989, 8–24, 32–34, 39, 19, MS 413, SSC.
58. Document 36, Marie Levinson Warner, "Birth Control and the Negro," 1934, "What Perspectives did African American Advocates Bring to the Birth Control Movement and How Did Those Perspectives Shape the History of the Harlem Branch Birth Control Clinic?" *Women and Social Movements in the United States, 1600–2000*, www.alexander-streetpress.com; Warner, "Contraception," 279–285.
59. Appel oral history, conducted by Chesler, 1989, 45; Chesler, *Woman of Valor*, 307; "Scientific Advice in Marriage Urged," *NYTimes*, July 5, 1947.
60. List of birth control clinics by state, 1934, Box 5, Folder 4, MSRB Records, MS 320, SSC; Mrs. Vine McCasland, San Franciso, to Dennett and Myra Gallert, March 3, 1930, Box 21, Folder 382, Reel 19, Mary Ware Dennett Papers, M-138, SL; Hajo, *Birth Control on Main Street*, 40–41.
61. Moses, *First Report of the Bureau for Contraceptive Advice*, 1929, Box 5, Folder 19, MSRB Records, MS 320, SSC.
62. Kleinman, Jamaica Plain, to Mr. Setter, May 3, 1932, Box 15, Folder "Kleinman, Elizabeth," Planned Parenthood League of Massachusetts Branch Papers, MS 359, SSC.
63. Transcript of interview of Lucile Lord-Heinstein conducted by Nils Bruzelius, 1976, Lucile Lord-Heinstein Papers, AL866h, SL; Wynn, "Lucile Lord-Heinstein," 4; Loraine Leeson Campbell, Boston, to Lord-Heinstein, Boston, December 14, 1936, Box 1, Folder 3, Lucile Lord-Heinstein Papers, MC 310, SL.
64. Transcript of interview of Lord-Heinstein conducted by Bruzelius; Lord-Heinstein's c.v., Box 1, Folder 1, Lord-Heinstein Papers, MC 310, SL.
65. Transcript of Elizabeth Cohen Arnold interview conducted by James Reed, August 1976, 8–11, 20–23, 33, Family Planning Oral History Project Records, OH-1, MC 223, SL; Robinson, *Seventy Birth Control Clinics*, 185.
66. The best recent overview of the gendered struggle for leadership is Engelman, *A History of the Birth Control Movement in America*, especially chap. 4 and the material on Robert Latou Dickinson and the Committee for Maternal Health.
67. Bertha Van Hoosen, Chicago, to BCCRB, New York, January 31, 1932, Box 12, Folder 28, Stone Papers, H MS c 157, HML.
68. Polls cited in Ray and Gosling, "American Physicians and Birth Control," 401. See also Benjamin, "Lobbying for Birth Control," 50.
69. Sanger, New York, to Wise, New York, October 31, 1931; Wise, New York, to Sanger, New York, November 1931; copy of Dennett, New York, to Henry Pratt Fairchild, New York, February 19, 1934, Box 69, microfilm reel 74–78, Wise Papers, P-134, AJHS. Dennett's book *Who's Obscene?* details her own legal struggles over sex education and birth control information.
70. Ernst, "Forward," in *Laws Relating to Birth Control in the United States and Its Territories*, 8–9; transcript of interview of Lord-Heinstein conducted by Bruzelius; "3 in Birth Control Case Found Guilty," *Boston American*, July 20, 1937.
71. "N.Y. to Help Birth Control Clinic Fight Here," *Boston Post*, August 9, 1937; Bromley, "Birth Control Stand Bay State Puzzle."
72. Wynn, "Lucile Lord-Heinstein," 17.
73. "Birth Controllers on Parade," *Time*, January 29, 1934.
74. "Birth Controllers on Parade," *Time*, January 29, 1934.
75. *Birth Control: Hearings Before a Subcommittee of the Committee on the Judiciary*, 5, 6, 8, 10–11, 13–14, 65–66, 68–69.

76. *Birth Control: Hearings Before a Subcommittee of the Committee on the Judiciary,* 74, 92.
77. For an overview of the *One Package* case, see Engelman, *A History of Birth Control in America,* 167–174.
78. Accounts of this court case include Benjamin, "Lobbying for Birth Control," 48; bound volume of papers related to *US v One Package,* MC 208, SL; Chesler, *Woman of Valor,* 372–373; and Tobin-Schelsinger, "The Religious Debate Over Contraception, 1916–1936," 312.
79. Chesler, *Woman of Valor,* 393–394.
80. Warner, "Contraception," 279–285.
81. Tobin-Schlesinger, "The Religious Debate Over Contraception," 168.
82. Yarros, "Some Practical Aspects of Birth Control," 188–189.
83. *The Churches and Birth Control.*
84. For example, Lake, "The Spiritual Aspect of Birth Control."
85. "The Future of Birth Control"; Sanger, "The Pope's Position on Birth Control."
86. Tobin-Schlesinger, "The Religious Debate Over Contraception," 255, 204.
87. Wise, New York, to S. Adolphus Knopf, New York, November 19, 1925, Box 69, Reel 74-48, Wise Papers, P-134, AJHS.
88. Goldstein and Israel quoted in Tobin-Schlesinger, "The Religious Debate Over Contraception," 272 and 299–300, respectively.
89. Quoted in "Birth Control: Council of Rabbis Passed on Subject," *New York Sun,* March 24, 1932.
90. Quoted in Wenger, *New York Jews and the Great Depression,* 76–77.
91. Interview Report Forms, NCFLBC, February 17, 1936, Box 18, Folder 12, Rose Papers, MS 134, SSC.
92. See Tentler, *Catholics and Contraception,* for more on developments within American Catholicism.
93. "Report of the Commission on Social Justice; Discussion of Recommendations," *CCAR Yearbook 1926,* 102–105, 110–115.
94. "Report of the Standing Committee on Cooperation with National Organizations," *CCAR Yearbook 1926,* 40.
95. *CCAR Yearbook 1927,* 145–146.
96. Lauterbach, "Talmudic-Rabbinic View on Birth Control," 369–384.
97. Lauterbach, "Talmudic-Rabbinic View on Birth Control,"
98. Lauterbach, "Talmudic-Rabbinic View on Birth Control," 377.
99. "Report of the Commission on Social Justice," *CCAR Yearbook 1927,* 137; "Report of the Commission on Social Justice," *CCAR Yearbook 1929,* 85–86.
100. Commission on Social Justice of the CCAR, "A Message of Social Justice, Tishri 5691/ September 1930," Box 81, Folder 3, Weil Papers, NCOA.
101. "Discussion," *CCAR Yearbook 1930,* 81–84.
102. Goldstein, *The Meaning of Marriage and the Foundations of the Family,* 4, 119–128.
103. Hoenig, *Jewish Family Life,* 54.
104. For more on this link, see Kline, *Building a Better Race* and Lovett, *Conceiving the Future.*
105. Robinson, *Seventy Birth Control Clinics,* 93–94.
106. Rosen, *Preaching Eugenics,* 37, 103–105; Pearl, *A Natural History of Population.* It should be noted, however, that Pearl did become a critic of some elements of eugenics.
107. Abrams, "Jewish Women in the International Suffrage Alliance, 1899–1926," 169.
108. These accusations continue to dog Sanger and, by extension, the entire birth control movement. They continue to play a role in contemporary population policy. The most basic Google search of Sanger's name immediately turns up countless websites accusing her of anti-Semitism and racism, and scholarly studies of Sanger and the birth control movement must all contend with the issue. While earlier treatments, such as Gordon, *The Moral Property of Woman,* and Kennedy, *The Birth Control Movement in America,* tended to criticize Sanger for her interest in eugenics as part of their larger critique of her

motivations and methods, more recent accounts, such as Chesler, *Woman of Valor*, Engelman, *A History of the Birth Control Movement in America*, and McCann, *Birth Control
Politics in the United States* have offered critiques from more nuanced approaches, taking
into account the widespread respectability of mainstream eugenics thinking during the
early twentieth century. For an example of a strongly polemical denunciation of Sanger,
birth control, and Planned Parenthood, see Franks, *Margaret Sanger's Eugenic Legacy*.

109. Chesler, *Woman of Valor*, 157.
110. This discussion follows McCann, *Birth Control Politics in the United States*, 100 ff.
111. Bound volume of materials related to *United States v. One Package*, Morris Leopold Ernst
papers, MC 208, SL.
112. Wise, "The Synagogue and Birth Control."
113. "Finds Race Aided by Birth Control," *NYTimes*, January 20, 1933.
114. American Eugenics Society Annual Meeting program, May 7, 1936, Box 2, Folder 29, Stone
Papers, H MS c 157, HML.
115. Yarros, *Modern Woman and Sex*, 169.
116. Haslett, "Hull House and the Birth Control Movement," 267.
117. Chesler, *Woman of Valor*, 344–345.
118. Quoted in Hajo, *Birth Control on Main Street*, 104.
119. Sanger, Introduction, in Linfield, *Laws Relating to Birth Control in the United States and
Its Territories*, 6.
120. *The Reconstructionist*, April 16, 1943, 8.

NOTES TO CHAPTER 5

1. Reyher, New York, to Graciela Valera de Franco, Lima, Peru, March 10, 1938, Box 5, Series
PMC/DRSA/Lectures, Other Professional Writings, PMC 1935–1950, Rebecca Hourwich
Reyher Papers, MC 562, SL.
2. "Women's Caravan to Fly for Peace," *NYTimes*, October 24, 1937; McCann, "The Women
of Both Americas Move to Prevent War"; Reyher, "Southward on Wings of Peace,"; Reyher, Rio de Janeiro, to Mabel Vernon, Washington, D.C., November 9, 1937, Series B, Box
7, Folder 8, PMC Records, DG 109, SCPC; Reyher's notebook on PMC Flying Caravan,
1937, Series PMC/DRSA/Lectures, Other Professional Writings, Box 5, Reyher Papers, MC
562, SL.
3. Reyher, "Search and Struggle," 190–192.
4. Debate over who knew what and when was initiated by Ross, *So It Was True* and Lipstadt,
Beyond Belief. Most agree that information was available to those who looked for it, but
media outlets often downplayed the targeting of Jews and relegated atrocity stories to back
pages. See Shapiro, ed., *Why Didn't the Press Shout* and Leff, *Buried by the Times*.
5. Reyher, "Search and Struggle," 200.
6. Oral history of Reyher by Peat, 64–66, SL; Reyher, "Search and Struggle," 27–28, 33–34.
7. Reyher, "Search and Struggle," 27–28; Marty Gertrude Fendall, Washington, D.C., to Morris Waldman, New York, September 23, 1935; Maurie Rose Fried, Youngstown, Ohio, to
WILPF, Washington, D.C., March 9, 1936, Series B, Box 11, Folder 16, PMC Records, DG
109, SCPC. For more on PMC, see Alonso, *Peace as a Women's Issue*, 135ff and Foster, *The
Women and the Warriors*, 143ff.
8. For rare treatments of Jewish pacifism—albeit without attention to women—see Wilcock,
Pacifism and the Jews and Young, "Facing a Test of Faith." Brettschneider, *Cornerstones of
Peace*, is valuable but does not really address the pre–World War II period.
9. Given the near invisibility of women in most historical accounts before the 1970s, it is
unsurprising that the earliest work to address the American Jewish response to the Holocaust excluded them. Prominent examples include Morse, *While Six Million Died*; Bauer,
My Brother's Keeper; Bauer, *The Holocaust in Historical Perspective*; and Feingold, *The Politics of Rescue*. During the 1980s, focus shifted to the limitations of American responses, as

in Breitman and Kraut, *American Refugee Policy and European Jewry, 1933–1945*; Marrus, *The Holocaust in History*; Penkower, *The Jews Were Expendable*; and especially Wyman, *The Abandonment of the Jews*. None of this work pays sustained attention to women or gender. Feingold, *Bearing Witness*, and Gurock, *America, American Jews, and the Holocaust*, generally argue that American Jews never had enough influence to accomplish much in the way of real aid to European Jewry, but women are missing from the evidence used to draw those conclusions. Nor do women make much of an appearance in a recent overview essay, Medoff, "American Jewish Responses to Nazism and the Holocaust," mostly because there is little research to draw on. Exceptions, such as Sheramy, "'There are Times When Silence is a Sin,'" have been slow to make their way into other accounts. As Sheramy points out, American Jewish response to the Holocaust has been measured largely in terms of the actions of Jewish defense organizations, with little attention to "ordinary" American Jews, much less women.

10. *National Council of Jewish Women Economic Audit*, 1930, Viola Hoffman Hymes Papers, 146.F.9.9(B), MHS; 1931 program, NCJW–Charleston Section Papers, MS 414, AJA; "A Peace Talk for You," NCJW–Minneapolis Section *Bulletin*, March 1931, Box 6, Folder 1, NCJW–Minneapolis Section Papers, #0545, JHSUM; Solomon, *Fabric of My Life*, 235; Blanche Marx, Mt. Carmel, Illinois, to NCJW Peace Chairmen, July 27, 1931, Series M, Box 504, Folder 25, NCPW Papers, DG 23, SCPC; Alonso, *Peace as a Women's Issue*, 118–120; "Convene Council of Jewish Women," *NYTimes*, March 28, 1932. Blanche Marx, Mt. Carmel, Illinois, to Carrie Chapman Catt, New Rochelle, New York, April 7, 1932, Box 19, Folder "NCJW," Committee on the Cause and Cure of War Records, 87-M111, SL. On the ICW, see *Women in a Changing World* and Rupp, *Worlds of Women*.

11. "Lillian Cantor Dawson's Story," in Marcus, ed., *The American Jewish Woman*, 771–775; NCJW–Baltimore Section Minutes, March 11, 1935, February 10, 1936, February 17, 1935, Box 17, Folder 645, NCJW–Baltimore Section Records, MS 124, JMM.

12. WILPF–New York branch board minutes, January 21, 1930, Box 1, Folder 3; October 19, 1931, Box 1, Folder 4; list of corporate WILPF Members for New York, August 1934, Box 7a, Folder 7; WILPF–New York State branch, to members, April 11, 1930, Box 3, Folder 10; Sophie Cohen, New York, to WILPF, New York, December 11, 1933, Box 6, Folder 23, Series B3, WILPF Collection, DG 043, SCPC; *Suggestions for Individual Efforts to Advance Peace*.

13. Korngold, *Judaism and International Peace*; Isaiah 2:4; Gittelsohn, "More Human Bondage," Box 53, Folder 4, Roland B. Gittelsohn Papers, MS 704, AJA.

14. For a useful overview, see Richardson, "The Geneva Disarmament Conference."

15. Blanche Marx, Mt. Carmel, Ill., to NCJW Peace Chairmen, July 27, 1931, Box 504, Folder 25, Series M, NCPW Papers, DG 23, SCPC; Box 3, Folder 7, Peace Collection, MS 437, SSC.

16. Alonso, *The Woman's Peace Union and the Outlawry of War*, 89, 135–137; Working Committee of the WPU, New York, to Frieda Langer Lazarus and Dorothy Prussian, New York, June 24, 1929, Box 1, Folder "Correspondence 1921–1933"; Lazarus, Geneva, to Elinor Byrnes, New York, February 1, 1932, Box 1, Folder "Correspondence 1921–1933," WPU Papers, NYPL.

17. Eagen, *Class, Culture, and the Classroom*, 59–61; Cohen, *When the Old Left Was Young*, 94–95. See also Wittner, *Rebels Against War*.

18. Wald, *Windows on Henry Street*, x; Eagen, *Class, Culture, and the Classroom*, 3–4, 12, 104–106, 120–121; *Bulletin of the Committee for Reinstatement*, April 1935, Series B3, Box 7, folder 19, WILPF Collection, DG 043, SCPC. For more on Hunter College and Jewish women's involvement in student protests, see Markowitz, *My Daughter, the Teacher*, chaps. 2 and 4.

19. Sternberger, "What Have Jewish Women Done for Peace?" 204; Britt, "The Boycott."

20. "Report of the Committee on International Peace," *CCAR Yearbook 1935*, 74–75.

21. "Report of the Committee on International Peace," *CCAR Yearbook 1935*, 68–70.

22. "Report of the Committee on International Peace," *CCAR Yearbook 1935*, 68, 74; Cronbach, *The Quest for Peace*, 151–154.

23. Cronbach, *The Quest for Peace*, 151–154.

24. PMC press release, August 23, 1936, Series A, Box 1, Folder 8, PMC Records, DG 109, SCPC.

25. List of allied organizations on NCPW letterhead, Box 3, Folder "Correspondence January–April 1938"; Tracy Mygatt, New York, to David de Sola Pool, New York, December 7, 1938, Box 4, Folder "Correspondence October 1938–February 1939," WPU Papers, NYPL; Cronbach, *The Quest for Peace*, 149–150; Young, "Facing a Test of Faith," 36; "Religion Urged as Guide to Peace," *NYTimes*, September 13, 1943.

26. April 10, October 26, November 9, 1930; January 28, March 12, March 27, April 9, April 11, April 14, October 22, 1933, Jennie Franklin Purvin diaries, Box 2278e, Jennie Franklin Purvin Papers, MS 502, AJA.

27. Pesotta, Boston, to David Dubinsky, New York, January 6, 1939, Box 3 Folder 3; Ralph Fol, New York, to Pesotta, Boston, November 28, 1939, Box 3, Folder 5, Rose Pesotta Papers, NYPL; Evans oral history transcript, 57–58, Jane Evans Collection, MS 745, AJA; Miller, New York, to Cronbach, Cincinnati, November 13, 1935, Box 3, Folder 3, Cronbach Papers, MSS 9, AJA.

28. "Mayor LaGuardia Exhorts Women to Fight Hitlerism," *American Hebrew*, February 2, 1934; Federation of Jewish Women's Organizations, New York, 1935 and 1936 programs, Box 1, Folder "Miscellaneous, 1919–1945," Federation of Jewish Women's Organizations Papers, I-208, AJHS; Reeve, Jr., "What Can Be Done for Peace?" 3–4; A.L. Manchee, New York, to Bertha Vera Corets, New York, October 8, 1937, Box 1, Folder 2, Bertha Vera Corets papers, MS 307, AJA; Kussy, "The Story of Miriam Auxiliary of Oheb Shalom," 6, Box 1, Folder "The Story of Miriam Auxiliary of Oheb Shalom," Sarah Kussy Papers, P-4, AJHS; Anna Moglowitz, New York, to WILPF, New York, February 29, 1940, Series B3, Box 7a, Folder 7, WILPF Collection, DG 043, SCPC.

29. Wolf, Wolf, and Feibel, "History of the Council, 1895–1964," SC 1961, AJA; NCJW–Fresno Section Minutes, December 15, 1937, SC-14320, AJA.

30. NCJW–Fresno Section Minutes, November 18, 1937, SC-14320, AJA; Peace Study Group of NCJW–Palisades Section, "The Peace Clinic," 1937, CDGA NCJW, SCPC; Mrs. Albert Melnik, "The Education of a Sceptic," ca. 1939, Box 1, Folder NCJW, Committee on the Cause and Cure of War Records, 87-M111, SL.

31. Brin, "Can a Boycott Help German Jewry?" undated, Box 1, Folder 4; Jewish Telegraphic Agency Reports, Box 2, Folder 10, Fanny Fligelman Brin Papers, A.B858, MHS; NCJW–New York Section Board Minutes, April 10, 1933, Box 3, Folder 7, NCJW Papers, I-469, AJHS; Unidentified biography of Brin, Fanny Brin Nearprint Box, AJA; Rogow, *Gone to Another Meeting*, 180. For a classic article on the proposed boycott, see Gottlieb, "The American Controversy Over the Olympic Games."

32. Syrkin, "The Pacifist Movements," 19–21; Hyman, *Economic Security and World Peace*, 20–24; Rees, *Heaven is Eternal Spring*, 20–22.

33. Zetzer, Baltimore, to Miss Marshall, June 22, 1940, Box 1, Folder 13, Rose Zetzer Collection, MS 86, JMM.

34. Chatfield, *For Peace and Justice*, 312; Randall, *Improper Bostonian*, 340, 351 (emphasis in original).

35. "Women's Group Joins Boycott of Products Imported from Reich," *Jewish Daily Bulletin*, February 1934; "Einstein Medals Awarded to Three," *NYTimes*, March 9, 1936; Westin, *Making Do*, 185.

36. Lyn Smith, New York, to Dorothy O. Hommel, Syracuse, December 18, 1936, Series B3, Box 6, Folder 3, WILPF Collection, DG 043, SCPC; Warburg, New York, to Mary E. Woolley, Westport-on-Lake Champlain, New York, February 9, 1938, Series B, Box 26, Folder 15, PMC Records, DG 109, SCPC.

37. Bernstein, "Hitlerism and World Peace"; Wise quoted in Cronbach, *The Quest for Peace*, 161; Wise, New York, to James G. Heller, Cincinnati, April 24, 1942, Box 37, Folder 12, reel 74–29, Stephen S. Wise Papers, P-134, AJHS; Magnes quoted in Szajkowski, "The Pacifism of Judah Magnes," 54.

38. Quoted in Alonso, *Peace as a Women's Issue*, 103–104.

39. Westin, *Making Do*, 276–277.

40. Dora Askowith, New York, to Meyer, February 10, 1934, Box 2, Folder 5, Annie Nathan Meyer Papers, MS 7, AJA; "Hitler Turned Playgirl Into Social Worker," *Evening Bulletin* (Providence), December 16, 1953; Koshland, "Citizen Participation in Government," 27; Bender, "Report of Tour of Mid-West Region–1939," 95, Box 2, Folder 1, Rose I. Bender Papers, MSS 020, HSP.

41. "Statement of Mrs. Arthur Brin," ca. 1939, Box 1, Folder 4, Brin Papers, A.B858, MHS; Sarna, *American Judaism*, 253–254. For more on the growth of Zionism, see Cohen, *The Americanization of Zionism*; Raider, *The Emergence of American Zionism;* and Urofsky, *American Zionism from Herzl to the Holocaust*.

42. October 22, 1933, Jennie Franklin Purvin diary, Box 2278e, Purvin Papers, MS 502, AJA (emphasis in original).

43. Lerner, "American Feminism and the Jewish Question," 310–312. See Storrs, *Civilizing Capitalism*, for the National Consumers' League during the 1930s. Rupp, *Worlds of Women*, 57, refers to anti-Semitism in international women's movements, but that is not the focus of her book and the subject remains poorly documented.

44. Van Voris, *Carrie Chapman Catt*, 175, 214; Catt, New Rochelle, to Frau Von Velsen, November 2, 1931, Box 5, Folder "Correspondence with IWSA," Committee on the Cause and Cure of War Records, 87-M111, SL; Catt, New Rochelle, to Manus, April 25, 1933, in Bosch and Kloosterman, eds., *Politics and Friendship*, 227; Nicholson, Mt. Vernon, Iowa, to Catt, New Rochelle, New York, July 1, 1933; Catt, New Rochelle, to Nicholson, Mt. Vernon, August 2, 1933; Box 1, Folder 10, Carrie Chapman Catt Papers, NYPL.

45. Catt, New York, to Ethel Dreier, Brooklyn, August 11, 1933, Box 2, Folder 3, Ethel Eyre Valentine Dreier papers, SSC; Gilman, Norwich Town, Connecticut, to Catt, New York, August 9, 1933, Box 1, Folder 10, Catt Papers, NYPL. On Gilman's anti-Semitism, see Lane, *To Herland and Beyond*.

46. "Mrs. Catt Gets 1933 American Hebrew Medal," *New York Herald Tribune*, November 24, 1933; Catt, American Hebrew Medal acceptance speech, February 13, 1934, Box 5, Folder 10; Office of the Secretary of State, Washington, D.C., to Catt, New Rochelle, November 19, 1938, Box 2, Folder 1, Catt Papers, NYPL; Catt, New York, to "Friend," January 29, 1934, Box 1, Folder 10, Edna Fischel Gellhorn Papers, A-113, SL. On U.S. refugee policy, see Breitman and Kraut, *American Refugee Policy and European Jewry* and the work cited in note 9.

47. WPU director Tracy Mygatt did say in 1938 that the WPU should make a "strong Jewish statement, pro-Jewish and not anti-Hitler." Quoted in Alonso, *Peace as a Women's Issue*, 141.

48. Mygatt, New York, to Lola Maverick Lloyd, Chicago, November 25, 1936, Box 2, Folder "Correspondence 1936, Nov–Dec," WPU Records, Accession #44 M 95, NYPL. For more on Mygatt, see Early, *A World Without War*.

49. Nathan, New York, to *The Nation*, April 1936, Reel 2, Maud Nathan Papers, M-83, SL.

50. Detzer, *Appointment on the Hill*, 220–221, 114ff.

51. Pais, "The U.S. Women's International League for Peace and Freedom and American Neutrality," 263, 277–278; Foster, *The Women and the Warriors*, 185–186, 188; Sternberger, "Women in Foreign Lands," 302.

52. May 1933 and March 1934 correspondence between American Jewish Congress and WILPF New York State Branch, Series B3, Box 4, Folder 8, WILPF Collection, DG 043, SCPC.

53. WILPF–Minnesota Branch, Board Minutes, April 11, 1933, 149.E.4.10(f), Folder "Minutes 1931–1935," WILPF–Minnesota Branch Records, MHS; WILPF, *Programs and Policies,*

1934–1935, Box 13, Folder 1; Brin, "Peace, A Condition of Survival," December 1934, Box 13, Folder 1, Brin Papers, A.B858, MHS; WILPF–Minnesota Branch, Newsletter, October 1938, Box 21, Folder 6, Peace Collection, MS 437, SSC.

54. Letter to Mrs. J. X. Cohen, March 13, 1934, Series B3, Box 4, Folder 10; Mrs. J.X. Cohen, Annual Report of Bronx Branch, March 9, 1934, Series B3, Box 1, Folder 7, WILPF Collection, DG 043, SCPC.

55. Lyn Smith, New York, to Dorothy O. Hommel, Syracuse, December 18, 1936, Series B3, Box 6, Folder 3; Annual Report of WILPF New York State Branch, March 3, 1938, Series B3, Box 1, Folder 11, WILPF Collection, DG 043, SCPC.

56. Smith, New York, to Detzer, Washington, D.C., April 12, 1938, Series B3, Box 5, Folder 9, WILPF Collection, DG 043, SCPC.

57. "Pacifists Split by Own War Over Policy of World Peace," *Philadelphia Record*, October 17, 1938.

58. Smith, New York, to Detzer, Washington, D.C., April 14, 1938; Smith, New York, to Detzer, Washington, D.C., October 11, 1938; Detzer, Washington, D.C., to Smith, New York, October 12, 1938, Series B3, Box 5, Folder 9; WILPF New York State Branch Annual Report, February 11, 1939, Series B3, Box 1, Folder 12, WILPF Collection, DG 043, SCPC.

59. "Peace Leader Urges U.S. Act to Save Jews," unidentified Rochester newspaper, Fall 1938; Detzer, *Appointment on the Hill*, 241–243; Hull and Detzer, Washington, D.C., to Franklin Delano Roosevelt, Washington, D.C., November 18, 1938, quoted in full in WILPF press release, November 18, 1938, Series II, Box 2, Mercedes M. Randall Papers, DG 110, SCPC; WILPF—Brooklyn Branch newsletter, November 18, 1939, Series B10, Box 21, Folder 12, WILPF Collection, DG 043, SCPC; Randall, *Improper Bostonian*, 361.

60. *National Council for Jewish Women Convention Crier*, 1938, Box 1, Folder NCJW (National), Committee on the Cause and Cure of War Records, 87-M111, SL; WILPF–New York State Branch press release, May 22, 1939, Series B3, Box 1, Folder 12, WILPF Collection, DG 043, SCPC.

61. NCJW press release, ca. 1940, Box 1, Folder 7, Brin Papers, A.B858, MHS; Report of the New York State Branch President and Executive Secretary, December 1, 1939, Series B3, Box 1, Folder 12; Sarah Lifton, Brooklyn, to Mary D. Brite, Cincinnati, February 26, 1941, Series B3, Box 4, Folder 11, WILPF Collection, DG 043, SCPC; Statement from the Executive Committee on the Program for 1940, October 22, 1940, Box 1, Folder "Statements of Principle," Committee on the Cause and Cure of War Records, 87-M111, SL.

62. Jennie Franklin Purvin diary, December 7, 1941, Box 2278e, Purvin Papers, MS 502, AJA.

63. "Statements on the War by the Women's International League for Peace and Freedom," December 10, 1941; Laura G. Rapaport, New York, to Brin, Minneapolis, December 12, 1941, Box 5, Brin Papers, A.B858, MHS.

64. Quoted in Paton-Walsh, "Women's Organizations, United States Foreign Policy, and the Far Eastern Crisis," 624.

65. Kubie, New York, to Chairmen of NFTS Peace Committees, January 29, 1942, Box 35, NFTS Circular File: Peace & World Relations, 1942–1952, Women of Reform Judaism Papers, MS 73, AJA.

66. Wise, New York, to James G. Heller, Cincinnati, April 24, 1942, Box 37, Folder 12, reel 74-29, Wise Papers, P-134, AJHS. See Chatfield, *The American Peace Movement* and DeBenedetti, *The Peace Reform in American History* for more on pacifists during World War II.

67. "Republican Plan on Nazi Surrender Urged by Women," *NYTimes*, June 22, 1944; Lazarus, undated speech, Box 1, Folder 6, Frieda Langer Lazarus Papers, Mss Col 1703, NYPL; Esther Eichel, Brooklyn, to Deena, February 8, 1983, Box 1, Folder 11, Eichel Family Collection, DG 131, SCPC.

68. Autobiographical notes, Series Articles, Biography, Novel, Autobio Notes, Reyher Papers, MC 562, SL.

69. Reyher, New York, to Setty Swartz Kuhn, Cincinnati, August 24, 1943, Series B, Box 20, Folder 26; Reyher's handwritten comment on Helen Raebeck, New York, to Mabel Vernon, Washington, D.C., September 27, 1943, Series B, Box 16, Folder 13, PMC Records, DG 109, SCPC.

70. Bennett, "'Free American Political Prisoners,'" 413–433; Women's Action Committee for Victory and Lasting Peace list of officers, Box 8, Folder 4, Brin Papers, A.B858, MHS.

71. Randall, New York, to WILPF members, April 19, 1943, Box 1039, Randall Papers, AJA.

72. Detzer, Washington, D.C., to WILPF members, December 15, 1943, Box 1039, Randall Papers, AJA.

73. Randall, Report on the Pamphlet *The Voice of Thy Brother's Blood*, October 12, 1944, Series III, Box 3, Folder 4, Randall Papers, DG 110, SCPC.

74. Report of the New York State President and Executive Secretary, December 1, 1939, Series B3, Box 1, Folder 12, WILPF Collection, DG 043, SCPC.

75. Schwimmer, New York, to Randall, New York, June 21, 1943, Series II, Box 1, Folder 19, Randall Papers, DG 110, SCPC.

76. Report of the National Committee on Service to Foreign Born, delivered by Kay Engel to NCJW Triennial Convention, Chicago, November 7–11, 1943, Box 1, Folder 7, Katharine Asher Engel Papers, MS 55, SSC.

77. *The Council Woman* 5 (September 1944): 3.

78. Eagen, *Class, Culture, and the Classroom*, 157; Cronbach, *The Quest for Peace*, 47; Oral history transcript, 54–58, Jane Evans Collection, MS 745, AJA; Esther Eichel, Brooklyn, to Deena, February 8, 1983, Box 1, Folder 11, Eichel Family Collection, DG 131, SCPC; Bennett, "'Free American Political Prisoners,'" 413.

79. "History of the Minneapolis Section," SC-8736, AJA; Box 13, Folder 1, Brin Papers, A.B858, MHS; Dinner program, January 9, 1947, Box 1, Folder 1, Carrie Chapman Catt Papers, MS 31, SSC.

NOTES TO CONCLUSION

1. Quoted in Perry, *Belle Moskowitz*, 14.

2. Nathan, *Once Upon a Time and Today*, 102–103.

3. Peterson, "Women to View Wide Progress in Past Century," *NYTimes*, November 24, 1940; "Woman's Centennial Session Ends," *NYTimes*, November 28, 1940.

4. Attendance List for Woman's Centennial Congress Banquet, Box 4, Folder 12, Carrie Chapman Catt Papers, NYPL. See also "Fight Dictators, Mrs. Catt Pleads," *NYTimes*, November 26, 1940, and "Woman's Congress Looks to Future," *NYTimes*, November 27, 1940.

5. For recent attention to the diversity of early feminism, see Hewitt, ed., *No Permanent Waves*.

6. This interpretation closely follows Hyman, *Gender and Assimilation in Modern Jewish History*.

7. Woocher explores this point in relation to all Jewish communal activism and its transformation later in the twentieth century into a "civil religion" in *Sacred Survival*.

BIBLIOGRAPHY

A NOTE ON YIDDISH SOURCES:

With very few exceptions, I did the research necessary to locate and roughly translate all Yiddish sources in the book. However, in cases when I wished to be able to quote these materials, several translators provided more literary renderings. The relevant endnotes provide full information about these translations.

PUBLISHED PRIMARY SOURCES

"3 in Birth Control Case Found Guilty." *Boston American*, July 20, 1937.

"250 Attend Rites Here for Dr. Stone." *New York Times* (*NYTimes* hereafter), July 14, 1941.

"1500 at Eugenics Sermon." *NYTimes*, November 29, 1915.

"An Act for the Suppression of Trade in, and Circulation of, Obscene Literature and Articles of Immoral Use, 1873." In N. E. H. Hull, Williamjames Hoffer, and Peter Charles Hoffer, eds., *The Abortion Rights Controversy in America: A Legal Reader*. Chapel Hill: University of North Carolina Press, 2004, 29–31.

Addams, Jane. *Newer Ideals of Peace*. New York: Chautauqua Press, 1907.

Advertisement for *Birth Control* by Kalmanowitz. *Forverts*, July 16, 1916.

"Air Tour Evokes Peace Pact Action." *NYTimes*, November 16, 1937.

American Jewish Year Book 5662/1901–1902. Philadelphia: Jewish Publication Society, 1901.

American Jewish Year Book 5666/1905–1906. Philadelphia: Jewish Publication Society, 1905.

"Annie Nathan Meyer, Wife and Mother, Opposes Woman Suffrage." *American Hebrew*, June 12, 1914.

"Anti-Semitism in the Medical Profession." *American Hebrew*, July 29, 1916.

"Are Women's Clubs 'Used' by Bolshevists?" *Dearborn Independent*, March 15, 1924.

Association for Peace Education. *An Analysis of the Emphasis Upon War in Our Elementary School Histories*. Chicago: Association for Peace Education, ca. 1924.

"Atlanta Social." *American Jewish Review* 3 (March 1914): 36.

Beard, Mary R. "The Legislative Influence of Unenfranchised Women." *Annals of the American Academy of Political and Social Science* 56 (November 1914): 54–61.

Beard, Mary R. "Women and the War Habit." *The Woman's Journal* (May 1930): 12–13, 44–45.

Belmont, Alva. "Jewish Women in Public Affairs." *The American Citizen* (May 1913): 181–182, 232.

Ben-Tsion, "Women Once Condemned Her; Today She is Honored in Washington." February 1936 article in unidentified Yiddish periodical. Box 2, Folder 46, Rose Zetzer Collection, MS 86, JMM.

Benjamin, Hazel C. "Lobbying for Birth Control." *Public Opinion Quarterly* 2 (January 1938): 48–60.

Bernstein, Herman. *Can We Abolish War?* New York: Broadview, 1935.

Bernstein, Herman. "Hitlerism and World Peace." *Jewish Daily Bulletin*, January 31, 1934.

"Big Meeting Moves for Birth Control." *NYTimes*, May 27, 1915.

"Birth Control Advocate Here." *Pocatello Tribune*, August 13, 1933.

"Birth Control: Council of Rabbis Passed on Subject." *New York Sun*, March 24, 1931.

Birth Control: Hearings Before a Subcommittee of the Committee of the Judiciary, United States Senate, Seventy-Third Congress, March 1, 20, and 27, 1934. Washington, D.C.: Government Printing Office, 1934.

Birth Control Issue. *The Nation*, January 27, 1932.

"Birth Controllers on Parade." *Time*, January 29, 1934.

"Birth Controllers Up Early for Trial." *NYTimes*, January 5, 1917.

Blacker, C.P. *Birth Control and the State: A Plea and a Forecast.* New York: Dutton, 1926.

Boeckel, Florence Brewer. "Women in International Affairs." *Annals of the American Academy of Political and Social Science* 143 (May 1929): 230–248.

Borochow, M.A. *The MAB Plan: International Peace Fund: A New Plan for Universal Peace.* New York: MAB Publishing, 1931.

Bosch, Mineke, and Annemarie Kloosterman, eds. *Politics and Friendship: Letters from the International Woman Suffrage Alliance, 1902–1942.* Columbus: Ohio State University Press, 1990.

"Boycott is Remedy of Woman for War." *NYTimes*, November 21, 1915.

Braden, Amy Steinhart. "Child Welfare and Community Service." Interview conducted by Edna Tartaul Daniel for the Regional Oral History Office, Bancroft Library, University of California, Berkeley, 1965.

Brin, Fanny. "The Jewish Woman in the American Scene." *Eve Magazine* (April 1936): 31–32.

Brin, Fanny. "A New International Habit of Mind." *Jewish Woman* 8 (July–September, 1928): 5–6.

Brin, Fanny. "Women and the Peace Movement." *Saturday Post* (Minneapolis/St. Paul), September 7, 1923.

Britt, George. "The Boycott: Peace Leader Sees It in Time Replacing War." *New York World-Telegram*, February 8, 1935.

Bromley, Dorothy Dunbar. *Birth Control: Its Use and Misuse.* New York: Harper & Brothers, 1934.

Bromley, Dorothy Dunbar. "Birth Control Stand Bay State Puzzle." *World-Telegram*, August 6, 1937.

Bromley, Dorothy Dunbar. "This Question of Birth Control." In N.E.H. Hull, Williamjames Hoffer, and Peter Charles Hoffer, eds., *The Abortion Rights Controversy in America: A Legal Reader.* Chapel Hill: University of North Carolina Press, 2004, 47–50.

Brooklyn Section–NCJW. *A History.* Brooklyn: n.p., 1977.

Campbell, Monroe. *The First Fifty Years: A History of the National Council of Jewish Women, 1893–1943.* NCJW, 1943.

Carrigan, Virginia. "National Woman's Party Subdivided in Congenial Groups." *Baltimore Sun*, February 11, 1936.

Catt, Carrie Chapman, and Nettie Rogers Shuler. *Woman Suffrage and Politics: The Inner Story of the Suffrage Movement.* Seattle: Washington, 1923.

CCAR. *Yearbook of Thirty-Sixth Annual Convention, October 20–23, 1925, Cincinnati.* Edited by Isaac E. Marcuson. CCAR, 1925.

CCAR. *Yearbook of Thirty-Seventh Annual Convention, June 22–26, 1926, Asheville.* Edited by Isaac E. Marcuson. CCAR, 1926.

CCAR. *Yearbook of Special Convention, January 17, 1927, Cleveland, and Thirty-Eighth Annual Convention, June 23–27, 1927, Cape May.* Edited by Isaac E. Marcuson. CCAR, 1927.

CCAR. *Yearbook of Fortieth Annual Convention, June 27–30, 1929, Detroit.* Edited by Isaac E. Marcuson. CCAR, 1929.

CCAR. *Yearbook of Forty-First Annual Convention, June 25–29, 1930, Providence.* Edited by Isaac E. Marcuson. CCAR, 1930.

CCAR. *Yearbook of Forty-Second Annual Convention, June 17–21, 1931, Wawasee.* Edited by Isaac E. Marcuson. CCAR, 1931.

CCAR. *Yearbook of Forty-Sixth Annual Convention, June 25–30, 1935, Chicago.* Edited by Isaac E. Marcuson. CCAR, 1935.

Chamberlain, Mary. "The Women at the Hague." *The Survey* 34 (June 5, 1915): 219–222, 236.

"Chelsea Woman Represents State." *Chelsea Evening Record,* April 15, 1921.

"Clergymen Back Peace Movement." *NYTimes,* August 31, 1941.

"Convene Council of Jewish Women." *NYTimes,* March 28, 1932.

"The Council of Jewish Women: Statements on the Work of the Council by the Chairmen of its Committees." *Jewish Tribune and Hebrew Standard,* November 2, 1923.

"Council Speaker Urges Action for No More War." *American Hebrew,* September 15, 1922.

Cronbach, Abraham. *The Jewish Peace Book for Home and School.* Cincinnati: Union of American Hebrew Congregations, 1932.

Cronbach, Abraham. *The Quest for Peace.* Cincinnati: Sinai, 1937.

Cronbach, Abraham. *War and Peace in Jewish Tradition.* 1936. Nearprint File. AJA.

Curti, Merle. *Peace or War: The American Struggle, 1636–1936.* New York: Norton, 1936.

Davis, Isabelle J. *Some Reasons Why the Jew Should Desire Woman Suffrage.* London: Jewish League for Woman Suffrage, 1914.

"D.C. Advocates of Birth Control Plan New Clinic." *Washington Post,* May 18, 1937.

De Ford, Miriam Allen. "In the Streets." In "The Suffragists from Tea-Parties to Prison." Interviews conducted by Sherna Gluck for the Regional Oral History Office, Bancroft Library, University of California, Berkeley, 1975. SSC.

Degen, Marie Louise. *The History of the Women's Peace Party.* Baltimore: Johns Hopkins University Press, 1939.

Dennett, Mary Ware. *Birth Control Laws: Shall We Keep Them, Change Them, or Abolish Them?* New York: Grafton, 1926.

Dennett, Mary Ware. *The Sex Side of Life: An Explanation for Young People.* New York: n.p., 1919.

Dennett, Mary Ware. *Who's Obscene?* New York: Vanguard, 1930.

Detzer, Dorothy. *Appointment on the Hill.* New York: Henry Holt, 1948.

"Dr. Aletta Jacobs Dies." *NYTimes,* August 13, 1929.

"Dr. Magnes Scored in Jewish Press." *NYTimes,* November 22, 1929.

"Dr. Stone, Pioneer in Birth Control." *NYTimes,* July 11, 1941.

"Dr. Stone Praised at Funeral Here." *NYTimes,* July 7, 1959.

Duffus, R. L. *Lillian Wald: Neighbor and Crusader.* New York: Macmillan, 1938.

"Dutch Suffragist Arrives." *NYTimes,* April 14, 1924.

"Dutch Suffragist Dies." *NYTimes,* June 28, 1942.

"Economic Woes Linked to Lack of Birth Control." *Seattle Daily Times,* August 25, 1933.

"Editorial." *American Hebrew,* October 29, 1915.

"Einstein Medals Awarded to Three." *NYTimes,* March 9, 1936.

Engelman, Uriah Zevi. " A Study of Size of Families in the Jewish Population of Buffalo." *University of Buffalo Studies* 16 (November 1938).

Ernst, Morris L. *The Best is Yet . . .* New York: Harper & Brothers, 1945.

Fairchild, Henry Pratt. "Family Limitation and the War." *Annals of the American Academy of Political and Social Science* 229 (September 1943): 79–86.

"Female Juries and Voting Rights." *Di Froyen Velt,* July 1913.

"Feminism Among Wives." *American Hebrew,* October 30, 1914.

"Finds Race Aided by Birth Control." *NYTimes,* January 20, 1933.

"Five Year's Progress." *Birth Control Review* 2 (June 1935).

Fleischman, Samuel. *A Plan for World Peace Based on a Permanent World Conference.* New York: n.p., 1925.

Frankel, Ida. *No More War: A Lecture on World Peace.* San Francisco: Ida Frankel, 1923.

Friedl, Bettina, ed. *On to Victory: Propaganda Plays of the Woman Suffrage Movement.* Boston: Northeastern University Press, 1987.

Friedlander, Alice G. "A Portland Girl on Women's Rights, 1893." *Western States Jewish Historical Quarterly* 10 (January 1978): 146–150.

"From the Women's World." *Di Froyen Velt*, April 1913.

"From the Women's World." *Di Froyen Velt*, June 1913.

Ganz, Marie, with Nat J. Ferber. *Rebels: Into Anarchy–And Out Again*. New York: Dodd, Mead, & Company, 1920.

Gittelsohn, Roland B. *The Jew Looks at War and Peace*. Cincinnati: NFTS, 1935.

Goldman, Emma. *Anarchism and Other Essays*. New York: Mother Earth, 1917.

Goldman, Emma. *Living My Life*, vol. 2. New York: Dover, 1970.

Goldstein, Israel. "Committee on Social Justice." *Proceedings of the Rabbinical Assembly of the Jewish Theological Seminary of America* 4 (1933): 358–364.

Goldstein, Sidney E. "Birth Control as a Moral Issue." *Free Synagogue Pulpit* 3 (December 1915): 210–222.

Goldstein, Sidney E. *The Meaning of Marriage and the Foundations of the Family*. New York: Bloch, 1942.

"Great Climax Marks Brilliant Campaign." *The Woman's Journal*, November 6, 1915.

Green, Max. *The Problem of Universal Peace and the Key to Its Solution*. Philadelphia: Buchman, 1924.

Greenberg, Hayim. "Jews Do Not Want War." *Jewish Exponent*, June 23, 1939.

Greenberg, Meyer. "The Reproduction Rate of the Families of Jewish Students at the University of Maryland." *Jewish Social Studies* 10 (July 1948): 223–238.

Grossman, Samuel B. *Di Flikhten fun a froy in Geburt Kontrol (A Woman's Duty in Birth Control)*, 1916.

Hapgood, Hutchins. *The Spirit of the Ghetto: Studies of the Jewish Quarter of New York*. New York: Schocken, 1966.

"Harriet Pilpel, Lawyer, Dies: An Advocate of Women's Rights." *NYTimes*, April 24, 1991.

Harris, Helen M. "Social Workers, Let's Lead the Parade!" *Birth Control Review* 3 (May 1936).

"Harry Kalmanowitz Dies at 81: Author of 20 Yiddish Plays, Musicals." *Jewish Telegraphic Agency*, October 14, 1966.

Haskell, Oreola Williams. *The Banner Bearers: Tales of the Suffrage Campaigns*. Geneva, NY: W. F. Humphrey, 1920.

Hay, Mary Garrett. "When Jewish and Christian Women Meet." *American Hebrew*, September 22, 1922.

Herrick, Genevieve Forbes. "Senators Hear Mother Tell How Birth Data 'Saved' Her." *Chicago Daily Tribune*, March 2, 1934.

Himes, Norman E. "Birth Control Must be Discussed." *Jewish Social Service Quarterly* 3 (June 1927): 61–63.

Hoenig, Sidney B. *Jewish Family Life: The Duty of the Woman*. Cleveland: Spero, 1946.

Holmes, John Haynes. "Should Jews be Pacifists?" *Opinion* (September 1940): 6–8.

Hornell, Hart. "Changing Social Attitudes and Interests." In *Recent Social Trends in the United States*, vol. 1. New York: McGraw Hill, 1933, 382–442.

Hourwich, Rebecca. "Malice In Palestine." *World Today* 56 (November 1930): 520–528.

"How American Women are Influencing the Peace Movement in England." *Jewish Exponent*, August 3, 1928.

Hyman, Sonia Zunser. *Economic Security and World Peace*. New York: League for Industrial Democracy, 1938.

"The Intelligence of Women." *Der Fraynd*, October 1917.

"The International Women's Congress." *Di Froyen Velt*, July 1913.

Irwin, Inez Haynes. *Angels and Amazons: A Hundred Years of American Women*. Garden City, NY: Doubleday, Doran & Company, 1934.

Irwin, Inez Haynes. *The Story of the Woman's Party*. New York: Harcourt, Brace & Company, 1921.

"It Took Nerve to be a Suffragette Then," *Philadelphia Record*, August 22, 1945.

Jacobi, Abraham. "Birth Control." *Free Synagogue Pulpit* 3 (December 1915): 181–209.

Jacobs, Aletta. *Memories: My Life as an International Leader in Health, Suffrage, and Peace.* Edited by Harriet Feinberg. Trans. Annie Wright. New York: Feminist Press, 1996.

Jaffe, A. J. "Religious Differentials in the Net Reproduction Rate." *Journal of the American Statistical Association* 34 (June 1939): 335–342.

Jaffe, H. "Dr. Hannah M. Stone." *Die Pionern Froy*, August 9, 1941.

"Jail Women Pacifists." *NYTimes*, April 1, 1915.

Jastrow, Morris. *The War and the Coming Peace: The Moral Issue.* Philadelphia: J. B. Lippincott, 1918.

"Jewesses as Suffragettes." *American Hebrew*, May 10, 1912.

"The Jewish Woman and the Suffrage Movement." *American Hebrew*, February 5, 1915.

"Jewish Women Doctors." *American Hebrew*, June 6, 1913.

"Jews Besiege the Theatre to Hear Suffrage Plea." *Philadelphia Record*, November 1915.

Jordan, Elizabeth, ed. *The Sturdy Oak: A Composite Novel of American Politics.* New York: Henry Holt, 1917.

Kahn, Morris H. "A Municipal Birth Control Clinic." *New York Medical Journal*, April 28, 1917.

Kalmanowitz, Harry. *Geburth Kontrol, oder, Rassen Zelbstmord (Birth Control or Race Suicide),* 1916.

Katz, Esther, ed. *The Selected Papers of Margaret Sanger, Vol. I: The Woman Rebel, 1900–1928.* Urbana: University of Illinois Press, 2003.

Katzenstein, Caroline. "Alice Paul, the Pankhurst of the Potomac: Her Personality and Her Characteristics." *Philadelphia Record*, November 4, 1917.

Katzenstein, Caroline. "'Cause' is Pledged to Shun Militancy." *Philadelphia Press*, December 6, 1913.

Katzenstein, Caroline. *Lifting the Curtain: The State and National Woman Suffrage Campaigns in Pennsylvania as I Saw Them.* New York: Dorrance & Company, 1950.

Keetley, Dawn, and John Pettegrew, eds. *Public Women, Public Words: A Documentary History of American Feminism* , vol. 2: 1900–1960. Lanham, MD: Rowman & Littlefield, 2002.

Kobre, Sidney. "Dr. Bessie Moses Believes Prejudice Against Women in Medicine is Less." *Baltimore Home News*, January 4, 1939.

Kohut, Rebekah. *As I Know Them: Some Jews and a Few Gentiles.* Garden City, NY: Doubleday, Doran & Company, 1929.

Kohut, Rebekah. *More Yesterdays: An Autobiography.* New York: Bloch, 1950.

Kohut, Rebekah. *My Portion: An Autobiography.* New York: Thomas Seltzer, 1925.

Kopp, Marie E. *Birth Control in Practice: Analysis of Ten Thousand Case Histories of the Birth Control Clinic and Research Bureau.* New York: McBride & Co., 1934.

Kornfeld, Joseph S. *Judaism and International Peace.* Cincinnati: Union of American Hebrew Congregations, ca 1930.

Koshland, Lucile H. "Citizen Participation in Government." Interview conducted by Harriet Nathan for the Regional Oral History Office, Bancroft Library, University of California, Berkeley, 1971. SC-6427. AJA.

Kramer, Sydelle and Jenny Masur, eds. *Jewish Grandmothers.* Boston: Beacon, 1976.

Kula, Witold, Nina Assorodobraj-Kula, and Marcin Kula. *Writing Home: Immigrants in Brazil and the United States, 1890–1891.* Edited and translated by. Josephine Wtulich. New York: Columbia, 1986.

Landes, Leonard. *Geburts-kontrol.* New York: Landes, ca. 1916.

Lauterbach, Jacob. "Talmudic-Rabbinic View on Birth Control," *Central Conference of American Rabbis Yearbook, Special Convention, January 17, 1927, Cleveland, and Thirty-Eighth Annual Convention, June 23–27, 1927, Cape May*, 369–384.

"Leaders in All Faiths Plan Jubilee for Rebekah Kohut." *New York Post*, October 28, 1935.

Lemlich, Clara. "Relieving Working Women of the Burdens and Responsibility of Life." n.d. M-950. SL.

Levin, Bertha. "The Place of Woman in Communal Life." *Jewish Times* (Baltimore), November 12, 1920.

Levy, J. Leonard. *War or Peace? A Sunday Lecture Before Congregation Rodeph Shalom.* Pittsburgh: Rodeph Shalom, 1904.

Liber, Ben Zion. *Dos Geshlekhts Lebn.* New York: n.p., 1918.

Linfield, Seymour L. *Laws Relating to Birth Control in the United States and Its Territories.* New York: BCCRB, 1938.

Lipsky, Abram. "The Foreign Vote on Suffrage." *American Hebrew*, November 26, 1915.

"'Little Corporal' of Woman Suffrage Party an Immigrant Jewess." *American Hebrew*, June 19, 1914.

Loeb, Sophie Irene, ed. "Shall Women Vote? A Symposium." *American Hebrew*, September 10, 1915.

"Louis D. Brandeis Brings Women In." *Woman's Journal and Suffrage News*, July 31, 1915.

Luria, Esther. "The Last Conquests on the Suffrage Front." *Der Fraynd*, June–July 1919.

Lurie, Harry L. "Sex Hygiene of Family Life." *Jewish Social Service Quarterly* 3 (December 1926): 19–24.

Malkiel, Theresa Serber. *The Diary of a Shirtwaist Striker.* Ithaca, NY: ILR, 1990.

Marcus, Jacob Rader, ed. *The American Jewish Woman: A Documentary History.* New York & Cincinnati: Ktav and AJA, 1981.

Matyas, Jennie. "Jennie Matyas and the I.L.G.W.U." Interview conducted by Corinne L. Gibb for the Institute of Industrial Relations, University of California, Berkeley, 1955. AJA.

Maxwell, Lucia. "Spider Web Chart: The Socialist-Pacifist Movement in America is an Absolutely Fundamental and Integral Part of International Socialism." *Dearborn Independent.* March 22, 1924.

Mayer, Eli. "War and Religion: A Sociological Study." PhD diss., University of Pennsylvania, 1918.

"Mayor Gaynor on Suffrage." *Di Froyen Velt*, June 1913.

McCann, Anabel Parker. "The Women of Both Americas Move to Prevent War." *Christian Herald*, December 17, 1940.

McCann, Carole, ed. "What Perspectives did African American Advocates Bring to the Birth Control Movement and How Did Those Perspectives Shape the History of the Harlem Branch Birth Control Clinic?" 2006. *Women and Social Movements in the United States, 1600–2000*, eds. Kathryn Kish Sklar and Thomas Dublin. <alexanderstreetpress.com>.

Metzker, Isaac, ed. *A Bintel Brief: Sixty Years of Letters from the Lower East Side to the Jewish Daily Forward.* New York: Schocken, 1971.

"Militants Hurting Cause." *NYTimes*, October 11, 1913.

"Miss Sanger Draws Crowd." *NYTimes*, June 19, 1916.

Moore, Edward Roberts. *The Case Against Birth Control.* New York: Century, 1931.

"More Marital Advice is Urged by Dr. Stone." *NYTimes*, February 8, 1947.

Moses, Bessie L. *Contraception as a Therapeutic Measure.* Baltimore: Williams & Wilkins, 1936.

"Mother Seeks Pardon for Son." *NYTimes*, August 23, 1957.

"Mother is a Judge." *National Business Woman* 38 (August 1959): 4–5, 29.

"Mrs. Gruenberg Takes Franchise Body Office." *Philadelphia Inquirer*, March 18, 1917.

"Mrs. Kohut Dead—Welfare Leader." *NYTimes*, August 12, 1951.

"Mrs. Pankhurst in America." *Di Froyen Velt*, November 1913.

"Mrs. Sanger's Aid is Found Guilty." *NYTimes*, January 9, 1917.

"Mrs. Stokes to Address the Jewish Council." *Brooklyn Eagle*, December 18, 1915.

Nathan, Maud. "Jewesses in the Suffrage Movement." *American Hebrew*, March 29, 1912.

Nathan, Maud. *Justice and the Expediency of Woman Suffrage.* New York: National Woman Suffrage Publishing Company, 1917. M-9162. SL.

Nathan, Maud. *Once Upon a Time and Today.* New York: G. P. Putnam, 1933.

Nathan, Maud. *The Story of an Epoch-Making Movement.* Garden City, NY: Doubleday, Page & Company, 1926.

Nathan, Maud. "The Wage Earner and the Ballot." *Political Equality Series* 3 (1908): 71–73. M-948. SL.

NCCCW. *Suggestions for Individual Efforts to Advance Peace.* New York: NCCCW, 1931.

National Council of Jewish Juniors. *War vs. Youth: Peace Knowledge Plus Action Program.* New York: National Council of Jewish Juniors, 1934.

NCJW. *Anti-Semitism: A Study Outline.* New York: NCJW, 1934.

NCJW. *Our Heritage and the World Today: A Symposium.* New York: NCJW/Contemporary Jewish Affairs, 1935.

National Council of Jewish Women Tenth Triennial Convention, St. Louis, Missouri, November Eleventh through Sixteenth, 1923. New York: NCJW, 1923.

"Need be No Conflict in Home and Career." *Cincinnati Times Star,* August 11, 1936.

"New York to Help Birth Clinic Fight Here." *Boston Post,* August 9, 1937.

New York Section–NCJW. *Year Book, 1906–1907.* New York: NCJW, 1907.

New York Section–NCJW. *Year Book, 1915–1916.* New York: NCJW, 1916.

New York Section–NCJW. *Year Book, 1918–1919.* New York: NCJW, 1919.

Official Report of the Council of Jewish Women Eighth Triennial Convention, Chicago, November 5–9, 1917. New York: NCJW, 1917.

"Pacifists Split by Own War Over Policy of World Peace." *Philadelphia Record,* October 17, 1938.

Palmer, Rachel Lynn, and Sarah K. Greenberg. *Facts and Frauds in Women's Hygiene: A Medical Guide Against Misleading Claims and Dangerous Products.* New York: Vanguard, 1936.

Paul, Alice. "Conversations with Alice Paul." Interview conducted by Amelia R. Fry for the Regional Oral History Office, Bancroft Library, University of California, Berkeley, 1976. SSC.

"Peace." *Jewish Woman* 6 (January 1926): 26–28.

"Peace." *Jewish Woman* 8 (July-September 1928): 16–17.

"Peace Delegates Reach the Hague." *NYTimes,* April 29, 1915.

"Peace Leader Urges U.S. Act to Save Jews." Unidentified Rochester newspaper, Fall 1938.

Pearl, Raymond. *The Natural History of Population.* New York: Oxford University Press, 1939.

Peck, Mary Gray. *Carrie Chapman Catt: A Biography.* New York: H. W. Wilson, 1944.

Pesotta, Rose. *Bread Upon the Waters.* Ithaca, NY: ICR, 1987.

Philadelphia Section–NCJW. *Twenty-Second Annual Report of Philadelphia Section, Council of Jewish Women.* Philadelphia: n.p., 1917.

Pierce, Bessie Louise. "The Political Pattern of Some Women's Organizations." *Annals of the American Academy of Political and Social Science* 179 (May 1935): 50–58.

"Pilgrims for Peace to Visit Congress." *NYTimes,* February 9, 1917.

Plotkin, Benjamin. "Present Day Plans for World Peace." *Proceedings of the Rabbinical Assembly of the Jewish Theological Seminary of America* 4 (1933): 312–321.

Pollitzer, Anita. "Pass the Equal Rights Amendment Now." *Equal Rights,* May 15, 1937.

Postal, Bernard. "Ernestine Rose: Pioneer Suffragette." *B'nai B'rith Magazine* 47 (February 1933): 141, 158.

Proceedings of the First Convention of the National Council of Jewish Women, Held at New York, Nov. 15, 16, 17, 18 and 19, 1896. Philadelphia: Jewish Publication Society, 1897.

"Prompt Mrs. Stokes in Yiddish Speech." *NYTimes,* September 30, 1908.

Purvin, Jennie Franklin. "The Illinois League of Women Voters." *Chicago Council of Jewish Women Monthly Bulletin* 2 (November 1920): 1.

"The Question of Birth Control." *Forverts,* October 23, 1916.

"Rabbi Goldstein: Save Children, Guard Mothers, Foster Nation." *Buffalo Courier-Express.* March 12, 1930.

"Rabbis Declare for Peace." *American Hebrew,* August 8, 1924.

Rabinowitz, Adele. "Deborah, the First Suffragette." *American Hebrew,* September 13, 1912.

"Raleigh's Educational Program." *Jewish Woman* 6 (January 1926): 24–25.

Randall, Mercedes. *Improper Bostonian: Emily Greene Balch.* New York: Twayne, 1964.

Rankin, Jeanette. "Jeanette Rankin: Activist for World Peace, Women's Rights, and Democratic Government." Interview conducted by Malca Chall and Hannah Josephson for the Regional Oral History Office, Bancroft Library, University of California, Berkeley, 1974.

Reese, Rose. *Heaven is Eternal Spring*. Minneapolis: Friday Study Club, 1935.

"Religion is Urged as Guide to Peace." *NYTimes*, September 13, 1943.

"Republican Plank on Nazi Surrender Urged by Women." *NYTimes*, January 22, 1944.

Reyher, Rebecca Hourwich. "Feminism and the Home." *The Suffragist*, April 1920.

Reyher, Rebecca Hourwich. "Rebecca Hourwich Reyher: Search and Struggle for Equality and Independence." Interview conducted by Amelia R. Fry and Fern Ingersoll for the Regional Oral History Office, Bancroft Library, University of California, Berkeley, 1977.

Reyher, Rebecca Hourwich. "Southward on Wings of Peace." *World Observer* (April 1938): 25–27.

Robinson, Caroline Hadley. *Seventy Birth Control Clinics*. Baltimore: Williams & Wilkins, 1930.

Robison, Sophia M., and Joshua Starr. *Jewish Population Studies*. New York: Conference on Jewish Relations, 1943.

"Rosa Manus Nazi Victim." *NYTimes*, August 12, 1942.

"Rose Pesotta, Early Organizer for Garment Union, Dies at 69." *NYTimes*, December 8, 1965.

"Rosika Schwimmer Appeals to Jewish Women." *American Hebrew*, December 18, 1914.

Rubinow, I.M. "Social Work and Birth Control: An Editorial." *Jewish Social Service Quarterly* 2 (June 1926): 316–318.

Sachar, Abram Leon, and Leo W. Schwarz. *Our Heritage and the World Today*. New York: NCJW, 1935.

Sanger, Margaret, ed. *Biological and Medical Aspects of Contraception*. Washington, D.C.: NCFLBC, 1934.

Sanger, Margaret. "The Birth Control Raid." *The New Republic*, May 1, 1929.

Sanger, Margaret. *Margaret Sanger: An Autobiography*. New York: W. W. Norton, 1938.

Sanger, Margaret. *Motherhood in Bondage*. New York: Brentano's, 1928.

Sanger, Margaret. *My Fight for Birth Control*. Elmsford, New York: Maxwell Reprint, 1959.

Sanger, Margaret. *The Pivot of Civilization*. New York: Brentano's, 1922.

Sanger, Margaret. *Woman and the New Race*. New York: Brentano's, 1920.

Sanger, Margaret, and Hannah M. Stone, eds. *The Practice of Contraception: An International Symposium and Survey*. Baltimore: Williams & Wilkins, 1931.

"Says Five Neutrals Consider Peace Plans." *NYTimes*, November 28, 1915.

"Says Week's Halt Would End the War." *NYTimes*, December 8, 1914.

Schwimmer, Rosika. "Women Pioneers of a New International Order." *Bnai Brith Magazine* 29 (April 1924): 231–233.

"Scientific Advice in Marriage Urged." *NYTimes*, July 5, 1947.

Schneiderman, Rose, with Lucy Goldthwaite. *All for One*. New York: Eriksson, 1967.

"Sex and Society." *Der Fraynd*, February 1913.

Simon, Kate. *Bronx Primitive: Portraits in a Childhood*. New York: Penguin, 1982.

Singer, Isidor. *A Religion of Truth, Justice, and Peace: A Challenge to Church and Synagogue to Lead in the Realization of the Social and Peace Gospel of the Hebrew Prophets*. New York: Amos Society, 1924.

"Single Standard." *Equal Rights* 21 (April 1935): 3.

Sippel, Mrs. John F. "Women and World Peace." *Ladies Home Journal*, February 1929, 11, 121.

Snowden, Ethel Annakin. *The Feminist Movement*. London: Clear Type Press, 1913.

Solomon, Hannah Greenebaum. *Fabric of My Life: The Story of a Social Pioneer*. New York: Bloch, 1946.

Solomon, Hannah Greenebaum. *A Sheaf of Leaves*. Chicago: n.p., 1911.

Solomons, Selina. *The Girl From Colorado, or the Conversion of Aunty Suffridge*. San Francisco: New Woman Publishing, 1911.

Solomons, Selina. *How We Won the Vote in California: A True Story of the Campaign in 1911*. San Francisco: New Woman Publishing, 1912.

Sporborg, Constance. "President's Message." In NCJW–New York Section *Year Book, 1918–1919*. New York: NCJW–New York Section.

Stanton, Elizabeth Cady. *Eighty Years and More: Reminisces, 1815–1897*. New York: Schocken, 1971.

A Statement from the American Institute on Judaism and a Just and Enduring Peace. Cincinnati: Hebrew Union College, 1942.

Sternberger, Estelle M. "Editorial." *Jewish Woman* 6 (January 1926): 20.

Sternberger, Estelle M. "For Women's Rights in the Jewish Community." *B'nai B'rith Magazine* 47 (May 1933): 238.

Sternberger, Estelle M. *The Supreme Cause: A Practical Book About Peace*. New York: Dodd, Mead & Company, 1936.

Sternberger, Estelle M. "What Have Jewish Women Done for Peace?" *B'nai B'rith Magazine* 47 (April 1933): 204.

Sternberger, Estelle M. "Women in Foreign Lands." *B'nai B'rith Magazine* 47 (July 1933): 302.

Stevens, Doris. *Jailed for Freedom*. New York: Boni & Liveright, 1920.

Stix, Regine K. "Contraceptive Service in Three Areas: Part 2: The Effectiveness of Clinical Services." *Milbank Memorial Fund Quarterly* 19 (July 1941): 304–326.

Stix, Regine K., and Frank W. Notestein. "Effectiveness of Birth Control: A Second Study of Contraceptive Practice in a Selected Group of New York Women." *Milbank Memorial Fund Quarterly* 13 (April 1935): 162–178.

Stix, Regine K., and Frank W. Notestein. "Effectiveness of Birth Control: A Study of Contraceptive Practice in a Selected Group of New York Women." *Milbank Memorial Fund Quarterly* 12 (January 1934): 57–68.

Stokes, Herbert, and David L. Sterling, eds. *"I Belong to the Working Class": The Unfinished Autobiography of Rose Pastor Stokes*. Athens: University of Georgia Press, 1992.

Stokes, Rose Pastor. *The Woman Who Wouldn't*. New York: G. P. Putnam's Sons, 1916.

Stone, Hannah Mayer. "The Birth Control Raid." *Eugenics* 2 (August 1929).

Stone, Hannah Mayer. *Contraceptive Methods: A Clinical Survey*. Paper read at Contraceptive Session of the Sixth International Neo-Malthusian and Birth Control Conference, March 29, 1925.

Stone, Hannah Mayer, and Abraham Stone. *A Marriage Manual*. New York: Simon & Schuster, 1935.

Stone, Hannah Mayer, and Henriette Hart. *Maternal Health and Conception: A Study of the Social and Medical Data of 2,000 Patients from the Maternal Health Center, Newark, New Jersey: Part 1, Social Data* (n.p., 1932).

Stone, Sylvia L. "Lifelong Volunteer in San Francisco." Interview conducted by Eleanor Glaser for the Regional Oral History Office, Bancroft Library, University of California, Berkeley, 1982. SC-12048. AJA.

"The Struggle for Women's Rights in the World." *Der Fraynd*, December 1914.

Stuhler, Barbara, ed. *For the Public Record: A Documentary History of the League of Women Voters*. New York: Praeger, 2000.

"Suffrage in New Jersey State." *Di Froyen Velt*, August 1913.

"Suffrage in the United States." *Di Froyen Velt*, June 1913.

"The Suffrage Movement in England." *Di Froyen Velt*, August 1913.

"Suffrage Secretary Praises Roosevelt." *Philadelphia North American*, August 30, 1912.

"Suffragists at Theatres." *NYTimes*, October 28, 1915.

"Suffragists Make Plea for Peace." *NYTimes*, October 14, 1914.

"Suffragists Raise $105,619 at Rally." *NYTimes*, November 7, 1914.

Suggestions for Individual Efforts to Advance Peace. New York: NCCCW, 1930.

Sutro, Florentine Scholle. *My First Seventy Years*. New York: Roerich, 1935.

Syrkin, Marie. "The Pacifist Movements." *Jewish Frontier* (November 1939): 19–22.

"Three Groups Join in Peace Week Here." *NYTimes*, May 8, 1926.

Thompson, Charles Willis. "What She is Like and What She Believes In: An Interview with Emma Goldman." *NYTimes*, May 30, 1909.

"Up to the Doctors." *The Survey*, April 15, 1925.

"Various Methods in the Struggle for Women's Rights." *Di Froyen Velt*, July 1913.

Vernon, Mabel. "Mabel Vernon: Speaker for Suffrage and Petitioner for Peace." Interview conducted by Amelia Fry for the Regional Oral History Office, Bancroft Library, University of California, Berkeley, 1976.

Vreeland, F. M. "Birth Control and Social Change." *Birth Control Review* 1 (March 1934).

Wald, Lillian. *The House on Henry Street*. New York: Holt, Rinehart & Winston, 1915.

Wald, Lillian. *Windows on Henry Street*. Boston: Little, Brown, and Company, 1941.

Waldman, Morris D. "Need for Birth Control." *Jewish Social Service Quarterly* 3 (December 1926): 25–31.

Warner, Marie Pichel. "Contraception: A Study of 500 Cases from Private Practice." *Journal of the American Medical Association* 115 (July 1940): 279–285.

Weinstein, Marion. "Madam Rosika Schwimmer: A Personal Impression." *American Hebrew*, May 5, 1916.

"Well Known Giver to Charity Says Prevention is Better than Relief." *Birth Control Herald*, December 21, 1923.

Wells, Marguerite M. "Some Effects of Woman Suffrage." *Annals of the American Academy of Political and Social Science* 143 (May 1929): 207–216.

What Doctors Have Learned About Birth Control: A Symposium. Girard, KS: Haldeman-Julius Publications, 1931.

"What is Going On This Week." *NYTimes*, May 6, 1934.

Wise, Stephen S. "The Synagogue and Birth Control." In Margaret Sanger, ed., *Religious and Ethical Aspects of Birth Control*. New York: ABCL, 1926, 31–36.

Wise, Stephen S. "Woman and Democracy." *Free Synagogue Pulpit* 3 (October 1915): 139–158.

Wolf, Rose, Hortense Wolf, and Ruth C. Feibel. "History of the Council, 1895–1965." SC-1961. AJA.

"The Woman After the War." *Der Fraynd*, October 1917.

"Woman Sells Peace with Advertisements." *McKeesport News*, October 16, 1936.

"Woman Suffrage Adopted by Jewish Congregation Here." *Union Bulletin*, January 1921.

"Women and Universal Peace." *American Hebrew*, November 13, 1914.

"Women Besiege Washington." *Di Froyen Velt*, August 1913.

"Women in Many Fields." *NYTimes*, December 8, 1897.

"Women in Seven Lands Plead for Peace." *NYTimes*, January 12, 1937.

"Women of Philadelphia Drive For Peace." *Jewish Exponent*, July 13, 1928.

"Women Receive Voting Rights in Illinois State." *Di Froyen Velt*, July 1913.

"Women's Caravan to Fly for Peace." *NYTimes*, October 24, 1937.

"Women's International League for Peace and Freedom Resolutions of the Zurich Conference, 1919." In Estelle Freedman, ed., *The Essential Feminist Reader*. New York: Modern Library, 2007, 199–203.

"Women's Rights Activists Convention." *Di Froyen Velt*, November 1913.

"Women's World Conference in Hamburg." *American Hebrew*, June 14, 1929.

World Congress of Jewish Women, Vienna, May 6–11, 1923. Vienna: Druckerei-U. Verlags-A.G., 1923.

Yarros, Rachelle S. "Birth Control and Its Relation to Health and Welfare." *Medical Woman's Journal* 32 (1925): 268–272.

Yarros, Rachelle S. "Experiences of a Lecturer." *Social Hygiene* 5 (1919): 205–222.

Yarros, Rachelle S. *Modern Woman and Sex: A Feminist Physician Speaks*. New York: Vanguard, 1933.

Yarros, Rachelle S. "Some Practical Aspects of Birth Control." *Surgery, Gynecology & Obstetrics* 23 (1916): 188–190.

Yarros, Rachelle S. "Statement of Dr. Rachelle Yarros, Hull House, Chicago." "Supplementary Statement to the Committee on the Social Security Act, by Dr. Rachelle Yarros, Hull House, Chicago." 1935. *Social Security Online*. www.ssaonline.us/history/pdf/s35yarros/pdf

Yiddish Writers' Group of the Federal Writers' Project of the WPA of the City of New York, *Yiddishe Familyes un Familye Krayz fun Nyu York* (*Jewish Families and Family Circles of New York*). New York: Yiddish Writers Union, 1939.

Zametkin, Adela Kean. "Around the Women's World." *Der Fraynd*, December 1917.

Zametkin, Adela Kean. "Around the Women's World." *Der Fraynd*, February 1917.

Zametkin, Adela Kean. "Around the Women's World." *Der Fraynd*, March 1917.

Zametkin, Adela Kean. *Di Froys Handbuch*. Jamaica, NY: Farfesser, 1930.

Zutner, Bertha. *Nider mit di Vafen* (*Down With Weapons*). New York: Worker's Voice, 1917.

Zylbercweig, Zalmen. *Leksikon fun Yidishn Teater*. New York: Elisheva and Hebrew Actors Union, 1931.

UNPUBLISHED PRIMARY SOURCES

Esther Myers Andrews Papers. A/A56. SL.

American Jewish Autobiographies Collection. RG 102. YIVO.

Cheri Appel Oral History. 1989. MS 413. SSC.

Association of Minneapolis Jewish Women's Organizations Papers. P755. MHS.

Jennie Loitman Barron Papers. MC 410. SL.

Rose I. Bender Papers. MSS 020. HSP.

Iphigene Bettman Papers. MS 667. AJA.

Jacob Billikopf Papers. MS 13. AJA.

Birth Control League of Massachusetts Records. B-20. SL.

Alice Goldmark Brandeis to Carrie Chapman Catt, 1920. SC-1305. AJA.

Fanny Brin. Nearprint File. AJA.

Fanny Fligelman Brin Papers. A.B858. MHS.

Carrie Chapman Catt Papers. NYPL.

Carrie Chapman Catt Papers. MS 31. SSC.

Committee on the Cause and Cure of War Records. 87-M111. SL.

Committee on Militarism in Education Records. DG 009. SCPC.

Bertha Vera Corets Papers. MS 307. AJA.

Sadie Jacobs Crockin Collection. MS 95. JMM.

Abraham Cronbach Papers. MSS 9. AJA.

Mina Kirstein Curtiss Papers. MS 250. SSC.

Mary Ware Dennett Papers. M-138; MC-392. SL.

Mary Ware Dennett, "A Special Message to the Council, Contributors, and Friends of the Voluntary Parenthood League." November 18, 1921. Margaret Sanger Papers. Series 2, Reel 2: 67-74, SSC.

Ethel Eyre Valentine Dreier Papers. SSC.

Eichel Family Papers. DG 131. SCPC.

Katharine Asher Engel Papers. MS 55. SSC.

Morris Leopold Ernst Papers. MC 208. SL.

Jane Evans Collection. MS 745. AJA.

Family Planning Oral History Project Records. MC 223; OH-1. SL.

Federation of Jewish Women's Organizations Papers. I-208. AJHS.

Sophia Goldberger Friedman Papers. MS 58. SSC.

Edna Fischel Gellhorn Papers. A-113. SL.

Roland B. Gittelsohn Papers. MS 74. AJA.

Emma Goldman, Chicago, to Margaret Sanger, New York, December 17, 1915. Margaret Sanger Papers, Manuscript Division, Library of Congress. www.loc.gov/exhibits/haventohome/haven-home.html (October 30, 2007).

Emma Goldman Collected Papers. CDG-A. SCPC.

Jonah J. Goldstein Collection. P-61. AJHS.

Bertha Sanford Gruenberg Papers. 837-69-31; 83-M196-86-M227. SL.

Rose Heiman Halpern Collection. In possession of Victor Garlin, Sonoma.
Ida H. Hyde Papers. Microfilm reels 3220–3221. AJA.
Viola Hoffman Hymes Papers. 146.F.9.9(B). MHS.
Judith Brin Ingber interview at Minnesota History Center, June 19, 2008.
Caroline Katzenstein Papers. Am. 8996. HSP.
Caroline Katzenstein Papers. Accession # 1246. PJAC.
Esther Loeb Kohn Collection. Unprocessed papers in possession of Jo Ann Rothschild, Boston.
Setty Swartz Kuhn Papers. MS 173. AJA.
Sarah Kussy Papers. P-4. AJHS.
Max Kohler Papers. P-7. AJHS.
Frieda Langer Lazarus Papers. Mss Col 1703. NYPL.
Ray Frank Litman Papers. P-46. AJHS.
Lucile Lord-Heinstein Papers. AL866h; MC 310; M-53. SL.
Kitty Marion Papers. Mss Col 6263. NYPL.
Annie Nathan Meyer Papers. MS 7. AJA.
Kate B. Miller Papers. SC-13647. AJA.
Jacob Moses Papers. MS 51. JMM.
Maud Nathan Papers. M-83. SL.
NAWSA Records. NYPL.
NCPW Papers. DG 023. SCPC.
NCJW Collected Records. CDG-A. SCPC.
NCJW. Nearprint file. AJA.
NCJW Baltimore Section Records. MS 124. JMM.
NCJW Charleston Section Papers. MS 414. AJA.
NCJW Dallas Section. Nearprint file. AJA.
NCJW Fresno Section Minutes. SC-14320. AJA.
NCJW. "History of Minneapolis Section." SC-8736. AJA.
NCJW Minneapolis Section Papers. #0545. UMJA.
NCJW New York Section Records. I-469. AJHS.
NCJW St. Paul Section Papers. P230. MHS.
NCJW St. Paul Section Papers. #0546. UMJA.
Pauline Newman oral history transcript. Box 696. AJA.
Pauline Newman Papers. MC 324. SL.
Amy Schwartz Oppenheim Papers. MS 116. SSC.
Peace Collection. MS 437. SSC.
Planned Parenthood of Minnesota Records. SW024. SWHA.
PMC Records. DG 109. SCPC.
Rose Pesotta Papers. NYPL.
Phillips Family Papers. P-17. AJHS.
Harriet Fleischl Pilpel Papers. MS 311. SSC.
Planned Parenthood League of Massachusetts Records. SSC.
Jennie Franklin Purvin Papers. MS 502. AJA.
Mercedes M. Randall Papers. Box 1039. AJA.
Mercedes M. Randall Papers. DG 110. SCPC.
Cecilia Razovsky Papers. P-290. AJHS.
Rebecca Hourwich Reyher Papers. Unprocessed at time of use. MC 562. SL.
Florence Rose Papers. MS 134. SSC.
Berta Ratner Rosenbluth Papers. A/R8132. SL.
Agnes Goldman Sanborn Papers. 85-M120. SL.
Hannah Greenebaum Solomon scrapbook. Box X-172. AJA.
Bella Weretnikow Rosenbaum Papers. MS 179. AJA.
Augusta Rothschild report. 91.126.1. JMM.

Margaret Sanger Research Bureau Records. MS 320. SSC.
Margaret Sanger Correspondence. SC-14901, AJA.
Schwimmer-Lloyd Collection. Accession # 88 M 23. NYPL.
Flora Spiegelberg Papers. Microfilm reel 511. AJA.
Estelle M. Sternberger. Nearprint file. AJA.
Rose Pastor Stokes Letter. A/5874. SL.
Rose Pastor Stokes Papers. Microfilm reels 3213–3219. AJA. (Originals at Yale)
Abraham Stone Papers. H MS c 157, HML.
Suffrage Collection. MS 447. SSC.
Maud Swarz, New York, to Carrie Chapman Catt, November 30, 1920. SC-12179. AJA.
Marie Syrkin Papers. MS 614. AJA.
United Way of Minneapolis Records. SW070. SWHA.
Elkan and Henrietta Voorsanger Papers. MS 256. AJA.
Lillian Wald Papers. NYPL.
Gertrude Weil Papers. NCOA.
Ira Solomon Wile Papers. MS 173. SSC.
Stephen S. Wise Papers. P-134. AJHS.
Stephen S. Wise, Portland, to Eva E. Dye, Oregon City, March 20, 1906. SC-13522. AJA.
WILPF U.S. Section Records. DG 043. SCPC.
WILPF Massachusetts Branch Records. 83-M23. SL.
WILPF Minnesota Branch Records. MHS.
WPU Records. Accession # 44 M 95. NYPL.
Women of Reform Judaism Papers. MS 73. AJA.
Women of Reform Judaism. Nearprint file. AJA.
Rose Zetzer Collection. MS 86. JMM.

SECONDARY SOURCES

Abrams, Jeanne. *Jewish Women Pioneering the Frontier Trail: A History in the American West.* New York: NYU Press, 2006.
Abram, Ruth, ed. *"Send Us a Lady Physician": Women Doctors in America, 1835–1920.* New York: W. W. Norton, 1985.
Abrams, Ruth. "Jewish Women in the International Woman Suffrage Alliance, 1899–1926." Ph.D. diss., Brandeis University, 1996.
Adams, Katherine H., and Michael L. Keene. *Alice Paul and the American Suffrage Campaign.* Urbana: University of Illinois Press, 2008.
Adickes, Sandra. *To Be Young Was Very Heaven: Women in New York Before the First World War.* New York: St. Martin's Griffin, 1997.
Albert, Marta. "Not Quite a 'Quiet Revolution': Jewish Women Reformers in Buffalo, New York, 1890–1914." *Shofar* 9 (Summer 1991): 62–77.
Alonso, Harriet Hyman. "Commentary: Why Women's Peace History?" *Peace & Change* 20 (January 1995): 48–52.
Alonso, Harriet Hyman. *Peace as a Women's Issue: A History of the United States Movement for World Peace and Women's Rights.* Syracuse: Syracuse University Press, 1993.
Alonso, Harriet Hyman. "Suffragists for Peace During the Interwar Years, 1914–1941." *Peace & Change* 14 (July 1989): 243–262.
Alonso, Harriet Hyman. *The Women's Peace Union and the Outlawry of War, 1921–1942.* Knoxville: University of Tennessee Press, 1989.
Amidon, Kevin S. "Carrie Chapman Catt and the Evolutionary Politics of Sex and Race, 1885–1940." *Journal of the History of Ideas* 68 (April 2007): 305–328.
Anderson, Kristi. *After Suffrage: Women in Partisan and Electoral Politics Before the New Deal.* Chicago: University of Chicago Press, 1996.

Antler, Joyce. *The Journey Home: How Jewish Women Shaped Modern America*. New York: Schocken, 1997.

Arian, Charles L. "'Disciples of Aaron': Pacifism in the Reform Rabbinate, 1924–1945." Hebrew Union College Term Paper, 1985. SC-480. AJA.

Baker, Paula. "The Domestication of Politics: Women and American Political Society, 1780–1920." *American Historical Review* 89 (June 1984): 620–647.

Baker, Zachary M. "Two Bibliographic Projects on the Yiddish Theatre." *Yiddish Theatre Forum 2001* (March 12, 2003). http://www.mendele.commons.yale.edu/ytf/ytf02001.htm.

Baker, Zachary M., with Bonnie Sohn. *The Lawrence Marwick Collection of Copyrighted Yiddish Plays at the Library of Congress: An Annotated Bibliography*. Washington, D.C.: Library of Congress, 2004. http://www.loc.gov/rr/amed/marwick/marwickbibliography.pdf.

Bauer, Yehuda. *The Holocaust in Historical Perspective*. Seattle: University of Washington Press, 1978.

Bauer, Yehuda. *My Brother's Keeper: A History of the American Jewish Joint Distribution Committee, 1929–1939*. Philadelphia: Jewish Publication Society, 1974.

Bayme, Steven. "American Jewish Leadership Confronts the Holocaust: Revisiting Naomi Cohen's Thesis and the American Jewish Committee." *American Jewish Archives Journal* 61 (2009): 163–186.

Beifield, Martin P., Jr. "Let Her Works Praise Her in the Gates." Paper presented March 17, 1984, at Gertrude Weil Conference. SC-12802. AJA.

Bennett, Scott H. "'Free American Political Prisoners': Pacifist Activism and Civil Liberties, 1945–48." *Journal of Peace Research* 40 (July 2003): 413–433.

Berkovitch, Nitza. *From Motherhood to Citizenship: Women's Rights and International Organizations*. Baltimore: Johns Hopkins University Press, 2002.

Bittel, Carla. *Mary Putnam Jacobi and the Politics of Medicine in Nineteenth-Century America*. Chapel Hill: University of North Carolina Press, 2009.

Blumberg, Janice Rothschild. "Sophie Weil Brown: From Rabbi's Wife to Clubwoman." *Southern Jewish History* 9 (2006): 1–33.

Bolksky, Sidney. *Harmony and Dissonance: Voices of Jewish Identity in Detroit, 1914–1967*. Detroit: Wayne State University Press, 1991.

Bolt, Christine. *Sisterhood Questioned: Race, Class, and Internationalism in the American and British Women's Movements, ca. 1880s–1970s*. London: Routledge, 2004.

Bordin, Ruth. *Woman and Temperance: The Quest for Power and Liberty, 1873–1900*. Philadelphia: Temple University Press, 1981.

Bosch, Mineke. "Gender and the Personal in Political Biography: Observations from a Dutch Perspective." *Journal of Women's History* 21 (Winter 2009): 13–37.

Brandes, Joseph. "From Sweatshop to Stability: Jewish Labor Between the World Wars." *YIVO Annual* 16 (1976): 1–149.

Bredbenner, Candice Lewis. *A Nationality of Her Own: Women, Marriage, and the Law of Citizenship*. Berkeley: University of California Press, 1998.

Breitman, Richard, and Alan M. Kraut. *American Refugee Policy and European Jewry, 1933–1945*. Bloomington: Indiana University Press, 1987.

Brettschneider, Marla. *Cornerstones of Peace: Jewish Identity Politics and Democratic Theory*. New Brunswick, NJ: Rutgers University Press, 1996.

Brin, Ruth Firestone. "She Heard Another Drummer: The Life of Fanny Brin and Its Implications for the Sociology of Religion." MA thesis, University of Minnesota, 1972.

Brodie, Janet Farrell. *Contraception and Abortion in Nineteenth-Century America*. Ithaca, NY: Cornell University Press, 1994.

Brodkin, Karen. *How the Jews Became White Folks and What That Says About Race in America*. New Brunswick, NJ: Rutgers University Press, 1998.

Bronner, Stephen Eric. *A Rumor About the Jews: Reflections on Anti-Semitism and the Protocols of the Learned Elders of Zion*. New York: St. Martin's, 2000.

Brown, Dorothy M. *Setting a Course: American Women in the 1920s.* Boston: Twayne, 1987.

Buechler, Steven M. *Women's Movements in the United States: Woman Suffrage, Equal Rights, and Beyond.* New Brunswick, NJ: Rutgers University Press, 1990.

Buhle, Mari Jo. *Women and American Socialism, 1870–1920.* Urbana: University of Illinois Press, 1981.

Burns, Gene. *The Moral Veto: Framing Contraception, Abortion, and Cultural Pluralism in the United States.* Cambridge: Cambridge University Press, 2005.

Butler, Amy E. *Two Paths to Equality: Alice Paul and Ethel M. Smith in the ERA Debate, 1921–1929.* Albany: SUNY Press, 2002.

Cantor, Milton. *The Divided Left: American Radicalism, 1900–1975.* New York: Hill & Wang, 1978.

Cassedy, Steven. *To the Other Shore: The Russian Jewish Intellectuals Who Came to America.* Princeton: Princeton University Press, 1997.

Chalberg, John C. *Emma Goldman: American Individualist.* 2nd ed. New York: Pearson/Longman, 2008.

Chatfield, Charles. *The American Peace Movement: Ideals and Activism.* New York: Twayne, 1992.

Chatfield, Charles. *For Peace and Justice: Pacifism in America, 1914–1941.* Knoxville: University of Tennessee Press, 1971.

Chatfield, Charles. "World War I and the Liberal Pacifist in the United States." In Charles F. Howlett, ed., *History of the American Peace Movement, 1890–2000: The Emergence of a New Scholarly Discipline.* Lewiston: Mellen, 2005, 54–80.

Chen, Constance M. *"The Sex Side of Life": Mary Ware Dennett's Pioneering Battle for Birth Control and Sex Education.* New York: The New Press, 1996.

Chesler, Ellen. *Woman of Valor: Margaret Sanger and the Birth Control Movement in America.* New York: Simon & Schuster, 1992.

Clar, Reva. "Dr. Sarah Vasen: First Jewish Physician of Los Angeles." *Western States Jewish History* 35 (2003): 110–120.

Clemens, Elisabeth S. "Securing Political Returns to Social Capital: Women's Associations in the United States, 1880s–1920s." *Journal of Interdisciplinary History* 29 (Spring 1999): 613–638.

Coates, Patricia Walsh. *Margaret Sanger and the Origin of the Birth Control Movement, 1910–1930: The Concept of Women's Sexual Autonomy.* Lewiston: Mellen, 2008.

Cobble, Dorothy Sue. *The Other Women's Movement: Workplace Justice and Social Rights in Modern America.* Princeton: Princeton University Press, 2004.

Cohen, Naomi W. *The Americanization of Zionism, 1897–1948.* Hanover, NH: Brandeis University Press, 2003.

Cohen, Robert. *When the Old Left Was Young: Student Radicals and America's First Mass Student Movement, 1929–1941.* New York: Oxford University Press, 1993.

Condran, Gretchen A. and Ellen Kramarow. "Child Mortality Among Jewish Immigrants to the United States." *Journal of Interdisciplinary History* 22 (Autumn 1991): 223–254.

Cook, Blanche Wiesen. "Female Support Networks and Political Activism: Lillian Wald, Crystal Eastman, Emma Goldman." In Nancy F. Cott and Elizabeth H. Pleck, eds., *A Heritage of Her Own: Toward a New Social History of American Women.* New York: Touchstone, 1979.

Cook, Blanche Wiesen. "The Woman's Peace Party: Collaboration and Non-Cooperation." *Peace & Change* 1 (Fall 1972): 36–42.

Cooper, Sandi E. *Patriotic Pacifism: Waging War on War in Europe, 1815–1914.* New York: Oxford University Press, 1991.

Coser, Rose Laub, Laura S. Anker, and Andrew J. Perrin. *Women of Courage: Jewish and Italian Immigrant Women in New York.* Westport, CT: Greenwood, 1999.

Costin, Lela B. "Feminism, Pacifism, and the 1915 International Congress of Women." *Women's Studies International Forum* 5 (1982): 301–315.

Cott, Nancy F. *The Grounding of Modern Feminism.* New Haven, CT: Yale University Press, 1987.

Cowan, Neil M., and Ruth M. Schwartz Cowan. *Our Parents' Lives: Jewish Assimilation and Everyday Life.* New Brunswick, NJ: Rutgers University Press, 1996.

Cummings, Kathleen Sprows. *New Women of the Old Faith: Gender and American Catholicisim in the Progressive Era.* Chapel Hill: University of North Carolina Press, 2009.

Daniels, Doris Groshen. *Always a Sister: The Feminism of Lillian D. Wald.* New York: Feminist Press, 1989.

Daniels, Doris. "Building a Winning Coalition: The Suffrage Fight in New York State." *New York History* 60 (January 1979): 59–79.

DeBenedetti, Charles. *The Peace Reform in American History.* Bloomington: Indiana University Press, 1980.

Diner, Hasia R., and Beryl Lieff Benderly. *Her Works Praise Her: A History of Jewish Women from Colonial Times to the Present.* New York: Basic, 2002.

Diner, Hasia R. *The Jews of the United States, 1654 to 2000.* Berkeley: University of California Press, 2004.

Diner, Hasia R. "Why American Historians Really Ignore Jewish History." *American Jewish History* 95 (March 2009): 33–42.

Diner, Steven J. *A Very Different Age: Americans of the Progressive Era.* New York: Hill & Wang, 1998.

Dinnerstein, Leonard. *Antisemitism in America.* New York: Oxford University Press, 1995.

D'Itri, Patricia Ward. *Cross Currents in the International Women's Movement, 1848–1948.* Bowling Green, OH: Bowling Green State University Press, 1999.

Drinnon, Richard. *Rebel in Paradise: A Biography of Emma Goldman.* Chicago: University of Chicago Press, 1961.

DuBois, Ellen Carol. *Feminism and Suffrage: The Emergence of an Independent Women's Movement in America, 1848–1869.* Ithaca, NY: Cornell University Press, 1978.

DuBois, Ellen Carol. *Harriot Stanton Blatch and the Winning of Woman Suffrage.* New Haven, CT: Yale University Press, 1997.

DuBois, Ellen Carol. "Woman Suffrage and the Left: An International Socialist-Feminist Perspective." *New Left Review* 186 (March-April 1991): 20–44.

DuBois, Ellen Carol. "Woman Suffrage Around the World: Three Phases of Suffrage Internationalism." In Caroline Daley and Melanie Nolan, eds., *Suffrage and Beyond: International Feminist Perspectives.* New York: NYU Press, 1994, 252–274.

Dye, Nancy Schrom. *As Equals and as Sisters: Feminism, the Labor Movement, and the Women's Trade Union League of New York.* Columbia: University of Missouri Press, 1980.

Dykeman, Wilma. *Too Many People, Too Little Love: Edna Rankin McKinnon: Pioneer for Birth Control.* New York: Holt, Rinehart, & Winston, 1974.

Eagen, Eileen. *Class, Culture, and the Classroom: The Student Peace Movement of the 1930s.* Philadelphia: Temple University Press, 1981.

Early, Frances H. *A World Without War: How U.S. Feminists and Pacifists Resisted World War I.* Syracuse: Syracuse University Press, 1997.

Edwards, Emma R. "History of the North Carolina Association of Jewish Women." (np, 1961). SC-9206. AJA.

Engelman, Peter C. *A History of the Birth Control Movement in America.* Santa Barbara: Praeger, 2011.

Epstein, Barbara Leslie. *The Politics of Domesticity: Women, Evangelism, and Temperance in Nineteenth-Century America.* Middletown, CT: Wesleyan University Press, 1986.

Epstein, Melech. *Jewish Labor in the United States: An Industrial, Political, and Cultural History of the Jewish Labor Movement, 1882–1952.* New York: Trade Union Sponsoring Committee, 1950, 1953.

Epstein, Melech. *The Jews and Communism, 1919–1941.* New York: Trade Union Sponsoring Committee, 1959.

Evans, Richard J. *Comrades and Sisters: Feminism, Socialism, and Pacifism in Europe, 1870–1945.* New York: St. Martin's, 1987.

Ewen, Elizabeth. *Immigrant Women in the Land of Dollars: Life and Culture on the Lower East Side, 1890–1925.* New York: Monthly Review, 1985.

Exler, Lisa Fran. "Birth Control Practices of Eastern European Jewish Women Immigrants to America." Senior Honors thesis, Brandeis University, 2000.

Falk, Candace. *Love, Anarchy, and Emma Goldman: A Biography*. New Brunswick, NJ: Rutgers University Press, 1990.

Feingold, Henry L. *Bearing Witness: How America and Its Jews Responded to the Holocaust*. Syracuse: Syracuse University Press, 1995.

Feingold, Henry L. *The Politics of Rescue: The Roosevelt Administration and the Holocaust, 1938–1945*. New Brunswick, NJ: Rutgers University Press, 1970.

Feingold, Henry L. *Zion in America: The Jewish Experience from Colonial Times to the Present*. New York: Dover, 2002.

Feld, Marjorie N. *Lillian Wald: A Biography*. Chapel Hill: University of North Carolina Press, 2008.

Feldman, David M. *Birth Control in Jewish Law: Marital Relations, Contraception, and Abortion as Set Forth in the Classic Texts of Jewish Law*. Northvale, NJ: Jason Aronson, 1998.

Finnegan, Margaret. *Selling Suffrage: Consumer Culture and Votes for Women*. New York: Columbia University Press, 1999.

Fishbein, Leslie. *Rebels in Bohemia: The Radicals of The Masses*. Chapel Hill: University of North Carolina Press, 1982.

Flamiano, Dolores. "The Birth of a Notion: Media Coverage of Contraception, 1915–1917." *Journalism & Mass Communication Quarterly* 75 (Autumn 1998): 560–571.

Flanagan, Maureen A. *America Reformed: Progressives and Progressivisms, 1890s–1920s*. New York: Oxford University Press, 2006.

Flanagan, Maureen A. *Seeing With Their Hearts: Chicago Women and the Vision of the Good City, 1871–1933*. Princeton, NJ: Princeton University Press, 2002.

Folbre, Nancy. "Sleeping Beauty Awakes: Self-Interest, Feminism, and Fertility in the Early Twentieth-Century." *Social Research* 71 (Summer 2004): 343–356.

Ford, Linda G. *Iron-Jawed Angels: The Suffrage Militancy of the National Woman's Party, 1910–1920*. Lanham, MD: University Press of America, 1991.

Foster, Carrie. *The Women and the Warriors: The U.S. Section of the Women's International League for Peace and Freedom, 1915–1946*. Syracuse: Syracuse University Press, 1995.

Foster, Catherine. *Women for All Seasons: The Story of the Women's International League for Peace and Freedom*. Athens: University of Georgia Press, 1989.

Fowler, Robert Booth. *Carrie Catt: Feminist Politician*. Boston: Northeastern University Press, 1986.

Frank, Dana. "Housewives, Protest, and the Politics of Food: The 1917 Cost-of-Living Protests." *Feminist Studies* 11 (Summer 1985): 255–285.

Frankel, Noralee, and Nancy S. Dye, eds. *Gender, Class, Race and Reform in the Progressive Era*. Lexington: University of Kentucky Press, 1991.

Frankel, Oz. "What Ever Happened to 'Red Emma'? Emma Goldman from Alien Rebel to American Icon." *Journal of American History* 83 (December 1996): 903–942.

Freeze, Chae Ran. *Jewish Marriage and Divorce in Imperial Russia*. Hanover, NH: Brandeis University Press, 2001.

Friedman-Kasaba, Kathie. *Memories of Migration: Gender, Ethnicity, and Work in the Lives of Jewish and Italian Women in New York, 1870–1924*. Albany: SUNY Press, 1996.

Galchinsky, Michael. *Jews and Human Rights: Dancing at Three Weddings*. Lanham, MD: Rowman & Littlefield, 2008.

Gamson, William A. "Commitment and Agency in Social Movements." *Sociological Forum* 6 (March 1991): 27–50.

Garlin, Victor. "Rose Halpern: Working-Class Activist in the Birth Control Movement." Unpublished paper in possession of author, 2007.

Genizi, Haim. "American Interfaith Cooperation on Behalf of Refugees from Nazism, 1933–1945." *American Jewish History* 70 (March 1981): 347–361.

Ginsburg, Amy Judith. "From Club Women to Progressive Philanthropists: The New York Section of the National Council of Jewish Women, 1894–1918." B.A. thesis, Harvard University, 1982.

Ginzberg, Lori D. *Elizabeth Cady Stanton: An American Life.* New York: Hill & Wang, 2009.

Ginzberg, Lori D. *Women and the Work of Benevolence: Morality, Politics, and Class in the Nineteenth-Century United States.* New Haven, CT: Yale University Press, 1990.

Glenn, Susan A. *Daughters of the Shtetl: Life and Labor in the Immigrant Generation.* Ithaca, NY: Cornell University Press, 1990.

Goldstein, Eric. *The Price of Whiteness: Jews, Race, and American Identity.* Princeton: Princeton University Press, 2006.

Golomb, Deborah Grand. "The 1893 Congress of Jewish Women: Evolution or Revolution in American Jewish Women's History?" *American Jewish History* 52 (September 1980): 52–67.

Goodier, Susan. "The Other Woman's Movement: Anti-Suffrage Activism in New York State, 1865–1932." PhD diss., University of Albany, SUNY, 2007.

Gordon, Linda. *The Moral Property of Women: A History of Birth Control Politics in America.* Urbana: University of Illinois Press, 2002.

Gordon, Linda. *Woman's Body, Woman's Right: A Social History of Birth Control in America.* New York: Grossman, 1976.

Gordon, Linda, ed. *Women, the State, and Welfare.* Madison: University of Wisconsin Press, 1990.

Gottlieb, Moshe. "The American Controversy Over the Olympic Games." *American Jewish Historical Quarterly* 61 (March 1972): 181–213.

Graham, Sara Hunter. *Woman Suffrage and the New Democracy.* New Haven, CT: Yale University Press, 1996.

Green, Nancy L., ed. *Jewish Workers in the Modern Diaspora.* Berkeley: University of California Press, 1998.

Guglielmo, Jennifer. *Living the Revolution: Italian Women's Resistance and Radicalism in New York City, 1880–1945.* Chapel Hill: University of North Carolina Press, 2010.

Gurock, Jeffrey S., ed. *America, American Jews, and the Holocaust.* New York: Routledge, 1998.

Gurock, Jeffrey S. "The Depth of Ethnicity: Jewish Identity and Ideology in Interwar New York City." *American Jewish Archives Journal* 61 (2009): 145–162.

Gurock, Jeffrey S. *When Harlem Was Jewish, 1870–1930.* New York: Columbia University Press, 1979.

Guthmann, Bernice J. *The Planned Parenthood Movement in Illinois, 1923–1965.* Chicago: Planned Parenthood, 1965.

Haarsager, Sandra. *Organized Womanhood: Cultural Politics in the Pacific Northwest, 1840–1920.* Norman: University of Oklahoma Press, 1997.

Hajo, Cathy Moran. *Birth Control on Main Street: Organizing Clinics in the United States, 1916–1939.* Urbana: University of Illinois Press, 2010.

Hardman, J.B.S. "The Jewish Labor Movement in the United States: Jewish and Non-Jewish Influences." *American Jewish Historical Quarterly* 62 (December 1952): 98–132.

Haslett, Diane C. "Hull House and the Birth Control Movement: An Untold Story." *Affilia* 12 (Fall 1997): 261–277.

Hawkins, Richard A. "'Hitler's Bitterest Foe': Samuel Untermyer and the Boycott of Nazi Germany, 1933–1938." *American Jewish History* 93 (March 2007): 21–50.

Henslely, Melissa Anne. "Feminine Virtue and Feminist Fervor: The Impact of the Women's International League for Peace and Freedom in the 1930s." *Affilia* 21 (May 2006): 146–157.

Hewitt, Nancy, ed. *No Permanent Waves: Recasting Histories of U.S. Feminism.* New Brunswick, NJ: Rutgers University Press, 2010.

Hollinger, David A. "Communalist and Dispersionist Approaches to American Jewish History in an Increasingly Post-Jewish Era." *American Jewish History* 95 (March 2009): 1–32.

Hollinger, David A. "A Yet More Capacious Expanse for American Jewish History." *American Jewish History* 95 (March 2009): 73–78.

Holton, Sandra Stanley. "'To Educate Women into Rebellion': Elizabeth Cady Stanton and the Creation of a Transatlantic Network of Radical Suffragists." *American Historical Review* 99 (October 1994): 1112–1136.

Holz, Rose. "Nurse Gordon on Trial: Those Early Days of the Birth Control Clinic Reconsidered." *Journal of Social History* 39 (Fall 2005): 112–140.

Horowitz, Helen Lefkowitz. *Rereading Sex: Battles Over Sexual Knowledge and Suppression in Nineteenth-Century America.* New York: Knopf, 2002.

Horvitz, Eleanor F. "Marion L. Misch: An Extraordinary Woman." *Rhode Island Jewish Historical Notes* 8 (November 1980): 7–65.

Howe, Irving. *World of Our Fathers: The Journey of East European Jews to America and the Life They Found and Made.* New York: Harcourt Brace, 1976.

Howlett, Charles F., ed. *History of the American Peace Movement, 1890–2000: The Emergence of a New Scholarly Discipline.* Lewiston: Mellen, 2005.

Howlett, Charles F., and Glen Zeitzer. *The American Peace Movement: History and Historiography.* Washington, D.C.: American Historical Association, 1985.

Hyman, Paula E. *Gender and Assimilation in Modern Jewish History.* Seattle: University of Washington Press, 1995.

Hyman, Paula E. "The Jewish Body Politic: Gendered Politics in the Early Twentieth Century." *Nashim* 2 (Spring 1999): 37–51.

Hyman, Paula E. "We are all Post-Jewish Historians Now: What American Jewish History Brings to the Table." *American Jewish History* 95 (March 2009): 53–60.

ICW. *Women in a Changing World: The Dynamic Story of the International Council of Women since 1888.* London: Routledge & Kegan Paul, 1966.

Jensen, Joan M. "The Evolution of Margaret Sanger's 'Family Limitation' Pamphlet, 1914–1921." *Signs* 6 (Spring 1981): 548–567.

Joselit, Jenna Weissman. *The Wonders of America: Reinventing Jewish Culture, 1880–1950.* New York: Hill & Wang, 1994.

Katz, Sherry J. "'Researching Around Our Subjects': Excavating Radical Women." *Journal of Women's History* 20 (Spring 2008): 168–186.

Katzman-Yungman, Mira. *Hadassah: American Women Zionists and the Rebirth of Israel.* Oxford: Littman, 2012.

Kennedy, David M. *Birth Control in America: The Career of Margaret Sanger.* New Haven, CT: Yale University Press, 1970.

Kern, Kathi. *Mrs. Stanton's Bible.* Ithaca, NY: Cornell University Press, 2001.

Kessler-Harris, Alice. "Organizing the Unorganizable: Three Jewish Women and Their Union." *Labor History* 17 (Winter 1976): 5–23.

Kessler-Harris, Alice. "Where Are the Organized Woman Workers?" *Feminist Studies* 3 (Autumn 1975): 92–110.

Klapper, Melissa R. *Jewish Girls Coming of Age in America, 1860–1920.* New York: NYU Press, 2005.

Kline, Wendy. *Building a Better Race: Gender, Sexuality, and Eugenics from the Turn of the Century to the Baby Boom.* Berkeley: University of California Press, 2001.

Kolmerten, Carol A. *The American Life of Ernestine L. Rose.* Syracuse: Syracuse University Press, 1999.

Koven, Seth, and Sonya Michel, eds. *Mothers of a New World: Maternalist Politics and the Origins of Welfare States.* New York: Routledge, 1993.

Kosak, Hadassah. *Cultures of Opposition: Jewish Immigrant Workers, New York City, 1881–1905.* Albany: SUNY Press, 2000.

Kraft, Barbara S. *The Peace Ship: Henry Ford's Pacifist Adventure in the First World War.* New York: Macmillan, 1978.

Kraut, Alan M. "Dispersionism, Pluralism, and the Nebulous Contours of Post-Jewish Identity." *American Jewish History* 95 (March 2009): 43–52.

Kraut, Alan M., and Deborah A. Kraut. *Covenant of Care: Newark Beth Israel and the Jewish Hospital in America.* New Brunswick, NJ: Rutgers University Press, 2007.

Kuzmack, Linda Gordon. *Woman's Cause: The Jewish Woman's Movement in England and the United States, 1881–1933*. Columbus: Ohio State University Press, 1990.

Ladd-Taylor, Molly. *Mother-Work: Women, Child Welfare, and the State, 1890–1930*. Urbana: University of Illinois Press, 1995.

Lambert, Joshua N. "'Unclean Lips': Obscenity and Jews in American Literature." PhD diss., University of Michigan, 2009.

Las, Nelly. *Jewish Women in a Changing World: A History of the International Council of Jewish Women, 1899–1995*. Jerusalem: Harman, 1996.

Laville, Helen. "A New Era in International Women's Rights? American Women's Associations and the Establishment of the UN Commission on the Status of Women." *Journal of Women's History* 20 (Winter 2008): 34–56.

Leavitt, Judith Walzer. *Brought to Bed: Childbearing in America, 1750–1950*. New York: Oxford University Press, 1986.

Leff, Laurel. *Buried by the Times: The Holocaust and America's Most Important Newspaper*. New York: Cambridge University Press, 2005.

Leinenweber, Charles. "The Class and Ethnic Basis of New York City Socialism, 1904–1915." *Labor History* 22 (Winter 1981): 31–56.

Lederhandler, Eli. "Guides for the Perplexed: Sex, Manners, and Mores for the Yiddish Reader in America." *Modern Judaism* 11 (October 1991): 321–341.

Lerner, Elinor. "American Feminism and the Jewish Question." In David A. Gerber, ed., *Anti-Semitism in American History*. Urbana: University of Illinois Press, 1986, 305–328.

Lerner, Elinor. "Jewish Involvement in the New York City Suffrage Movement." *American Jewish History* 52 (June 1981): 442–461.

Lifson, David S. *The Yiddish Theatre in America*. New York: Yoseloff, 1965.

Linder, Doris H. "Jennie Matyas." In Susan Ware, ed., *Notable American Women: A Biographical Dictionary Completing the Twentieth Century*. Cambridge. MA: Harvard University Press, 2004.

Lipstadt, Deborah E. *Beyond Belief: The American Press and the Coming of the Holocaust, 1933–1945*. New York: Free Press, 1986.

Litt, Jacquelyn. "Mothering, Medicalization, and Jewish Identity, 1928–1940." *Gender and Society* 10 (April 1996): 185–198.

Lovett, Laura L. *Conceiving the Future: Pronatalism, Reproduction, and the Family in the United States, 1890–1938*. Chapel Hill: University of North Carolina Press, 2007.

Lumsden, Linda J. *Rampant Women: Suffragists and the Right of Assembly*. Knoxville: University of Tennessee Press, 1997.

Lunardini, Christine A. *From Equal Suffrage to Equal Rights: Alice Paul and the National Woman's Party, 1910–1928*. New York: NYU Press, 1986.

Manor, Ehud. *Forward: The Jewish Daily Forward (Forverts) Newspaper: Immigrants, Socialism, and Jewish Politics in New York, 1890–1917*. Brighton: Sussex, 2009.

Marcellus, Jane. "My Grandmother's Black Market Birth Control: 'Subjugated Knowledges' in the History of Contraceptive Discourse." *Journal of Communication Inquiry* 27 (January 2003): 9–28.

Marchand, C. Roland. *The American Peace Movement and Social Reform, 1898–1918*. Princeton: Princeton University Press, 1972.

Markowitz, Ruth Jacknow. *My Daughter, the Teacher: Jewish Teachers in the New York City Schools*. New Brunswick, NJ: Rutgers University Press, 1993.

Marrus, Michael R. *The Holocaust in History*. Hanover, NH: UPNE, 1987.

Marsh, Margaret. *Anarchist Women, 1870–1920*. Philadelphia: Temple University Press, 1981.

Marshall, Susan E. *Splintered Sisterhood: Gender and Class in the Campaign Against Woman Suffrage*. Madison: University of Wisconsin Press, 1997.

Masel-Walters, Lynn. "'To Hustle with the Rowdies': The Organization and Functions of the American Woman Suffrage Press." *Journal of American Culture* 3 (Spring 1980): 167–183.

McGerr, Michael E. *A Fierce Discontent: The Rise and Fall of the Progressive Movement in America, 1870–1920.* New York: Oxford University Press, 2005.

Meyer, Jimmy Elaine Wilkinson. "Birth Control Policy, Practice and Prohitibion in the 1930s: The Maternal Health Association of Cleveland, Ohio." PhD diss., Case Western Reserve University, 1993.

McCammon, Holly J. "'Out of the Parlors and Into the Streets': The Changing Tactical Repertoire of the U.S. Women's Suffrage Movements." *Social Forces* 81 (2003): 787–818.

McCann, Carole R. *Birth Control Politics in the United States, 1916–1945.* Ithaca, NY: Cornell University Press, 1994.

McCune, Mary. "Creating a Place for Women in a Socialist Brotherhood: Class and Gender Politics in the Workmen's Circle, 1892–1930." *Feminist Studies* 28 (Fall 2002): 585–610.

McCune, Mary. "Formulating the 'Women's Interpretation of Zionism': Hadassah Recruitment of Non-Zionist American Women, 1914–1930." In Shulamit Reinharz and Mark A. Raider, eds., *American Jewish Women and the Zionist Enterprise.* Hanover, NH: Brandeis University Press, 2005.

McCune, Mary. *"The Whole Wide World Without Limits": International Relief, Gender Politics, and American Jewish Women, 1893–1930.* Detroit: Wayne State University Press, 2005.

McGerr, Michael E. "Political Style and Women's Power, 1830–1930." *Journal of American History* 77 (December 1990): 864–885.

McGuire, John Thomas. "Two Feminist Visions: Social Justice Feminism and Equal Rights, 1899–1940." *Pennsylvania History* 71 (Autumn 2004): 445–478.

McLaren, Angus. *A History of Contraception: From Antiquity to the Present Day.* Oxford: Blackwell, 1990.

Mead, Rebecca J. *How the Vote Was Won: Woman Suffrage in the Western United States, 1868–1914.* New York: NYU Press, 2004.

Medoff, Rafael. "American Jewish Responses to Nazism and the Holocaust." In Marc Lee Raphael, ed., *The Columbia History of Jews and Judaism in America.* New York: Columbia University Press, 2008.

Michels, Tony. "Communalist History and Beyond: The Potential of American Jewish History." *American Jewish History* 95 (March 2009): 61–72.

Michels, Tony. *A Fire in Their Hearts: Yiddish Socialists in New York.* Cambridge, MA: Harvard University Press, 2005.

Millen, Rochelle. *Women, Birth, and Death in Jewish Law and Practice.* Hanover, NH: Brandeis University Press, 2004.

Miller, Sally M., ed. *Race, Ethnicity, and Gender in Early Twentieth-Century American Socialism.* New York: Garland, 1996.

Mohr, James. *Abortion in America: The Origins and Evolution of National Policy, 1800–1900.* New York: Oxford University Press, 1978.

Mononson, S. Sara. "The Lady and the Tiger: Women's Electoral Activism in New York City Before Suffrage." *Journal of Women's History* 2 (Fall 1990): 100–135.

Moore, Deborah Dash. *At Home in America: Second Generation New York Jews.* New York: Columbia University Press, 1981.

Morantz-Sanchez, Regina Markell. *Sympathy and Science: Women Physicians in American Medicine.* New York: Oxford University Press, 1985.

More, Ellen S. *Restoring the Balance: Women Physicians and the Practice of Medicine, 1850–1995.* Cambridge, MA: Harvard University Press, 1999.

Morgan, S. Philip, Susan Cotts Watkins, and Douglas Ewbank. "Generating Americans: Ethnic Differences in Fertility." In Susan Cotts Watkins, ed., *After Ellis Island: Newcomers and Natives in the 1910 Census.* New York: Russell Sage, 1994, 83–124.

Morton, Lauren P. "Baltimore's First Birth Control Clinic: The Bureau for Contraceptive Advice, 1927–1932." *Maryland Historical Magazine* 102 (Winter 2007): 300–319.

Muncy, Robyn. *Creating a Female Dominion in American Reform, 1890–1935.* New York: Oxford University Press, 1994.

Nadell, Pamela S., and Rita J. Simon. "Ladies of the Sisterhood: Women in the American Reform Synagogue, 1900–1930." In Maurie Sacks, ed., *Active Voices: Women in Jewish Culture*. Urbana: University of Illinois Press, 1995, 63–75.

Nahshon, Edna. "The Yiddish Theater in America: A Brief Historical Overview." In Zachary M. Baker, with Bonnie Sohn, eds. *The Lawrence Marwick Collection of Copyrighted Yiddish Plays at the Library of Congress: An Annotated Bibliography*. Washington, D.C.: Library of Congress, 2004. http://www.loc.gov/rr/amed/marwick/marwickbibliography.pdf.

Newman, Louise. *White Women's Rights: The Racial Origins of Feminism in the United States*. New York: Oxford University Press, 1999.

Orleck, Annelise. *Common Sense and a Little Fire: Women and Working-Class Politics in the United States, 1900–1965*. Chapel Hill: University of North Carolina Press, 1995.

Orleck, Annelise. "'We Are That Mythical Thing Called the Public': Militant Housewives During the Great Depression." *Feminist Studies* 19 (Spring 1993): 147–172.

Pastorello, Karen. *A Power Among Them: Bessie Abramowitz Hillman and the Making of the Amalgamated Clothing Workers of America*. Urbana: University of Illinois Press, 2008.

Paton-Walsh, Margaret. "Women's Organizations, U.S. Foreign Policy, and the Far Eastern Crisis, 1937–1941." *Pacific Historical Review* 70 (2001): 601–626.

Patterson, David S. "An Interpretation of the American Peace Movement, 1898–1914." In Charles Chatfield, ed., *Peace Movements in America*. New York: Schocken, 1973.

Patterson, David S. *The Search for Negotiated Peace: Women's Activism and Citizen Diplomacy in World War I*. New York: Routledge, 2008.

Penkower, Monty Noam. *The Jews Were Expendable: Free World Diplomacy and the Holocaust*. Urbana: University of Illinois Press, 1983.

Perlman, Selig. "Jewish American Unionism: Its Birth Pangs and Contribution to the General American Labor Movement." *Publications of the American Jewish Historical Society* 41 (1951/1952): 297–338.

Perry, Elisabeth Israels. *Belle Moskowitz: Feminine Politics and the Exercise of Power in the Age of Al Smith*. New York: Oxford University Press, 1987.

Petit, Jeanne. "'Organized Catholic Womanhood': Suffrage, Citizenship, and the National Council of Catholic Women." *U.S. Catholic Historian* 26 (Winter 2008): 83–100.

Pois, Anne Marie. "The U.S. Women's International League for Peace and Freedom and American Neutrality, 1935–1939." *Peace & Change* 14 (July 1989): 263–284.

Pratt, Norma Fain. "Culture and Radical Politics: Yiddish Women Writers, 1890–1940." *American Jewish History* 52 (September 1980): 68–90.

Pratt, Norma Fain. "Transitions in Judaism: The American Jewish Woman Through the 1930s." *American Quarterly* 30 (Winter 1978): 681–702.

Raider, Mark A. *The Emergence of American Zionism*. New York: NYU Press, 1998.

Ray, Joyce M., and F. G. Gosling. "American Physicians and Birth Control, 1936–1947." *Journal of Social History* 18 (Spring 1985): 399–411.

Reagan, Leslie J. *When Abortion Was a Crime: Women, Medicine, and Law in the United States, 1867–1973*. Berkeley: University of California Press, 1997.

Reed, James. *The Birth Control Movement and American Society: From Private Vice to Public Virtue*. Princeton: Princeton University Press, 1983.

Reinharz, Shulamit, and Mark A. Raider, eds. *American Jewish Women and the Zionist Enterprise*. Hanover, NH: Brandeis University Press, 2004.

Rich, Jacob C. *60 Years of the Jewish Daily Forward*. New York: Forward Association, 1957.

Richardson, Dick. "The Geneva Disarmament Conference, 1932–1934." In Dick Richardson and Glyn Stone, eds., *Decisions and Diplomacy: Essays in Twentieth Century International History*. London: Routledge, 1995, 61–84.

Rischin, Moses. "The Jewish Labor Movement in the United States: A Social Interpretation." *Labor History* 4 (August 1963): 227–247.

Rischin, Moses. *The Promised City: New York's Jews, 1870–1914.* New York: Cambridge University Press, 1962.

Roberts, Dorothy. "Margaret Sanger and the Racial Origins of the Birth Control Movement." In Bruce Baum and Duchess Harris, eds., *Racially Writing the Republic: Racists, Race Rebels, and Transformations of American Identity.* Durham, NC: Duke University Press, 2009, 196–213.

Rochelson, Meri-Jane. "Israel Zangwill and Women's Suffrage." *Jewish Culture and History* 2 (Winter 1999): 1–17.

Rodgers, Daniel. *Atlantic Crossings: Social Politics in a Progressive Age.* Cambridge, MA: Belknap Press, 2000.

Rodrique, Jessie M. "The Black Community and the Birth Control Movement." In Darlene Clark Hine, Wilma King, and Linda Reed, eds., *"We Specialize in the Wholly Impossible": A Reader in Black Women's History.* New York: Carlson, 1995, 505–520.

Rogow, Faith. *Gone to Another Meeting: The National Council of Jewish Women, 1893–1993.* Tuscaloosa: University of Alabama Press, 1993.

Rojanski, Rachel. "Socialist Ideology, Traditional Rhetoric: Images of Women in American Yiddish Socialist Dailies, 1918–1922." *American Jewish History* 93 (September 2007): 329–348.

Rosen, Christine. *Preaching Eugenics: Religious Leaders and the American Eugenics Movement.* New York: Oxford University Press, 2004.

Rosen, Robyn. "The Shifting Battleground for Birth Control: Lessons from New York's Hudson Valley in the Interwar Years." *New York History* 90 (Summer 2009): 187–215.

Rosenbaum, Judith. "'The Call To Action': Margaret Sanger, the Brownsville Jewish Women, and Political Activism." In Marion Kaplan and Deborah Dash Moore, eds., *Gender and Jewish History.* Bloomington: Indiana University Press, 2010, 251–266.

Ross, Robert W. *So It Was True: The American Protestant Press and the Nazi Persecution of the Jews.* Minneapolis: University of Minnesota Press, 1980.

Ruddick, Sara. *Maternal Thinking: Toward a Politics of Peace.* Boston: Beacon, 1989.

Rupp, Leila J. "Constructing Internationalism: The Case of Transnational Women's Organizations, 1888–1945." *American Historical Review* 99 (December 1994): 1571–1600.

Rupp, Leila J. *Worlds of Women: The Making of an International Women's Movement.* Princeton: Princeton University Press, 1997.

Rupp, Leila J., and Verta Taylor. "Forging Feminist Identity in an International Movement: A Collective Identity Approach to Twentieth-Century Feminism." *Signs* 24 (Winter 1999): 363–386.

Sandrow, Nahma. *Vagabond Stars: A World History of Yiddish Theater.* New York: Harper & Row, 1977.

Sarna, Jonathan D. "American Jewish History." *Modern Judaism* 10 (October 1990): 343–365.

Sarna, Jonathan D. *American Judaism: A History.* New Haven, CT: Yale University Press, 2005.

Sarna, Jonathan D. *A Great Awakening: The Transformation that Shaped Twentieth-Century American Judaism and Its Implications for Today.* Council for Initiatives in Jewish Education, 1995.

Scharf, Lois, and Joan M. Jensen, eds. *Decades of Discontent: The Women's Movement, 1920–1940.* Westport, CT: Greenwood, 1983.

Schloff, Linda. "Fanny Fligelman Brin." In Paula E. Hyman and Deborah Dash Moore, eds., *Jewish Women in America: An Historical Encyclopedia.* New York: Routledge, 1997, 184–185.

Schoen, Johanna. *Choice and Coercion: Birth Control, Sterilization, and Abortion in Public Health and Welfare.* Chapel Hill: University of North Carolina Press, 2005.

Schott, Linda. "The Woman's Peace Party and the Moral Basis for Women's Pacifism." *Frontiers: A Journal of Women's Studies* 8 (1985): 18–24.

Scott, Anne Firor. "Gertrude Weil and Her Times." *Southern Cultures* 13 (Spring 2007): 87–102.

Scott, Anne Firor. *Natural Allies: Women's Associations in American History.* Urbana: University of Illinois Press, 1992.

Seller, Maxine Schwartz. "Defining Socialist Womanhood: The Women's Page of the Jewish Daily Forward in 1919." *American Jewish History* 76 (June 1987): 416–438.

Seller, Maxine Schwartz. "The Housewife Who Would 'Fly With Wings': The Emotional Life of the East European Jewish Woman." *Shofar* 9 (Summer 1991): 47–61.

Seller, Maxine Schwartz. "Putting Women into American Jewish History." *Frontiers: A Journal of Women's Studies* 5 (Spring 1980): 59–62.

Seller, Maxine Schwartz. "World of Our Mothers: The Women's Page of the Jewish Daily Forward." *Journal of Ethnic Studies* 16 (Summer 1988): 95–118.

Shaffer, Robert. "Women and the Communist Party USA, 1930–1940." *Socialist Review* 45 (May 1975): 73–118.

Shapiro, Robert Moses, ed. *Why Didn't the Press Shout: American and International Journalism During the Holocaust.* New York: Yeshiva University Press, 2003.

Sharer, Wendy B. *Vote and Voice: Women's Organizations and Political Literacy, 1915–1930.* Carbondale: Southern Illinois University Press, 2004.

Sheramy, Rona. "'There are Times When Silence is a Sin': The Women's Division of the American Jewish Congress and the Anti-Nazi Boycott Movement." *American Jewish History* 89 (2001): 105–121.

Silver, M.K. "Selina Solomons and Her Quest for the Sixth Star (Woman's Suffrage)." *Western States Jewish History* 31 (Summer 1999): 301–318.

Simmons, Erica B. *Hadassah and the Zionist Project.* Lanham, MD: Rowman & Littlefield, 2006.

Singerman, Robert. "The American Career of the Protocols of the Elders of Zion." *American Jewish History* 71 (Spring 1980): 48–78.

Sklar, Kathryn Kish. *Florence Kelley and the Nation's Work: the Rise of Women's Political Culture, 1830–1900.* New Haven, CT: Yale University Press, 1995.

Skok, Deborah A. "The Historiography of Catholic Laywomen and Progressive Era Reform." *U.S. Catholic Historian* 26 (Winter 2008): 1–22.

Skocpol, Theda. *Protecting Mothers and Soldiers: The Political Origins of Social Policy in the United States.* Cambridge, MA: Belknap Press, 1992.

Smith, Judith E. *Family Connections: A History of Italian and Jewish Immigrant Lives in Providence, Rhode Island, 1900–1940.* Albany: SUNY Press, 1985.

Sneider, Allison L. *Suffragists in an Imperial Age: U.S. Expansion and the Woman Question, 1870–1929.* New York: Oxford University Press, 2008.

Solomon, Martha M., ed. *A Voice of Their Own: The Woman Suffrage Press, 1840–1910.* Tuscaloosa: University of Alabama Press, 1991.

Soloway, Richard. "The 'Perfect Contraceptive': Eugenics and Birth Control Research in Britain and America in the Interwar Years." *Journal of Contemporary History* 30 (1995): 637–664.

Sorin, Gerald. *The Prophetic Minority: American Jewish Immigrant Radicals, 1880–1920.* Bloomington: Indiana University Press, 1985.

Steinson, Barbara J. *American Women's Activism During World War I.* New York: Garland, 1982.

Steinson, Barbara J. "The Mother Half of Humanity: American Women in the Peace and Preparedness Movements in World War I." In Carol R. Berkin and Clara M. Lovett, eds., *Women, War, and Revolution.* New York: Holmes & Meier, 1980.

Storrs, Landon R. Y. *Civilizing Capitalism: The National Consumers' League, Women's Activism, and Labor Standards in the New Deal Era.* Chapel Hill: University of North Carolina Press, 2000.

Stuhler, Barbara. "Fanny Brin: Woman of Peace." In Barbara Stuhler and Gretchen Kreuter, eds., *Women of Minnesota: Selected Biographical Essays.* St. Paul: Minnesota Historical Society, 1977.

Summy, Ralph, and Malcolm Saunders. "Why Peace History?" *Peace & Change* 20 (January 1995): 7–38.

Szajkowski, Zosa. "The Pacifism of Judah Magnes." *Conservative Judaism* 22 (Spring 1968): 36–55.

Tax, Meredith. *The Rising of the Women: Feminist Solidarity and Class Conflict, 1880–1917.* New York: Monthly Review, 1980.

Taylor, A. Elizabeth. "The Woman Suffrage Movement in North Carolina: Part 1." *North Carolina Historical Review* 38 (January 1961): 45–62.

Taylor, A. Elizabeth. "The Woman Suffrage Movement in North Carolina: Part 2." *North Carolina Historical Review* 38 (April 1961): 173–189.

Taylor, Verta. "Social Movement Continuity: The Women's Movement in Abeyance." *American Sociological Review* 54 (October 1989): 761–775.

Tentler, Leslie Woodcock. *Catholics and Contraception: An American History.* Ithaca, NY: Cornell University Press, 2004.

They Dared to Dream: A History of National Women's League, 1918–1968. New York: National Women's League of the United Synagogue of America, 1967.

Thurner, Manuela. "'Better Citizens Without the Ballot': American Antisuffrage Women and Their Rationale During the Progressive Era." *Journal of Women's History* 5 (Spring 1993): 33–60.

Tobin-Schlesinger, Kathleen. "Population and Power: The Religious Debate Over Contraception, 1916–1936." PhD diss., University of Chicago, 1994.

Tone, Andrea. "Black Market Birth Control: Contraceptive Entrepreneurship and Criminality in the Gilded Age." *Journal of American History* 87 (September 2000): 435–459.

Tone, Andrea. *Devices and Desires: A History of Contraceptives in America.* New York: Hill & Wang, 2001.

Tyrell, Ian E. *Woman's World/Woman's Empire: The Women's Christian Temperance Union in International Perspective, 1880–1930.* Chapel Hill: University of North Carolina Press, 1991.

Urofsky, Melvin I. *American Zionism from Herzl to the Holocaust.* New York: Bison, 1995.

Urofsky, Melvin I. *A Voice that Spoke for Justice: The Life and Times of Stephen S. Wise.* Albany: SUNY Press, 1981.

Van Voris, Jacqueline. *Carrie Chapman Catt: A Public Life.* New York: Feminist Press, 1987.

Vellacott, Jo. "A Place for Pacifism and Transnationalism in Feminist Theory: The Early Work of the Women's International League for Peace and Freedom." *Women's History Review* 2 (1993): 23–56.

Waldstreicher, David. "Radicalism, Religion, Jewishness: The Case of Emma Goldman." *American Jewish History* 80 (Autumn 1990): 74–92.

Watkins, Susan Cotts, and Angela D. Danzi. "Women's Gossip and Social Change: Childbirth and Fertility Control Among Italian and Jewish Women in the United States, 1920–1940." *Gender and Society* 9 (August 1995): 469–490.

Weigand, Kate. *Red Feminism: American Communism and the Making of Women's Liberation.* Baltimore: Johns Hopkins University Press, 2001.

Weinberg, Sydney Stahl. "'The World of Our Mothers: Family, Work, and Education in the Lives of Jewish Immigrant Women." *Frontiers: A Journal of Women's Studies* 7 (1983): 71–79.

Weinberg, Sydney Stahl. *The World of Our Mothers: The Lives of Jewish Immigrant Women.* Chapel Hill: University of North Carolina Press, 1988.

Wenger, Beth S. "Jewish Women of the Club: The Changing Role of Atlanta's Jewish Women 1870–1930." *American Jewish History* 76 (March 1987): 311–333.

Wenger, Beth S. *New York Jews and the Great Depression: Uncertain Promise.* Syracuse: Syracuse University Press, 1999.

Wenger, Beth S. "Radical Politics in a Reactionary Age: The Unmaking of Rosika Schwimmer, 1914–1930." *Journal of Women's History* 2 (Fall 1990): 66–99.

Westin, Jeanne. *Making Do: How Women Survived the '30s.* Chicago: Follett, 1976.

Wexler, Alice. *Emma Goldman: An Intimate Life.* New York: Pantheon, 1984.

Wheeler, Marjorie Spruill, ed. *One Woman, One Vote: Rediscovering the Woman Suffrage Movement.* Troutdale, OR: NewSage, 1995.

Wilcock, Evelyn. *Pacifism and the Jews.* Gloucester: Hawthorn Press, 1994.

Wilson, Jan Doolittle. *The Women's Joint Congressional Committee and the Politics of Maternalism, 1920–1930.* Urbana: University of Illinois Press, 2007.

"With Eye on Future, A Suffragette Takes Time to Look Back." *Maine Sunday Telegram,* September 16, 1979.

Wittner, Lawrence S. *Rebels Against War: The American Peace Movement, 1933–1983*. Philadelphia: Temple University Press, 1984.

Woocher, Jonathan. *Sacred Survival: The Civil Religion of American Jews*. Bloomington: Indiana University Press, 1996.

Wynn, Judy. "Lucile Lord-Heinstein: Breaking Trails." *Sojourner* (September 1977): 4, 17.

"'Yes I Can!' Says Pioneer Woman Doctor." *Cleveland Jewish News*, June 25, 1971.

Young, Louise. *In the Public Interest: The League of Women Voters, 1920–1970*. Westport, CT: Greenwood Press, 1989.

Young, Michael. "Facing a Test of Faith: Jewish Pacifists During the Second World War." *Peace & Change* (Summer/Fall 1975): 34–40.

Zeiger, Susan. "Finding a Cure for War: Women's Politics and the Peace Movement in the 1920s." *Journal of Social History* 24 (Autumn 1990): 69–86.

Zelizer, Viviana A. *Pricing the Priceless Child: The Changing Social Value of Children*. New York: Basic, 1985.

Zipser, Arthur. *Fire and Grace: The Life of Rose Pastor Stokes*. Athens: University of Georgia Press, 1990.

Melissa R. Klapper is Professor of History at Rowan University in Glassboro, New Jersey. She is the author of *Jewish Girls Coming of Age in America, 1860–1920* (NYU Press, 2005) and *Small Strangers: The Experiences of Immigrant Children in the United States, 1880–1925.*